MR. ATOMIC ENERGY

Chester Earl Holifield

MR. ATOMIC ENERGY
Congressman Chet Holifield and
Atomic Energy Affairs, 1945–1974

Richard Wayne Dyke

Contributions in Political Science, Number 241
Bernard K. Johnpoll, Series Editor

GREENWOOD PRESS
NEW YORK • WESTPORT, CONNECTICUT • LONDON

Library of Congress Cataloging-in-Publication Data

Dyke, Richard Wayne.
    Mr. Atomic Energy : Congressman Chet Holifield and atomic energy
affairs, 1945-1974 / Richard Wayne Dyke.
        p.   cm.—(Contributions in political science, ISSN 0147-1066
; no. 241)
    Bibliography: p.
    Includes index.
    ISBN 0-313-26244-6 (lib. bdg. : alk. paper)
    1. Holifield, Chet, 1903-   —Views on nuclear energy. 2. United
States. Congress. Joint Committee on Atomic Energy. 3. Nuclear
industry—Government policy—United States. 4. Nuclear energy—
Government policy—United States. I. Title. II. Title: Mister
Atomic Energy. III. Series.
HD9698.U52H634   1989
333.792'4'092—dc20   89-12005

British Library Cataloguing in Publication Data is available

Library of Congress Catalog Card Number: 89-12005
ISBN: 0-313-26244-6
ISSN: 0147-1066

First published in 1989

Greenwood Press, Inc.
88 Post Road West, Westport, Connecticut 06881

Printed in the United States of America

The paper used in this book complies with the
Permanent Paper Standard issued by the National
Information Standards Organization (Z39.48-1984).

10 9 8 7 6 5 4 3 2 1

To my wife
Paula Radcliffe Dyke

Contents

Photos follow page 213

Abbreviations

ABM	antiballistic missile (system)
ACRS	Advisory Committee on Reactor Safety
AEC	Atomic Energy Commission
AFL-CIO	American Federation of Labor-Congress of Industrial Organizations
BPA	Bonneville Power Administration
CIA	Central Intelligence Agency
DENR	Department of Energy and Natural Resources
DNR	Department of Natural Resources
DOT	Department of Transportation
EPA	Environmental Protection Agency
ERDA	Energy Research and Development Administration
FBI	Federal Bureau of Investigation
FEA	Federal Energy Administration
GAC	General Advisory Committee
HUD	Department of Housing and Urban Development
JCAE	Joint Committee on Atomic Energy
JCS	Joint Chiefs of Staff
LMFBR	Liquid Metal Fast Breeder Reactor
MLF	Multilateral Force
MPCA	Minnesota Pollution Control Agency
NATO	North Atlantic Treaty Organization

NCRP	National Committee on Radiation Protection and Measurement
NDRC	National Defense Research Committee
NEC	Nuclear Energy Commission
NEPA	National Environmental Policy Act of 1969
NRC	Nuclear Regulatory Commission
NSC	National Security Council
OSRD	Office of Scientific Research and Development
OWMR	Office of War Mobilization and Reconversion
PG&E	Pacific Gas and Electric Company
PRDC	Power Reactor Development Company
SANE	National Committee for a Sane Nuclear Policy
SEC	Securities and Exchange Commission
SEFOR	Southwest Experimental Fast Oxide Reactor
SNAP	Special Nuclear Auxiliary Power (satellite)
TVA	Tennessee Valley Authority
WPPSS	Washington Public Power Supply System

Preface

During his years in Congress, Chet Holifield
became known as "Mr. Atomic Energy"[1] among
his friends and colleagues in the House of
Representatives. There was and still is
good reason for the title. From 1946
through 1974, Holifield was a key national
figure, and probably the most important and
prominent House leader, in atomic energy
affairs. He earned the distinction first as
a member, and later as chairman, of the
House-Senate Joint Committee on Atomic
Energy (JCAE), which was created by the
Atomic Energy Act of 1946. This congressional committee established policy for the
nation's military and civilian atomic energy
programs and closely monitored the activities of the Atomic Energy Commission (AEC),
which was also established by the 1946 act
to implement atomic energy programs. As
Harold P. Green and Alan Rosenthal have
demonstrated, the JCAE had a profound effect
on the course and content of atomic energy
development in the United States in its
formative period, and Holifield was one of
its most active members. He served for over
twenty-eight years[2] on the committee, longer
than any of the other charter members, with
the exception of one representative.[3] He

once wrote matter-of-factly that "I believe I can say, without reservation, that I have personally given more years and days and hours to the Joint Committee than any other single member."[4]   In fact, Holifield's career as a JCAE member encompassed nearly the entire period of the JCAE's and AEC's existence in the national arena.   The AEC ceased to exist simultaneously with Holifield's retirement in 1974, and the JCAE was dissolved by Congress just three years later.

This study documents Holifield's significant contributions to the field of atomic energy development, particularly its peaceful uses, throughout his twenty-eight years as a member and ten years as formal House leader of the JCAE.   The first chapter is a biographical sketch of Holifield's life prior to his career in Congress; succeeding chapters cover the period primarily from 1945, when atomic energy first came to national attention, until the end of 1974, when Holifield retired from Congress.   During these years, Holifield participated actively in every major issue affecting atomic energy development.   In 1946, the California congressman was in the forefront of efforts to shape the first Atomic Energy Act as a civilian, rather than military, enterprise.   Three years later, he was appointed to a JCAE subcommittee to investigate the feasibility of the hydrogen bomb and advise President Harry Truman on the issue.   During the first years of the Eisenhower presidency, Holifield was one of the chief Democratic spokesmen and critics of the Republican-inspired Atomic Energy Act of 1954 and the ill-fated Dixon-Yates contract. In Eisenhower's second term, Holifield and the JCAE Democrats went on the offensive. In the Gore-Holifield bill, they proposed a massive governmental development program for nuclear power.   Although the Gore-Holifield proposal was never enacted into law, Holifield nonetheless gained his objectives gradually through the back door of annual authorizing legislation for the AEC budget. By the Kennedy years, Holifield and the JCAE had also won a lengthy and hard-fought battle to convert a military reactor, the Hanford N-reactor, to the dual function of plutonium and electricity production. During his final decade in Congress, Holifield maintained his commitment to nuclear power development, but he also promoted both atomic safety as an issue and efforts to reduce radiation and other environmental hazards associated with atomic power plants. As a finale to his career, the veteran congressman presided over the development of legislation to restructure the nation's atomic energy programs, thus extending his influence in atomic energy affairs well beyond his retirement.

It would not do to conclude this preface without giving grateful acknowledgement to those persons who had a role in making this book possible. I am particularly grateful to my wonderful parents, Hastin O. and Margaret M. Dyke, who provided the initial building blocks for this work through their steadfast emphasis on the value of education and encouragement of my educational pursuits. I received my initial formal training in history and political science from Pasadena College, now Point Loma Nazarene College in San Diego, California. Dr. Raymond M. Cooke, through his excellent teaching, was a heavy influence in kindling within me the desire to become a student of history and politics. Drs. Thomas Andrews, Larry Hybertson, and Ronald Kirkemo were also an inspiration. At California State University, Long Beach, I studied under the wise and able tutelage of Dr. James F. Ragland and Dr. Toivo Raun in American and Russian history. It was Dr.

Ragland in particular who sharpened my interest in modern American history; this book reflects that interest. At the University of Southern California, I was privileged to study under very able and committed scholars. Very special thanks is due Dr. Franklin D. Mitchell for his valuable counseling and guidance throughout my doctoral studies. His contribution is considerable. Dr. Terry L. Seip was also a valued source of encouragement and wise counsel. I am also truly appreciative for the advice and suggestions given to me by Drs. John A. Schutz, A. Lloyd Moote, Steven Kerr, and Daniel Straub during my graduate studies. Sincere thanks and appreciation also to both Mr. and Mrs. Holifield, who opened their home to me and helped to give an additional perspective to the writing of this book. Mr. Holifield explored atomic energy issues in detail with the author, and Mrs. Holifield was especially helpful on the biographical aspects of this study. Mr. Holifield also provided documents I could not have obtained elsewhere.

This book would not have been possible without the excellent technical support I received from Greenwood Press. Mildred Vasan, Politics and Law Editor at Greenwood, was a veritable pillar of support in this project. Her prompt and thoughtful responses to my many letters were very much appreciated and helpful in keeping me on the right track. I am also indebted to Patricia A. Meyers, my production editor, who was extremely helpful in pointing the way on the many technical issues that arise during the process of publishing a book.

Finally, I want to thank my wife, Paula, to whom this book is dedicated. She knows better than anyone how much I wanted to complete this work. Its completion is her triumph as well as mine. Without her cooperation, understanding, and patience,

the road would have been much longer and
harder, and our mutual sacrifices perhaps
too great.

Los Angeles, California   R. W. D.
                                   August 1989

MR. ATOMIC ENERGY

1

Before Atomic Energy: The Making of a Liberal Democratic Congressman

In the early morning hours of December 3, 1903, Chester Earl Holifield became the firstborn son of Erscie V. and Bessie Lee Holifield. An early winter had brought snow and bitter cold to the Holifield home in Mayfield, Kentucky. Erscie had stacked extra wood on the fire at midnight before he trudged with his lantern the half mile up the hill to the home of the country doctor, who was also Erscie's father, John R. Holifield. Chester was delivered by his grandfather.[1]

Chester or Chet, as he was to be called from boyhood and through his adult years, experienced many contrasting influences during his boyhood and youth in the Ozark Mountains of Arkansas, where the family moved when he was a year old. His exposure to socialist ideology, Christian fundamentalism, the Puritan ethic with its business practicality, and a good measure of common sense all combined to make Holifield a successful businessman in California early in his life. At the same time, Holifield developed a liberal outlook, which made him a New Deal Democrat when he was elected to Congress in 1942. A congressional career had not been an early ambition. It took the catastrophic events of the Great Depression and a debilitating leg injury that left time for reading and reflection to provide the impetus for Holifield's journey into politics.

By birth, Holifield was the product of a modest southern planter family with roots that stretched back to the colonial period. Holifield is an English name, and the family had immigrated to the colonies of Virginia and the Carolinas before the revolutionary war. William Holifield, the first known descendant of the family, served under George Washington during the American Revolution. In step with the general westward movement of the early 1800s, segments of the family moved into Kentucky and later into what became the states of Tennessee, Arkansas, Oklahoma, and Texas.[2] Chet's great grandfather was the first Holifield to move to Kentucky, and his grandfather John and father, Erscie, were both born there. John Holifield and his father before him were slaveholders and raised tobacco on the family farm near Pryorsburg, Kentucky. During the Civil War, John Holifield served as a cavalry officer in the Confederate Army under General Nathan B. Forrest. At the battle of Shiloh, a minie ball shattered John's left wrist, permanently restricting the use of his hand.[3]

After the Civil War, John Holifield returned home to find the family farm in ruins. The house and barn had been burned, and all of the livestock were gone. Together with Tom Holifield, his emancipated slave, John began to rebuild his home and replant his fields. In spite of the economic hardships of the Reconstruction era, John was able to restore his home place and maintain a modest standard of living. He also found time to obtain a degree in medicine and to practice as a country doctor. For Tom's loyalty, John later provided Tom's son an education in pharmacy. Tom and his wife Mary lived on the Holifield farm until their deaths.[4]

During the immediate postwar years, John Holifield married Julia Ann Dodson, of English parentage. Chet's father, Erscie, was born to the couple in 1883, one of five sons in the family.[5]

Like his father, Erscie was an enterprising man. Growing up on the family farm, he became proficient at carpentry and built his own home, in which Chet was born. Erscie utilized his carpentry skills in the Kentucky State Guard around the turn of the century. In 1902, at the age of nineteen, he married Bessie Lee Brady, a seventeen-year-old Irish girl. Chet was born about a year later.[6]

Restless and looking to improve his lot, Erscie moved his family from his father's farm to Paragould, Arkansas, when Chet was about a year old. There he worked for a relative in the cleaning and pressing business and learned the trade of a "bushelman"--an alterations man who was not really a full-time tailor. When he had learned the trade well enough, Erscie moved his family again, this time clear across the state to Springdale, a town in the Ozark Mountains. Erscie also became a lay minister in the fundamentalist Church of Christ. Chet spent most of his boyhood in Springdale.[7]

Until he was fifteen years old, Chet attended school and learned his father's trade. Already he exhibited some of the characteristics of a successful politician, if not the desire to become one. Gregarious and a leader among his peers, Chet distinguished himself on the Springdale High School football team and as a member of the high school newspaper staff.[8] He was also a voracious reader, a practice at least partially instilled by his father. He later wrote that "my father was a minister in the

Christian Church, and before I was twelve years old, I had read through the Old Testament under his direction two times."[9]   This training not only helped to imbue him with strong fundamentalist religious beliefs, but also helped to compensate for the years of high school that he never completed.[10]

In addition to his education, Chet also received practical exposure to the world of work in his father's shop.   When he was old enough, he spent his after-school hours and his vacations in the shop, where he learned cleaning, pressing, alterations, and other aspects of the business.[11] His father paid him according to the amount of work he performed, so Chet learned early about the value of money and hard work.

His father's shop also provided Chet with another important influence in the growth and development of his outlook on society.   The shop was a favorite gathering place for the men of the town, who came to discuss and debate their theories of society and how things ought to be run.   Erscie was an "avowed socialist,"[12] and Chet was treated to many lively discussions between his father and the other independent-minded thinkers of the area.   What developed in Chet from these experiences was not so much a crystalized political philosophy as a liberal attitude toward social issues.   His early exposure to Christian fundamentalism helped to instill in him a concern for each person as an individual, while his exposure to "radical" theories of society impressed upon him the importance of fashioning a government responsive and beneficial to all of its members.

Holifield's childhood was not without its dark moments.   His younger sister Madge died at the age of four from typhoid fever. Later, when Chet was nine, his mother died of "consumption" (tuberculosis) at the age of twenty-seven years.   Erscie, with Chet and Chet's younger brother and sister to raise, soon married Hazel Osterland. Three additional children were added to the family from this union.[13]

Youthful adventurousness and the Spanish influenza epidemic of 1918 accounted for Chet's first long trek from home at the age of fifteen. As Chet remembered it, "It was December, my birthday month, and the schools were closed because so many people were dying."[14] Chet read in the paper that pressers were being recruited for jobs in Springfield, Missouri, so he rode the rails to Springfield, and applied for, and got a job pressing pants for a firm that had a contract for Marine uniforms. Riding the rods became a familiar form of transportation for him in his numerous journeys away from home in his teens. As he explained it:

> It was also a trade which had to be learned. The box cars on a train had three sets of rods underneath. You hooked your foot on one and your knee on another and let your butt be between--with your arms hanging on the side. You didn't go to sleep. If you were really lucky, you found a plank your butt and back could rest on. Anyway, you were protected from the rain. Also, if you could find an empty box car which was open, you got in and stayed really dry. Or if you found a coal car, you got in from the top and stood and hooked over [i. e., pulled down] the blind. The blind collapsed and two of them made a complete enclosure.[15]

Chet was in and out of his father's home after his Springfield job. The job and his other short jaunts away from home to

Oklahoma and Missouri had shown him he could support himself, and his growing independence put him at odds with his father. Finally, in the spring of 1919, he decided to go to California. As he put it, "I'd read of the romance of the forty-niners and, California was a kind of golden legend to young people in the Middle West. So I went there."[16] He made his way west with two of his boyhood chums and finally reached the Los Angeles area. Once there, his friends decided to return home at the end of the summer. "But for me," Holifield later explained, "California was the land of glamour, the finding of gold and oil, the setting for the Wild West novels--G. A. Henty's *Bound to Succeed*, *Sink or Swim*--the books which, more than the Bible, really made poor kids want to succeed."[17]

If a bit romantic in his impressions of California, Chet was also practical. In keeping with his previous work experience, he obtained employment as a presser in a Pasadena cleaning and dyeing shop. He wrote letters home, but rather than expressing homesickness, he described the abundant opportunities available in his new environment and urged his father to bring the rest of the family and establish his cleaning business in California.[18]

Like his father and grandfather, Chet was too restless and ambitious to remain long in the employ of others. Within a few months of settling in California, he persuaded his father to help him to finance a modest pressing business in nearby Montebello, a booming oil town with a population of eighteen hundred. Starting the business required a cash outlay of two hundred dollars. With the money, Chet bought a used press and rented space for the "shop," which consisted of the press and a counter made of packing crates. He also bought an old Model-T truck, which he used for his early morning commutes to the dry cleaners in downtown Los Angeles and then back again for the pressing of his customers' clothes. The job often entailed working late into the night. Still, the young Holifield persisted and succeeded as a businessman when he was only in his teenage years.[19]

Meanwhile, Chet's optimistic letters to his father made their impact. Soon Erscie moved the rest of the family to Montebello, and together father and son operated a men's cleaning and haberdashery shop. This arrangement lasted for about a year, until Chet and his father clashed over Chet's attempts to strengthen the business through a new window display and advertising. Erscie considered the window display foolish and advertising a waste of money. The disagreement ended amicably by Chet's buying his father's portion of the business.[20]

During the year he was in business with his father, Chet met Vernice ("Cam") Caneer, a local girl who had come into the shop with a friend to sell tickets to a senior class play. When she left the shop, Chet pointed her out to his father: "You know the dark-haired girl on the right? That is the one I am going to marry." And marry her he did. The two were wed on September 14, 1922. Chet had to ask his father's permission because he was not twenty-one years old; in fact, he had not quite reached his nineteenth birthday. From 1923 to 1933, the couple produced a family of five daughters: Lois Anita, Betty Lee, Patricia Jean, Willa Mae, and Jo Ann.[21]

After his father left the business and moved to Oregon, Chet directed his energies toward expanding and improving his business. One of his first endeavors was growing the mustache that thereafter became a permanent fixture of his appearance. As he put it, "In that way, people coming in and seeing a 19-year-old youth would stop asking 'Where's

the boss?'"[22]   Holifield also turned heavily
toward advertising and promotionals, including a drawing at which he gave away a new
Ford.   Such activities were unusual in Montebello in the 1920s,   and Holifield became
well known among the people of the area.   By
1927, Holifield was able to borrow $1,750
and convert his business into a full men's
wear store.   His wife and Cotton Lavender, a
boyhood chum, helped in the management of
the expanded business.[23]

In addition to his business enterprise,
Holifield also turned gradually to civic
activities.   He joined the Montebello Lions
Club, the Chamber of Commerce, and the YMCA.
In 1934, after his election as president of
the Montebello Lions Club, he was instrumental in setting up Lions clubs in Monterey
Park, East Los Angeles, Vernon, and Pico
Rivera.[24]   Despite his status as a businessman, Holifield supported union activities,
in keeping with the liberal outlook he had
developed over the years.   He helped organize food drives for strikers at the Goodrich
Tire Plant during a strike there in the
twenties, and during the thirties he also
helped to organize food drives to assist
Works Progress Administration workers in the
area.[25]

By the late 1920s, Holifield was relatively well known by the people of his area.
The recognition of his name that he achieved
through his business and civic activities
probably assisted him in later years when
his interests turned to politics.   During
the 1920s, however, Holifield did not possess any ambitions in the political arena.
Without a "conspiracy of events" in the
thirties--both a serious injury that left
him bedridden for three years with plenty of
time for reading and reflection and also the
emotional and economic traumas that he experienced during the Great Depression--
Holifield probably never would have turned

his attention to politics at all.

The years 1931 through 1934 were any-thing but pleasant for Holifield. During those years he suffered a serious leg in-jury, one of his young daughters died sud-denly, and the Great Depression literally wiped him out financially. His troubles began on March 29, 1931, during a hunting expedition with a friend on Catalina Island. A stray shot struck Holifield in the right leg, seriously wounding him. (Although the origin of the shot was never determined, Holifield theorizes that the shot came from careless hunters on another ridge, who broke the rule about never firing across ridges.)[26] Holifield's friend, Gene Mar-zoff, walked for two to three hours as he led the stricken Montebello businessman on horseback out of the hills for medical at-tention. At one point, it was doubtful whether he would survive because of the loss of blood. A Dodge delivery truck and a Packard ambulance completed Holifield's trip to the hospital in Avalon, where he called for the sheriff so he could sign papers absolving his friend Marzoff of any blame in the incident. Two quarts of saline solution later, Holifield was able to rest comfort-ably, but he would not walk again for two years without the aid of crutches.[27]

A few months later, Holifield and his wife experienced a second family tragedy. Their seemingly healthy third daughter, Patricia Jean, was suddenly stricken with an unknown illness at the family home on Cedar Street, and died shortly thereafter. The grief of losing a very young loved one com-pounded the hardship placed on the family by Chet's injury. These were dark times, but the family worked together to make the prob-lems as livable as possible--Cam worked with Cotton Lavender in the clothing store, and the two older daughters did the housework and prepared dinner after school. Chet did

what he could, saving the five-dollar cost
of a trip to the doctor by heating a twenty-
pound nail over the gas stove, carefully
scraping off the dead flesh of the wound,
which did not seem to want to heal, and
dressing the wound himself, using a sanitary
napkin for a bandage. Chet had always been
frugal in order to expand the business, but
frugality became increasingly necessary as
the Great Depression made its way west and
his business declined.[28]

Haberdasher Holifield adjusted relatively well to the decline in his business,
partly because he had had the foresight
three months before his accident to purchase
an accident insurance policy from a customer
who had just gone into the insurance business. The monthly stipend helped out for a
time while he was recuperating. Holifield
was unprepared, however, for the full effects of the Great Depression, as were other
Montebello businessmen. In 1931 the First
Bank of Montebello closed its doors. Holifield had written a total of fifteen hundred
dollars in checks to his creditors, all of
which became worthless with the closure of
the bank. To save his business, Holifield
mortgaged the family home on Cedar Street,
which he finally lost because he could not
keep up with the mortgage payments. His
business, at one point, "was down to zero."
Without a generous landlord and creditors
who believed his word that he would repay
all of his debts, Holifield would have had
to close his business. At the height of his
financial woes, Holifield faced debts worth
twice his assets, and he was three years
behind in paying the rent for his store.
His business had all but collapsed, and he
had lost the home on Cedar Street, forcing
the Holifields to the status of renters.
They moved, ironically enough, to a house on
California Street.[29]

Holifield's economic ruin followed in

rapid succession upon his hunting accident
and the death of his daughter. The economic
losses came when Holifield's mental state
was probably at its lowest ebb. As he recu-
perated, Holifield had plenty of time to
reflect upon the things that were happening
to him, and this particular configuration of
events turned the businessman's interests to
politics. As he put it, "I had done everything right. I had worked like a son of a
gun to build the business. We had saved our
money."[30] But all of his efforts had
counted for nothing. "I realized that,
regardless of a man's personal ability,
economic depression could take away all of
his gains through years of hard work."[31]

During his convalescence, Holifield
began to read and speak out. Always an
enthusiastic reader, he turned his attention
to political and economic works, including
histories of the United States, Thorsten
Veblen's *The Theory of the Leisure Class*,
the liberal economic writings of Stewart
Chase, Adam Smith's *The Wealth of Nations*,
and Upton Sinclair's Lenny Budd books.
Holifield decided there must be something
wrong with America's economic system, which
was "the real crucible for my future political beliefs."[32] He began to attend political meetings and took a course in public
speaking. His bedside, during the years he
could not walk, became a gathering place for
political and economic discussions.[33] By
1934, Holifield had become a thoroughly
primed liberal Democrat in largely Republican Montebello, and it required only a small
amount of encouragement to get him into the
political arena.

Significantly, the prompting for Holifield's entry into politics came from a
socialist. Socialists were hardly anathema
to Holifield, whose father had espoused
socialism; Chet, too, had undoubtedly accepted some of the philosophical and prac-

tical tenets of socialism. According to
Holifield, his neighbor W. P. Caulkins urged
him in 1934 to run for a seat on the Los
Angeles County Democratic Central Committee
for the Fifty-first State Assembly District.
Caulkins offered to pay the dollar filing
fee. Holifield accepted Caulkins's offer
and had his name placed on the ballot. During the election of 1934, Holifield took to
the stump for himself and his candidate for
governor, Upton Sinclair. Holifield believed Sinclair had good ideas, even if he
was only nominally a Democrat. Sinclair
lost his bid for the governorship, but Holifield was elected to the County Democratic
Central Committee seat by the largest plurality of any candidate.[34]

Holifield soon became acquainted with
another rising star in Southern California
Democratic circles, Jerry Voorhis. Voorhis
had spoken at a monthly meeting of the Los
Angeles County Democratic Committeemen's
Association and so impressed Holifield that
he told his wife that Voorhis reminded him
of Abraham Lincoln.[35] The two men quickly
became close friends as well as political
associates.

As the Great Depression slowly eased
its grip on the economy, Holifield's business began to improve. To increase his
sales, Holifield moved his store to East Los
Angeles, where he changed the store's name
from "Chet's Men's Wear" to "Chet Holifield's." Once again the business thrived,
and Holifield was able to recoup the losses
he had suffered. Somewhat after the manner
of the haberdasher who succeeded Franklin
Roosevelt--Harry S Truman--Holifield paid
off every debt and obligation he had in-
curred during the Great Depression. By the
mid-1930s, he had repaid the three years of
rent due on his Montebello store, and he was
the first to make good on his business loans
with Montebello's First State Bank. During

the 1950s, when he was a congressman, Holifield moved his business a final time to
11711 Rosecrans Avenue in Norwalk to increase his sales volume and obtain additional parking for his customers. From 1952
to 1976, the family home was at 2001 Lincoln
Avenue in Montebello.[36]

The Great Depression had left a permanent imprint on Holifield and his future
career. Never again was Holifield only a
businessman; he was heavily involved in
politics as well. In 1936, when his friend
Jerry Voorhis decided to run for Congress,
Holifield served as codirector of the forty
Democratic state and county committeemen who
managed Voorhis's successful campaign. For
Holifield's service and loyalty, the new
congressman Voorhis appointed Holifield to
the State Democratic Central Committee for
the Twelfth Congressional District, a position that Holifield held from 1938 to
1940.[37]

Holifield's appointment to the State
Democratic Central Committee enlarged his
range of contacts and the scope of his political experience. Always an innovator,
Holifield took the opportunity to arrange an
association of all local central committees
in the district, which he called the Twelfth
Congressional District Association. "If
there ever was a 'Holifield machine,'" he
recalled in later years, "the Association
was it."[38] Holifield's leadership abilities
and political acumen were recognized and
appreciated by his political colleagues. In
1938, Voorhis urged him to take his first
step into elective politics by running for
the post of Los Angeles County supervisor.
He told Holifield that it was very unlikely
that he would win, but "nevertheless, I want
you to get campaign experience because if I
run for the Senate [in 1940] my congressional seat will be open." Holifield spent
his total savings of five hundred dollars on

the campaign for posters and traveling expenses and finished among the top four out of seventeen candidates for the position. The savings had been intended as the beginning of an education fund for his young daughters, and when his wife found out that the money had been spent, Holifield "had a lot of explaining to do."[39]

Jerry Voorhis, as it turned out, did not run for the Senate in 1940, so there was no congressional seat for Holifield. Instead, Holifield contented himself with attending the 1940 Democratic National Convention in Chicago. This was the first of many national conventions Holifield attended as a delegate. At the convention, Holifield, in keeping with his liberal Democratic outlook, enthusiastically supported Franklin D. Roosevelt for a third term as president. Holifield fully supported the New Deal, particularly the economic and social programs designed to improve the framework of America's economic system and provide assistance to those who were genuinely in need.[40]

While 1940 did not bring a congressional race for Holifield, it did provide the necessary events for a future race. The census taken in 1940 brought about reapportionment of congressional districts in California. As a result of the reapportionment, a new Nineteenth Congressional District was formed, which contained a large portion of Jerry Voorhis's old Twelfth District. The constituency was mainly Democratic, and the majority of the people were union and non-union laborers and small-business men. Since there was no incumbent, the Nineteenth District was "up for grabs" in the 1942 election.[41]

By 1942, Holifield was well known and liked in the Nineteenth District. His business and civic activities, as well as his political activities, had given him the

reputation and name-recognition necessary
for winning the post of congressman. The
constituency of the district identified with
his party affiliation and liberal Democratic
views. Moreover, Holifield had leaned toward a career in politics since the Great
Depression and was prepared to enter elective politics in 1942. Finally, Voorhis and
other friends urged him to declare for the
position. Holifield accepted the challenge.

In the primary and general elections
that followed, Holifield triumphed over his
opponents. In the Democratic primary, Holifield had to contend with seven opponents,
the chief of whom was George Wheeler, a
newspaper editor from the city of Bell.
Holifield's win in the primary election was
by plurality, but his win over Republican
Max Ward in the November election was by a
decisive 65 percent majority. Both Holifield and Ward were members of the Lions
Club. Both men studiously avoided personal
attacks on each other, a campaign formula
Holifield would continue to follow in his
remaining fifteen elections.[42]

The election of 1942 launched Holifield
on a thirty-two-year congressional career,
one of the longest of any congressman from
California. By the time he entered Congress
in January 1943, Holifield had already received an extensive political education
through his associations as a committeeman
and his friendship with Voorhis. He would
be able to adjust to the job of congressman
easily, and he would work at it tirelessly,
giving up the golf, hunting, and other
sports that once filled his spare hours.[43]
At the same time, he would enjoy the luxury
of a "safe" district on which he could depend to return him to Congress every two
years without any significant opposition in
most election campaigns.[44] This situation
made it easier for Holifield to become heavily involved in the field of atomic energy

during its fledgling stage when it promised
no short-term benefits for his district.
Holifield's interest in atomic energy, however, did not arise from his political perceptions of his district.   His interest was
closely aligned with the liberal Democratic
outlook he had developed over the years.
Events and his liberal Democratic responses
to these events, not prior motivation, eventually placed him in the forefront of atomic
energy affairs.   But in 1942, the country
was at war with Germany and Japan, and
atomic energy was not yet a matter of widespread political discussion.

2

Present at the Dawning:
Holifield and the Passage of the
Atomic Energy Act of 1946

It was bitter cold in Washington when Holifield arrived with his family in January 1943 to assume his new duties as a freshman congressman. The press took note of him almost immediately, if only because of the cold weather. The *New York Sunday News* of January 10, 1943, featured a picture of the Holifield family bundled in sweaters and overcoats around the kitchen table in their new Washington home because they had been unable to obtain any heating fuel.[1] Even congressmen felt the impact of shortages caused by the war with the Axis powers.

Holifield was not even aware of atomic energy when he began his first term in Congress. The atomic bombings of Hiroshima and Nagasaki were over two years away, and the development of the atom bomb was a closely guarded secret. Holifield's career began uneventfully with his appointment to the House Committee on Post Offices and Roads, hardly a vantage point from which to influence important national issues. A chance appointment to the Military Affairs Committee late in 1944, however, coupled with his own intense interest in the new field of atomic energy when it became a public matter, eventually brought Holifield into the

legislative controversy over passage of the
nation's first atomic energy legislation.
Holifield's outspoken opposition on the
Military Affairs Committee to the initial
proposal, the May-Johnson bill, and his
other contributions to passage of the Atomic
Energy Act of 1946 provided the impetus for
establishing him as an important congressional influence in national atomic energy
affairs over the next three decades. In
recognition of his contributions to the 1946
act, he was appointed to the Joint Committee
on Atomic Energy established by the legislation, where he remained as a member for the
remaining twenty-eight years of his career
and served as chairman several times.

Standing committees essentially ruled
Congress in 1943, as they do today and have
since the late nineteenth century. Although
Holifield was no political novice, he entered a new political environment in the
House of Representatives, with its powerful
committee chairmen, jurisdictional rival-
ries, and rule by seniority. Holifield's
election by the people of his district assured him only of entry-level status in his
new profession. With regard to committee
assignments, he had to start at the bottom;
as he later expressed it, "When you first
come to Congress, you take anything you can
get."[2]

In view of his freshman standing in the
Seventy-eighth Congress, Holifield was assigned to a minor committee, the Committee
on Post Offices and Roads. This standing
committee was established in the nineteenth
century when the federal government began
subsidizing construction of roads between
towns to facilitate mail delivery. By the
time Holifield entered Congress, the committee's major responsibility was the annual
review of the financial status of the post
office and the salaries of its employees.
Throughout his career, Holifield voted con-

sistently in favor of salary increases for postal employees, thus demonstrating his liberal Democratic outlook and friendly attitude toward public employees and labor in general. Although Holifield did not stay on the committee long, he evidently impressed the House leadership with his careful attention to his committee duties. In 1955, he was again asked by Speaker Sam Rayburn to sit on the successor to the committee, the Committee on Post Office and Civil Service--as it turned out, for six years--to work toward modernization of postal personnel policies. During the Johnson administration, Speaker John McCormack again called upon Holifield's expertise in the field by naming him chairman of the Committee of the Whole House on the State of the Union for consideration of the 1964 Postal Salary Act.[3]

A chance appointment to an influential House committee late in 1944, the second year of Holifield's career, placed the freshman congressman in a position to consider atomic energy legislation when it became a matter for public political discussion about a year later. In 1944, a vacancy occurred on the powerful Military Affairs Committee because of the death of one of its members. Holifield, who was never able to serve in the nation's armed forces because of his earlier leg wound, expressed an interest in joining the committee, which had the responsibility for oversight on all military matters and legislation. With the support of the California congressional delegation, Holifield was able to gain the vacant post. He quickly established strong rapport with the committee's chairman, Andrew J. May (D-Kentucky), as he had with most House leaders. Good relations with his fellow native Kentuckian, however, were to last only until committee consideration of the May-Johnson bill. After their disagree-

ment over the proper content for the nation's first atomic energy legislation,
Holifield and May were never again on very
friendly terms.[4]

Long before Holifield began his tenure
on the Military Affairs Committee, the stage
was being set for the entry of atomic energy
as a national issue. In January 1939, the
distinguished Danish theoretical physicist
Neils Bohr, on a visit to the United States,
brought to the attention of U.S. scientists
his knowledge of a new discovery--fission.
German scientists Otto Hahn and Fritz
Strassman, working at the Kaiser Wilhelm
Institute in Berlin in late 1938, were the
first scientists to split a uranium nucleus
into two lighter elements by bombarding it
with neutrons. The separation resulted in a
consequent release of part of the energy
that had held the component neutrons and
protons together in the original nucleus.
That fission had occurred was confirmed by
the experiments of two of Hahn's Austrian
colleagues, who brought it to the attention
of Bohr. Avid discussion of the new discovery at the Fifth Washington Conference on
Theoretical Physics in late January and an
authoritative article by Bohr in the *Physical Review* on February 15 brought the concept of fission into the center of American
scientific discussion. The process of fission was even more important because it
suggested the possibility of a chain reac-
tion--that the split uranium nucleus might
release neutrons that might in turn split
other uranium nuclei, resulting in an energy
release of great magnitude. Scientists
immediately perceived that fission might be
manipulated for use as a powerful explosive
or be harnessed as a power source if the
chain reaction could be controlled.[5]

With the outbreak of World War II,
scientists in the United States became increasingly concerned about fission's poten-

tial use as an explosive. Leo Szilard, a
Hungarian physicist working at Columbia
University, was worried enough about Germany's possible development of an atomic
bomb to prod Albert Einstein to send his
famous 1939 letter to President Roosevelt,
in which Einstein asserted that "This new
phenomenon would also lead to the construction of bombs." Alexander Sachs, a Lehman
Corporation economist with personal access
to the president, carried the letter to
Roosevelt and persuaded him of its importance. In response, Roosevelt created the
Advisory Committee on Uranium, the first
governmental body to consider the potential
use of nuclear energy as an explosive.
Roosevelt's later creation of the National
Defense Research Committee (NDRC) in June
1940, which included the Advisory Committee
as part of the organization, provided an
enlarged government framework and funding to
begin vigorous research into the potential
of nuclear energy as an explosive. The NDRC
and the Advisory Committee were subsumed
about a year later in still another of
Roosevelt's creations, the Office of Scientific Research and Development (OSRD). The
OSRD helped to intertwine basic research
with practical applications and testing of
the new resource under the protective arm of
the president. The large-scale construction
projects that the development of atomic
energy required were implemented by the army
under the ultra-secret Manhattan Engineer
District.[6]

     U.S. scientists considered four major
approaches for development of fissionable
material in their quest for the bomb. They
experimented with three different processes
in their effort to separate enough fissionable uranium (uranium 235) for a bomb.
These processes included electro-magnetic
separation, gaseous diffusion, and centrif-
ugal force. They also tried a fourth proc-

ess, involving a nuclear reactor fueled by
the unusable uranium 238, to produce plutonium, a highly fissile isotope. Scientists
ultimately settled on the gaseous diffusion
and nuclear reactor processes and pushed
them vigorously. The development of fissionable materials by these methods became
the impetus for the creation of two new
American cities--Oak Ridge, Tennessee, and
Hanford, Washington. The Hanford reactor
became operational in late 1944 and supplied
the fissionable material for the world's
first atomic blast at Alamogordo, New Mexico, on July 16, 1945. The empire of Japan
soon felt the wrath of this awesome new
power; on August 6, 1945, a uranium 235
bomb leveled the city of Hiroshima, and a
plutonium bomb destroyed Nagasaki and most
of its inhabitants three days later. World
War II came to an end, and atomic energy
became a new and urgent matter for public
discussion in the United States and elsewhere.[7]

The utter destruction of Hiroshima and
Nagasaki by the new atomic weapons came as a
surprise as much to Chet Holifield as to the
rest of the American public. During World
War II, only the chairmen of the House and
Senate committees on Appropriations and on
Military Affairs knew about the funding for
the Manhattan Engineer District. These four
congressional leaders passed upon funding
for the development of atomic bombs without
the knowledge of or consultation with the
members of their committees. Thus, Holifield's first exposure to atomic energy was
the same as that of other Americans. On
August 6, 1945, he listened with fascination
to President Truman's statement to the American people, announcing that an American
airplane had dropped a bomb on Hiroshima
with more power than twenty thousand tons of
TNT. Truman proclaimed "a new era in man's
understanding of nature's forces." He also

announced that he would ask Congress to establish a commission on atomic energy to control and regulate the development and use of atomic energy in the United States, while he prepared plans for eventual international control of this new force.[8]

Holifield became an avid student of atomic energy almost immediately in the days after Hiroshima and Nagasaki. As he put it, "I was fascinated by the explosion of that bomb, and I got everything I could to read on the explosion."[9] He was one of only two national legislators (the other was Democratic Senator William Fulbright of Arkansas) to read the Smyth Report in the early days after its issuance. Henry Dewolf Smyth's classic *General Account of the Development of Methods of Using Atomic Energy for Military Purposes* was issued by the government on August 9, 1945, to provide the public a summary of the wartime program. The Smyth Report became Holifield's primer, although he admitted that "you about had to be a physicist" to understand all of the technical aspects of atomic bomb development.[10]

Although he worked at becoming an informed layman on atomic energy matters, Holifield, as a cautious junior member of Congress with little real power or influence, did not attempt to introduce legislation on atomic energy. Nor was he given to particularly fatuous overstatements about the new force, such as that of the freshman Democratic senator from Connecticut, Brien McMahon, who declared that the bombing of Hiroshima was the greatest event in world history since the birth of Jesus Christ.[11] Still, Holifield realized the significance of atomic energy and its potential applications. Seldom a grandstander, Holifield characteristically worked at becoming conversant with the subject so that he could respond intelligently to the proposals that were sure to be forthcoming from the Truman administration and other sources. He knew instinctively that the Military Affairs Committee would have a hand in deciding the fate of any atomic energy proposal.

Legislative action on this new public issue was not long in coming. On September 6, 1945, Senator McMahon grasped at the opportunity to become a senatorial influence in atomic energy matters by introducing the nation's first piece of atomic energy legislation. McMahon's bill essentially proposed a control board made up of cabinet officers and other federal officials. The bill, however, was a hastily prepared and makeshift measure that lacked Truman administration or other support. McMahon's proposal, somewhat audacious for a freshman senator, was countered on the same day of its introduction by a concurrent resolution by Arthur Vandenburg (R-Michigan). Vandenburg proposed that a joint committee of six senators and six representatives make a complete study of atomic energy matters and report back to Congress with proposals for "the development and control of the atomic bomb." The resolution passed the Senate on September 27, 1945, but became stalled in the House because of the introduction of the administration proposal on October 3, 1945.[12]

The original administration proposal became known as the May-Johnson bill, since it was introduced in the House by Andrew Jackson May (D-Kentucky), chairman of the House Military Affairs Committee, and in the Senate by Edwin C. Johnson (D-Colorado), the ranking member of the Senate Military Affairs Committee. The May-Johnson bill (H. R. 4280), which proposed an administrative apparatus for controlling atomic energy on the domestic front, had its origins in the work of various organizations and persons associated with the Manhattan Engineer District but was basically a product of the War Department.[13]   Brigadier General   Kenneth Royall   of the Army Service   Forces (later under secretary of war) and William L.   Marbury,   chief counsel on War Department   contracts,   jointly prepared the version of the bill   originally introduced in the House and the Senate.   Basically,   the bill   provided for   a part-time Atomic Energy Commission of nine members appointed by the president   for nine-year   terms   and an   administrator   and deputy   administrator to serve as   executive officers with essentially the same powers as the   commission.   In addition to   full-time staff to be hired for commission work, advisory boards for various activity areas could be   designated by the president to make recommendations to the commission.   The Atomic Energy   Commission   was also   given   plenary power over all atomic energy research, materials, and equipment, with authority to hire without reference to civil service laws,   to adopt   and administer security   regulations, to make contracts,   to create   corporations, and   to acquire property by purchase or eminent domain.   Given such wide powers and the commission-administrator-staff   framework proposed,   the War Department bill   appeared to   request   authorization for the   continuance,   in only slightly different   form,   of the administrative structure embodied in the Manhattan Engineer District,   which was composed of the Military Policy Committee, with General Leslie R.   Groves as the head administrator,   and various research and development staffs.[14]

Robert P. Patterson, successor to Henry Stimson as secretary of war on September 22, 1945,   intended   to push for quick action on the   administration bill,   given the   smooth working relationship that the War Department had   established with the   military   affairs committees   of both houses.   In the Senate, however,   Senator Vandenburg blocked by parliamentary maneuver the referral of the May-Johnson bill to any committee, pending action on his concurrent resolution in the House. In the House, Andrew May agreed to hold a hearing on October 9, anticipating that the bill would be reported out of committee quickly. Neither Secretary Patterson nor the Senate and House chairmen expected the outcry that the bill would arouse, both from the public and from members of both houses of Congress.[15]

Perhaps the biggest mistake the War Department made in formulating and introducing the May-Johnson bill was that it had failed to consult the scientists who had worked for the Manhattan Engineer District and other organizations responsible for developing the bomb. Scientific organizations sprang up all over the country in protest to the bill, charging initially that the proposal placed intolerable restrictions on scientific research and damaged efforts to establish international control. Newly organized scientists at Chicago, Oak Ridge, and Los Alamos made their views known. In Washington, D.C., in late October, the Federation of Atomic Scientists was formed, followed in short order by the Federation of American Scientists and the National Committee for Atomic Information. Although such scientific luminaries as J. Robert Oppenheimer, Ernest O. Lawrence, and Enrico Fermi continued to support the May-Johnson bill, equally prominent scientists such as Leo Szilard, Harold Urey, and Edward U. Condon denounced it.[16]

As a member of the Military Affairs Committee, Holifield was in a strategic position to register his opposition to the May-Johnson bill. His opposition evolved as much from his study of the bill as from his support of the scientists and the senatorial opponent of the bill, Brien McMahon. Holifield was also offended by the lack of fairness in the October 9 hearing, in which only proponents of the bill were called to testify. He demonstrated his unhappiness with the hearing in an uncharacteristic act of brashness. Visiting the chairman in his office, Holifield rapped his knuckles on May's desk and demanded an additional day of hearings to allow the opposing scientists to be heard. He later characterized his exchange with May as "brisk."[17]

Chairman May, of course, was being pressured from other quarters as well to reopen the hearings. Bowing to pressure from within and without the administration, Secretary Patterson urged an additional day of hearings. Pressure was also mounting in the Senate, where McMahon and Vandenburg had allied around McMahon's October 9 resolution to create a Special Committee on Atomic Energy not only to study the subject, but to consider all bills and resolutions related to it. May reluctantly scheduled another hearing for October 18. At the new hearing, he hardly disguised his contempt for the bill's opponents, opening the hearing with a sarcastic declaration that the hearing had been reopened "for the purpose of permitting a group of interested people, known as scientists, to present their views." In contrast to the favorable views of Secretary Patterson, Manhattan Engineer District head General Groves, OSRD Chief Vannevar Bush, and NDRC Chairman James B. Conant at the October 9 hearing, the committee now heard the diverse views of Leo Szilard, Herbert Anderson, Arthur Compton, and J. Robert Oppenheimer and received a written, opposing view from Harold Urey, who had temporarily left the hearing room.[18]

The October 18 hearing did little to change the committee report on the May-Johnson bill, which was issued on November 5, 1945. H. R. 4280, rewritten as H. R. 4566, totally subordinated the administrator under the Atomic Energy Commission, which could delegate powers to the administrator as it saw fit. In addition, the committee had made an attempt to change the research provisions to reassure the scientists that basic research on atomic energy could continue without commission oversight as long as the byproducts of the research did not constitute a national hazard or prove to be of commercial or industrial value.[19] On other central questions, however, May and most of his committee were unmoved. The committee's failure to make substantial amendments prompted Holifield to pencil a number of recommendations for changes to the bill. He persuaded Melvin Price (D-Illinois) to sign the recommendations with him and had them attached to the report as "Dissenting Views of Members of the Military Affairs Committee on H. R. 4566."[20]

Holifield's objections to the May-Johnson bill were fundamental. Instead of the part-time commission proposed in the bill, Holifield believed that the commission "should be composed of full-time, well-paid members," since "the Nation deserves to have the full-time services of high-caliber well-paid men to direct the development and application of this great power which will affect the destiny of every man, woman, and child in the United States, and possibly the world." In place of the staggered, nine-year terms of the commissioners, Holifield proposed that the commissioners be removable by the president "whenever he deems it in the national interest." Holifield pointed out that the commission appointment provisions in the May-Johnson bill meant that "the President would have to be elected for two successive terms before he would be in a position to appoint a majority of the Commission." Holifield also proposed that the administrator, "the principal full-time executive who will in fact, under this bill,

direct the Nation's activities in the atomic
energy field," should be appointed by the
president with consent of the Senate and
"serve at his pleasure." Moreover, Holifield emphasized that the administrator
should be a civilian, since "the constructive possibilities of the use of atomic
energy in our civilian life far exceeds
[sic] the importance of atomic energy for
military purposes." For Holifield, "to
consider the field of atomic energy as one
of primarily military significance [was to]
overlook totally the tremendous possibilities which it offers for improving the public welfare, increasing the standard of
living, and generally easing the daily bur-
dens of each of us." In a final technical
amendment, Holifield suggested that the
federal government "should be the exclusive
producer and owner of plutonium and such
other fissionable materials as may be defined from time to time in regulations issued by the Commission." Holifield's point
was that such atomic energy materials were
so vital to the nation's welfare that the
licensing of any private firm to produce,
refine, or process such materials should be
prohibited, "except on a research basis."[21]

Holifield's "Dissenting Views" were
perhaps his single greatest contribution to
the passage of the Atomic Energy Act of 1946
in its final form. His views provided a
rallying point for opponents of the May-
Johnson bill not because his views represented a behind-the-scenes consensus strategy of the bill's opponents, but because
Holifield's personal objections to the bill,
based upon his study of it, coincidentally
mirrored the opinions of many of the bill's
opponents. In particular, Holifield's insistence that the administrator be a civilian helped cast the "military versus civilian control" issue into broad relief for
future public discussion. This issue later

became the cutting edge of the movement by scientists, senators, and finally the White House to set aside the May-Johnson bill in favor of legislation that would ensure that qualified civilians, rather than the military, would decide the future of the atom.[22] Almost all of Holifield's "Dissenting Views" would turn up in some form in the Atomic Energy Act of 1946.

In November 1945, however, the passage of the Atomic Energy Act of 1946 was over eight months away. Holifield found himself allied with a motley array of scientists, a handful of congressmen, and the opposition centering around Brien McMahon in the Senate. He was contacted frequently by scientific opponents of the May-Johnson bill, including the Federation of Atomic Scientists, the Federation of American Scientists, the National Committee on Atomic Information, and many individual scientists, including Henry Dewolf Smyth, Leo Szilard, Harold Urey, Edward Condon, and Thorofin Hogness. In discussing his close relationships with scientists opposed to the War Department bill, Holifield noted later that Henry Smyth, as an example, "used to come in and out of my back door and give stuff to me on the q-t because he was still on the Government payroll and didn't want to be charged with lobbying."[23]

Although Holifield helped to solidify and extend opposition to the May-Johnson bill, he was not the prime mover in changing the course of atomic energy legislation. The major impetus for the change came from the Senate and Brien McMahon, in particular. McMahon enlisted the aid of Arthur Vandenburg, whose concurrent resolution for a joint congressional study committee had failed in the House. Together, with the help of Majority Leader Alben Barkley (D-Kentucky), McMahon and Vandenburg succeeded in winning Senate acceptance on October 23,

1945, of McMahon's October 9 resolution to
establish an eleven-member Senate Special
Committee on Atomic Energy to study atomic
energy and consider all bills and resolutions related to the subject. On October
26, President Pro Tempore Kenneth McKellar
(D-Tennessee) appointed as chairman of the
committee none other than McMahon himself,
who had tactfully advanced to McKellar his
chairmanship claim based on his introduction
of the resolution. In addition to McMahon
and Vandenburg, McKellar appointed four
Democrats and five Republicans, almost all
of them conservative supporters of the military.[24]

McMahon's Special Committee formulated
the major provisions of the Atomic Energy
Act of 1946. Special Committee hearings on
atomic energy were opened for thirteen days
between Thanksgiving and Christmas, 1945,
and were continued after the holiday season
from January 22 until April 19, 1946. Mc-
Mahon obtained the services of James R.
Newman, head of the Science Section of the
Office of War Mobilization and Reconversion
(OWMR), as his committee's special counsel
and persuaded him to develop legislation
that could serve as McMahon's alternative to
the May-Johnson proposal. With the help of
an associate in OWMR, Byron S. Miller, Newman completed a draft bill in consultation
with various interested scientific groups
across the country. Senator McMahon introduced the Newman-Miller draft in the Senate
as S. 1717 on December 20, 1945. Representative Helen Gahagan Douglas (D-California)
introduced the McMahon measure in the House,
a fact that led Newman in later writings to
refer to the proposal as the McMahon-Douglas
bill, although most historians have referred
to it as the McMahon bill.[25] From his strategic position on the House Military Affairs
Committee, Holifield also showed his support
for the McMahon initiative by formally in-

troducing it again in the House on February 4, 1946, as H. R. 5365, even though the measure did not yet contain the civilian administrator concept advocated by Holifield in his opposition statement on the May-Johnson proposal.[26]

Acceptance of McMahon's new bill by the Senate Special Committee was not a foregone conclusion. The freshman senator's publicity-mongering and his one-sided views in support of the scientists were not appreciated by the conservative, promilitary majority on the committee. His open squabbles with the War Department to obtain classified information further widened the breach. This latter situation and continued attempts by Patterson to salvage the May-Johnson bill soon led to the military versus civilian control issue which dominated public debate over passage of atomic energy legislation. Gradually, a deepening rift developed between McMahon and the military-oriented majority on the Special Committee. The same alignment of viewpoints was also mirrored in the House, where relatively junior members such as Holifield, Helen Gahagan Douglas, Jerry Voorhis, and Melvin Price supported McMahon's and the scientists' views, while Andrew May and most of the Military Affairs Committee still supported the War Department proposal. The fundamental disagreement was even apparent in the president's official family. Secretary of Commerce Henry Wallace, Secretary of the Interior Harold Ickes, and spokesmen in OWMR found themselves opposed to Secretary of War Patterson, Secretary of the Navy James Forrestal, and General Leslie Groves of the Manhattan Engineer District.[27]

At the heart of the dispute over military versus civilian control was disagreement over the extent to which active military officers should serve on the commission and advisory boards and in staff positions

certain to be created by the final legislation. Scientific groups, especially the
associations of scientists at the various
Manhattan District sites who longed to be
free of the military, publicized the problem
as the major issue to be resolved in the
legislation and sought support in Congress
and elsewhere to dramatize their campaign.
Following a public relations stint by the
McMahon group on behalf of the scientists,
Marquis Childs wrote a series of articles in
the *Washington Post* beginning on January 4,
1946, which brought into broad relief the
turbulent relations between those in Congress who opted for an entirely civilian
administration of atomic energy and those
who believed the military should be made a
significant part of the organizational
framework. As time and circumstances
changed, the McMahon forces advocated nothing short of military exclusion, while the
opposing side was equally determined that
the military should have a major role in
governing the atom.[28]

In executive sessions early in 1946,
the Special Committee accepted McMahon's
proposal as the basis for discussion, an
acceptance that was no small victory for the
senator. Before reporting the bill favorably, however, committee members attached
several significant amendments to the bill.
One amendment created the post of general
manager for the commission. Made at the
suggestion of the Bureau of the Budget, the
change was easily accepted by both McMahon
and his opponents. Committee members also
included in the bill an additional administrative framework, the Joint Committee on
Atomic Energy. Although some historians
have seen this addition as "growing out of
Vandenburg's initial approach to atomic
energy legislation," it was probably also a
result of Senator Edwin C. Johnson's singular insistence during the hearings on some

form of continued congressional control over the development of atomic energy. As a member of the Special Committee, Johnson became the principal advocate for congressional controls on atomic energy development. Johnson, in fact, introduced a bill calling for a commission composed of five members from each house of Congress.[29]

The most controversial amendment attached to McMahon's bill came to be known as the Vandenburg Amendment. As a solution to the military versus civilian control issue, committee member Vandenburg proposed creation of a Military Liaison Committee as an adjunct to the commission to oversee the national security aspects of atomic energy affairs. Basically, the Military Liaison Committee would be vested with "power to advise and consult with the Commission on all matters *it* deemed to affect security, to know of all matters within the Commission and, where it felt any action or proposed action was 'inimical to the common defense and security,' to appeal the question to the President, whose decision would be final."[30]

The battle over the Vandenburg Amendment was the last major confrontation during passage of the Atomic Energy Act of 1946 in which Holifield had a direct and significant role. Holifield and some thirty congressmen, the McMahon committee staff, and the various scientific organizations took up the Vandenburg challenge to civilian control of the atom by forming an ad hoc committee to work toward elimination or modification of this offensive addition to the McMahon bill. Holifield was among the founders of this committee, which included Senator McMahon; James Newman and Byron Miller of the McMahon committee staff; Rachel Bell, executive secretary of Americans United for World Organization; Albert Cahn, representing the Atomic Scientists of Chicago; William Higinbotham of the Federation of Atomic

Scientists;   Joseph Rauh, a Washington law-
yer;   scientists Edward U. Condon, Thorofin
Hogness,   and   Edward Levi;   and Representative Helen Gahagan Douglas.[31]   A brainchild
of   this ad hoc committee was the   Emergency
Conference   for Civilian Control   of   Atomic
Energy,   which   was   held in   Washington   on
March   21,   1946,   as   the   spearhead   of   a
nationwide   protest   against the   Vandenburg
Amendment in particular and military control
of the atom in general.   Attesting to Holifield's   importance among the   advocates   of
civilian   control   were   the facts   that   he
arranged the meeting place (the House caucus
room)   and   also   chaired   the   organization
session of the Emergency Conference.[32]   The
opening   session of the conference witnessed
the   gathering   of between one   hundred   and
three   hundred   persons involved   in   atomic
energy   affairs,   including   many   prominent
scientists   and   about   thirty   congressmen.
With   Holifield at the opening   session   was
the   president of the Emergency   Conference,
the   Reverend A.   Powell Davies of All Souls
Unitarian   Church (and   a   member,   inciden-
tally,   of   the National Committee on Atomic
Information),   who described the   conference
aim.   Rachel Bell,   who served as executive
secretary,   explained   the conference's program   of   assault   on   the   military-control
viewpoint.   In addition,   several scientists
and nine congressmen made brief   statements.
The   morning   session   was followed   in   the
evening   by   a public rally of   about   eight
hundred   people at the Press   Club   building
auditorium.   From   there,   members   of   the
Emergency   Conference   returned home to   fan
the   flames of opposition to the   Vandenburg
Amendment.[33]
     The intensity of the opposition did not
fail   to impress Vandenburg,   who faced   reelection.   He   softened   his   amendment   to
subordinate   clearly   the   Military   Liaison
Committee   to the Atomic Energy   Commission,

with lessened review and potential override powers over only the "military applications of atomic energy." This compromise was reluctantly accepted by both the advocates and the opponents of civilian control. With this major hurdle cleared, the amended McMahon bill was reported and passed the Senate easily by unanimous voice vote on June 1, 1946, "a relatively quiet Saturday afternoon in the Senate."[34]

There was to be no quiet Saturday afternoon in the House for the amended McMahon proposal. From June 10, when it was referred to the Military Affairs Committee, the bill faced formidable opposition. The McMahon group did, of course, enjoy the support of Holifield, but there was really very little that the junior congressman and other McMahon supporters could do to resist the flurry of promilitary amendments that besieged the bill in committee. Amendments to the proposal at this stage included a provision assuring one seat, but not more than two seats, on the commission for military representatives and a requirement that the director of the military applications staff division allow active military officers to serve in any position on the commission's staff. Holifield continued to meet with McMahon supporters to discuss legislative strategies and solidify public support for civilian control during this time. Holifield and his allies agreed that floor and conference action would be the most important opportunities for stemming the promilitary tide.[35]

In the end, action on the floor and in conference did thwart the military initiatives that arose in the Military Affairs Committee and continued to receive support in the Rules Committee. The civilian control forces ultimately succeeded in eliminating most of the military-oriented aspects of the House bill, although they were

obliged to endure some minor concessions to
the War Department. While military officers
were allowed to direct the military applications staff division and serve in other
staff positions, the commission was made
all-civilian in the final version of the
bill.[36]

Ironically enough, however, the vocal
Holifield was not a party to the complex
legislative maneuvering that rescued the
all-civilian-commission provision in the
original McMahon bill. Instead, he was a
witness to another atomic energy event in
the Pacific at the behest of President
Truman--the July 1 and 25, 1946, nuclear
tests in the Bikini Islands. On July 2,
when Chairman May announced that the amended
McMahon proposal had been reported out of
the Military Affairs Committee, Holifield
was inspecting the damage to a fleet of
obsolete naval vessels caused by the first
atomic blast since Nagasaki; also present
were another congressman, two senators, and
five civilians who comprised the President's
Civilian Evaluation Commission. Again on
July 26, the day the conference version of
the Atomic Energy Act of 1946 passed both
houses of Congress, Holifield and the others
aboard the U.S.S. *Haven* were, as he wrote in
his Bikini notebook, "waiting for radioactivity to subside" before conducting an
inspection of the effects of the second
atomic explosion in the Bikinis.[37]

The Bikini tests were the first atomic
experiments witnessed by Holifield. Operation Crossroads, the code name for the
tests, featured two atomic explosions, one
above water and one underwater. Holifield
was impressed enough by what he called "the
impending historic event" to keep a notebook
of his daily activities and impressions
during his month in the Pacific. Holifield
particularly noted the general "feeling of
anxiety" that preceded the first Bikini

explosion, which he pointed out was "the fourth Atomic bomb explosion in history and the first Atomic bomb explosion over naval vessels and ocean water." Throughout the operation, in which "more than 34,000 personnel were participating in various capacities," Holifield detected "an air of suppressed excitement and waiting for the great experiment" as the day for the blast approached. The excitement turned to wonder on July 1. Of this first atomic blast he witnessed, Holifield wrote:

This is it! 8:59 A. M. Bomb Away! Tense, breathless waiting for 63 seconds that seemed minutes. A horizon enveloping [sic] flash--even through our special goggles it takes a few seconds to re-focus our eyes. The danger to our eyes is now passed, we jerk our goggles off and with naked eyes watch the great column of fire and smoke start skyward--a violent writhing upsurge of orange, rose-pink and yellow-cream colored tower of turbulent fire and smoke against a "Maxfield Parish" sky of azure blue. Slowly it seems to us, 18 miles away, the column grows 10, 20, 30 thousand feet high; at about 20 thousand feet a mushroom top starts to form, turbulent, boiling, spreading out like the top of an umbrella folding. The under half of the umbrella top seems to be boiling and tumbling, the upper half is smooth as the top of an ice cream cone.
     Two minutes after the flash, we hear the detonation, muffled and deep like thunder. We continue to watch the great towering column

with the mushroom top, amazed at
the multi-colored phenomena, fearful in its beauty against the
cloudless azure sky. For 10 or 12
minutes it holds its shape . . .[38]

Although the underwater test of July 26 was
somewhat less colorful in its display because of the position of the blast, Holifield was nonetheless awe-struck by the
power of the explosion, which displaced
"millions of tons of water" and sank several
ships, including an old aircraft carrier, on
the surface near the area of the blast.[39]

    If anything, the Bikini tests sharpened
Holifield's interest in atomic energy.
Holifield believed the tests ultimately
would prove constructive, since they would
reveal "many scientific facts of beneficial
value to mankind." As he viewed the subject, "I believe that as many of the facts
[as possible] about atomic energy must be
discovered, and that [should occur] as soon
as possible." As for the military implications of the tests, Holifield would restate
his position again and again in the coming
years: "The people of the world must know
and believe that a force has been discovered
that is so different in degree of power, so
many times greater in its malevolent fury
that Atomic war cannot be tolerated."[40]

    Although Holifield was away on the
momentous occasion of the passage of the
Atomic Energy Act of 1946, the House leadership did not forget his intense interest in
atomic energy affairs and his contributions
to the Atomic Energy Act when it came time
to select members for the Joint Committee on
Atomic Energy created by the new law. Holifield and his close associate on the Military Affairs Committee, Melvin Price, who
had joined Holifield in his dissenting report on the May-Johnson bill, were among the
five Democratic House members chosen by

Speaker Rayburn to serve on the Joint Committee, along with four Republican House members. Such was the well-deserved reward Holifield received despite his lack of seniority for his early and continuing interest and work in atomic energy affairs.[41]

Holifield eventually gained the reputation as "Mr. Atomic Energy" in the House of Representatives through his work on the Joint Committee on Atomic Energy (JCAE). Unlike other standing and joint committees, the JCAE was created by statute rather than by the rules of the House and the Senate. The Atomic Energy Act of 1946, moreover, gave the JCAE sweeping jurisdiction over atomic energy affairs. It specified that the committee was to have exclusive jurisdiction over "all bills, resolutions, and other matters in the Senate or the House of Representatives relating primarily to the [Atomic Energy] Commission or to the development, use, and control of atomic energy." The Atomic Energy Commission, which replaced the Manhattan Engineer District as the administrative body for the nation's development and use of atomic energy, was enjoined to keep the JCAE "fully and currently informed with respect to the Commission's activities."[42] From his important vantage point in a new and growing field, Holifield became well known and influential in a way that congressmen on the traditional committees could not. He was aided, of course, by these factors: atomic energy was an area in which there was continuing public interest; atomic energy was national in scope and many people were involved nationwide in atomic energy programs; and a Democratic Congress, most of his career, and his committee seniority brought him the JCAE chairmanship by 1961.

Both Holifield's studious consideration of atomic energy issues and his vociferousness in making his views known figured in his rise to prominence in the debate over passage of the Atomic Energy Act and in his subsequent appointment to the JCAE. These traits, plus a keen eye for political opportunity, placed Holifield in the forefront of national atomic energy affairs. These attributes would also characterize his performance later on the JCAE. Holifield was more than a political opportunist, however; he had quickly recognized the implications atomic energy had for the future of the nation, and he became an avid student of atomic energy, seeking to know as much as he could about this new force. He was certainly not unmindful of the importance of atomic energy's military uses, but he concentrated his attention on peaceful applications, a focus evidenced by his criticisms of the May-Johnson bill and his liberal Democratic push for civilian control. Although he was a only a junior congressman, Holifield already had become a recognizable force in atomic energy affairs by virtue of his activities during passage of the Atomic Energy Act of 1946. In time, he would become one of the most knowledgeable and influential national legislators in the atomic energy field.

3

In Defense of the Nation:
Holifield and the Hydrogen
Bomb Decision

For most Americans, the first four years after passage of the Atomic Energy Act of 1946 were disquieting ones abroad. They watched with dismay and apprehension as Communism spread in Europe and the Far East. In 1947, Communist insurgencies threatened Greece and Turkey. In February 1948, a Communist coup overthrew the government of Czechoslovakia; shortly afterward, the Soviet Union began the Berlin Blockade. In the fall of 1949, America witnessed the flight of Chiang Kai-shek to Formosa and the victory of Mao Tse-Tung in China. At the same time, the American government and public were shocked to learn that the Soviets had detonated a nuclear device. Nuclear arms were no longer to be the possession solely of the United States.

These international events added further gravity to the already weighty responsibilities of those charged with administering atomic energy at home. Both the fledgling Joint Committee on Atomic Energy (JCAE), of which Holifield was a member, and the new Atomic Energy Commission, which replaced the Manhattan Engineer District, struggled to meet the responsibilities of managing a growing atomic energy program.

The Cold War developing between the United States and the Soviet Union brought development of weapons and the issue of security uppermost in congressional minds and also provided opportunities for the opponents of civilian control of the atom to attempt to retrieve control for the military. Holifield, a staunch supporter of the civilian-controlled AEC, opposed these moves. As a result of the Soviet detonation, however, Holifield did join with JCAE Chairman Brien McMahon against the AEC commissioners in advocating a new weapons policy, development of the "super weapon" or hydrogen bomb, as the nation's newest line of defense. Holifield played a pivotal role as chairman of an ad hoc JCAE subcommittee appointed by McMahon to investigate the feasibility of proceeding with development of the hydrogen bomb. Holifield's subcommittee recommended unanimously to the JCAE that the hydrogen bomb be developed as quickly as possible, and the JCAE began promoting the project. Holifield accompanied McMahon to the White House in an effort to persuade President Harry S Truman that development of the new bomb was essential to national security. The JCAE's influence on Truman's "hydrogen bomb decision" was the beginning of a unique relationship between the JCAE and the AEC, in which the JCAE emerged as an equal, if not superior, partner in initiating and implementing atomic energy policy. To Holifield, participation in the JCAE's recommendation to the president was of lasting importance personally as a "high mark" in his career and also helped to solidify his reputation as an important congressional influence in atomic energy affairs.

The three years prior to the H-bomb controversy were formative ones for the administrative framework created by the Atomic Energy Act of 1946. The act created the JCAE and the AEC as the principal organizations for managing the atomic energy program. The AEC consisted of five commissioners appointed by the president with the advice and consent of the Senate. Manhattan Engineer District personnel provided staff for the new organization's statutory divisions of Military Applications, Research, Production, and Engineering. In addition, the act provided for two advisory bodies to assist the AEC. A General Advisory Committee of nine scientists appointed by the president was responsible for advising the commission on scientific and technical matters relating to materials, production, research and development policies, and other matters. To provide expertise and recommendations on military aspects of atomic energy, Congress also added a Military Liaison Committee consisting of appointees of the secretaries of war and navy.[1]

The JCAE was organized long before the AEC and its attendant organizations were in full operation. On August 2, 1946, the day after President Truman signed the Atomic Energy Act, both the House and the Senate leadership appointed members to the committee. In the Senate, eight of the eleven members of the Senate Special Committee on Atomic Energy, which drafted the act, won seats on the JCAE. These included Brien McMahon (D-Connecticut), Richard B. Russell (D-Georgia), Edwin C. Johnson (D-Colorado), Tom Connally (D-Texas), Harry F. Byrd (D-Virginia), Arthur Vandenburg (D-Michigan), Eugene D. Milliken (R-Colorado), and Bourke B. Hickenlooper (R-Iowa). Senator William F. Knowland (R-California) was the lone appointee who had not been on the Special Committee. In the House, Speaker Sam Rayburn (D-Texas) appointed Holifield and Melvin Price (D-Illinois), along with R. Ewing Thomason (D-Texas), Carl T. Durham (D-North Carolina), Aime Forand (D-Rhode Island), Charles H. Elston (R-Ohio), J.

Parnell Thomas (R-New Jersey), Carl Hinshaw (R-California), and Clare Booth Luce (R-Connecticut). Of the nine House appointees, only Forand and Hinshaw had not been on the Military Affairs Committee, although Hinshaw had contributed to the floor debate on the McMahon bill. All eighteen appointees met together on August 2 and elected McMahon as the first JCAE chairman just before the Seventy-ninth Congress adjourned. Senator Hickenlooper was selected as vice-chairman.[2]

When the Eightieth Congress convened in January, 1947, the JCAE was reconstituted to reflect the Republican victory in the election of 1946. For the first time since the days of Herbert Hoover, Republicans won majorities in both houses of Congress. As a result, Senator Hickenlooper gained the chairmanship of the committee, and a newcomer to the committee, Representative Sterling Cole (R-New York), became vice-chairman. Of consequence for Holifield's seniority on the committee, two Democratic House members senior to him, Thomason and Forand, did not return to the committee. Thomason, who had been floor manager of the McMahon bill in the House, resigned from Congress late in 1947 and was replaced by Congressman Lyndon Johnson (D-Texas). Forand left the committee to pursue other interests, including the chairmanship of the House Democratic Caucus. Thus, in the first full session of Congress for the JCAE, Holifield was elevated to second in seniority among Democratic House members (Durham was first), a position that greatly improved his chances for becoming chairman in future Democratic-controlled sessions of Congress.[3]

The first issue before the JCAE, confirmation of the first AEC commissioners, created divisiveness within the committee, especially on the Senate side, which had the responsibility for making the recommendation for confirmation to the full Senate. In a spirit of nonpartisanship, President Truman had nominated a self-described Independent and four Republicans for the AEC posts. The Independent, David Lilienthal, was chairman of the Tennessee Valley Authority, created during the New Deal years. The Republicans included Admiral Lewis L. Strauss, a navy reservist who had played an important part in the wartime ordnance program; Sumner T. Pike, a former member of the Securities and Exchange Commission; Robert F. Bacher, a prominent scientist at Los Alamos Laboratory during the war who had worked on the atomic bomb; and William W. Waymack, Pulitzer-Prize-winning editor of the *Des Moines Register and Tribune* who had also served as a public director of the Federal Reserve Bank of Chicago.[4] Strauss would later prove to be the renegade on the commission, if there was any, through his opposition to many AEC majority decisions, including the question of developing the H-bomb.

Lilienthal's nomination brought the biggest fire from Senate opponents, who variously charged that he was a Communist, that his leadership would endanger free enterprise, and that he was "soft" on Communism and would be an unworthy guardian of atomic secrets. Lilienthal's opponents, including former Senate President Pro Tempore Kenneth McKellar (D-Tennessee), Robert Taft (R-Ohio), John Bricker (R-Ohio), and Republican Whip Kenneth S. Wherry (R-Nebraska), were unable to defeat Lilienthal's confirmation, although Bricker, as a new member of the JCAE, did prevent a unanimous recommendation from the Senate side of the JCAE. After almost five months of hearings and debate, the Senate confirmed the five AEC commissioners. The confirmation controversy made clear that many members of Congress were still disgruntled and unhappy with the prospect of a civilian commission to oversee atomic energy affairs. Senator Taft, a presidential candidate in the upcoming election of 1948, actually called for return of the atomic energy enterprise to the military during the debate on Lilienthal's confirmation. By mid-1947, six pending bills proposed renewed military jurisdiction over atomic energy affairs.[5]

The members of the JCAE spent most of the remainder of 1947 educating themselves in the field of atomic energy. They accomplished this objective through study of relatively scarce resource materials, joint meetings with the AEC, public and private hearings to gather information, and visits to the atomic energy installations around the country. The AEC commissioners were not particularly successful in educating JCAE members, and the two bodies quite naturally began to drift apart as a result of each institution's attention to protecting, preserving, and even expanding its bureaucratic turf.[6] The AEC had formally assumed control of all atomic energy installations on January 1, 1947, and was preoccupied with problems of administration and setting of program priorities for the various projects. The JCAE's interests increasingly centered on oversight and protection of national security and the nation's monopoly of nuclear weapons. According to Commissioner Waymack:

> Joint meetings, public hearings and private hearings became infrequent and limited to specific subjects, usually controversies and fears of the moment. . . . The greater part of communication became "paper work." It centered increasingly on security matters. It tended to take the form of time-consuming replies to letters apparently designed to make a written record.[7]

Questions of security became increasingly significant, indeed, as the United States and the Soviet Union drew farther apart from their World War II alliance. Congressional opponents of a civilian commission took this opportunity to expose and magnify the supposed weaknesses of civilian control of the atom.   In May 1947, Representative J. Parnell Thomas (R-New Jersey), who had opposed the McMahon bill in the Rules Committee and as a House conferee had refused to sign the conference report on the bill, charged in *American* magazine that most of the atomic energy patents that the army had withheld from publication during the war were now available to the Russians and anyone else through the Patent Office.   Thomas followed this article with another one on June 21 in *Liberty* magazine.   In his second article, Thomas attacked the commission's security system at its installations in Oak Ridge, Tennessee.   Thomas claimed that all production plants and the Clinton Laboratories at Oak Ridge were "heavily infested" with "Communist suspects," and he called for repeal of the Atomic Energy Act and resumption of army control.   At about the same time, the Federal Bureau of Investigation (FBI) received a tip that secret documents were missing from the Los Alamos, New Mexico, weapons laboratory.   Although the Thomas articles did not have their intended impact and the FBI concluded that the Los Alamos incident only involved two army sergeants taking "souvenirs," a *New York Sun* article on July 9, 1947, sensationalized the Los Alamos investigation by reporting the theft of "highly secret data on the atomic bomb."   The *Sun* story received a wide public hearing;   even the *Washington Post* gave it prominent space.   AEC Chairman Lilienthal experienced difficulty calming the nerves of some JCAE members.   A joint meeting of the JCAE and the AEC commissioners on July 22,

however, appeared to resolve this crisis and
put an end to the wave of newspaper "revelations" about weak AEC security.[8]

As an unwavering supporter of the AEC,
Holifield had doubts from the beginning
about the genuineness of the charges leveled
at the AEC.   Immediately after the July 22
joint meeting, he delivered a lengthy and
forceful speech on the floor of the House
entitled, "Smearing the Scientists: Attempt
to Discredit Civilian Atomic Energy Control."   He placed blame for the Los Alamos
incident squarely on the army, pointing out
that "it has been shown that the recently
discovered leak was due to two Army men
working during the period of Army control at
Los Alamos--a leak which was not discovered
until a year later when the civilian commission took over." Holifield concentrated his
remarks on a defense of Dr. Edward U.
Condon, director of the Bureau of Standards
and formerly scientific advisor to McMahon's
Special Committee.   A July 17, 1947, *Washington Times-Herald* article had attempted to
discredit Condon, using information from
Representative Thomas's earlier writings in
American and *Liberty* magazines.   Holifield,
who considered Condon a personal friend
since the two had witnessed the 1946 Bikini
tests together as members of the President's
Civilian Evaluation Commission, provided a
point-by-point rebuttal of the article,
exposing weaknesses in the facts and method-
ology employed.   Furious at what he believed
to be smear tactics used against Condon,
Holifield brusquely challenged the "rumor-
mongering character assassins" to "put up or
shut up."[9]

In March 1948, Thomas personally assumed the offensive against Condon, this
time in his capacity as chairman of the
House Committee on Un-American Activities.
He published a special subcommittee report
highly critical of the scientist, alleging

Communist associations by Condon and calling
him "one of the weakest links of our atomic
security." Holifield angrily defended the
scientist again on the House floor in a
stinging attack on the methods, facts, and
conclusions used in the report. This time
he was more specific in his theory of the
motives behind the attack on Condon. Holifield wondered aloud whether "a certain
military clique" was using Thomas's committee "to so discredit civilian control that
the Army will be handed back the atomic
energy platter appropriately stained with
the sacrificial blood of lopped-off heads of
our scientists who advocated civilian control."[10] Before and after the Condon report,
Holifield was highly critical of violations
of civil liberties by congressional committees, especially the House Committee on Un-
American Activities. He voiced concern
about those citizens who "suffered character
assassination without recourse" and declared
at one point that protection of civil liberties "is THE crucial issue facing the people
of the United States."[11] To emphasize his
position, Holifield introduced legislation
in several sessions of Congress to prescribe
specific procedures for investigating committees, in order to protect citizens under
investigation.[12]

The second round of confirmations for
AEC commissioners in 1948 brought more controversy to atomic energy affairs. The
Atomic Energy Act provided a two-year trial
period for the first commissioners, followed
by staggered terms of one to five years for
each. On April 20, President Truman renomi-
nated the five original commissioners and
proposed five years for Lilienthal, four for
Pike, three for Strauss, two for Waymack,
and one for Bacher. Opposition senators
immediately attacked Truman's proposal.
Senator Robert Taft, who had objected to
Lilienthal's original confirmation and had

called for resumption of army control, announced as chairman of the Senate Republican
Policy Committee that confirmation would go
slowly and that those facing this slow process "included Lilienthal." With the election of 1948 near, partisan politics, as
well as dislike of the civilian commission,
figured in Taft's posture, since he harbored
hopes of becoming president. On another
front, JCAE Chairman (Senator) Hickenlooper
proposed a two-year extension for the commissioners on the grounds that the trial
period had been shortened because of the
earlier, drawn-out confirmation hearings.
Although Democratic Senator Edwin Johnson
cosponsored Hickenlooper's compromise bill,
Holifield and the other Democratic JCAE
members opposed it, charging the Republicans
with "partisan politics." Nonetheless, the
JCAE supported Hickenlooper's proposal and
reported it favorably. The vote was largely
along party lines, with the ten JCAE Republicans and Johnson in favor and the Democratic minority opposed. Holifield thus
participated in another minority report,
charging partisan politics and using Taft's
statements as justification.[13] The House
and the Senate easily passed the measure,
and Truman reluctantly signed the bill,
noting that the measure was "not in the best
public interest, since it invests the atomic
energy program with an aura of uncertainty
and partisan politics." Hickenlooper, who
was no friend of the commissioners, believed
that he had possibly averted a renewed
battle over the civilian/military control
issue.[14]

The outcome of the election of 1948
came as a surprise to Republicans. The
nation's voters returned Truman to the presidency and created Democratic majorities in
both the House and the Senate. On the JCAE,
Senator McMahon resumed the chairmanship and
Representative Carl Durham (D-North Caro-

lina) became vice-chairman, making Holifield
the ranking House member.[15] Almost immediately, the tenor of the JCAE changed.
McMahon and his new staff director, William
L. Borden, took unprecedented interest in
the AEC's weapons production plans. Borden,
an attorney and World War II B-24 pilot who
participated in the bombing of Germany, met
with AEC staff to ascertain present and
future weapons production capabilities of
the AEC. The JCAE scrutinized development
efforts for the hydrogen bomb, or "super" as
it was then called, almost from the beginning of McMahon's chairmanship in the
Eighty-first Congress. On behalf of Chairman McMahon, Borden requested a status report from the AEC on the development of the
hydrogen bomb for presentation at a JCAE
hearing on March 10, 1949. McMahon also
prodded the Joint Chiefs of Staff to increase production goals for the AEC.
McMahon, who hoped to make the JCAE an instrument of national policy, complained to
Secretary of Defense Louis Johnson that past
military requirements submitted to the AEC
"merely reflected an estimate of what the
Atomic Energy Commission was capable of
producing with existing or planned
facilities--and did not reflect an independent judgment as to what we need in the event
of war." McMahon urged "the fabrication of
more and better (nuclear) weapons," believing that the military's projection of military requirements should recognize that
strategic bombing with nuclear weapons had
become "the keystone of our military policy
and a foundation pillar of our foreign
policy as well." McMahon further argued in
the press that the United States should
reveal the number of nuclear weapons in its
arsenal as a warning to the Soviet Union
against reckless activities on the European
continent.[16]
　　　While McMahon contented himself with

exploring avenues for making atomic energy a
centerpiece of the nation's military and
foreign policies, security controversies
continued to plague the AEC. Holifield
continued his role of defending the organization he had helped to create. When the
AEC published its fifth semiannual report to
the Congress in January 1949, Democratic
senators Connally and Millard E. Tydings of
Maryland complained to the AEC and to President Truman that too much sensitive information had been made public. In rebuttal,
Holifield pointed out that the so-called
sensitive information, mostly photographs,
had been published earlier.[17]

The spring and summer months of 1949
brought even more serious controversies. On
April 13, the AEC commissioners learned that
a bottle of 289 grams of uranium was missing
from the Argonne National Laboratory at the
University of Chicago. Only days later, on
April 25, Senator Clyde Hoey (D-North Carolina) wrote to AEC Chairman Lilienthal to
inquire whether it was AEC policy to award
fellowships to Communists, and the senator
called for an investigation of the fellow-
ship program. These events and other considerations led former JCAE Chairman Hickenlooper to accuse the AEC and Chairman
Lilienthal in particular of "incredible
mismanagement" and to demand Lilienthal's
resignation.[18]

Holifield met these crises with the
same "coolness of judgment and calmness of
reason" that he had asked the House Committee on Un-American Activities to exercise in
investigating potential Communist subver-
sives. Although the *New York Daily News*
screamed banner headlines of "Atom Bomb
Uranium Vanishes," the Argonne loss turned
out to be a case of mishandling, not theft,
with all but four grams of the uranium soon
accounted for.[19] With regard to the AEC
fellowships, Holifield wrote the Princeton

Association of Scientists that he thought it best to eliminate the AEC fellowships on nonsecret work for the present because he believed that congressional opinion would not support them "unless a great deal of 'thought-control' is included in the program." He explained to the scientists that "such a strategic retreat is wise at this time because of the hysterical nature of the atomic project in the public press."[20] As for the Hickenlooper charges against Lilienthal and the consequent hearings, which dragged on through the summer months, Holifield first characterized them as a fiasco.[21] The California congressman was even more condemnatory of Hickenlooper's efforts in a 1950 speech:

> Senator Hickenlooper abused his privilege. Apparently on the half-baked advice of some persons formerly employed by the Atomic Energy Commission, he charged the Commission with "incredible mismanagement."
>   This was a serious charge....
>   For days and days our Joint Committee on Atomic Energy held hearings, some public, some secret, to get at the truth of the matter. In the end, we found nothing of importance wrong with the Atomic Energy Commission. Its administration was sound; its accomplishments large. But precious time was wasted, at the taxpayers' expense, and the business of the Atomic Energy Commission was disrupted because a Senator eager for some publicity in a pre-election year and bearing a grudge against Commission Chairman Lilienthal, made rash and unwarranted accusations.

I shudder to think what would have happened in the investigation if Senator Hickenlooper were still the Chairman of the Atomic Energy Committee, as he was during the 80th Congress. Probably a Republican majority would have handed atomic energy control back to the military.[22]

As the Hickenlooper probe was drawing to a close with its last session on August 25, an event of far greater significance was about to unfold over the Pacific. On September 3, 1949, a WB-29 weather reconnaissance plane on routine patrol from Japan to Alaska picked up some measurable radioactivity. A filter paper that had been exposed for three hours at eighteen thousand feet over the North Pacific east of the Kamchatka Penninsula produced evidence of an amount of radioactivity sufficient to constitute an official alert. Monitoring personnel promptly notified the air force's Long Range Detection System. The military conducted further tests and concluded tentatively that the radioactivity was the result of a nuclear explosion. They notified the AEC on September 8. The AEC hurriedly assembled a "blue ribbon" panel to examine the evidence, and the panel concluded by September 19 that the Soviet Union had detonated a nuclear device on or about August 29, 1949. Vacationing AEC Chairman Lilienthal rushed back to Washington on September 20 to urge President Truman to inform the public immediately of the event. Truman, who had been kept informed by the Central Intelligence Agency and the Joint Chiefs, was reluctant to make an immediate announcement because of several factors, including the potentially adverse effects the announcement might have on the recent devaluation of the British pound and on the first United Nations General Assembly meeting then in progress in the United States. On September 21, however, Truman sent for JCAE leaders McMahon and Hickenlooper. Hickenlooper was out of town, so Truman delivered the news solely to McMahon on September 22, announcing his intention to inform the public the next day. On September 23, the president informed the American people that the United States had evidence that "within recent weeks an atomic explosion occurred in the U.S.S.R." To allay public anxiety, however, Truman emphasized that "the eventual development of this new force by other nations was to be expected" and that "this probability had always been taken into account by us."[23]

JCAE members were shocked and alarmed as they hastily assembled in a special session on September 23 to hear the news of the Soviet detonation. William Webster, deputy for atomic energy to Secretary of Defense Louis Johnson, explained the discovery to the JCAE. Simultaneously, the president informed the cabinet, and the presidential press secretary, Charles Ross, distributed a carefully worded statement to the press.[24]

The news of the Soviet achievement spurred the JCAE into action. On the day of the president's announcement, McMahon conferred with AEC Commissioner Gordon Dean, his close friend and onetime law partner, who had replaced Waymack on the commission. After the meeting, Dean drafted a memorandum for the other commissioners suggesting the need for "some tangible response to the Soviet challenge." On Thursday, September 28, and Friday, September 29, the JCAE held the first two of many hearings with the AEC on the subject of America's response to the Soviet detonation. At the September 29 meeting, which was closed to the public, McMahon read aloud a staff report by Borden on increasing military strength. The report concluded that "the atomic armaments race, in its present phase, makes primacy in developing a thermo-nuclear [sic] super-weapon a dominant consideration."[25]   This report was the first solid indication that the JCAE would be considering development of the hydrogen bomb as an option to counter the new Soviet threat.

In his JCAE endeavors, McMahon counted on Holifield as an ally.   This attitude was less because of a close personal friendship than because of what Holifield later termed "our common philosophies."[26]   The two men seldom found themselves opposed to each other in atomic energy matters, and the new situation was no exception.   On October 1, 1949, Holifield publicly described the news of the Russian blast in a radio broadcast as "the most serious public announcement since the first revelation of the first atomic bomb explosion at Almagorde [sic], New Mexico."   He emphasized, however, that "the verification of the Russian bomb explosion was not a surprise to us except in point of time," adding that "most of our members would have set the date of discovery forward a year or two."   The Soviet detonation, Holifield said, required "a renewed attempt to evolve a system of international control of atomic energy."   Until this objective could be achieved, he urged expansion of the U.S. atomic energy program.   Holifield perhaps referred cryptically to hydrogen bomb development when he added, "This expansion is not only in the field of physical production of atomic weapons, but it also lies in the field of scientific research and development."[27]

Any reference by Holifield to building the hydrogen bomb had to be vague, since the public was unaware of development in this area.   Actually, the possibility of a hydrogen, or fusion, weapon had been a topic for scientific, if not public, discussion since 1934 in the United States.   Ironically, the

first scientist to suggest the fusion reaction was a Russian immigrant, George
Gamow, who had joined the physics department
at George Washington University. Upon
Gamow's recommendation, Edward Teller also
joined the department, and together the two
men started the first pure research on the
subject. It became for them "a kind of
game, an intellectual exercise."[28] This
attitude was because of the nature of the
fusion reaction, which was the opposite of a
fission reaction. In a fission reaction,
which was the concept used in the atomic
bomb, the nucleus of a heavy element (usually uranium) is bombarded by neutrons,
causing it to split into two nuclei of
lighter elements with a resultant release of
energy. In a fusion or thermonuclear reaction, two light nuclei (isotopes of hydro-
gen--deuterium and tritium--are most suitable) collide and fuse together to form the
nucleus of a heavier element, again producing energy as a by-product. The consequent
energy release is about one thousand times
more powerful than that in a fission reaction. Since nuclei are positively charged
particles, they naturally repel each other
and collide only at high speeds, which can
be generated only by very high temperatures
approaching those in stars such as the sun.
Thus, in 1934, with the atomic bomb still
eleven years away, Gamow and Teller's work
was necessarily theoretical, since the high
temperatures generated by fission reactions
would be required to produce a fusion reaction, and even fission itself was only an
abstraction at the time.[29]
    The achievement of a fission reaction
in Germany in 1938, America's entry into
World War II, the establishment of the Manhattan Engineer District for developing the
atomic bomb, and the achievement of a chain
reaction by scientist Enrico Fermi at the
famous Chicago "pile" in December 1942 all

brought the hydrogen, as well as the atomic bomb closer to reality. Working with Fermi, Teller by mid-1942 had overcome most of the theoretical obstacles to a hydrogen bomb and had suggested that the uranium bomb being developed would provide the high temperatures necessary to trigger the fusion reaction. Since the atomic, or uranium, bomb was the key to the hydrogen bomb, it had to be developed first. The newly created Los Alamos Laboratory gave the atomic bomb first priority, with the hydrogen bomb, among other projects, assigned a secondary position. Teller went to work at Los Alamos. By September 1944, development of the hydrogen weapon became a visible project at the laboratory. Wartime technical reports on the hydrogen bomb were optimistic that the super-weapon project could be accomplished in a relatively short period of time. In a 1946 report, Teller suggested that only one or two years of vigorous development similar to the atomic bomb endeavor would be needed. A 1945 study by J. Robert Oppenheimer and 1947 and 1948 reports of the AEC's General Advisory Committee (chaired by Oppenheimer), however, became increasingly discouraging, the enthusiasm of Teller and his allies notwithstanding. Thus, the AEC and the military were deluged with negative information on the super weapon in the two or three years immediately preceding the Soviet detonation. They did not know that the 1944-1946 positive reports by Teller even existed. Such was the situation when McMahon and Borden began advocating expansion of the nation's weapons programs and touting the super weapon as a possible subject for priority consideration.[30]

The president's September 23, 1949, message on the Soviet explosion produced little immediate official activity outside of the JCAE except for separate efforts by AEC commissioners Dean and Strauss and sci-

entist Teller. Gordon Dean had conferred
with McMahon and had begun preparation of
the memorandum to his fellow commissioners
asserting the need to respond to the Soviet
action, but he had not been specific about
what the response should be. Strauss, on
the other hand, had concluded that the
United States should develop the super
weapon, based on information he had gathered
at the September JCAE hearings and in discussions with his fellow commissioners. In
a memorandum begun on September 30 and submitted to his colleagues on October 5,
Strauss maintained that "the time has now
come for a quantum jump in our planning,"
meaning that the United States "should now
make an intensive effort to get ahead [of
Russia] with the super." Strauss was thinking of "a commitment in talent and money
comparable, if necessary, to that which
produced the first atomic weapon." Strauss
believed that development of the fusion
bomb, not expansion of the existing atomic
arsenal, was "the way to stay ahead" of the
Soviet Union. He concluded that the AEC
should "immediately consult the General
Advisory Committee to ascertain their views"
on expediting development of the super.[31]
Strauss notified the White House of his
actions through Truman's military aide,
Admiral Sydney W. Souers, and learned that
Truman knew nothing of the super-bomb project but expressed an immediate interest in
it and wanted the matter forced up to the
Oval Office quickly. The AEC agreed to
Strauss's request. AEC Chairman Lilienthal
asked General Advisory Committee (GAC)
Chairman Oppenheimer to call a meeting on
the issue. Oppenheimer set the meeting of
the nine-member GAC for October 28-30, when
member Enrico Fermi would be back from
Italy.[32]
    JCAE Chairman McMahon received
Strauss's October 5 memorandum on October 6.

This timing was testimony to the coincidence of McMahon's and Strauss's views on the hydrogen weapon and indicates they may have conferred. Shortly after the president's September 23 announcement, probably before October 6, McMahon also met with Teller, who was at AEC headquarters in Washington from September 23 on a work-related trip. Upon hearing of the Soviet nuclear test, Teller had called Oppenheimer to see what he could do to meet the Soviet challenge. Oppenheimer told Teller to "keep your shirt on," but Teller, with his tremendous enthusiasm for the hydrogen project, may have interpreted the comment liberally or, possibly, his friend Lewis Strauss may have introduced the scientist to McMahon.[33]

Whatever the precise timing or motivation behind Teller's lunch with McMahon in McMahon's office, the meeting brought Chet Holifield to center stage in the JCAE's efforts to expedite development of the hydrogen bomb. Holifield received a telephone call from McMahon inviting him to join the senator and Teller in McMahon's office for lunch. Holifield remembered that McMahon ordered steaks delivered to his office from the Senate restaurant, a move that impressed Holifield because "we couldn't do anything like that over in the House."[34] During lunch, Teller explained the dynamics of the thermonuclear reaction to McMahon and Holifield and made forceful arguments for development of the hydrogen bomb based on the threat of Russia's obtaining the super weapon before the United States. After Teller's presentation, McMahon explained to Holifield that he wanted the congressman to chair an ad hoc subcommittee to look into feasibility of developing the hydrogen weapon. The mission of the subcommittee would be to visit the weapons laboratories and reach a conclusion on what scientists in general thought about possibilities of de-

veloping the hydrogen bomb. Holifield readily agreed to the assignment and learned
that McMahon had appointed representatives
Melvin Price (D-Illinois), Henry Jackson (D-
Washington), Carl Hinshaw (R-California),
and Senator William F. Knowland (R-California) as the other subcommittee members.
Holifield's group scheduled visits to the
Los Alamos Weapons Laboratory in New Mexico
and the Lawrence Radiation Laboratory in
Berkeley for late October, during the upcoming congressional recess.[35]

McMahon kept busy through mid-October
in his efforts to ascertain the climate of
opinion on the hydrogen bomb within government circles. On October 10, the senator
(and Carl Hinshaw) lunched with Berkeley
scientists Ernest Lawrence and Luis Alvarez
and came away convinced more than ever that
the super was the answer to the Russian
threat.[36] On October 14, the JCAE held a
closed hearing with the military to ascertain their opinions on the super. The
witnesses, including generals Omar Bradley,
Hoyt S. Vandenburg, and Kenneth Nichols,
expressed their view that the hydrogen bomb
should be developed as soon as possible
because the Russians might also be building
one. At another closed hearing on October
17, McMahon and other JCAE members discovered with some chagrin that the Central
Intelligence Agency (CIA) was unable to
assert conclusively whether or not the Soviets were working on the hydrogen bomb or
what their progress might be. On October
17, McMahon wrote AEC Chairman Lilienthal
that "it is the sense of the Joint Committee
that the current situation dictates unusual
and even extraordinary steps," and he urged
that efforts on the super be "as bold and
urgent as our original atomic enterprise."
McMahon also asked for a detailed history of
the hydrogen bomb effort before January.
Specifically, he wanted to know "what is now

being done and planned to be done; whether
or not an all-out, supreme effort comparable
to the Manhattan District wartime effort is
contemplated; [and] how you believe the
Joint Committee and Congress might help
accelerate this program."   Lilienthal did
not reply until November 28 and did not send
the requested information until December 30.
By then, McMahon had already obtained most
of the information from the Holifield subcommittee   visits   to   Los   Alamos   and
Berkeley.[37]

Holifield's group, minus Senator Knowland but including JCAE Staff Director Borden and JCAE staff member Walter Hamilton,
assembled at Los Alamos on October 27.   Dr.
Norris Bradbury, head of the Los Alamos
Laboratory after Oppenheimer's resignation
in October 1945, gave the subcommittee members, in an extensive morning lecture, their
first concrete data on the hydrogen weapon.
Bradbury provided a technical overview of
the history of the atomic weapons program.
He outlined weapons development from the
early days of the atomic bomb project up to
the present and provided projections of
future tests and other developments.   Bradbury also briefed the congressmen on the
differences between fission and fusion bombs
and discussed the various types of fission
weapons that had been developed.   He then
discussed the hydrogen project in detail.
Bradbury declared that there was virtually
no upper limit on the destructive power of
hydrogen bombs, but that present technology
dictated that bombs with greater destructive
capability would have to be larger in size.
Because of the size constraint, he indicated
that "deliverability immediately appears as
a critical problem in the use of such a
weapon."   Bradbury estimated that the current, step-by-step development program
"would carry the U.S. forward to a super
weapon by about 1958 or 1960."[38]

Soviet work on the super bomb was the other important subject of Bradbury's lecture. He verified that the Soviets had a plutonium weapon, and that they had obtained the services of approximately five hundred German physicists captured in World War II who were particularly well acquainted with heavy water reactor design (critical to the production of the light isotopes of hydrogen). Moreover, Dr. Kapitsa, a leading Russian scientist and the world's foremost expert on high pressures, probably was also assisting in the Soviet hydrogen project. Bradbury believed that "it is logical to assume that Dr. Kapitsa would be considering or even have worked out a high pressure super weapon using deuterium and tritium." Since the Russians possessed heavy water plutonium production facilities that were "almost perfect for tritium production," Bradbury concluded that "it is logical to believe that the Russians now possess both the basic idea for a super weapon and the most critical production facilities and brain to execute that idea." He also pointed out that the radioactivity of the atomic bomb used to trigger a hydrogen weapon would be completely dissipated by the blast, and hence "in all probability the super weapon could not be detected by radioactive measurement if the Soviets tested it." Using these somber conclusions, Bradbury outlined an accelerated development program that would yield a "workable super" by mid-1952. He emphasized, however, that "even with a workable super, the problem of how to deliver such a weapon to its target was very great and might negate the utilization of the bomb."[39]

As a follow-up to his morning lecture, Bradbury scheduled an afternoon meeting with himself and Teller as speakers. The primary subject of this meeting was the moral and political aspects of producing a thermo-

nuclear weapon. Teller did most of the
talking. As his major theme, he emphasized
that it would not be possible to carry out
hydrogen bomb development effectively "unless firm moral and political assurance was
given perhaps by the President himself as
well as by the Congress to the men who would
be working on the program." Scientists
would have to be assured that such a bomb
"would be used in a positive and perhaps
even a dramatic manner to achieve Russian
compliance with Western aims." Teller acknowledged that already a number of prominent scientists had serious reservations
about the moral and political feasibility of
the super weapon.[40]

Teller's assessment of possible scientific resistance to the super particularly
interested the subcommittee members. They
queried the scientist about whether the
project would still be possible if large
numbers of scientists and technicians were
opposed. Teller indicated that he thought
development would still be possible. Bradbury pointed out, however, that his projection of a workable bomb by mid-1952 probably
would depend upon complete cooperation from
principal scientists in the United States
and from about twelve of those in Great
Britain and Canada. Bradbury estimated that
about thirty additional scientists would be
needed at Los Alamos for the project, as
well as "several hundred" more staff.[41]

That evening, Holifield chaired an
informal meeting of the subcommittee at
Bradbury's home. The four subcommittee
members and the two JCAE staff present recognized the importance of the information
they had obtained. It both alarmed them and
spurred them to action. The subcommittee
agreed that Hinshaw should head immediately
back to Washington and ask McMahon for an
executive session of the full JCAE within
two weeks to present Bradbury's proposal for

an accelerated program. The specific purpose of the meeting "would be to free the
State Department in order that it might firm
up an agreement with Britain and Canada" to
permit the United States to use certain
scientists in the hydrogen development effort. In addition, the subcommittee agreed
to start legislative preparations for amending the Atomic Energy Act "to permit export
of enriched material to Chalk River, Canada,
in order that the United States might get
the benefit of possible tritium from the
Chalk River heavy water pile." Finally, the
subcommittee instructed JCAE Staff Director
Borden to phone McMahon in preparation for
Hinshaw's visit and to call Senator Knowland
to ask him to meet the group in Berkeley the
next day.[42]

The subcommittee assembled in Berkeley
the next day for a meeting with Dr. Ernest
Lawrence (head of the Lawrence Radiation
Laboratory), several of his associates, and
two members of the AEC. The legislators
were anxious to know Lawrence's views on the
hydrogen bomb, as an important supplement to
what they had learned at Los Alamos. Lawrence's presentation served to reinforce the
subcommittee's growing sense of urgency
about developing the fusion weapon. Lawrence averred that the super was "entirely
feasible," that the Russians were already or
soon would be developing the super bomb, and
that the United States had "no time to lose"
in getting its own development program underway. The scientist essentially reiterated Bradbury's analysis of Soviet work
on the super and also mentioned Dr. Kapitsa.
He then outlined three methods by which the
United States could obtain enough tritium
for a test in 1952. Lawrence also favored
the use of British and Canadian scientists
in the project.[43]

The meeting with Lawrence essentially
ended the subcommittee's tour. Holifield

and the two JCAE staff members, however, continued to Idaho Falls to discuss with AEC staff there the capability of the new Idaho office to take on construction of a tritium production facility. Holifield may have been prompted to make the trip because of Lawrence's suggestions at Berkeley for increasing tritium production. As a result of this trip, Holifield concluded that there did not appear to be any problems in Idaho Falls that would hamper rapid construction of a tritium production facility at the site.[44]

For two important reasons, the Holifield subcommittee trip turned out to be a pivotal event in the JCAE's attempts to expedite hydrogen bomb research and development. First, as a result of the trip, the JCAE now possessed more information than it had ever had before on the fusion weapon. The JCAE was probably the best informed body on the project inside the government, with the exception of the Los Alamos scientists, and certainly was better informed than some of the AEC commissioners or the military.[45] The subcommittee brought back to McMahon the information he requested from AEC Chairman Lilienthal, information Lilienthal would not provide until December 30 and, even then, only in abbreviated form. Armed with considerable information and advised by subcommittee messenger Hinshaw to convene the JCAE in executive session to hear Bradbury's proposal for a crash program, McMahon was able to parry the future thrusts of various opponents of the super and successfully advance the JCAE's cause of expediting hydrogen bomb development.

Second, the Holifield subcommittee trip helped to unite the JCAE in support of the hydrogen program. During the trip, Holifield and the other subcommittee members had learned that the project might be crucial for maintaining America's lead in weapons

development and that an accelerated program
was possible for accomplishing this goal.
Given these facts, the Holifield subcommittee of three Democrats and two Republicans
returned to Washington unanimous in their
recommendation to expedite hydrogen bomb
development. Of the eighteen JCAE members,
only Republican representatives Sterling
Cole of New York and Charles Elston of Ohio
remained unconvinced of the need to develop
the bomb quickly.[46] Thus, McMahon was armed
not only with considerable facts, but with
almost unanimous support of the JCAE in his
efforts to persuade the AEC, the military,
the State Department, and ultimately the
president that an accelerated hydrogen bomb
project was essential to national security.

The AEC was not unaware or unmindful of
the JCAE's foray into its territory. AEC
Chairman Lilienthal kept a watchful eye on
the subcommittee and other McMahon "machina-
tions," which increasingly filled him with
dread and disgust. In his journal, he
noted:

> Reports from Los Alamos and
> Berkeley are rather awful: the
> visiting firemen saw a group of
> scientists who can only be de-
> scribed as drooling with the pros-
> pect and "blood-thirsty." E. O.
> [Lawrence] quite bad: there's
> nothing to think over; this calls
> for the "spirit of Groves," and
> the ground is laid for the Joint
> Committee members to come back and
> demand that we plunge ahead and
> think about it, if at all, on
> vacation or something.[47]

Lilienthal and McMahon soon became
embroiled in a bitter controversy over the
hydrogen bomb. Oppenheimer's GAC was the
first body, however, to assault the JCAE's

efforts to expedite the hydrogen project.
On the same day that the Holifield subcommittee was concluding its trip, the GAC met
in Washington to consider the hydrogen bomb
question. The eight prominent scientists
present for the meeting held hearings and
conducted discussions on the super from
October 28 through October 30. On October
30, the scientists issued their report to
the AEC, recommending unanimously against a
crash program. Their major reasons included
the uncertain feasibility of the super
weapon, the lack of nonmilitary applications
of the weapon, the limited targets and situations for which the bomb would be appropriate, and the immorality of constructing a
weapon that "would bring about the destruction of innumerable human lives." The scientists wanted the United States to seek an
agreement with Russia to forswear hydrogen
bomb development by both nations.[48]

On October 31, the AEC commissioners
met with McMahon and gave him a copy of the
GAC report. The report alarmed the senator.
In a meeting with Teller two days later,
McMahon averred that the report "just makes
me sick." Almost immediately, McMahon wrote
a letter to President Truman asking to be
heard before Truman made any final decision.
Truman replied on November 2 that he would
be happy to hear from McMahon on the matter,
but that it had not yet reached his desk.[49]

Indeed, it had not; the AEC did not
send the report to the president until November 9, at which time the commissioners
attached their individual views to the document. Commissioners Lilienthal, Henry
Dewolf Smyth, and Sumner T. Pike basically
agreed with the GAC, while absent commissioners Dean and Strauss predictably lined
up later with McMahon. Lilienthal gave the
GAC report as broad a coverage within the
government as possible to block the McMahon
steamroller. On November 1, he had met with

Secretary of State Dean Acheson because he
regarded the matter "not as one for the
commission merely, or chiefly, but essentially a question of foreign policy for him
[Acheson] and the President." Lilienthal
also warned the president that McMahon would
try to "blitz" the White House in favor of
the hydrogen bomb.[50]

McMahon was busier than usual during
the first two weeks of November preparing
his case for presentation to the president.
Possibly because of the Holifield subcommittee suggestion that the whole committee hear
Dr. Bradbury's proposal and partly because
he wanted to hear the information firsthand,
McMahon made two trips to Los Alamos with
Borden on November 8 and November 15. On
November 8, McMahon listened to essentially
the same lecture by Dr. Bradbury that the
Holifield subcommittee had heard about a
week before. On November 15, McMahon and
Borden returned to Los Alamos for what
turned out to be unproductive discussions
with John Manley, secretary to the GAC and
acting laboratory director in Bradbury's
absence. Manley was also an opponent of the
super. McMahon and Borden met with Teller
in the afternoon, however, and the scientist
repeated the information he had presented to
the subcommittee. After meeting with
Teller, McMahon traveled to Los Angeles,
where he began revising a draft report to
the president written by Borden and
Hamilton.[51]

The draft report took the form of a
five-thousand-word letter from McMahon to
President Truman. It was probably the most
comprehensive restatement and discussion of
the hydrogen bomb question presented to
Truman. In the letter, Borden and Hamilton
refuted the reasons given by the GAC for
repudiating a crash program for the super.
More importantly, they used the Holifield
subcommittee findings both to challenge the

GAC's arguments and to advocate the accelerated hydrogen bomb project.

In the completed letter, McMahon assailed the GAC's reasons for rejecting the super. With regard to the GAC's contention that the feasibility of the bomb was uncertain, McMahon countered that "my information, in contrast, is that . . . intensive work *short* of wartime methods might reach fruition in early 1952." As for the GAC's opinion that there were no nonmilitary applications for the hydrogen bomb, McMahon declared that "this contention flouts all past experience," since "there never has been research and development of any type or character that failed to increase human capacity for constructively harnessing the forces of nature." McMahon also disputed the GAC's contention that there were only limited targets for such a bomb by pointing out that the GAC "admits that at least two or three urban targets tailored to the super do in fact exist--and rapid Soviet industrialization may soon increase the list." McMahon also argued that there were "additional targets, many of them tactical, which only the super might successfully destroy" and that the use of super bombs on still other targets would free up fission bombs for other targets. Finally, as to the immorality of constructing the hydrogen bomb, McMahon asserted that "there is no moral dividing line that I can see between a big explosion which causes heavy damage [hydrogen bomb] and many smaller explosions causing equal or still greater damage [fission or conventional weapons]." As McMahon viewed the matter, "Modern warfare, even if waged with pre-atomic weapons only, is the real instrument of genocide--not a single agent like the super."[52]

For McMahon, even the path toward mutual renunciation of the fusion weapon by the United States and the Soviet Union was

fraught with danger. He advised against
dependence on "a mere paper pledge" and
pointed out that "the need for a tight control system of the kind approved by the UN
General Assembly is now intensified, since
the secret manufacture of just one fission
bomb might furnish an initiator for a super
and since the necessary tritium might be
produced in dozens of small reactors difficult to locate through inspection." Drawing
upon the information obtained by the Holifield subcommittee, McMahon emphasized that
"if Russia elected to test merely the initiating assembly, she would gain essential
information; she would know that, in all
probability, her scientists had mastered the
super; and the experimental explosion--if
we detected it at all--would appear to us as
an ordinary fission bomb." McMahon warned
Truman that "if we let Russia get the super
first, catastrophe becomes all but certain--
whereas, if we get it first, there exists a
chance of saving ourselves."[53]

    McMahon's letter thus included all of
the major findings of the Holifield subcommittee. The belief that the hydrogen weapon
was feasible, the conclusions that an orderly completion of the existing development
program was possible by 1958 and a crash
program by 1952, and the possibility that a
Soviet fusion bomb might go undetected were
all ideas that were interspersed in the
letter among the criticisms of the GAC's
position. McMahon sent copies of his November 21 letter to Secretary of State Acheson,
Secretary of Defense Johnson, and AEC Chairman Lilienthal. Within the government,
there was no longer any question at all of
the course the JCAE was pursuing.[54]

    The influence of the Holifield subcom-
mittee did not end with the McMahon letter.
Together with Vice-Chairman Durham and subcommittee members Holifield, Price, and
Jackson, McMahon visited the president to

solicit his support for the JCAE's position on the super. Holifield recalled the occasion vividly and remembered "staring at the President's naval aide, Admiral Sydney W. Souers, and being amazed that he could sit by the President of the United States dressed in an informal dark blue shirt." McMahon chose Holifield to give the oral presentation to the president. At the conclusion of the nearly hour-long meeting, McMahon gave Truman his five-thousand-word letter, and the president indicated that he would give the JCAE an answer very soon.[55]

On November 18, at about the time McMahon was revising his voluminous letter and preparing for his meeting with Truman, the hydrogen bomb issue, which had involved only discussions within the government, was suddenly injected into the public arena. Alfred Friendly reported in a feature article in the *Washington Post* that Senator Edwin Johnson had mentioned the super weapon on a local New York television show on November 1. A later, possibly less-kind commentator, Margaret Truman, explained that the senator had "blabbed the information about the H-bomb debate on a television show." In any event, Friendly's announcement of Senator Johnson's action brought the glare of publicity to the hydrogen bomb debate and also brought the need for a much quicker presidential decision.[56]

Actually, by the end of November, the JCAE, the AEC and its GAC, and the military had all provided their opinions to Truman on the need for hydrogen bomb development. In addition, Karl T. Compton, a respected scientist and early atomic energy administrator, had also written to the president on the issue. (Truman had offered Compton the chairmanship of the AEC, but the scientist had declined for health reasons.) Compton believed that development of the super weapon should be pushed if an effective international control agreement could not be obtained. Probably because he was distrustful of the majority views of the AEC and the GAC, Truman asked on November 18 for a special subcommittee of the National Security Council (NSC) to study hydrogen bomb development. Truman wanted as soon as possible a full assessment of the political and military, as well as technical, aspects of the project. The president chose Secretary of State Acheson, Defense Secretary Johnson, and Lilienthal as the three members of the special NSC subcommittee.[57]

The appointment of the special subcommittee essentially brought an end to the hydrogen bomb debate, with the decision in favor of the JCAE. Lilienthal now found himself in the minority, outvoted by Acheson, who found the moral argument "less persuasive as one examined it critically," and by Johnson, who disliked Lilienthal personally and espoused the slowly emerging Pentagon position in favor of all-out hydrogen bomb development.[58] Acheson later wrote that "due to the ascerbity of Louis Johnson's nature, the Committee held only two meetings." These were on December 22, 1949, and on January 31, 1950. By January 31, the special subcommittee had decided on a recommendation and immediately took it to the president. Truman brushed aside Lilienthal's reservations about the subcommittee's decision and immediately adopted and delivered the subcommittee's findings to the press. In the recommendation, which became known as the hydrogen bomb decision, Truman directed the AEC "to continue its work on all forms of atomic weapons, including the so-called hydrogen or super-bomb."[59] Actually, the term *continue* was deceptive, since "there was certainly an implication that they [the AEC] should approach the task with a greater sense of urgency than had heretofore been the case."[60] In the details of

his decision, Truman ordered that a vigorous
effort should be made to determine the technical feasibility of the hydrogen bomb, that
the rate and scale of effort should be determined jointly by the AEC and the Department of Defense, and that the departments of
State and Defense should concurrently review
the nation's foreign and military policies
with respect to the Soviet Union's nuclear
capabilities. The decision was supplemented
about two months later on March 10 by another Truman directive to accelerate the
hydrogen bomb development and production
program.[61]

Warner Schilling has aptly characterized Truman's hydrogen bomb decision as a
"minimal" decision, since it failed to resolve any of the major issues in the hydrogen bomb debate, such as the feasibility of
the weapon, its military value, or the intensity of the research and development
effort.[62]   What has been overlooked by many
historians, however, is that the decision
was also pro forma, made several weeks after
Truman decided the course he would pursue.
According to Holifield, McMahon and he knew
by "late December or early January" that the
president had decided to order development
of the H-bomb. Truman phoned McMahon, as he
promised he would when he finally reached a
decision, and an excited McMahon related the
news to Holifield.[63] The fact that the
decision had already been made by January 31
may also help to explain why Truman did not
want to discuss Lilienthal's reservations
about the special NSC subcommittee's recommendation when subcommittee members met with
him on January 31. It may also help to
explain comments of AEC historians Richard
G. Hewlett and Francis Duncan in their discussion of a closed JCAE hearing on January
20, 1950. Hewlett and Duncan write that
"the committee's frequent references to
possible costs of tritium production and

talk about a 'crash' effort suggested an
assumption on the Hill that development of
the Super was already an accepted fact."[64]
Indeed, McMahon and Holifield probably knew
by this time that Truman would soon announce
in favor of the accelerated hydrogen effort.

When Truman announced his hydrogen bomb
decision on January 31, Holifield broke the
news simultaneously in the House of Representatives, also suggesting that he had been
informed beforehand. Interrupting debate on
a cotton acreage bill, Holifield announced
the president's decision. After explaining
the content of Truman's directive, Holifield
dramatically told his colleagues that "in my
opinion, it is the most important announcement of our time."[65]

The hydrogen bomb decision was, indeed,
an important one in the history of atomic
energy affairs. The decision served notice
to the Soviet Union that the United States
would not renounce unilaterally the development of the super bomb. As such, the decision was an important origin of the atomic
armaments race.[66] On the domestic front,
Truman's order established the JCAE as an
important force in atomic energy affairs.
From 1947 to 1949, the JCAE had played a
relatively passive and silent role. During
the hydrogen bomb debate and after, the JCAE
emerged as an important partner in the nation's atomic energy program, largely because of the efforts of Senator McMahon.
Holifield, still a relatively junior member
of Congress, assisted McMahon probably more
than any other JCAE member in McMahon's
efforts to make the JCAE a force to be
reckoned with.

The hydrogen bomb decision was also a
very important (perhaps the most important)
event personally for Holifield during his
long tenure as a congressman. He always
looked back proudly to his participation as
one of the high points of his career. In

1957, when he was asked to write an article for *Reader's Digest* on the subject of "The Day I was Proudest to be an American," Holifield chose his participation in the hydrogen bomb decision as his topic.[67] In 1969, when he was chairman of the JCAE, Holifield reacquainted himself with the hydrogen project as part of his preparations for the Anti-Ballistic Missile (ABM) debates. As a result, he asked the JCAE staff to prepare a history of the JCAE's influence on Truman's decision to develop the hydrogen bomb. Although the history was never completed because of the heavy workload of the committee, a JCAE staff member did complete a draft of approximately 150 pages. Holifield retained a censored copy of the draft report among his congressional papers.[68]

On November 1, 1952, after almost two years of vigorous research and development on the super, the United States successfully tested its first thermonuclear device. Tragically, Senator McMahon did not live to see the results of his handiwork. But Holifield did. When the Soviet Union announced on August 8, 1953, that the United States no longer had a monopoly of the super weapon, Holifield was particularly thankful for the effort the JCAE had made to assure development of the bomb by the United States. "Had we failed to éxplore the hydrogen weapon potential," Holifield wrote later, "the Soviets would have bested us, and we might now be on our knees before them."[69]

Public Power on the Defensive:
Holifield and the Passage of the
Atomic Energy Act of 1954

Chet Holifield's prominence in atomic energy
affairs did not diminish in the years after
the hydrogen bomb decision. He remained an
avid student of all aspects of atomic energy. As the weapons issue receded and the
peaceful uses of atomic energy became the
dominant concern of lawmakers during the
Eisenhower administration, Holifield stayed
at the forefront of atomic energy discussions. As a harbinger of policy, however,
he was largely on the defensive from 1952
through 1954, as Republicans gained control
of both Congress and the White House.
    Several events in 1952, some of them
unsettling, brought significant changes that
altered the course of atomic energy affairs
in the United States. On July 28, Senator
Brien McMahon died from cancer. The dominant JCAE chairman had been a driving force
in the nation's atomic energy affairs and an
ardent advocate of weapons development in
the contest with Russia. As a result of
McMahon's death, Vice-Chairman Carl Durham
became the first House member to be chairman
of the JCAE.[1] On November 1, the United
States successfully tested the first hydrogen bomb device, thus assuring the nation of
a continuing lead over Russia in nuclear

weapons.   Also in November, General Dwight
Eisenhower and the Republicans overturned
twenty years of Democratic rule, gaining the
presidency and majorities in both houses of
Congress.   Thus, Republicans looked forward
to recapturing the chairmanship and majority
on the Joint Committee when Congress convened in January 1953.

With McMahon gone, the weapons issue
temporarily in the background, and a Republican majority on the JCAE, the new Republican administration sought to redirect the
activities of the emerging atomic energy
establishment to its own ends.   Early in
1953, Eisenhower took steps to bring the AEC
directly under his control. The administration also announced plans to amend substantially the Atomic Energy Act of 1946, with
the intent of bringing private industry into
partnership with the government in the quest
to develop commercially competitive electrical power from atomic energy.   As a consequence of the debate and passage of the
Republican-inspired Atomic Energy Act of
1954, the public versus private power issue
was injected into atomic energy affairs,
where it remained the paramount domestic
policy concern of the nation's atomic energy
lawmakers throughout the Eisenhower administration and into the Kennedy years.   This
issue involved the traditional struggle for
control of electric-generating power between
private utilities and municipal, cooperative, and other publicly owned utilities.
It also concerned the question of the role
the federal government should play in the
development of this new source of electrical
power and the distribution of its benefits.
Although not strictly a party policy matter,
the issue engendered bitter controversy
between Republicans and Democrats, as well
as among other public and private power
advocates, with the Republicans generally
favoring private power and most Democrats

supporting public power.

Holifield remained an active and vociferous member of the JCAE despite the fact that he was in the Democratic minority. He was one of the first congressmen to take a serious interest in policy questions involving scientific efforts to create commercially competitive electrical power from atomic energy. In keeping with his liberal Democratic outlook, Holifield leaned philosophically toward the public power persuasion. He vigorously resisted Republican attempts during passage of the Atomic Energy Act of 1954 to allow private industry to monopolize the benefits of atomic energy research and development, activities that had been paid for by American taxpayers. In fact, Holifield was the chief opponent in the House to the Eisenhower administration's efforts to pass the new legislation. Although Holifield was unsuccessful in thwarting the Republicans, he nonetheless emerged, even more than before, as a primary Democratic spokesman and leader on atomic energy matters. The Atomic Energy Act of 1954, moreover, was in some ways a different piece of legislation than it would have been without Holifield's criticisms.

Holifield might never have been chairman of the JCAE by 1961 but for a concerted effort by other JCAE Democrats and himself at the beginning of the Eisenhower administration to assert equality with the Senate in selection of JCAE chairmen. Up through the Eighty-second Congress, the Senate had held the chairmanship, and Senator McMahon himself had been chairman, except in the Eightieth Congress, when Republican control of the Senate permitted selection of Bourke Hickenlooper of Iowa. The tradition of deference to senators in selection of JCAE chairman had been based on the fact that the Senate Special Committee of Atomic Energy had formulated the original Atomic Energy

Act.[2]

   With McMahon's death, House members, particularly the Democrats, were less predisposed to defer to their senatorial colleagues. They were dissatisfied with Senate dominance of the committee because, as Holifield viewed it, "[w]e were doing the work, and they were getting the glory." In conversations with the other three House Democrats, Holifield proposed that the House fight for the principle of alternate chairmanships when the Joint Committee convened for its organizational meeting in January 1953. This proposal appeared to be a just solution to the problem, since the JCAE was made up equally of representatives and senators. After agreeing among themselves, the House Democrats appealed to the five House Republicans, arguing "from the standpoint of the prestige of the House and from the standpoint of justice." Sterling Cole (R-New York), who stood to gain the chair, was receptive to the idea, and the Republicans agreed to join with the Democrats.[3]

   When the JCAE met in January 1953, members were unable to agree upon a chairman. The Senate members unanimously supported Senator Hickenlooper for the post, while their House counterparts unanimously backed Cole. The impasse was not to be broken easily, since the Republican Senate was equally determined to continue Senate dominance on the committee. When Holifield left Washington for three weeks beginning on March 24, 1953, the disagreement was still unresolved. In a letter to Carl Durham, Holifield asked Durham to "see that my proxy is used along with your vote" if any meetings were held in Holifield's absence. Holifield concluded that "if Stub Cole withdraws his nomination . . . I believe that it should be used as a bargaining point to secure an agreement, duly recorded in the minutes of the Committee, that the Senate

acquiesces in the principle of alternate
chairmanships."4   Ultimately, Cole did not
have to retire as a candidate;   in April,
the Senate agreed to the House's demands.
Sterling Cole became the first House member
to be elected chairman of the JCAE,   and the
principle of alternate chairmanships was
later given the force of law in the Atomic
Energy Act of 1954.5

The   end of the struggle over the JCAE
chairmanship cleared the way for the JCAE to
consider substantive atomic energy issues.
Under the McMahon chairmanship, the weapons
contest with Russia had been the paramount
concern.   By the end of 1952,   however, the
weapons issue had begun to recede as the
major consideration because preparations for
development of the hydrogen bomb were well
underway. Development of tritium facilities
had begun on the Savannah River near Aiken,
South Carolina,   along with construction of
additional gaseous diffusion facilities at
Paducah, Kentucky.   Congress had also authorized construction of five additional
plutonium-producing reactors at Hanford,
Washington,   for the expanded plutonium
weapons program.   Acting Chairman Durham
thus was able to turn his attention to a
subject that had received a secondary priority in previous years: the production of
commercially competitive electricity from
atomic reactors.   On August 19,   1952, less
than a month after McMahon's death,   Durham
sent a letter to the AEC indicating the
JCAE's keen interest in and plans for hearings in 1953 on industrial participation in
atomic power development.   Durham also requested a report from the AEC reviewing its
policies in this area.   Chairman Cole, who
took over from Durham in April 1953, continued to prod AEC Chairman Gordon Dean for
a policy statement and added an additional
request that the AEC recommend legislation
to permit private industrial participation

in atomic power development.   Dean's delay
in responding to Durham's and Cole's requests can be partly attributed to the fact
that the first Republican administration in
twenty years needed time to consider its
approach to atomic energy affairs.[6]
     The JCAE's interest in atomic power
development grew from the absence of any
urgent weapons issues and, probably more
importantly, from the AEC's growing activities in this field.   In its first report to
Congress, the AEC declared that a broad
program initiated by the Manhattan Engineer
District to produce electric power from the
atom was already underway with Monsanto
Chemical and the General Electric Company.
The AEC also announced that it planned con-
sultations with utilities, with electrical
manufacturing and chemical companies, and
with other segments of private industry "to
assure broad participation by private enterprise in . . . the industrial application of
atomic energy."[7] Actually, however, the
AEC's "broad program" was more good intentions than fact.   The problems of organizing
and staffing the newly created AEC, the
emphasis on weapons, the shortage of uranium, and the concern with secrecy all im-
peded the development of atomic power in the
early years.   By early 1950, the AEC could
boast of only two approved power reactor
projects, the Experimental Breeder Reactor
under construction at the Argonne National
Laboratory and the Homogeneous Reactor being
developed at the Oak Ridge National Laboratory.   Beginning in 1951, however, the AEC
initiated a program of industrial participation in reactor development studies.   The
first four industrial teams, selected by the
AEC in 1951, reported separately in classified studies on a survey of dual-purpose
(plutonium and electricity production) reactor technology.   By 1953, there were ten
authorized study groups made up of utili-

ties, equipment manufacturers, chemical companies, architectural-engineering firms, and other industries. These groups were allowed access to AEC laboratories, plants, and contractor engineers and scientists in studying various aspects of reactor technology. The companies spent three million dollars of their own funds surveying the technology, making preliminary designs and economic studies, and performing various types of research and development activities.[8]

The Republican leadership of the JCAE recognized that full participation of industry in atomic power development would entail significant revisions to the Atomic Energy Act of 1946, which required governmental ownership and operation of all atomic plants and fissionable materials. Among other things, full participation by industry in the development and use of atomic reactors "raised policy and contractual problems over such matters as ownership of nuclear plants, licensing and use of fissionable materials, secrecy, patent rights, public safety, competition, and liability in case of disaster."[9] With such issues in mind, JCAE Chairman Cole and Vice-Chairman Hickenlooper announced hearings in June of 1953. Indicative of their interest in quickly opening up atomic energy to private enterprise was their assertion that the hearings would "develop a public understanding of the subject" and that "in the next session of Congress we will be able to direct our attention to the question of the desirable legislative language." The purpose of the hearings, according to Cole and Hickenlooper, would be to assess the effect of the development of atomic power on national security and American leadership in the "Free World," and both the amount and source of money and also the type of policy that would be called for in order to enlist the efforts of pri-

vate enterprise to develop atomic power
while protecting the public's multi-billion-
dollar investment in the national atomic
energy program.[10]

Even before the 1953 hearings began,
Holifield stated his views on industrial
participation in a lengthy speech on the
floor of the House. On June 1, 1953, the
California congressman declared, perhaps as
a warning to the Republicans, that he did
not intend "to sit idly by and give silent
assent to a give-away program in atomic
energy." Although Holifield believed that
"private industry should participate to the
fullest extent possible in atomic activities," he asserted that "I do not believe
that private industry should go the whole
hog and insist on private ownership of bomb-
making materials and the facilities for
producing them." Holifield pointed out that
"the law as it now stands does not prevent
private industry from going ahead with
atomic reactor research and development" and
that "a great deal of thinking, investigating, experimenting, and building remains to
be done before private industry can see any
investment opportunities and realize any
legitimate profit in the atomic-energy
field." Holifield reminded his colleagues
that all funds invested in atomic energy
"came from the public Treasury," and he
characterized the atomic energy program as
"a monument to cooperative endeavor by public and private agencies and enterprises in
a free society." Holifield concluded that
"the time is not yet at hand, atomic technology is not far enough advanced, to tear
down the legislative structure which sup-
ports our atomic programs" and that "drastic
revision of the Atomic Energy Act at this
time would be premature, ill-considered and
unwise."[11]

The 1953 hearings began on June 24 and
lasted until the end of July. In twenty-six

sessions, the JCAE heard from more than fifty witnesses, including business executives, government administrators, labor representatives, scientists, and public and private power spokesmen. Business, private utilities, and the AEC vigorously urged revision of the McMahon Act to allow fuller industrial participation in atomic power development. Public power associations and labor organizations, on the other hand, were fearful of hasty revisions to the act. Samuel Morris of the American Public Power Association, for example, favored participation by both public and private power and warned against patent policies that might result in monopolies. Edgar Dixon, chairman of the Edison Electric Institute's Atomic Power Committee, advocated changes to enhance the private sector's role, including private ownership of nuclear facilities and fissionable materials, workable licensing procedures, "fair" patent rights, and incentives for new developments.[12]

Although Chairman Cole announced that the 1953 hearings had paved the way for preparation of legislation to change the 1946 act in the next session of Congress, Holifield remained highly skeptical of the Republican initiative. Near the end of the hearings, Holifield reiterated in the House his belief that "basic changes in the Atomic Energy Act now would be premature and ill-advised." Holifield indicated that he would be "strongly opposed to any legislative course that would entail huge Government subsidies to private firms or restrict the participation through patent devices or otherwise, to a small segment of industry." He asserted that "government should proceed under existing legislation to develop atomic reactors and advance reactor technology until private industry was willing and able to invest its own funds on an independent footing and participate on the basis of

equal opportunity for all." According to
Holifield, further study by the AEC and the
JCAE would be necessary "before we arrive at
the stage of formulating new legislation on
atomic-power development."[13]   In place of
new legislation, Holifield introduced House
Joint Resolution No. 317, cosponsored by his
JCAE associate Melvin Price. The resolution
proposed a series of activities for both the
AEC and the JCAE.   It directed the AEC to
expedite the reactor development program and
to review its restricted data with a view
toward making more information available to
private industry and other interested parties.   It also required the AEC to complete
a report on the projected effects of atomic
power use and make formal recommendations
for necessary supplemental legislation. The
measure also called for continued studies by
the JCAE, including additional public hearings, if necessary, on the need for new
legislation, and directed the JCAE to submit
a report to Congress on its findings and
recommendations. Holifield was advocating a
careful, studious approach toward overhaul-
ing the McMahon Act in order to protect the
public investment in the atomic energy program and ensure equitable participation by
public and private organizations. His approach conflicted with Republican desires
for quick action, and his vociferousness in
offering a viable alternative made Holifield
an opponent to be reckoned with.[14]

Holifield might have been more successful in thwarting what appeared to him to be
a determined and somewhat audacious attempt
to redirect atomic energy activities to
benefit large corporations, but for now the
Republicans had the votes.   The election of
1952 had produced a rather firm Republican
majority in the House and a somewhat tenuous
one in the Senate.[15]   The White House was
also occupied by the first Republican in
twenty years.   President Eisenhower moved

quickly to bring atomic energy affairs under
Republican control.   Early in his administration   he   appointed   Admiral   Lewis   L.
Strauss,   a   former AEC commissioner,   as   his
atomic   energy   advisor.   Rumors   that   AEC
Chairman   Gordon Dean would soon resign surfaced   shortly   after   the   election,   even
though his term would not expire for another
year.   In June, Dean departed from the commission, and Eisenhower appointed Strauss as
AEC chairman.   Strauss,   by his own   admission,   "was   on record in opposition to continuing government monopoly in the   civilian
uses   of   atomic energy as far back   as   the
beginning of the Commission."[16]   At the 1953
hearings,   Strauss   testified   that   he   had
hoped,   as early as 1947,   that in his life-
time   "conditions will improve to the   point
where   atomic energy can be freed of government   monopoly and placed in a framework   of
[the] American system of   free,   competitive
enterprise."[17]   With Strauss in a dual role
as   presidential advisor and   AEC   chairman,
the   Eisenhower   administration developed   a
hold   on atomic energy affairs that was   not
even contemplated in the Truman   administration.

Holifield, certain that the Republicans
intended   to   alter , atomic   energy   affairs
mainly   for   the benefit of   business,   continued   with his criticisms even after   Congress adjourned.   At a National   Industrial
Conference   Board   panel   at   New   York's
Waldorf-Astoria Hotel in October,   Holifield
maintained that the 1953 hearings were   "ex-
ploratory   rather than conclusive" and   that
the AEC draft legislation was "hastily drawn
and   incomplete,"   overlooking many   complex
problems.   In   keeping   with   his   proposed
House   joint   resolution,   Holifield   urged
"more homework" by the AEC on its   recommendations   and   suggested that greater   industrial   participation was possible under   the
existing law if the AEC would heed his   pro-

posal to disseminate more information on the industrial uses of atomic energy.[18]   On November 17 at a roundtable discussion of the Washington chapter of the Federation of American Scientists, Holifield told a participating AEC representative that if the AEC was not intentionally trying to give away the benefits of atomic energy to private industry, "I, for one, will be happy to hear it, and in the meantime you can be sure I will do my best to prevent a give-away." He pointed out that a giveaway could be subtle, such as allowing large corporations to monopolize the industry through granting patents in the usual way, a procedure that would effectively "limit the access of all American industry to the technical information that is now public property." Other subtle giveaways, according to Holifield, could be the guaranteed buy-back by the government of plutonium produced by private industry, as proposed in the AEC draft legislation, and tax benefits and other incentives for new power developments. Holifield emphasized that "atomic energy was born a public enterprise" and that "there is ample room for public _and_ private advance in this field." He concluded that "before we change its birthright, it must be demonstrated that the public interest and the national welfare would be better served thereby." Holifield was plainly not convinced that a change was needed.[19]

By the end of 1953, the Eisenhower administration provided an additional impetus to the Republican congressional drive for new atomic energy legislation. On December 8, 1953, the president gave his now-famous "Atoms for Peace" speech before the General Assembly of the United Nations, calling for the establishment of an international atomic energy agency to promote peaceful uses of atomic energy. In three other speeches in early 1954, Eisenhower

made additional recommendations for changes
in the existing legislation.   In his State
of the Union address in early January, the
president proposed that the United States
share information with its allies on the
tactical uses of nuclear weapons.   Eisenhower's budget message on January 29, 1954,
called explicitly for three basic changes in
atomic energy legislation. In international
affairs, the chief executive wanted legislative authorization first, to allow the exchange of more classified information with
the United States' allies, and second, to
permit the transfer of fissionable materials
to allies for "peace-time atomic-power development." On the domestic front, Eisenhower called for changes in atomic energy
laws to encourage wider participation by
private industry in the development of
atomic power.   The specifics of the president's proposals were contained in a special
atomic energy message that Eisenhower sent
to Congress on February 17, 1954. He recommended fifteen basic changes to the Atomic
Energy Act.   These included relaxation of
restrictions against ownership and leasing
of fissionable materials and   production
facilities for these materials;   permission
for private ownership, manufacturing, and
operation of power-producing atomic   reactors; liberalization of the patent provisions of the 1946 act;   and authority for
the AEC to supply special materials and
services to the new industry at prices adequate to remunerate the government.   The
president also asked for authorization for
the AEC to establish minimum security and
safety regulations governing the use of
fissionable materials.   Simultaneously with
the president's special message, the AEC
sent draft legislation to Congress embodying
Eisenhower's recommendations.[20]
     The import of the president's addition
of an international aspect to atomic energy

law revision efforts was not lost upon Holifield. He took the opportunity of an address on January 13, 1954, before the National Rural Electric Cooperative Association in Miami, Florida, to suggest that
Eisenhower's "Atoms for Peace" proposal be
given first priority for passage. Holifield
asserted that Congress "would be extremely
ill-advised to consider *in one package* legislative amendments to further the President's plan and to promote private industry." He emphasized that "there is a compelling urgency about concerted efforts for
peace; no compelling urgency about authorizing Consolidated Edison or Monsanto Chemical to own an atomic reactor." Holifield
warned that the United States "must take
care lest other nations see us preoccupied
with seeking ways to make a profit from the
atom instead of seeking ways to advance the
welfare of mankind." The California congressman characterized the AEC's domestic
proposals as "half-baked" in any event and
noted that the JCAE in the 1953 hearings had
advised the AEC to "go back and finish the
baking process."[21]

In his speech before his Miami public
power audience, Holifield suggested an alternative to the AEC's domestic recommendations while the president's international
proposals were being considered. Holifield
now declared that the federal government
"must move ahead boldly in several lines of
atomic power development." He recommended a
diversified program of large and small reactor construction, which would improve
atomic power technology and could provide
power to service large atomic installations,
emergency needs, remote civilian and military installations, and areas with high
power costs. Holifield cited with pride
recent congressional approval of funding for
"a real, honest-to-goodness atomic power
project which would produce large amounts of

electricity." He noted that it was approved only because of "the prodding of our Joint Committee and of the Congress." "We did not propose," he said, "to see the atomic power program bogged down in idle debate, nor wait upon the uncertain responses of private industry while other nations pushed ahead in the atomic power field." Holifield claimed that the AEC was "not a power-minded agency" and that it had backed away from government programs in the atomic power field. He also criticized Eisenhower's budget cuts in atomic energy and implied that the adminis- tration was acting hypocritically because it proposed expansion in activities with other nations while cutting funds at home.[22]

As a final major point, Holifield de- scribed the active conflict existing between public and private power. He declared:

> Today there is a massive head-on assault against the public power policies that enable your rural electric systems to live and grow and prosper--policies ham- mered out during the last 20 years by administrations dedicated to the public welfare and determined to bring the blessings of elec- tricity to all areas and to all segments of the population. . . .
> The assault comes from inside and outside of government--from the administration now in office, from those in Congress who block appropriations for needed proj- ects, from the lobbying organiza- tions of the private utilities rushing in for the kill with a desperate cry of "now or never," from others who hope that their self-seeking endeavors will be sanctified by the reports of spe- cial Commissions.[23]

Holifield urged the National Rural Electric Cooperative Association to be on guard and to give close attention to atomic energy legislation.

As with his speech of January 13 in response to Eisenhower's "Atoms for Peace" plan, Holifield was also ready with a response to the president's special atomic energy message of February 17, 1954. After studying Eisenhower's recommendations, the California congressman delivered a speech on the floor of the House in which he reiterated the previous positions he had taken, criticized elements of Eisenhower's proposals, and outlined an alternative set of principles for amending the McMahon Act. Holifield seized upon the president's statement in the president's message that the 1946 act "in the main is still adequate to the Nation's needs." He declared that Eisenhower's admission supported his own contention that "the time is not ripe for fundamental changes in the basic legislation." Holifield wondered aloud about the incongruity of the president's statement, specifically whether Eisenhower was fully aware that his proposal to confer private ownership rights was "a radical departure from the concept that has guided atomic development to date." Holifield also renewed his suggestion that the international proposal be considered first and separately from the domestic recommendations. As additional support for this suggestion, the congressman pointed out that if private industry acquired vested interests in atomic facilities, these might conflict with international commitments and requirements of the international proposal, thus making it more difficult to establish international control of atomic weapons in the future.[24]

Holifield concentrated his attack on three of the president's domestic proposals: private ownership of atomic facilities, private ownership of fissionable materials, and liberalization of the patent provisions of the 1946 act. With regard to ownership of atomic installations, Holifield feared that such a situation might eventually conflict with international requirements for implementing the "Atoms for Peace" initiative. On the subject of fissionable materials, he felt a better alternative would be government leasing of the materials to private firms, instead of outright sale. As for patents, Holifield disagreed with Eisenhower's prediction that only about five years would be required before the industry would be broad-based enough to allow for normal patents. He characterized the prediction as "unduly optimistic and unwarranted by the present state of atomic technology." Pointing out that it took (at that time) three or four years to build a reactor, he asserted that it would be "at least 10 years before we can reasonably expect to see reactors of sufficient diversity in design and techniques of operation to determine the economics of the industry." Holifield recommended that "the use of all inventions should be made readily available to all interested and qualified businesses for a period of not less than 10 years." He was particularly concerned about patents because they held the key to how the atomic power industry would develop and grow.[25]

Holifield was willing to talk about specifics and recommend practical alternatives because he was never under any illusion that the Republicans would pass up their opportunity to amend the domestic features of the 1946 act. In his speech, he proposed eight "guiding principles for atomic energy legislation" to be used in any revision of the McMahon Act. Overriding considerations for Holifield were that any new law should contain a clear declaration of congressional policy with respect to

atomic power development and that firm maintenance of civilian control over the atomic
energy program should be retained.   If industrial participation was to be encouraged,
Holifield proposed that there should be no
subsidies to private businesses, a ten-year
ban on basic patent privileges, positive
measures to prevent monopolistic trends, and
wide distribution of atomic power benefits.
Holifield also stressed that labor's rights
should be protected in atomic activities
where security measures were necessary with
a right of appeal to an impartial review
board on licensing and other actions of the
AEC.[26]

Holifield was not the only congressman
who was critical of the AEC draft legislation.   JCAE Chairman Cole and Vice-Chairman
Hickenlooper were also unhappy with the
draft proposal because it conferred, in
their view, too much power on the president.
They decided to write their own version of
the "bill" before submitting it for formal
introduction.   The two congressmen ultimately introduced a revised draft of the AEC
proposal, which thus became known as the
Cole-Hickenlooper bill.[27]

The Cole-Hickenlooper bill, introduced
in the House on April 15, 1954, as H. R.
8862 and in the Senate on April 19 as S.
3323, was similar to Eisenhower's proposal,
but it did contain some significant changes.
In keeping with the president's recommendations, the bill provided for private ownership of reactors and production facilities
for fissionable materials.   However, the
bill followed Holifield's suggestion that
there be no private ownership of fissionable
materials or "special materials," a term
that indicated the new, broadened definition
of fissionable materials in the bill. Also,
the bill extended immediate normal patent
rights to "peaceful applications of atomic
energy."   In addition, much to Holifield's

chagrin, the bill contained provisions for implementing Eisenhower's international proposals. Cole and Hickenlooper had decided that the McMahon Act was "in dire need of being overhauled and modernized and brought up-to-date," and they concluded that the president's domestic and international proposals "would be treated as 1 [sic] bill."[28]

Predictably, Holifield had something to say about the Cole-Hickenlooper bill after studying it for a few days. On April 20, he again charged that the bill was premature, and he urged Congress to be on guard against an "atomic 'giveaway' program." He still did not believe a drastic overhaul of the McMahon Act was necessary, and he reminded his colleagues of the president's statement that the 1946 act was still adequate. The congressman continued to insist on the "two-package approach to proposed changes in the atomic energy law" and asserted that "defense and peace requirements . . . should be first on the agenda." With regard to specific criticisms of the Cole-Hickenlooper bill, Holifield noted that "government responsibilities in the production and distribution of atomic power are not spelled out" and that there were no standards "to chart the troublesome course of management-labor relations in this new industry hedged in by difficult security requirements." On the critical subject of patents, Holifield complained that the bill "proposed to grant normal patents in a new industry which is not normal by any standard and which is susceptible to monopolistic control by a few large corporations."[29]

The Cole-Hickenlooper bill became the basis for consideration of changes to the Atomic Energy Act, and public hearings were held by the JCAE on the bill in May and June of 1954. Opposition from Holifield centered as much on Chairman Cole's conduct of the hearings as on the content of the legisla-

tion.   Holifield objected to the continual
revisions   of   the bill to the   point   where
witnesses   and even JCAE members (including
Holifield) did not know what version of   the
bill   was being considered at any particular
time.   When Holifield suggested that   additional   hearings   might be required on   the
revised   bill,   Cole curtly replied that the
full committee,   not Holifield, would determine the course to be followed.   This reply
did   nothing   to lessen   the   objections   of
Holifield, who was perhaps the most persistent critic of the bill at the hearings.[30]

Before the close of the hearings, Holifield   and other public power advocates   did
manage   to amend the bill in their favor   on
some points.   During the discussion of congressional   policy,   Holifield asked to have
inserted into the record that the intent   of
the legislation was to include participation
by "government, private, and public institutions,   both   profit   and   nonprofit."   The
section   on   patent rights stirred the   most
controversy, and President Eisenhower's proposal   for a five-year period before   insti-
tuting   normal   patents was   ultimately   inserted   into the bill.   This insertion   won
even the approval of Holifield,   who sarcas-
tically commented that he "would like to see
the principles that the President enunciated
written into this bill," probably because he
believed them to be preferable in some areas
to   the provisions of the bill the   Republicans   were pushing through   the   JCAE.   The
public   power advocates also won   acceptance
of a "public power preference clause," which
authorized   the AEC to give priority to public   power groups in the sale of any   excess
power it generated.[31]

The JCAE favorably reported the revised
bill,   H.   R.   9757 (S.   3690),   on June 30,
1954,   for   consideration by the   full   Congress.   Holifield, in an action reminiscent
of his opposition in 1946 to the May-Johnson

bill, submitted a lengthy minority report,
again with the support of his close friend
Melvin Price.[32] Most of Holifield's major
criticisms of the administration's revision
efforts were included in the report. Holifield's objections to the one-step domestic
and international legislative approach, his
dislike for "government subsidies" to private businesses inherent in the plutonium
buy-back provisions, and his insistence on a
minimum ten-year transition period for patents were listed among the eight major
points of the minority report. Holifield
and Price also recommended that the AEC
complete a comprehensive study, as required
in the 1946 act, on the "practical value" of
any utilization or production facility
before issuing an appropriate license. This
recommendation was probably designed to slow
the transition to private ownership of nuclear reactors. The two congressmen also
called for changes in the atomic energy law
to conform procedures more closely to those
in the Federal Power Act of 1920, which
accorded preferred consideration to public
bodies where their applications were in
conflict with those of privately owned systems. In seeking to align nuclear power
with hydropower development, Holifield and
Price advocated the insertion of a provision
that would subject an agency's application
for a construction permit to the same safeguards as similar applications before the
Federal Power Commission, thus assuring
interested parties (especially public power
groups) full opportunity for notice, hearings, and appeal before the AEC issued a
license. On another point particularly
reflective of Holifield's concentration on
peaceful uses of atomic energy, the two
congressmen proposed organizational changes
in the AEC to give the development of atomic
power equal footing with weapons development. They proposed a Division of Civilian

Power Application and an Electric Power
Liaison Committee to correspond to the existing Division of Military Applications and
the Military Liaison Committee. Finally,
Holifield and Price listed two other objections to the Republican bill that were pe-
ripheral in terms of the act itself, but
still very important. Although they had
succeeded during the hearings in watering
down the position of AEC chairman to "official spokesman"--the Republican members had
tried to make the AEC chairman the "principal officer" among the five commissioners--
the two legislators wanted even this reference deleted, partially because they believed AEC Chairman Strauss had been heavy-
handed in his dealings with the other commissioners, allegedly limiting their access
to important and sensitive information.
Finally, the two lawmakers objected strenu-
ously to the Dixon-Yates contract, a power
agreement involving the AEC and private
utilities recently concluded by the Eisenhower administration. Holifield and Price
declared that the contract had made the AEC
a "power broker" through its purchasing of
power from a private utility to service an
area (Memphis) "far removed from its [the
AEC's] activities."[33] The Dixon-Yates controversy was itself a major public versus
private power issue both during and after
passage of the 1954 act and is discussed in
detail in the next chapter.

During the House floor debate over
passage of the revised Cole-Hickenlooper
bill, "Holifield was a key strategist for
the opposition and Cole a key defender of
his own legislation."[34] Because Holifield
and the liberal Democrats did not have a
majority, they could hope only to damage and
delay the Republican bill through amendments. Holifield and his colleagues alone
proposed thirty-three changes to the bill
and called for extended debates on each

issue. Holifield's proposals calling for
establishment of governmental *and* private
production and distribution of atomic power
and establishment of an Electric Power Liaison Committee, as well as several other
proposals of his, all met with defeat. The
most significant Democratic-inspired vote
prior to passage of the legislation was
Holifield's motion to recommit the bill to
the JCAE for further study. This proposal
failed passage on July 26, 1954, by a vote
of 222 to 165. On the Republican side,
Representative Cole managed to amend the
bill on July 24 by a vote of 203 to 154 to
include his desire for immediate normal
patent rights for private industry. The
Cole-Hickenlooper bill, with Cole's amendment, passed the House on July 26 by a
substantial margin of 231 to 154.[35]
In contrast to the 1946 act proceed-
ings, the most vigorous debate on the Cole-
Hickenlooper measure took place in the Senate rather than in the House, partly because
Republican senators held only the slim majority of one over Democratic senators.[36] A
group of about twenty senators under the
leadership of Warren G. Magnuson (D-Washington), Lister Hill (D-Alabama), Clinton Anderson (D-New Mexico), and Albert Gore (D-
Tennessee) organized a public power filibuster from July 14 to July 26 in an attempt to
void the Dixon-Yates contract and win concessions for public power in the Cole-
Hickenlooper bill. While the filibuster
failed to void the contract, Republicans
were equally unsuccessful in their efforts
to end debate. Senator William Knowland (R-
California), in particular, complained that
the filibuster had put a "crimp" in the
administration's legislative program. On
July 26, the filibuster ended because of
pressure from Senate Minority Leader Lyndon
Johnson (D-Texas), and on July 27, the Senate passed its version of the bill by a vote

of 57 to 28. Public power advocates did manage to win some ground. Senator Edwin Johnson (D-Colorado) successfully sponsored an amendment authorizing the AEC to produce atomic power and requiring that preference be given to public bodies and cooperatives in disposing of excess electricity from AEC plants. The latter half of Johnson's amendment became known as the "public power preference clause." In addition, Robert Kerr (D-Oklahoma) won majority support for his amendment, which enlarged the period before issuance of normal patents from five to ten years.[37]

Holifield was a member of the conference committee made up of JCAE members who met on August 4 to iron out differences between the House and Senate versions of the Cole-Hickenlooper bill. The major differences concerned patents, the public power clause, and the conditions under which the AEC could produce power. Representative Cole, who was also a conferee, insisted on retaining his normal patent provisions, while Holifield and other Democrats vainly opposed him, supporting the Senate version. Cole carried his point with the assistance of the Republican majority on the conference committee. As a concession to the Democrats, Cole and the Republicans agreed to insert Johnson's public power clause into the final bill, but with the proviso that "insofar as practicable" be inserted as a qualifier. Senator Johnson's bid to allow the AEC to produce power was dropped in favor of a similar House amendment by Cole to allow the AEC to generate power itself only as a necessary by-product of its research and development activities. By August 6, the majority of the conference committee had voted approval of the changes and sent the conference report back to the House and the Senate for summary acceptance or rejection.[38]

Holifield was very unhappy with the compromise version of the bill and, along with Senators Edwin Johnson and Clinton Anderson, refused to sign the conference report. He gave his reasons in a House floor speech on August 9. Holifield characterized the conference version of Cole-Hickenlooper as "a thoroughly bad bill from the standpoint of farm, labor, rural electric co-op, public power and consumer organizations." He charged the bill reflected "the objectives of the drive of powerful private interests to oust the Federal Government from future development of the new atomic industry and [to] take over." He criticized the final provisions on Dixon-Yates, patents, public power preference, and authorization for the AEC to produce power, noting that the conferees had "left just enough of the language of constructive amendments . . . to mislead the people into believing that some protection would be afforded." In essence, however, he pointed out that "the substance has been effectively removed."[39]   Holifield attached a lengthy statement by himself and Melvin Price stating their opposition to the conference report because it contained "no effective measures preventing monopoly control of atomic energy." Holifield and Price warned against "the danger of creating a twilight zone of inaction, where the Federal Government fails to take responsibility and private industry is not prepared to assume it." The two congressmen proposed a five-year "billion dollar crash program" by the federal government for peaceful development of atomic energy to demonstrate to the world that the United States was "serious about putting the atom to work for peace." In closing, Holifield and Price expressed hope that a change in the congressional majority by the election of 1954 would cause Congress to "re-examine the atomic energy legislation, plug the loopholes against monopoly, and make it plain that the Federal Government as well as private industry should produce electrical power from atomic energy." In the meanwhile, the two congressmen declared that "we take this means of serving notice that we do not intend to let the matter of atomic power policy fall by the wayside."[40]

It came as no surprise to Holifield when the House on August 9 approved the conference report by voice vote. He was undoubtedly jubilant, however, when the Senate voted on August 11 by a vote of forty-eight to forty-one to send the bill back to conference. The almost unanimous Democrats under Minority Leader Lyndon Johnson and five dissenting Republicans made the action possible. The upshot was a second conference in which Cole's normal patent provisions were delayed for five years (as Eisenhower had suggested months before). Conferees also deleted the "insofar as practicable" phrase from the public power clause. The Senate approved these changes by a vote of fifty-nine to seventeen on August 16, and the House signified its acceptance of the amendments by voice vote the next day. Two weeks later, President Eisenhower signed the Atomic Energy Act of 1954 into law.[41]

The 1954 act opened a new era in atomic energy affairs. In the area of international affairs, the new act provided for "agreements for cooperation" between the United States and its allies whereby the United States could provide materials and technical know-how to assist other nations in the peaceful applications of atomic energy or could share information on the defensive use of atomic weapons. Domestically, the law authorized private ownership of atomic power reactors and production facilities for fissionable materials. The federal government retained title to all fissionable materials, now called "special materials" under a broadened definition, but allowed private firms to lease the materials for use in their atomic power projects. As in other industries, the 1954 act also provided for near-normal patents after the initial period of five years. The AEC grew enormously because of the new law, in order to carry out its new licensing, security, and safety functions as controls on private industry.[42]

The new atomic energy law also conferred significant new powers on the JCAE, although these new prerogatives were not treated as issues and were seldom discussed during the debates on passage of the act. The JCAE strengthened its right to be "fully and currently informed" by inserting in the committee report that it was the "intent of Congress that the Joint Committee be informed while matters are pending, rather than after action has been taken." This statement was a reference to AEC Chairman Strauss's failure to follow former Chairman Gordon Dean's example of making information available in a timely fashion. The act extended this new obligation to the Department of Defense, and the JCAE added a further provision that required *any* government agency to furnish information requested by the JCAE about an agency's atomic energy activities. The committee also added a clause that authorized and required it to hold hearings within sixty days of the opening of each Congress on the "development, growth, and state of the atomic energy industry." Here the JCAE clearly indicated that it intended to be a solid and inquisitive partner in atomic energy development. In addition, the committee injected itself into determinations of what constituted "source materials" and "special materials," into the "agreements for cooperation" ap-

proval process, and into long-term utility
contracts involving the AEC. The new act
required the AEC to lay before the JCAE for
thirty days prior to final action all AEC
determinations of "source materials" and
"special materials," all "agreements for
cooperation" negotiated by the AEC and/or
the Department of Defense (after approval by
the president), and all long-term utility
contracts, including those negotiated by the
AEC for electricity at the Oak Ridge, Paducah, and Portsmouth installations. Finally,
the act gave the JCAE authorization power
for "plant construction or expansion" and
for "acquisition or condemnation of real
property." The committee would acquire full
program authorization power by 1963, enabling it to direct the AEC to begin particular programs.[43]

Although Holifield had been unable to
prevent passage of the new atomic energy
law, he could identify some end products
resulting from his involvement. Holifield
had personally ensured that public power
interests were included as a part of the
stated intent of the legislation. He also
fought successfully, along with other JCAE
Democrats, to include a public power clause,
to delay normal patent rights, and to provide for leasing, rather than ownership, of
fissionable materials. As a result, the new
law provided an opening wedge, rather than
an open field, for private development of
atomic power. If he was often repetitious
in his criticisms of the Republican plans
for atomic power, Holifield served nonetheless as an effective educator and a key
public power spokesman in the debate over
the passage of the 1954 act. Not seeking to
be a member of the opposition simply for its
political value, he hammered out a viable
public power program as an alternative to
the Republican bill. Most importantly, in
proposing a billion-dollar crash program for

atomic power, Holifield presaged the course
to be taken when Democrats were once again
in control of atomic energy.

5

Public Power Fights Back: Holifield and the Dixon-Yates Controversy

At the same time Holifield resisted Republican efforts to change the Atomic Energy Act of 1946, he became embroiled in another, related confrontation involving the public versus private power issue. This confrontation, known as the Dixon-Yates Controversy, or simply as Dixon-Yates, was a primary, if not the most important, issue during the passage of the Atomic Energy Act of 1954; it was also, however, a separate and distinct dispute that both preceded and outlasted the debate over passage of the 1954 law. Dixon-Yates involved an attempt by the Eisenhower administration to reduce, in effect, the electricity service area of the Tennessee Valley Authority (TVA) through a complicated contract between the AEC and a private utility combine.

The complex maneuvering of the Eisenhower administration on Dixon-Yates did not mislead Holifield. He studied the contract carefully and was the first congressman to call for hearings and a multifaceted investigation of the matter, actions that eventually forced Eisenhower to order cancellation of Dixon-Yates. Until the contract's demise, Holifield remained at the forefront of the controversy. His analysis of the contract and numerous speeches and actions on the subject easily made Holifield the Eisenhower administration's chief opponent in the House on the issue. Although success did not come readily or quickly, Dixon-Yates was eventually a triumph for Holifield and his allies.

The overall public versus private power controversy, involving the struggle for service area among municipal, cooperative, and other public electric providers and private utilities, has existed since electrical power became an economic resource in the late nineteenth century. The origins of the Dixon-Yates Controversy, however, can be traced to the creation of the TVA in 1933 during President Franklin D. Roosevelt's New Deal. From 1934 to 1945 the TVA became the major promoter of electrification in the Tennessee Valley, which spans almost all of Tennessee and parts of Kentucky, Virginia, North Carolina, Georgia, Alabama, and Mississippi. In the process of expanding its electrical service area over the Tennessee Valley, the TVA forced many private utilities, unable to compete with TVA's prices, to sell out to the growing public utility. This result engendered bitter hostility from private utilities near or bordering the TVA service area, which viewed the TVA and public utilities in general as "shady purveyors of alien socialist doctrines and practices."[1] The animosity of private utilities increased during World War II as the TVA exhausted its hydroelectric power sites and added coal-burning steam plants to its system, thus eliminating the natural factors that had limited expansion of its service area. The private utilities, with the help of the Republican-controlled Eightieth Congress, managed to kill appropriations for TVA's first giant steam plant project at New Johnsonville, Tennessee, only to see the Democratic majority in the Eighty-first

Congress reinstate the funds. The Korean War added further steam plants to the TVA system, but appropriations for new steam plants continued to produce heated debates, along with a growing resistance to additional TVA outlays, a resistance that came from southern Democrats who were not in the TVA service area.[2]

The TVA's proposal for a new steam plant at Fulton, Tennessee, to serve Memphis, Tennessee, provided the immediate stimulus for the Dixon-Yates Controversy. As part of the TVA service area, Memphis had voted as early as 1934 to build transmission lines to accept TVA power and had an exclusive contract with the TVA for its power needs. The TVA's request for the new electricity installation at Fulton was made in order to provide for the growing power requirements of Memphis. The city needed additional electricity by 1957, and the TVA did not have the capability to provide the additional power without the new plant. The Fulton proposal met with stiff resistance from the private utilities bordering the TVA service area. Edgar H. Dixon, president of Middle South Utilities, was particularly fearful that the additional plant would be used as a springboard to encroach on private utility territory. A subsidiary of Middle South offered to sell power to the TVA to eliminate the need for the new plant. This offer was similarly interpreted by the TVA as a foray into *its* service area.[3]

Dixon's views found favor in the White House, where Eisenhower sought a solution that would not involve additional appropriations to the TVA, in keeping with his budget-cutting efforts. Because Memphis insisted it could not build its own plant and had an exclusive contract with the TVA and because the three-man TVA board (originally appointed by President Roosevelt for staggered nine-year terms) refused to buy

private power, the Republican president
ultimately settled upon the solution of
reducing the TVA's vast power commitments to
the AEC's gaseous diffusion facilities at
Paducah, Kentucky, in order to allow the TVA
to shift the electricity to Memphis. Eisenhower announced his decision in his December
24, 1953, budget message. He indicated that
the AEC would contract with private utilities for electricity to replace the TVA's
power and promised to submit a supplemental
appropriation request for the Fulton plant
if this new arrangement did not work.
Eisenhower believed this approach would
succeed with the support of his appointee,
AEC Chairman Lewis Strauss.[4]

An embarrassing situation confronted
the Eisenhower administration, however, when
the Bureau of the Budget sought to work out
the specifics of the president's proposal.
Private utilities refused to build an additional steam plant at Paducah for the necessary additional electricity, fearing that
the AEC would cancel its requirements at
some future date, leaving them with a huge
plant in a remote location without other
customers. In order to avoid the Fulton
steam plant appropriation, the Eisenhower
administration was forced into a complex
contractual arrangement where "the utilities
would sign a contract with AEC but would
provide the power at Memphis." Thus, "TVA
(which would not be a party to the contract)
would not directly receive the power," since
"the power . . . supplied to Memphis would
be considered in replacement of power which
TVA continued to supply to AEC at Paducah."[5]

The Eisenhower administration moved
quickly to complete a contract. By January
20, 1954, Edgar Dixon of Middle South Utilities had agreed verbally to advance a proposal. He was joined on February 19 by
Eugene A. Yates, chairman of the board of
the Southern Company, a utility holding

company with subsidiaries operating near the
TVA's southwestern border.   Dixon and Yates
jointly advanced a detailed proposal on
February 25, which was considered too costly
by the Bureau of the Budget.   A second proposal advanced on April 10, however, won
initial approval by the Bureau and began its
journey for approval through a number of
affected federal agencies.   Reviewing agencies included the TVA, the AEC, the Federal
Power Commission, the Securities and Exchange Commission, the Treasury Department,
the General Accounting Office, and the Department of Justice.   Agency reviewers were
asked to approve a proposal in which Dixon
and Yates would form a new combine, the
Mississippi Valley Generating Company, to
provide 600,000 kilowatts of power to the
TVA through construction of a coal-burning
steam plant in West Memphis, Arkansas, at a
total cost of about $107 million.   Funding
would be provided through a 5 percent cash
investment, and the remainder, through bonds
with a guaranteed interest rate of 3.5 percent.[6]
    The Dixon-Yates proposal faced opposi-
tion from both the TVA and the AEC.   The TVA
viewed it as an attempt by a private utility
to take over part of the TVA service area.
The AEC disagreed vigorously with the TVA
over what costs the proposal would entail
and was incensed by a reminder from the
TVA's manager for power that the AEC would
be bearing all of the extra costs in order
to keep the TVA from having to subsidize the
AEC or the Dixon-Yates group.   In addition,
AEC Commissioners Henry Dewolf Smyth and
Eugene M. Zuckert, both Truman appointees,
expressed their displeasure with the Bureau
of the Budget's brainchild in a letter to
Budget Director Rowland Hughes on April 16,
1954.   The two commissioners decried the use
of the AEC as a vehicle for supplying power
to Memphis, noting that this use involved

the AEC in "a matter remote from its responsibilities." They believed the AEC was
being drawn into the power business "in an
awkward and unbusinesslike way."[7]

About two weeks after the Dixon-Yates
proposal won initial Bureau of the Budget
approval, it came to the attention of Congress through a speech by Senator Albert
Gore (D-Tennessee). In the opening speech
of the Dixon-Yates Controversy, Gore alleged
that the Dixon-Yates proposal had three
purposes. It was being implemented, first
of all, "to strike a death blow forever at
the proposed . . . Fulton steam plant." It
was also being used to "lay claim to the
supply of electricity to the Memphis TVA
service area." Finally, Gore declared that
the third purpose was to "have a subsidy
paid to private power interests by the
American taxpayers through the Atomic Energy
Commission."[8]

Holifield became the first House member
and JCAE member to take an interest in the
Dixon-Yates proposal. Senator Gore's speech
helped to stir him to action, as did a
conversation with a professional staff member who assisted several committees. The
staff person told Holifield that the Dixon-
Yates proposal appeared to be an attempt by
the Eisenhower administration to use the AEC
to enable private utilities to invade the
TVA service area. This information prompted
Holifield to investigate the Dixon-Yates
arrangement. He sent requests for information to the TVA, the AEC, and the General
Accounting Office. By the end of May, Holifield was convinced that something was
amiss. He informed and enlisted the support
of his close friend and JCAE associate
Melvin Price. Holifield also prepared a
formal statement for presentation at the
June 4, 1954, JCAE hearing.[9]

At the June 4 JCAE session, Holifield
(with the support of Price) formally asked

Chairman Sterling Cole to hold hearings on the Dixon-Yates contract. He pointed to the growing concerns of Senator Gore and other TVA advocates and questioned whether explicit authority for the AEC to enter into long-term utility contracts should be included in the Cole-Hickenlooper bill. Noting that he had studied the Dixon-Yates proposal carefully, Holifield emphasized that his investigation had led him to conclude that the Dixon-Yates arrangement was "an administrative device to use the Atomic Energy Commission for purposes neither contemplated nor authorized by the Atomic Energy Act."[10]

As a matter of congressional courtesy, Chairman Cole reluctantly agreed to Holifield and Price's request to hold hearings. The Eisenhower administration, however, was undaunted. On June 16, the day before the JCAE Dixon-Yates hearings were scheduled to begin, Eisenhower directed the AEC to negotiate a contract with the private utilities.[11]

The Holifield-inspired hearings on Dixon-Yates began on June 17 and continued through the next day. Although they did not produce any revelations that might be used as a deathblow to the Dixon-Yates proposal, they did provide an education for Holifield and the other JCAE members. The hearings also revealed the depth of the dispute within the government over the proposed contract. AEC Commissioners Thomas E. Murray, Zuckert, and Smyth (all Truman appointees) stated their opposition to Dixon-Yates. Smyth mirrored the opinions of the AEC majority when he declared that he did not want to see the AEC getting "into the business of being a broker for the supply of power for the Memphis area." Eisenhower's appointees, AEC Chairman Strauss and Commissioner Joseph Campbell, spoke vigorously in favor of the proposed contract, emphasizing

that the president had decided that the
arrangement was in the national interest.
After a heated exchange between TVA and AEC
staffs, the hearings adjourned.[12]

Holifield was not satisfied by the
results of the hearings. He widened the
controversy by writing to Ralph Demmler,
chairman of the Securities and Exchange
Commission (SEC), urging him to conduct
hearings on Dixon-Yates on matters within
the SEC's jurisdiction. Holifield believed
the SEC should investigate "whether the
public interest is adequately protected
according to the terms of the Holding Company Act." Using Smyth's term, Holifield
charged that Dixon-Yates would make the AEC
"a 'power broker' involving it in transac-
tions for utility services not necessary for
its own program . . . [and] not authorized
by the Atomic Energy Act." He also warned
Demmler that the Dixon-Yates proposal "cannot rely upon . . . [the national defense]
argument," as in the case of two existing
AEC utility contracts,[13] since "the additional power supply proposed to be created
would not serve directly any atomic energy
project but would be utilized for the commercial, industrial and domestic needs of
the Memphis area." Holifield released his
letter to Demmler to the press.[14]

In three House floor speeches during
July 1954 (just prior to House passage of
the Atomic Energy Act of 1954), Holifield
sought to educate his colleagues and the
public the illegality and shortcomings that
he believed inherent in the proposed Dixon-
Yates contract. On July 6, Holifield read
sections of the 1953 hearings to his colleagues to show that the Eisenhower administration was misinterpreting (or interpreting
very liberally) Section 12 (d) of the Atomic
Energy Act of 1946, which was used as the
authority for Dixon-Yates. The Eisenhower
administration had interpreted Section 12

(d), which authorized twenty-five-year
utility contracts "in connection with the
construction or operation of the Oak Ridge,
Paducah and Portsmouth installations," to
signify authority for Dixon-Yates, since the
proposed utility contract was "in connection
with," if not directly related to, operation
of the Paducah facility.   Holifield averred
that "the hearings, the remarks of the committee members, the statement of the [AEC]
general manager before us, and other testimony which I have presented" clearly showed
that the utility contracts provision was
"limited to the power requirements for those
three installations."   Holifield emphasized
that "it was never contemplated that the
Atomic Energy Commission should be given the
authority to make electric utility contracts
three facilities named in the section."   He
concluded that Eisenhower had been "ill-
advised and misinformed when he was persuaded or advised to recommend that the
[AEC] . . . become in effect a power broker
to contract with a private utility to supply
electrical energy to . . . the [TVA]."[15]

Although Holifield mentioned some of
the unsavory aspects of the proposed Dixon-
Yates contract in his July 6 speech, he
saved his full-blown assessment for July 8.
On that date he presented an eighteen-point
analysis to his colleagues showing how the
proposed contract was damaging to the government and a subsidy to private power.
Comparing TVA and AEC estimates, Holifield
pointed out that Dixon-Yates would cost the
government from approximately $3.7 million
to $5.6 million more per year for the elec-
tricity than if the same power was available
from the TVA, a fact that would mean a total
additional cost of $90 million to $140 million over the life of the contract.   Holifield also noted that the government assumed
a maximum cancellation liability of over $40
million on the $107 million contract if the

agreement was to be abrogated for any reason. In addition, the government would be obligated for an additional $5 million in construction costs if overruns exceeded 9 percent of the total contract amount. The government would also be contributing about $9 million to construct transmission lines for the TVA to accept the power from the Dixon-Yates combine, would be paying all operation and maintenance costs of the transmission lines for the life of the contract, and would be foregoing all federal, state, and local taxes for the project. Holifield also pointed out that the government would also have to ensure a 9 percent return on the portion of the investment not raised through bonds and would have to take at least 93 percent of Dixon-Yates power at point of delivery at all times or be penalized. The AEC would be prohibited from assigning its power to other government agencies at contract rates and would be liable for increases in power costs if they were the result of increased fuel, labor, or construction costs. Finally, Holifield emphasized that 95 percent of the total contract amount for the project would be financed through the sale of bonds with a guaranteed interest rate of 3.5 percent.[16] Holifield greatly disliked seeing the "bonding power of the Government" placed in the service of private industry.[17]

On July 21, 1954, Holifield delivered his last major speech on the proposed contract prior to its passage as a part of the 1954 act. He again criticized the Eisenhower administration's determination to pursue Dixon-Yates and to justify it through a loose interpretation of Section 12 (d) of the 1946 act. Of the administration's interpretation of Section 12 (d), Holifield declared that the administration was guilty of "straining the English language beyond the point of forbearance." With mounting sarcasm, he suggested that Dixon-Yates "might well be termed, as the President of the United States is well acquainted with military terms, an invasion of the public power area which the Tennessee Valley Authority has been serving and is seeking to serve in the State of Tennessee."[18] Holifield inserted into the *Congressional Record* an article composed by himself, entitled "Dixon-Yates Contract Contains a Boobytrap [*sic*] for TVA." Pointing to the Dixon-Yates prerogative to cancel the power arrangement upon three years' notice, as well as other provisions in the proposed contract, Holifield claimed the contract "means, in effect, that TVA can be put in the position of building a $9 million transmission line . . three years, and then have a gun placed to its head through legal right to withdraw the 600,000 kilowatts" unless the TVA would agree to increased prices for the power. If the TVA agreed, and it would have little choice during "this anti-public-power administration," TVA costs would rise. This increase "would destroy the [TVA] yardstick on rates." Holifield concluded:

> This is the boobytrap [*sic*] designed for TVA by cunning legal minds.
> Afraid to come out in the open and make a frontal attack, they, like all cowards, have resorted to devious and tricky methods to accomplish their end.
> Their end is to prevent TVA [from] building the Fulton plant; use the credit and administrative devices of the Government to subsidize a favorite public utility; pad upward the TVA yardstick rate; and thereby extort from the pockets of the American people many hundreds of millions of dollars

annually for the benefit of private utility groups operating under monopoly franchises.[19]

The Republican majority in the House
was unimpressed by Holifield's words; an
amendment to the Cole-Hickenlooper bill to
void the proposed Dixon-Yates contract was
soundly defeated on July 23 by a vote of 172
to 115. In the Senate, Clinton Anderson (D-
New Mexico) offered a similar amendment,
which the Republicans eliminated handily on
July 21 by a vote of 55 to 36. In place of
the Anderson amendment, Homer Ferguson (R-
Michigan) acted as the administration
spokesman in proposing an amendment to authorize the AEC specifically to execute the
Dixon-Yates contract. Ferguson agreed to
change his amendment at the suggestion of
Sam Ervin (D-North Carolina), who wanted to
include the part of Anderson's proposal that
specified that the proposed contract was to
lie before the JCAE for thirty days before
becoming effective. Ferguson agreed, with
the understanding that the JCAE could act to
waive the thirty-day requirement. Republicans, fearing setbacks in the elections of
1954, were determined to use their JCAE
majority before the end of the Eighty-third
Congress to ensure that the contract became
effective. The Ferguson/Ervin amendment
passed the Senate on July 21 by a vote of 56
to 35 and became part of the approved
House/Senate conference version of the
Atomic Energy Act of 1954 sent to President
Eisenhower in late August for his signature.
Conferees Holifield and Price denounced the
contract in part of their minority report on
the 1954 act.[20]
The Ferguson/Ervin amendment set the
stage for the Republican administration's
attempt to win JCAE approval to waive the
thirty-day review requirement before the end
of the Eighty-third Congress. On August 18,

Bureau of the Budget Director Rowland Hughes
wrote to JCAE Chairman Cole to urge an early
waiver action to permit the Dixon-Yates
combine to begin work before flood conditions on the Mississippi made construction
impossible and "so that the contract will
not be delayed until Congress returns next
January." With the 1954 elections near,
Cole was cautious, but the Democrats were
only too happy to oblige, hoping to make
Dixon-Yates a campaign issue. Holifield was
among those who advocated early hearings.
On September 22, 1954, he issued a press
release in which he indicated that he had
written Cole to urge a "thorough-going ex-
amination" of the Dixon-Yates contract.
Probably in an attempt to draw out the hearings for the benefit of the Democrats, Holifield wanted to hear from eleven federal
agencies involved in the contract or potentially involved, expressing the view to Cole
that all "preliminary contingencies and
conditions" be "definitively settled" before
JCAE action. Holifield solemnly warned that
the prestige of the JCAE was at stake in the
controversial matter and that the Joint
Committee should discharge its duty "fully
and faithfully." Cole's response to Holifield's and other Democrats' pressure was to
appoint Vice-Chairman Bourke B. Hickenlooper
as chairman of the whole committee for the
upcoming "JCAE waiver hearings." Hickenlooper thereupon declared the Democratic
overtures to be "political noise" and scheduled the hearings right after the November
elections.[21]

The elections of 1954 created Democratic majorities in both the Senate and the
House, but when the Joint Committee began
its waiver hearings on November 4, a lame-
duck Republican majority still controlled
the committee. Nonetheless, the Democrats
did their best to destroy Republican credibility. Holifield, for one, who was proba-

bly aware by this time of rumors circulating that a consultant for the Bureau of the Budget had later joined the Dixon-Yates group, asked AEC Chairman Strauss, "Do you know if Mr. [Joseph] Dodge [who was budget director before Hughes] was advised by a consultant who is now employed by any of the Dixon-Yates utility companies?" Strauss replied negatively. During the hearings, Holifield's views also received unexpected support from the General Accounting Office, which submitted a report for the hearings indicating that the Dixon-Yates combine might reap excessive profits under the contract as it stood. As a result, the Eisenhower administration pressed the utility companies for a contract amendment limiting profits and also, quite significantly, for a change allowing the AEC to recapture the plant at cost within three years, thus responding to Holifield's "booby trap" objection.[22]

In spite of Democratic attempts to discourage the waiver, the soon-to-be-ousted Republicans stood firm and voted as a block on November 13 to waive the thirty-day requirement and allow the contract to become effective. Holifield responded to the action with an announcement that he would introduce a resolution "dumping" the Dixon-Yates contract at the first session of the Democratically controlled JCAE in January, 1955. The Republicans and Democrats wrote majority and minority reports, respectively, on the waiver action. The Republicans saw the issue as rejecting a national policy of expanding the TVA, while the Democrats protested the Eisenhower administration's misuse of the AEC as a power broker for Memphis and the TVA. Characteristically, Holifield enlisted Price's support in filing a long, separate minority report, which concurred with the Democratic minority's report but at the same time made a point of "blasting the

Dixon-Yates contract from all sides," using Holifield's eighteen-point analysis and other accumulated criticisms of the agreement.[23]

Early in January 1955, Holifield let it be known that he was indeed drafting a resolution to cancel Dixon-Yates. "The leader of the fight against the controversial private power deal in the House last year," as one reporter characterized him, indicated that the resolution would be ready soon after "some minor revisions." Holifield also indicated that his resolution had the support of the House and Senate leadership.[24] The action was not long in coming. On January 28, 1955, the ten JCAE Democrats voted unanimously (with the eight JCAE Republicans dissenting) for a resolution finding that Dixon-Yates was not in the public interest and recommending that the AEC cancel it. The resolution also rescinded the waiver granted by the JCAE Republican majority in November. As such, the JCAE resolution did not actually cancel Dixon-Yates, since the contract was already in effect and interpreted by the Eisenhower administration as authorized by the Atomic Energy Act of 1954. It did, however, express the opposition of the JCAE majority and the opposition of the Democratic leadership of Congress to the Dixon-Yates deal. Senator Henry M. Jackson (D-Washington), a JCAE member, quipped, "We're in a legal no-man's land. This will keep the lawyers busy for six months or more."[25]

The JCAE resolution represented one of many attempts by the Democrats in both houses of Congress during the early months of 1955 to damage the Dixon-Yates contract, while avoiding any floor votes on the issue. Democratic leaders feared that southern Democrats in favor of the contract would join with Republicans in a floor vote and that any legislation rescinding the contract would be vetoed by Eisenhower. One damaging tactic employed was to pack relevant House and Senate appropriations subcommittees with public power advocates. Another was to encourage further investigations and speeches denouncing the contract. Holifield continued to do his share in blasting the contract. In a February 14, 1955, floor speech entitled, "Cancel Dixon-Yates Contract and Restore Unity to the A. E. C.," Holifield charged that the AEC had been "diverted from its statutory function by Presidential directive" and had been "plunged into the boiling hot cauldron of partisan political controversy." Having "lost its statutory independence and . . . become subservient to direction from so-called 'higher authority,'" the AEC had "lost the high regard of many members of Congress." Holifield noted with regret the heated exchanges among commissioners, which to him were a major symptom of the loss of unity in the AEC. The congressman urged President Eisenhower to end the Dixon-Yates contract in order to restore harmony to the AEC and let it continue with the job it was established to do.[26]

As the months wore on, it became increasingly clear that the Dixon-Yates contract was in trouble. In February, Joseph Volpe, Jr., attorney for the State of Tennessee in the Dixon-Yates matter, informed JCAE Chairman Clinton Anderson that there appeared to be a conflict of interest on the part of Adolphe Wenzell, a vice president of First Boston Corporation. Wenzell had advised Dixon and the Bureau of the Budget on financial aspects of the contract, and yet First Boston Corporation had become a financial consultant later for the Dixon-Yates group. Senator Lister Hill (D-Alabama) also learned of the potential conflict of interest at the same time as Anderson and exposed the apparent relationship between Wenzell and Dixon-Yates in a speech on February 18 on the Senate floor. A subsequent investigation by the JCAE also established that Wenzell had been involved in meetings on the contract at the AEC.[27] Wenzell was grilled in June and July at subsequent hearings of the SEC and Estes Kefauver's (D-Tennessee) Judiciary Subcommittee on Anti-Trust and Monopoly. If these activities were not enough to kill the contract, in March the legislature of Tennessee passed a law forbidding construction of the transmission lines to send Dixon-Yates power to the TVA. This law was followed on June 23, 1955, by a decision of the city of Memphis to build its own municipal power plant, thus eliminating the need for the Dixon-Yates plant. By July 8, Wenzell had testified that the Dixon-Yates contract could not have been completed without the financial information he had supplied.[28] In a May 5, 1955, address before the American Public Power Association, an increasingly confident Holifield had quipped that when he was aboard the navy's first nuclear-powered submarine (the *Nautilus*) in April 1955, "one of my colleagues suggested, as the ship dove sharply toward the bottom of the ocean, that this would be a good time to dispose of the Dixon-Yates contract." For the Eisenhower administration, the time to dispose of Dixon-Yates came on July 11, 1955, when President Eisenhower abruptly ordered cancellation of the contract. The Wenzell episode and the Memphis plan were the major contributing factors to his decision.[29]

The JCAE Democrats, who had fought Dixon-Yates actively for nearly a year, were unforgiving when the time came to consider cancellation costs for the combine. Holifield was among this group and agreed with JCAE Chairman Anderson's decision that "not one dollar" should be paid in termination fees. The AEC reluctantly, and somewhat slowly, adopted this view. The Dixon-Yates group sued the government on December 13, 1955, for $3.5 million in costs incurred before cancellation of the contract. Eisenhower's Justice Department responded, ironically, that the contract had been "unlawful, null and void" because of, among other things, Wenzell's conflict of interest and the JCAE's action on January 28, 1955, rescinding the waiver. The United States Court of Claims, in a three to two decision on July 15, 1959, decided in favor of Dixon-Yates for $1.87 million in termination costs.[30]

For a final time, Holifield took up the gauntlet against Dixon-Yates. In a speech before the House of Representatives, the California congressman called for an appeal to the Supreme Court on the Dixon-Yates case. Holifield cited a letter from the comptroller general, who recommended appeal of the Claims Court's decision. Holifield emphasized the close vote by the court and indicated his concern that the decision might become a precedent "in a vital area of public interest."[31]

In response to the urgings of Holifield and others, the government appealed the case to the Supreme Court. On January 9, 1961, the Court ruled six to three that the Dixon-Yates contract was unenforceable because of a conflict of interest on the part of Adolphe Wenzell. After one year of fierce political warfare and six years of litigation, the Dixon-Yates Controversy was thus settled to the satisfaction of Holifield and his fellow public power advocates.

6

Silent Victory:
The Gore-Holifield Bill
and Its Aftermath

Holifield and his Democratic associates on
the JCAE had been reduced to fighting a rear
guard action against the Eisenhower administration's private power initiatives in the
Republican-controlled Eighty-third Congress.
They could but protest against passage of
the Atomic Energy Act of 1954 and for a time
only decry Republican heavy-handedness in
pursuing the Dixon-Yates contract. The
election of 1954, however, turned the tables
in Congress, permitting Holifield and the
new Democratic majority to take the initiative in atomic energy affairs.

In 1956, Holifield and the other JCAE
Democrats launched a major drive to involve
the government directly in the development
of economically competitive atomic power.
This offensive centered on a bill cosponsored by Senator Albert Gore (D-Tennessee)
and Holifield. Among other things, the
Gore-Holifield bill directed the government
(the AEC) to build large-scale atomic power
plants as a supplement to efforts by private
industry in order to gain practical construction, design, and operation experience
needed to perfect the art of producing economic atomic power. Holifield and his allies sought to accelerate the atomic power

program allegedly because of the slow pace
of the AEC in concluding its partnership
arrangements with private industry under the
1954 act. Most Republicans and private
power spokesmen, however, interpreted the
"real" motive as a desire to inject the
public power philosophy and framework on
atomic power development by involving the
government as a power producer and competi-
tor with private enterprise. Although Holifield, Gore, and other JCAE Democrats
amended the Gore-Holifield bill during committee hearings to avoid the public versus
private power controversy, the Republican
administration, Republican members of Congress, private utilities and other segments
of private industry, and even some Democrats
remained firm in their opposition to the
measure as a threat to various private interests, particularly the coal industry.
While the bill passed the Senate, it failed
later in the House amid intensified opposition.

Although the Gore-Holifield bill did
not become law, it did accelerate the AEC's
atomic power program. Fearing another assault, the AEC became very attentive to the
JCAE's wishes to speed development of the
power program where possible. In addition,
Holifield eventually acquired some of the
programs he had sought in the bill. In 1957
and subsequent years, Holifield and his
Democratic JCAE colleagues secured some of
the development projects they had desired
through a "backdoor approach," namely, increased JCAE oversight and authorization
powers over the AEC's Power Demonstration
Reactor Program. Holifield would thus gain
his victory, although it would be hardly
noticed and without fanfare.

Holifield had announced intentions
similar to the Gore-Holifield bill as early
as August 1954. In the minority report on
the 1954 Atomic Energy Act, he and Repre-

sentative Melvin Price had called for a
five-year, billion-dollar "crash" program by
the government to develop atomic power. The
Gore-Holifield bill had its immediate legislative origins, however, in a bill (S. 2725)
introduced by Senator Gore in the Senate on
July 30, 1955.[1] To supplement efforts by
private firms to develop atomic power, Senator Gore proposed that the government also
build some nuclear power plants. S. 2725
authorized and directed the AEC to construct
six nuclear power facilities of different
designs in six different geographical areas
of the United States. The bill stipulated
that the reactor construction program was to
supplement other AEC power programs, and it
authorized such sums as necessary to finance
the program.[2]

By July 1955, Senator Gore's unhappiness with AEC efforts under the 1954 act
stemmed from the fact that the AEC had offered only one opportunity by then for business to participate in atomic power development. This opportunity was "Round One" of
the new Power Demonstration Reactor Program,
established by the AEC to implement the
atomic power development provisions of the
1954 law. Announced in January 1955, Round
One called for competitive proposals by
April 1 from businesses willing to assume
the risks of construction, ownership, and
operation of large-scale reactors. Although
four businesses responded with acceptable
proposals by the deadline, the AEC still had
not signed contracts with any of the four by
the end of July. Senator Gore thus felt
that additional effort was necessary to
supplement the AEC's private industry effort.[3]

Holifield deliberated much longer than
Gore before deciding to press the AEC for
more action. This delay was probably due to
his practical attitude toward legislating,
because, as he noted later, he "wouldn't

handle a bill we couldn't get passed," since he didn't want to "get my ass whipped and lose my prestige as a guy who couldn't get his bill through." Not until April 25, 1956, did Holifield introduce H. R. 10805 in the House. His bill was identical to the Gore measure, and by then, he was reasonably certain that the bill would have substantial support in the JCAE and on the floor.[4]

By April, Holifield had many reasons for joining Senator Gore. The continuing lack of any signed contracts from Round One of the Power Demonstration Reactor Program undoubtedly figured in his decision. In addition, Round Two of the program, announced in September 1955, had also produced no contracts after nearly seven months.[5] Holifield's deep concern that Russia and Great Britain might soon assume world leadership in the development of atomic power also helped to push him openly into Gore's camp.[6] There was also extensive discussion by then among JCAE Democrats of the AEC's lethargy and Chairman Strauss's alleged despotic rule at the AEC, and Holifield seemed the logical choice for sponsoring the bill in the House. During the debate on the 1954 act, he had continuously and vociferously asserted that the act was premature in involving private firms as the major vehicle for atomic power development. During the Dixon-Yates Controversy in July 1955, Holifield had also joined with JCAE Chairman Clinton Anderson (D-New Mexico) to introduce legislation to curb Strauss's alleged "one-man rule" of the AEC; this legislation was an amendment to the 1954 act to ensure that all AEC commissioners would have equal access to all information on AEC business.[7] Holifield may also have been influenced by a citizens' group empaneled by the JCAE to report on the peaceful uses of atomic energy. One of the panel's conclusions was that if private industry would not assume

the risks of constructing various reactor
designs to test their economic feasibility,
then "the Commission should support expeditious development, if necessary, even up to
and including construction of one demonstration plant of each size and type with public
funds." This support would be essential,
because the panel believed that "the United
States must lead" in development of the
peaceful uses of atomic energy. These panel
findings paralleled the philosophy behind
the Gore-Holifield bill.[8]

The fact that JCAE Chairman Anderson
announced hearings on the Gore-Holifield
bill (S. 2725 and H. R. 10805) the day after
Holifield introduced his bill tends to indicate that the JCAE Democrats had consciously
planned action on the bill as an assault on
the Strauss AEC's and the Eisenhower administration's handling of atomic power development. At the Gore-Holifield bill hearings
in late May, Anderson quickly brought out
the point that "the real policy issue involved" in the hearings was "the pace of our
atomic development." He noted that "it has
been alleged that the pace of our development is lagging" and cited the facts that
only one prototype power reactor (the Experimental Breeder Reactor Number One at the
National Reactor Testing Station in Idaho)
was in operation in the United States and
that no commercial power reactors had been
planned. In contrast, Anderson noted that
Great Britain and Russia were "going full
steam ahead with the construction and operation of full-scale central station atomic
powerplants [sic]." He believed that these
facts raised the "fundamental question of
whether AEC has abdicated some of its responsibilities to private industry." In
addition to exploring the issue of American
leadership and the best way to maintain it,
Anderson hoped the hearings would touch on
the practical questions of technical road-

blocks to atomic power development that needed to be removed, the realities of when American firms would achieve their schedules for prototype development, and the kinds of reactors needed if Congress decided to authorize government-financed reactors.[9]

In his opening comments on the first day of the hearings, Holifield reiterated the position he had taken during the debate on the 1954 act. He reminded his JCAE colleagues that he had made it "quite clear" that "the timeliness of throwing open the atomic energy development to private industry was in error." Holifield declared that "the events of the last 2 years have proven that to be a fact." He pointed out that there was now "confusion" in the atomic power development field and "a holding back on the part of industries, private industry, in making investments for the very good reason that they could not make them on the basis of a profitable investment." Holifield further asserted that if the government had gone ahead ahead with the crash program he had proposed, "we would have been in a better position today, a further advanced position today, than we are." He concluded that "if we are going to obtain the lead in the development of electrical kilowatts on an economic basis in the world, it must be through a crash effort of the government much as we used in the development of weapons."[10]

Political and ideological alignments that would show up later in the debate over passage of the Gore-Holifield bill were already evident at the hearings. Strauss's AEC, which considered itself under attack from the Democrats, maintained that enough was being done to maintain American leadership in atomic power development and that private industry should continue to "take the initiative and assume the major responsibility for full-scale prototype reactors."[11]   Individuals in private industry, particularly the private utilities, were fearful that the Gore-Holifield bill was an attempt to make the government a power producer and potential economic rival, as they believed had happened in the Tennessee Valley. They opposed the bill on various grounds, arguing variously that the United States was in the lead in testing several types of reactors, that the AEC had done an excellent job in covering the field while working with private industry, that an additional program might divert manpower from other projects, and that premature construction of controversial designs might lead to nuclear accidents.[12] Public power groups, labor, and the JCAE's consultant, Dr. Walter H. Zinn, former director at Argonne National Laboratory, stressed that the United States was falling behind Great Britain and the USSR and that more and bigger types of reactors needed to be built by the government. In linking the Gore-Holifield bill with the need to stay ahead of the Soviets, William F. Schnitzler of the American Federation of Labor-Congress of Industrial Organizations (AFL-CIO) argued that the bill "would be an important step for freedom-loving people everywhere."[13]

With the possibility of a public versus private power fight just around the corner, Holifield and most of the other JCAE Democrats sought compromises on controversial portions of the bill during their markup sessions on the legislation. Their objective was to produce an acceptable bill that would avoid the public versus private power controversy and appease the AEC, while ensuring an accelerated program of testing new reactor designs suggested by Dr. Zinn and others at the hearings. In discussing the section of the bill that was alleged to contain authority for the government to become a competitive power producer, Holi-

field declared that "I have no desire to see
this [section] get into this public versus
private power squabble" and was quick to
compromise.[14]   The major point on which
Holifield and the other JCAE Democrats refused to budge was the language that the AEC
was "authorized and directed" to carry out
the bill, instead of simply "authorized."
AEC Chairman Strauss personally appeared
before the JCAE and complained that such
terminology was "the kind of an expression
you use to your valet" and that "we are
anxious to go forward, but we hate to be
flogged as tardy schoolboys for not having
done a better job." Strauss's remonstrance
was to no avail, however, because the JCAE
majority believed the wording was necessary
to distinguish clearly the urgency and sepa-
rateness of the accelerated program.[15]

By the end of the hearings and markup
sessions, the JCAE members felt they had a
bill that could be reported out of committee
for consideration on the floors of the Senate and the House.   The JCAE voted fourteen
to nothing, with the four Senate Republicans
abstaining, to report the Gore-Holifield
bill.   In view of their claims to prior
sponsorship, Senator Gore and Holifield
introduced the revised bill as S. 4641 and
H. R. 12061 in the Senate and the House,
respectively, on June 29, 1956.[16]

The revised Gore-Holifield bill was a
significantly changed version of the original bill and reflected the clear intent of
the JCAE to avoid the public versus private
power issue and neutralize potential opposition from the AEC and the White House.   The
revised bill, known formally as the Atomic
Power Acceleration Amendment of 1956, authorized and directed the AEC to construct
"large-scale prototype reactor demonstration
facilities" to test the feasibility of various reactor designs to produce economically
competitive electricity.   However, to ap-

pease the AEC, the bill gave the commission the discretion to determine the number of reactors and the particular types that would be built. Rather than directing that six types of reactors be placed in six different regional areas, the bill specified only that however many reactors the AEC decided to construct were to be placed at sites of major AEC production facilities. In an attempt to defuse the public versus private power issue, the bill further dictated that the electricity produced by the reactors was to be used exclusively for the operation of the AEC facilities where the reactors were located. As a final concession to the AEC, the revised Gore-Holifield bill emphasized that the new activities would be supplementary and would not restrict or interfere with the AEC's Power Demonstration Reactor Program.[17]

In addition to the "Accelerated Power Reactor Program," the revised Gore-Holifield bill contained other important programs and provisions. Under a new "Advanced Design and Development Program," the AEC was authorized and directed to proceed with the development of promising reactor designs and to construct, as soon as practicable, smaller-scale prototype reactors (capable of producing up to fifty thousand kilowatts of electricity) at AEC sites of the commission's choice. An international component of the bill, titled "Foreign Atomic Power Assistance," gave the AEC responsibility for "a vigorous program of international cooperation and assistance in the design, construction and operation of power reactors and related matters." Intended as an enticement for the Eisenhower administration, the purpose of the program was "to carry out [effectively] the Atoms for Peace Plan of the United States." In addition, the bill authorized the AEC to construct, own, and operate any support facilities necessary to carry out the Accelerated Atomic Power Reactor Program, the Advanced Design and Development Program, and the Foreign Atomic Power Assistance Program. Finally, in contrast to the original bill, which authorized "such sums as may be necessary" to carry out its provisions, the revised bill provided $400 million for the programs authorized in the legislation.[18]

The JCAE did not expect problems with the Gore-Holifield bill in the Senate. The Eisenhower administration apparently began to lobby quietly against the measure, however, prior to its consideration. Still, Senate debate on the bill on July 12, 1956, was relatively mild. Neither the Democrats nor the Republicans suggested substantial amendments to the legislation, and neither side sought to delay the vote. When the vote was taken, Gore-Holifield passed by a vote of forty-nine to forty-one, without any amendments attached to it. Significantly, the vote was virtually along party lines. No Democrat voted against the measure, and only three Republicans voted for it.[19]

In the House, trouble brewed on two fronts. One problem area was the conservative Rules Committee, chaired by Judge Howard W. Smith (D-Virginia), who was no particular friend of Holifield or other liberal Democrats and their liberal legislation. Although Holifield formally requested a rule on July 7, he did not receive a reply from Smith until July 10, and even then the powerful Rules Committee chairman was noncommittal. He wrote Holifield that "there are many applications pending for rules which have come in ahead of your request, but we will endeavor to give you a hearing if possible."[20] After the Senate passed S. 4641 on July 12, the Rules Committee did agree to consider the Senate-passed bill briefly on July 17 but failed to give it a rule so it could be taken to the floor. In

fact, Smith continued to be noncommittal,
telling Gore that the Rules Committee might
or might not clear the Senate bill for House
floor consideration. The next day, July 18,
the situation was clarified, because of
pressure on Smith from the Democratic leadership. They wanted Gore-Holifield to come
to the floor in order to pin the blame
squarely on the Republicans if the bill
failed, rather than on Democrats controlling
the Rules Committee. The leadership's
strategy was clear: if the bill was defeated, Republican congressmen could be
blamed; if it passed and was vetoed by
President Eisenhower, the administration
could be accused of slowing the progress of
economic atomic power development. Accordingly, the Rules Committee gave the Gore-
Holifield bill a rule on July 18 by a vote
of five Democrats for and four Republicans
against.[21]

Smith's reluctance to consider the
measure may have been related to the second
emerging front of opposition to the Gore-
Holifield bill. Both Republicans and Democrats from the coal regions of Pennsylvania,
Virginia, and West Virginia were under heavy
pressure from the United Mine Workers union
to oppose the bill. On July 17, Representative John P. Saylor (R-Pennsylvania) circu-
lated a letter to all House members to "call
attention to what we feel are objectionable
features in S. 4641 (Atomic Power Acceleration Program) and its House counterpart
HR12061 [sic]." Attached to his letter was
a list of seventeen "Obvious Objections to
Atomic Power Acceleration Program - S.
4641."[22] The first seven objections dealt
with criticisms of accelerating the program
before results of the current program were
known, before radiation and atomic waste
disposal problems were "licked," and before
economic kilowatts were a clearly foreseeable possibility. The last two points

explained the opposition of the AEC and its
reluctance to be "directed" to accelerate
the program. The intervening eight points,
however, constituted the crux of the opposition of the "coal region congressmen."
Points eight through eleven projected problems for coal and related industries, while
points twelve through fifteen attacked the
Gore-Holifield bill as a "public power
bill." Specifically, coal region congressmen believed that the proposed reactors,
which would supply electricity to AEC installations, would mean reduced coal consumption because of this "government-
financed competition." The reactors would
also mean cancellation of substantial coal
contracts at AEC installations, resultant
capital investment losses for railroads that
had built tracks and other supporting facilities for AEC installations for transportation of coal, and consequent job losses
for coal mine and railroad employees. In
their criticisms of Gore-Holifield as a
public power measure, the opposition congressmen charged that the accelerated program represented "the threat of complete
socialization of the power industry." Another point was that "in the future, the
argument will most certainly be advanced
that Government ownership will have to be
continued to 'protect' the Government's
'past investment.'" Saylor and his allies
also noted that private electric companies
were also opposed to the government's construction of all but experimental-scale
reactors. Finally, the coal region congressmen charged that the Gore-Holifield
proposal "was conceived as a possible public
power empire using the popular atomic energy, rather than flood control, as the
justification." Republicans from the coal
region, if not also Democrats, evidently
feared the possibility of another TVA.[23]
    Saylor's charges, coming after the

success of the bill in the Senate, concerned JCAE Democrats enough to elicit a reply. The task fell to Vice-Chairman Carl Durham, who wrote on July 19 a similar "Dear Colleague" letter refuting Saylor's charges. Durham pointed out that the Gore-Holifield bill had "passed the Senate without amendment as S. 4641." He asserted that the JCAE believed that the bill represented "a balanced non-controversial bill which will speed our atomic program forward." Durham emphasized that the proposal was "reported out of the Joint Committee by a vote of 14-0, with all House members of both parties voting in favor of the bill," and that the objections to the bill "have not come from Members of the Joint Committee on Atomic Energy who have studied the need for this program so carefully." With regard to the coal issue, Durham cited the testimony of Tom Pickett, "a leading spokesman for the coal industry," who had asserted at a 1956 JCAE hearing that "we do not fear inroads upon our market by nuclear power." As for the public power issue, Durham averred that the JCAE had "made every effort to obtain a bill which will promote atomic power development under safe conditions, and without putting the government in the power business." This goal was accomplished, he pointed out, "by locating the reactors at isolated AEC production and testing sites and providing that the intermittent power produced would go into the system for operations at the sites."[24]

On the day that Saylor sent his letter to House members, Holifield delivered in the House his major speech on the Gore-Holifield bill. Waxing both sarcastic and eloquent at different points, Holifield presented a lengthy, wide-ranging critique on the opposition to his bill. In his talk, he plainly showed his irritation with the Eisenhower administration, the AEC, and the private utilities for their attempts to defeat his and Senator Gore's proposal. Holifield began his speech by noting that Eisenhower and AEC Chairman Strauss had declared that America's leadership in atomic power development was essential and that AEC Commissioner Willard Libby had recently declared that loss of America's leadership would be catastrophic. "Unfortunately," Holifield continued, "for more than three years these gentlemen have seemed more interested in making declarations than in taking action to assure our leadership." Holifield declared that "we have had a spate of speeches, plans and proposals--and more recently, the beginning of a lavish self-seeking advertising campaign--but we are still waiting for effective action." He also noted that the United States' expenditures for military reactors, almost three times as much as for civilian reactors, "must look to the world as though we talk about 'Atoms for Peace' but put our dollars into atoms for war." With mounting sarcasm, Holifield alluded to criticisms of the Gore-Holifield proposal as he discussed military reactor development.[25] He pointed out that there were "no complaints that manpower shortages make greater efforts impossible, no crocodile tears shed about technical problems that defy rapid solution, and no reluctance to choose reactor types to be developed and get on with the job." These attitudes were "entirely different," however, when it came to atomic power development. Holifield said he understood that Strauss was reluctant to pursue an accelerated government program of reactor development because of a desire to "avoid the production of electric energy by the AEC," but it could certainly not have been because of a "fear of involving [the] AEC in power marketing problems, since Admiral Strauss was quite ready to involve the AEC in the Dixon-Yates Affair, certainly the

most distracting issue in the history of the
Commission." In attacking another criticism
of the Gore-Holifield bill, Holifield lamented that Strauss and the other AEC commissioners (except Thomas Murray) had "been
taken in by propaganda that the private
utilities, and not the government must build
these large developmental plants or else by
some mysterious process the electric power
industry in this country will be 'social-
ized.'" The California congressman declared
that "I know of no plot to socialize the
electric power industry" and pointed out
that the government's much-criticized accelerated program would "speed the day when
atomic power becomes practical" and also
"save the utilities and the consumers some
very large sums of money."[26]
     The major focal point of Holifield's
speech was his criticism of an advertisement
by 123 private electric companies entitled,
"How America Will Keep Its Lead in Atomic-
Electric Power," which appeared "in at least
36 of the large metropolitan papers" on June
13. Holifield launched into a lengthy and
biting analysis of the June 13 advertisement, which he described as a "collection of
half-truths" and a "cynical effort to mislead and misinform the American public." He
claimed that "America's Independent Electric
Light and Power Companies," which sponsored
the advertisement, were playing a "numbers
game" when they compared fifty-five completed reactors and thirty-five planned ones
for the United States with twenty-three
completed ones and fifty-eight planned for
the rest of the world. He noted sarcasti-
cally that the sponsors had included the
Fermi pile and about seven other reactors
that had outlived their usefulness and been
dismantled. Holifield also noted that
forty-six of the fifty-five completed reactors had been entirely financed by the
government. In addition, he pointed out

that thirty of the finished reactors were research reactors, two others were testing-only facilities, thirteen were the production reactors at Hanford and Savannah that produced plutonium for weapons, and three were military reactors. Only seven, he maintained, had "a direct connection with atomic power development," and he emphasized that of the fifty-five completed reactors, "not one single reactor of any size has been built by a private power company--not one." Holifield scolded the private companies, saying, "The officers of the companies which sponsored this advertisement know better," meaning that "most of them know that the number of all types and sizes of reactors built is a largely meaningless figure as far as progress in atomic power technology is concerned." Holifield added that the companies "could almost have financed a small research reactor with the money they spent for their misleading advertisement," and then "they could say we had built 56 reactors."[27]

In terms of American leadership in the atomic energy field, Holifield brought out what he believed were disquieting qualitative, rather than quantitative facts about English and Russian atomic power development. He observed that the British expected to complete a two-reactor power plant in October 1956 with a capacity of sixty thousand kilowatts and that "one of the reactors is already in experimental operation." Holifield also noted a recent statement by the chairman of Japan's atomic energy organization, who favored importing British reactors because of his impression that Britain was ahead of the United States in reactor development. As for the Soviets, Holifield emphasized that the USSR had had a five-thousand-kilowatt nuclear power plant operating since June 1954, and as a result of having an operating power reactor, the

Soviets "apparently have learned some things
we did not know." In addition, the Soviets
were using their plant as a propaganda tool.
In contrast to British and Russian achieve-
ments, Holifield pointed out that in the
United States "there is not one reactor,
other than a military reactor, which will
produce more than 5,000 kilowatts of electric power."[28]

Holifield used the advertisement's final question, "Where do we go from here?" to
explain his own solution, embodied in his
and Senator Gore's proposal. He criticized
the advertisement's answer of appointing a
task force to evaluate the U.S. program as
unnecessary and meaningless, since the JCAE
was already well informed and "we have all
the information needed to decide whether we
want to coast along with a modest research
and development program . . . or . . .
whether we want to launch a vigorous program
with some positive goals." In his conclusion, Holifield declared that passage of the
Gore-Holifield bill would be important for
developing the economic kilowatt at home and
would have important economic, political,
psychological, and prestige ramifications in
international affairs. Overall, the proposal would be "a step forward in maintaining the leadership for America in the field
of atomic power" and "make possible on an
economic and competitive basis an almost
unlimited new source of power for mankind's
use."[29]

Holifield's speech did little to calm
the fears of opponents of his bill. When
the measure came up for consideration in the
House on July 24, the attitudes of most
congressmen were already established. Despite the JCAE's efforts to avoid the public
versus private power controversy and its
attempts to assuage the fears of at least
the Democrats from the coal regions, the
opposition remained firm, and the public

power and coal issues surfaced as the major concerns during the debate.[30]

The few statements allowed before formal debate showed that the Gore-Holifield measure was going to experience rough sledding in the House. Congressman Smith from the Rules Committee, who called up the rule to open the debate, noted that the proposal was "quite a controversial subject," and he personally was "very unhappy" with it. Former JCAE Chairman Sterling Cole had voted for the bill in committee but now shifted his original position by introducing a letter he had received the previous week from AEC Chairman Strauss. In the letter, Strauss indicated that he was inviting a number of distinguished scientists to Washington to evaluate the AEC's reactor development program and promised quick action to correct any deficiencies, although he emphasized the thoroughness of the AEC's exploration of viable reactor designs. Cole now declared that "this legislation is not necessary" and announced that he would introduce several amendments to the bill. Four other Republicans followed Cole and denounced Gore-Holifield as a public power bill and/or a threat to the nation's coal industry.[31]

To counter these claims, Holifield and JCAE Vice-Chairman Durham emphasized the research nature of the proposed programs. Durham used the history of the airplane to show that government assistance had been used before to advance a new art. He also pointed out the potential future benefits to business from government research proposed in the bill. He vigorously denied that the measure was a public power bill and predicted a lag in atomic energy development if the proposal failed to pass. Holifield agreed with Durham, arguing that the money expended for the nation's first nuclear power plant at Shippingport, Pennsylvania, was essentially "government money that is being spent for the benefit of the advancement of the art and the technology." "This [government aid to advance nuclear technology]," he averred, "is exactly what this bill plans to do." Holifield declared that his proposal was "not a public power bill and . . . not a private power bill." Rather, it was "a subsidy to the art" and "completely an experimental job." He pointed out that the technology developed would be turned over eventually to both private and public power companies for their use.[32]

In the formal debate that followed, Holifield attempted to allay the fears of the private power interests and the coal industry. He stressed that the power produced by the reactors would be used only by the government and that the electricity would be intermittent anyway, since the reactors would have to be shut down for tests and experiments. Thus, the program would be "an experimental and research operation completely; it is not a production, commercial type of operation." In response to the coal issue, Holifield believed that "a false conception has been planted deliberately in the minds of the Members from the coal regions to get them to oppose this bill." He declared that it would be "many years before we reduce this to a cost where it will be competitive with coal."[33]

Although opponents raised many issues during the House debate on the Gore-Holifield bill,[34] the most persistent opposition themes continued to be that the proposal was a public power bill and that it would damage the coal industry. With regard to the public power question, Representative James Van Zandt (R-Pennsylvania), a JCAE member, now indicated that he would join former Chairman Cole in opposing the bill although he had favored the measure in committee. Van Zandt charged that the major effect of the bill would be "a further extension of subsidized Federal power into the atomic energy field" and that "creation of these atomic TVAs would be very, very expensive." John Saylor, organizer of the coal protest, stated his opposition on both the public power and coal issues. As for the bill's public power features, Saylor declared that "the Federal Government does not belong in private business" and that "we can not afford to become involved in any more spurious blueprints produced on socialistic drawing boards." With regard to the coal issue, Saylor felt that "the proposal is unfair to American citizens who produce coal and other fuels now used in the generation of electricity." Van Zandt's and Saylor's views were reiterated in various forms by several other congressmen during the debate.[35]

The amendments proposed after formal debate made it clear that the Republicans would attempt to weaken, if not block, passage of the bill. Former JCAE Chairman Cole, on behalf of the Republicans, sought acceptance of a series of twelve amendments to the measure. Among other things, Cole asked and obtained approval for changes eliminating the directive language in the bill, requiring the AEC to issue a public invitation for private and public groups to build the proposed reactors before building them itself, prohibiting the AEC from building, owning, or operating reactors in foreign countries under the Foreign Atomic Power Assistance Program (although these activities were allowable under other existing foreign AEC programs), and requiring the AEC to sell all reactors authorized in the bill after fifteen years of operation. Cole also asked (unsuccessfully) for a reduction in the authorization amount for the bill from $400 million to $50 million. This proposal drew a blast from Holifield, who

had opposed most of Cole's amendments without success. Holifield termed the authorization reduction amendment "the final act"
and declared that it showed that the Republicans were "not willing to accelerate the
peace-time application of atomic power."
Actually, however, the final act came later
in the debate, when Van Zandt made a motion
to recommit the bill to the JCAE. Although
it had escaped by four votes an earlier,
somewhat mysterious attempt by Clarence
Cannon (D-Missouri) to kill the bill by
striking out the enacting clause, this time
the Gore-Holifield bill did not survive. On
a roll call vote, Van Zandt's motion to
recommit was approved by a vote of 203 to
191, with thirty-eight other members present
but not voting.[36]

The Democrats from the coal regions
proved to be the "swing vote" that made the
Republican recommittal effort a success.
There were at least sixteen coal area Democrats who voted, or were paired, against the
bill, including seven from Virginia, five
from Pennsylvania, and four from West Virginia. A switch of six of these votes would
have brought about a tie vote, and seven
would have preserved Gore-Holifield for
conference. Except for the coal region
Democrats, the vote was largely along party
lines, with Republicans the more cohesive.
Of the 202 Republicans then in the House,
176 voted for recommittal, 17 voted against,
and 9 did not vote. Out of 230 Democrats,
27 voted for recommittal, 174 voted against,
and 29 did not vote.[37]

Holifield placed the blame for the
failure of his bill squarely on the Eisenhower administration and AEC Chairman
Strauss. In House speeches on July 26 and
27, he castigated the Republicans for damaging their own administration's Atoms for
Peace initiative and declared that the Gore-
Holifield bill was not a dead issue.[38] In

his speech of July 27, Holifield attributed his bill's failure largely to "the vehement opposition of the Republican administration at the behest of private utilities" and declared that the utilities had "put their own business affairs ahead of the national interest in maintaining American leadership in the peaceful uses of atomic power." He also noted the "conspicuous part" played by AEC Chairman Strauss. The defeat of the bill signified to Holifield that the administration's Atoms for Peace program was "little more than an empty gesture, a windy exercise in rhetoric." He concluded his speech with a declaration that the Gore-Holifield fight was not over:

> If the peaceful potentials of atomic energy are to be realized, the Federal Government must proceed boldly and constructively to build reactors and to promote research and development. Therefore, I believe that the Holifield-Gore bill will be a crucial item on the agenda of the next Congress.[39]

Holifield's "belief" that the Gore-Holifield bill would be reconsidered was actually more in the nature of a warning to the Republican administration. The bill itself proved to be in a permanent legislative grave. It was to have some major effects, nonetheless, on the course of atomic power development in the United States.

The death of the bill had immediate effects on two other important atomic energy bills that the Republicans considered vital to private industry initiatives in atomic power development. These bills included the Price-Anderson bill, which would have provided up to $500 million in government indemnification to supplement private industry

liability insurance against nuclear accidents, and an amendment to the Public
Utility Holding Company Act, which would
have exempted utilities working in large
groups on atomic power projects from prose-
cution as illegal combines. Piqued at the
defeat of the Gore-Holifield bill, House
Democrats determined that the two laws the
Republicans wanted to see enacted would die
along with the Gore-Holifield measure, so
they could be used as bargaining points in
the next Congress when the accelerated reactor program presumably would be reconsidered. When Majority Leader John McCormack
(D-Massachusetts) on July 25 demurred on
setting a date for consideration of the
Price-Anderson bill, and Holifield and
Melvin Price (D-Illinois--cosponsor of the
Price-Anderson bill) personally objected on
July 26 to consideration of the Public
Utility Holding Company Act amendment, it
became clear to Republicans that the two
bills were doomed. Even a letter from
Eisenhower calling for consideration of the
Price-Anderson measure had no effect on the
determined Democrats. Former Republican
JCAE Chairman Cole complained to no avail
that "real progress will be seriously hin-
dered."[40]

The defeat of the Gore-Holifield bill
led to action in the AEC as well as in
Congress. The Eisenhower administration,
taking note both of the Democrats' quashing
of the two atomic energy bills desired by
Republicans and of Holifield's threat of
another Gore-Holifield initiative in the
Eighty-fifth Congress, acted to head off the
possibility of another such confrontation.
The AEC hastily developed a "Third Round"
for the Power Demonstration Reactor Program.

Round Three was announced conspicuously
on January 7, 1957. Like Round One, Round
Three invited proposals for reactors with no
limitation on size. AEC terms of assistance

were to be largely the same as for Round
One, except the AEC indicated that it would
consider loaning heavy water to projects
requiring it.   Round Three had no cutoff
date for receiving proposals, but construction of reactors had to be completed by June
30, 1962. On August 30, 1962, the AEC modified Round Three to require reactors under
the program to have a minimum capacity of
400,000 kilowatts, which were distinctly
large reactors. Eight proposals received
AEC approval under Round Three, including
those for such large-scale plants as the
Connecticut Yankee Atomic Power Station in
Haddam Neck, Connecticut (600,000 kilowatts), and the San Onofre Nuclear Generating Station near San Clemente, California
(450,000 kilowatts).   Significantly, Round
Three was the last program of direct government subsidies to private industry for developing atomic plants, except for a few
extraordinary design and development efforts, such as the Liquid Metal Fast Breeder
Reactor in the 1970s.[41]

Another major effect of the failure of
the Gore-Holifield bill was its influence on
future JCAE activities.   The bill's defeat
signaled a change in strategy on the part of
JCAE Democrats: the measure was the last
attempt by them to legislate a broad program
in atomic energy.[42] The resistance in Congress because of the public versus private
power issue and the coal issue put a damper
on Democratic enthusiasm for another such
venture in 1957 despite Holifield's personal
determination.   There would be, however,
some consolation for the California congressman.   The Democrats now sought to influence the AEC's programs through another
means, namely, authorization of individual
reactor projects.   Chet Holifield would
become a major, if not the major, player in
this effort also.

At the time of the Gore-Holifield defeat, the JCAE did not have authorization power over individual reactor projects. The 1954 act was the first atomic energy law to grant to the JCAE authorization power over the AEC budget. Section 261 of that act required authorization for funds "necessary for acquisition or condemnation of any real property or any facility or for plant or facility acquisition, construction or expansion."[43] This provision essentially gave the JCAE the power to review various line budget items requested by the AEC and approved by the Bureau of the Budget and to establish a measure of control over AEC expenditures related to the acquisition of property, plants, and facilities. In 1955, Holifield had become chairman of the new JCAE Subcommittee on Authorizing Legislation created to perform this function. Holifield's subcommittee, however, initially had no control over power reactors. The reactors were not subject to authorization because the AEC, with support from the comptroller general, had determined that these projects were experimental and temporary in nature and could not, therefore, be interpreted as a "plant" or "facility" within the scope of the JCAE's authorization power.[44]

By early 1957, JCAE Democrats had explored alternative methods to accomplish their goal of influencing atomic power development. In April, an "extremely fortuitous or cleverly planned event" occurred. In a House speech on April 16, 1957, House Appropriations Committee Chairman Clarence Cannon, who somewhat inexplicably had advanced the motion to strike out the enacting clause during debate on the Gore-Holifield bill, now initiated an equally mysterious attack on the AEC. Cannon complained that the AEC had obtained 80 percent of its funds as "operating expenses" in 1956 and 1957 without proper legislative authorization. In Cannon's view, research and development appropriations, as well as funds for plants and facilities, should be authorized. Cannon clearly implied that he would block appropriation of funds for the AEC unless its reactor programs were specifically authorized by Congress.[45]

Whether he had been informed in advance or not, Holifield was quick to respond. At the Fiscal Year 1958 authorization hearings then in progress before Holifield's JCAE Subcommittee on Legislation, Holifield announced that, as a result of Cannon's remarks, consideration of the reactor program items in the AEC budget would be delayed until after the Easter recess. In place of review of the AEC budget, Holifield and members of his subcommittee busied themselves with informal meetings with the AEC to draft legislation to meet Cannon's "objections." The full subcommittee met in late May, and the JCAE decided in early June to consider the draft measure.[46]

During these hearings on "Congressional Review of the Atomic Power Program," Subcommittee Chairman Holifield made it clear he still felt stung by the AEC's involvement in the Republican defeat of the Gore-Holifield bill. When Commissioner Libby appeared to argue for maximum flexibility for the AEC under the proposed legislation, JCAE Vice-Chairman Clinton Anderson retorted with reference to the Gore-Holifield bill that "it was wrong when a congressional subcommittee sponsored it, but it was right when the AEC sponsored it," since "the Commission was down to the Bureau of the Budget asking for authority to build something very similar." Holifield was immediately caught up in the argument, emphasizing that the AEC had lost the "high esteem" of his colleagues and himself and could be expected to be treated like any other governmental agency in the future:

Some time ago your Commission was
warned that the Atomic Energy
Commission had lost its high estate in the minds of the Congress;
that it had gotten itself embroiled in political areas and had
made political decisions. . . .
You are face to face with the grim
fact of just exactly how you are
going to be treated. You are
going to be treated like the Agriculture Department and like the
rest of the agencies from here on
out, in my opinion, by the Congress. So you have to either make
up your mind to work under that
condition or not to work under
it.[47]

Holifield continued that the AEC might need
"15 percent latitude to change" and was
"going to be in the same position that the
Defense Department is in when it comes back
and wants to change from three destroyers to
a submarine." When Commissioner Libby attempted to appease Holifield by asserting
that "we are not in an uncooperative mood as
far as the committee is concerned," Holifield made it clear that he did not intend
to be embarrassed again on the floor by the
AEC:

I want to be very sure about that
because personally I am not going
to take a bill to the floor along
this line if the Commission is
going to buck the bill that goes
to the floor. I will let the
other members do as they wish to
do, but I will resign from the
subcommittee before I will do
that. I will let you go before
the Appropriations Committee and
do your fighting with them.[48]

Thus subdued, the AEC reluctantly went along with the JCAE's recommended amendments to existing authorization procedures. There was no AEC opposition even to Holifield's stated intentions of scrutinizing all reactor programs, including those already under contract. AEC Chairman Strauss appeared before the JCAE on June 10 to indicate that "we believe we can live with the proposed changes, but we will not be happy with them, and candor compels us to say that." Under questioning, Strauss made it clear that the AEC would not oppose the proposed bill when it went to the floor. Later in the day, the JCAE voted unanimously to report the bill, which was contained in a House report filed on June 14.[49]

Action on the "Durham bill," introduced in the House by JCAE Chairman Durham on June 7, 1957, as H. R. 7992 and in the Senate by Vice-Chairman Anderson on June 10, 1957, as S. 2243, was swift. Only nine days after Senator Anderson introduced his bill, the Senate passed S. 2243 by voice vote without debate. Five days later on June 24, the House also passed the bill. On July 3, 1957, President Eisenhower signed the bill into law as Public Law No. 85-79.[50]

The new law greatly expanded the authorization powers of the JCAE. First and foremost, the bill required the AEC to obtain authorization from the JCAE for funds for all nonmilitary reactors with thermal outputs of ten thousand kilowatts or greater and for those to be used for the generation of electrical power. Also, the measure required that the AEC obtain authorization for all funds to be used for the Power Demonstration Reactor Program with industry. Finally, it required the AEC to submit to the JCAE for forty-five days any plans to establish or revise either prices or periods for buy-back materials and any criteria for waiving charges for use of special nuclear materials.[51]

Holifield did not lose any time in using the new powers conferred upon the Joint Committee. As chairman of the Subcommittee on Legislation, he immediately resumed hearings on the Fiscal Year 1958 funding authorization for the AEC. As he had forewarned, Holifield scrutinized all aspects of the reactor development program and found much to criticize. Holifield's major criticism of the AEC at the hearings was the same as it had been during the Gore-Holifield effort: the AEC was displaying a lack of sufficient progress in the development of atomic power.[52]

At the conclusion of the hearings, Holifield played the major role in shaping the Fiscal Year 1958 authorization bill. With the help of JCAE staff, he proposed a bill that met the AEC's requests and then provided $165 million for an additional four reactors: a heavy-water reactor, a plutonium-recycle reactor, a dual-purpose reactor (plutonium/electricity production), and a gas-cooled, graphite-moderated reactor. Holifield's reasons for this action are not hard to find. The Canadians were concentrating their efforts on heavy-water reactor development, the British were working on a gas-cooled, graphite-moderated reactor, and the Russians were known for their dual-purpose reactors. Holifield wanted to be sure that the United States was also working in these fields to ensure its continued world leadership.[53] In addition--and not very ironically--Holifield was bringing in a reduced Gore-Holifield through the back door with the JCAE's new powers of the purse.

The AEC and the Republicans were not fooled by Holifield's backdoor assault. Appearing before the subcommittee on July 9, with only a day's notice to review and comment on the new proposal, AEC Chairman

Strauss objected to the four additional
reactors because they had not been requested
by the AEC nor approved by the Bureau of the
Budget. He also objected to another Holifield addition altering conditions for Round
Two of the Power Demonstration Reactor Program. Republicans on the JCAE, except for
Senator Henry Dworshak (R-Idaho), were also
opposed to this Democratic attempt to impose
programs and conditions on the Republican-
controlled AEC.[54]

Although Holifield was determined to
get some of his 1956 program ideas through
the JCAE, he did show a willingness to compromise on some points in order to woo Republican support for the bill when it came
to the floor. Together with JCAE Chairman
Durham, he met with Strauss in an attempt to
defuse as much of the AEC's opposition as
possible. He also showed a similar disposition in his bargaining with the Republican
members of his subcommittee. As a result,
the final version of the subcommittee's bill
reduced the funding for developing the additional reactors from $165 million to $107
million. The heavy-water reactor was
dropped, and the dual-purpose reactor was
funded for only a development-design and
engineering study.[55]

Despite Holifield's attempts to garner
Republican support for his additions, the
JCAE Republicans remained steadfastly opposed. On July 23, the subcommittee voted
four to three along party lines for the
amended authorization bill. The full JCAE
sustained the action of Holifield's subcommittee on July 25 by a vote of eleven to
seven, with Senator Dworshak joining the
Democrats in favoring the measure. The
majority report, filed on August 2, specified technical requirements for various
reactor projects and even designated the
location, contractor, and branch chief
within the AEC who should be responsible.

This type of "direction" was even more severe than that in the Gore-Holifield bill
and served to alienate further the AEC and
the Republicans.[56]

Official opposition was not long in
coming. On August 6, Republican legislative
leaders meeting with President Eisenhower
made the decision to fight the authorization
bill on the basis of "public power favoritism." A meeting of the Republican Policy
Committee buttressed this action on the same
day. Minority Leader Joe Martin thereafter
announced that almost all of the members had
agreed to support the administration's effort to defeat the Democratic additions to
the authorization bill.[57]

Holifield and his Democratic associates
on the JCAE were in a stronger position than
they had been during the Gore-Holifield
confrontation. By effecting changes through
authorization bills rather than substantive
program legislation such as Gore-Holifield,
they knew, as did the Republicans, that the
Republicans could not afford to kill or
recommit an authorization bill because this
action would imperil all of the AEC's funding. Likewise, President Eisenhower could
ill afford to veto such a measure. In any
event, Holifield and his House cohorts could
be sure as a last resort that the more
liberal Senate would enact an authorization
bill with additions to the JCAE leadership's
liking and attach these to the conference
version, which had to be rejected or accepted in toto by each house of Congress.[58]

To add to their strength, the Democrats
countered the vocal Republican opposition by
lecture and threat. Holifield spoke on the
House floor on August 5 and emphasized that
the JCAE had often been right in its recommendations even when the AEC protested. He
cited the often-mentioned examples of the
hydrogen bomb decision, the weapons expansion program of the early 1950s, the Five-

Year Reactor Program, and other instances in which the JCAE had prodded a reluctant AEC. Vice-Chairman Anderson took the Senate floor the next day and threatened the Republicans with the loss of other important legislation should the authorization bill fail.[59]

As expected, Holifield's additions to the proposed AEC measure encountered stiff opposition in the House when they were considered on August 9, 1957. In fact, there were clear parallels with the debate on the Gore-Holifield bill. The Republicans charged the Democrats with public power favoritism, socialism, and atomic-power federalism, while the Democrats emphasized that the reactor program was at a standstill. Although the Republicans did not attempt to kill or recommit the bill, they did try to eliminate Holifield's additions. When it passed the House by a vote of 383 to 14, only the $3 million for the development design and engineering study for the dual-purpose reactor was retained, because of successful Republican amendments to the measure supported by conservative southern and coal region Democrats.[60]

Holifield's proposals fared better, as he knew they would, in the Senate. On August 16, the Senate rejected all Republican attempts to amend the authorization bill and then passed it by a voice vote. Thus, in conference the JCAE Democrats were able, as the committee majority, to salvage additional parts of their proposals. As a result, some work was authorized on all three proposed reactor projects. Construction of the plutonium-recycle reactor was authorized, the $3 million study for the dual-purpose reactor was retained, and the gas-cooled, graphite-moderated reactor was also approved, although only for a $3 million design and engineering study.[61] Nonetheless, the authorization bill finally passed by Congress represented something of a be-lated Gore-Holifield triumph for Holifield and affirmed the strength of the public power philosophy in power reactor development.

The JCAE's intervention in the power reactor field from 1958 until 1961 did not result in public versus private power disputes of the magnitude of the 1956 Gore-Holifield and 1957 reactor authorization battles, because of two important reasons. First, the JCAE had clearly established itself as a partner in power reactor development. This position was openly acknowledged by AEC General Manager Kenneth E. Nichols at the Fiscal Year 1959 authorization hearings before Holifield's subcommittee.[62] Secondly, the departure of AEC Chairman Strauss and his replacement by John McCone significantly reduced tensions between the AEC and the JCAE. Because they wanted to avoid bruising fights like those of the past and because they recognized the realities of Democratic strength, the Eisenhower administration and its new atomic energy spokesman sought accommodation with the JCAE.[63]

In this new environment of tenuous cooperation, Holifield was able to further the advancement of the reactor concepts he had championed. The Fiscal Year 1959 authorization bill reported by his subcommittee included $145 million for construction of a full-size, dual-purpose reactor and funding to construct a number of prototype reactors, including a gas-cooled, graphite-moderated reactor and a heavy-water reactor. Holifield also increased the total authorization for the AEC's programs from $193,379,000 to $386,679,000.[64]

The enhanced authorization bill encountered much less opposition than the JCAE's proposals of 1956 and 1957. Republican members of the JCAE, including even staunch conservatives such as Representatives

Van Zandt and James T. Patterson (R-Connecticut), joined with the JCAE Democrats to report the measure unanimously. When the bill was considered in the House on July 14, 1958, the only vocal opposition came from West Virginia Democrat Cleveland M. Bailey, who charged that the legislation would damage the coal industry. Bailey also introduced a letter from Eisenhower stating the chief executive's opposition to nearly every feature in the bill added by Holifield's subcommittee. Notwithstanding the president's objections, the House passed the measure by voice vote. During Senate debate on the bill the next day, Senators Leverett Saltonstall (R-Massachusetts) and Bourke Hickenlooper (R-Iowa) staged a small-scale attack on the legislation as favoring public power, but to little avail. Although some minor amendments to the Senate version necessitated a House-Senate conference, the final version essentially retained the additions of Holifield's subcommittee, and President Eisenhower signed it readily, if reluctantly.[65] With the signing of the Fiscal Year 1959 authorization bill, Holifield thus gained inconspicuously and without much fanfare much of the rest that he had sought in the Gore-Holifield bill. It was a silent victory, but a victory nonetheless.

7

To Waste Energy or Not:
Holifield and the Hanford
Steam Plant Controversy

The Gore-Holifield bill and its aftermath
left no question of Holifield's public power
leanings. Indeed, Holifield had remained
consistent throughout the public versus
private power disputes of the Eisenhower
years in his beliefs that the government
should remain a vital partner in atomic
energy development and that public power
interests should be given equal consideration with private electric companies in
atomic power development. Holifield was
not, however, an ideologue; rather, he was
a practical, commonsense politician who
believed in politics as the art of the possible.[1] He remained open-minded to compromises he believed were workable and necessary, as shown by his willingness to compromise on Gore-Holifield. In the last major
eruption of the public versus private power
controversy--the Hanford Steam Plant Controversy of 1961-1962--Holifield again showed
his willingness to compromise his original
position in order to reach agreement with
his fellow congressmen. Ultimately, but not
at first, Holifield was successful in shep-
herding a compromise proposal to passage.
    The Hanford Steam Plant Controversy
erupted at the beginning of the John F.

Kennedy administration and revolved around a
JCAE proposal to install electricity-generating facilities on a dual-purpose (plutonium and electricity production) reactor at
the AEC's Hanford, Washington, reactor complex. As the new chairman of the JCAE,
Holifield included the project in the Fiscal
Year 1962 AEC authorization bill with the
full support of the AEC and the Kennedy
administration. The Hanford provisions of
the bill proposed that the government construct, own, and operate the generating
facilities at a total construction cost of
$95 million in order to use the waste steam
from the reactor for electricity production.
The Hanford steam plant proposal came under
attack by private power interests and the
coal industry, who feared further federal
encroachments in the electric power field
and damage to the coal industry. As with
Gore-Holifield, the Senate approved the
project, while a coalition of Republicans
and southern and coal-region Democrats rejected the measure in the House. Despite
clever parliamentary maneuvering and scaling
down of his proposal, Holifield failed to
gain House approval of the project in 1961.
In 1962, however, he launched a successful
compromise proposal with enough support to
secure passage after an initial defeat by
determined opponents. Although Holifield
did not win a clear public power victory, he
salvaged the practical point at issue, which
had been his major personal objective all
along. He ensured that the waste heat of
the Hanford "N-reactor" would be put to use
to provide needed, economical power for the
Pacific Northwest.

     The roots of the Hanford Steam Plant
Controversy stretched back into the Eisenhower years. Ironically, the Fiscal Year
1959 AEC authorization bill--Holifield's
backdoor, Gore-Holifield triumph--contained
the seeds of the Hanford controversy. This

bill authorized $145 million for a dual-
purpose reactor to be built by the AEC at
Hanford, Washington. The New Production
Reactor or "N-reactor," as the dual-purpose
reactor was also known, was to be constructed as an additional plutonium producer
for the nation's defense needs, with the
intent of converting it later to production
of electricity through the use of the waste
steam generated by the reactor. Of the $145
million authorized for development of the
reactor, $25 million had been added to pro-
vide this convertibility feature in the
reactor's design, making it similar in concept to the numerous dual-purpose reactors
constructed by the Soviets.[2]

While the Fiscal Year 1959 AEC authorization bill passed Congress easily, the
dual-purpose reactor already had its opponents before, during, and after passage of
the bill. Before the bill's passage, the
Strauss AEC predictably had disagreed with
the opinions of General Electric management
at Hanford that the reactor should have the
convertibility feature. The Eisenhower AEC
preferred a single-purpose, plutonium-
production reactor, clearly hoping to fore-
stall any additional power generation by
government-owned reactors.[3] When Holifield's JCAE Subcommittee on Legislation
resolved the issue in favor of the convertibility feature, the dispute was transferred
to the floor debates on the authorization
bill. In the Eisenhower letter introduced
by Representative Cleveland M. Bailey (D-
West Virginia) during House debate (see
chapter 6), Eisenhower objected to both the
New Production Reactor and its convertibility feature as unnecessary. During Senate debate on the bill, senators Leverett
Saltonstall (R-Massachusetts) and Bourke
Hickenlooper (R-Iowa) attempted to rescind
authorization for the dual-purpose design,
charging that it would eventually be used

for the benefit of public power interests. Even after Eisenhower reluctantly signed the authorization bill, he issued a strongly worded statement contending that it was unsound to proceed with the reactor. As with other JCAE addenda to the original AEC bill, the Republican president decried the Democratic effort to add what he believed were unnecessary programs to the budget.[4]

The N-reactor continued to be a subject of dispute even after construction began in March 1959. Several studies conducted during 1958-1961 disagreed over whether the reactor would be an economical producer of electricity if converted. Studies sponsored by the AEC tended to be cautious and even pessimistic, thus spurring the JCAE to appoint its own consultant to do a study. The JCAE study, conducted by R. W. Beck and Associates, optimistically reported that the New Production Reactor would be an economical producer of electricity. The report thus served as a spearhead for the JCAE drive in 1961 to tap the source of waste steam from the reactor for power generation.[5]

Holifield became chairman of the JCAE for the first time in January 1961 as a result of the retirement of Representative Carl Durham (D-North Carolina). Under the auspices of his chairmanship and the Kennedy administration, a $95 million authorization was proposed in the Fiscal Year 1962 AEC authorization bill for construction of electricity-generating facilities to convert the waste steam from the N-reactor to usable power. The proposal called for the AEC to construct, own, and operate the "steam plant." The electricity produced was to be sold to the Bonneville Power Administration, which would in turn sell the electricity and use the profits from the sale to reduce its capital investment, this assuring lower power costs to Pacific Northwest consumers of Bonneville power.[6]

Aside from supporting the Kennedy administration, Holifield had several practical reasons for promoting the steam plant in
the authorization bill. His principal concern was that he did not want to see the
steam generated by the N-reactor go to waste
when it could be used easily for productive
purposes.[7] In a letter to colleagues responding to critics of the Hanford proposal,
Holifield also asserted that the project was
justified from the five viewpoints of economic advantages, national defense, national
prestige, nuclear power technology advancement, and benefits to both public and private power enterprise. With regard to economic advantages, Holifield believed that
the steam plant would pay for itself in time
and would benefit Pacific Northwest consumers at no cost (eventually) to the government. In terms of national defense, the
N-reactor, by being kept in operation for
electricity generation, could be more
quickly converted back to plutonium production, argued Holifield, than if the reactor
was shut down completely when plutonium was
not needed. As for national prestige, Holifield observed that the proposed steam plant
would have the largest electrical capacity,
800,000 kilowatts, of any nuclear power
plant in the world. Holifield also believed
that construction and operation of the generating facilities would lead to various
technical advances in nuclear power technology.   Finally, in terms of benefits to public and private enterprise, Holifield asserted that the power produced from the
Hanford steam plant would meet an expected
shortfall in the Pacific Northwest area and
would also enhance the financial position of
the Bonneville Power Administration, resulting in lower rates to Bonneville consumers.
In refuting the counterclaims of his opponents, including five Republican JCAE mem-

bers who promised a floor fight, Holifield concluded that opposition arguments "were an attempt to obscure, by an irrelevant public versus private power controversy, the real benefits to national security and well-being which can be realized from this project."[8]

Holifield's opposition on the JCAE did not believe that the public versus private power issue was irrelevant. Led by Representative James E. Van Zandt (R-Pennsylvania), the staunch private-power conservative who had been successful in his motion to recommit the Gore-Holifield bill, the five JCAE Republicans opposed the Hanford proposal on ten grounds, which they stated in a minority report on the Fiscal Year 1962 authorization bill. Besides denying categorically all of the points advanced by Holifield and the JCAE majority in support of the steam plant, Van Zandt and his allies charged that the steam plant eventually would be used to justify the construction of transmission lines leading to another TVA-type electric power grid in the Pacific Northwest and that it would also "constitute a precedent for the further encroachment of Government in private business." They also asserted that the steam plant was unnecessary for the Pacific Northwest's present power requirements, that it would attract businesses from other regions and damage the coal industry, and that it violated the spirit and intent of the Atomic Energy Act of 1954, which authorized the AEC to produce and distribute only power incidental to its research and development programs and its production activities.[9]

The anticipated House debate on the Hanford proposal occurred on July 13, 1961. Holifield acknowledged that the steam plant project would probably be the only controversial item in the authorization bill. He averred that there had been "a great deal of misinformation spread about this particular item" and charged that the private utilities claimed falsely that the Hanford steam plant would lead to the socialization of the power industry and would replace coal. He declared that the utilities "are taking a dog-in-the-manger attitude that they do not want to see this heat used; they want to see it wasted." Further, he observed that coal was an almost nonexistent fuel source in the Pacific Northwest, which depended on hydroelectric power and oil and gas for its power needs. For Holifield, the issue was thus not public power or damage to the coal industry; rather, it was a question of energy waste and sound economics:

> You can blow the heat into the air, you can turn it into the Columbia River and heat the Columbia River, or you can run it through a generator and produce between 700,000 and 800,000-kilo-watt-hours of electricity. . . .
> . . . And who profits by it? The Government profits by it because it gets a return from it. The private utilities profit by it because they participate in the distribution. The consumers profit because they get electricity from this hydroelectric power at reduced rates.[10]

Congressman Van Zandt, leader of the opposition during the debate, discounted Holifield's universal benefit reasoning and repeated the arguments advanced in the Republicans' minority report. The Hanford steam plant, he charged, was the opening wedge for another TVA. As he viewed it, the Hanford project revolved around the question of "Should the AEC take its place alongside the Department of Interior and TVA as a major producer of government-generated

power?"   For Van Zandt,   the   estimated
800,000-kilowatt capacity of the proposed
facility would make the AEC a major power
producer, especially in view of the fact
that the steam plant would be the biggest
electricity-generating nuclear plant in the
world.   Such a capacity, argued Van Zandt,
would hardly be an "incidental" by-product
of other AEC activities as authorized in the
power provisions of the 1954 act.[11]

With the battle lines thus drawn, the
House debate on the Hanford steam plant
accomplished little except to demonstrate
the depth of the division over the proposal.
At one point, the heated nature of some of
the exchanges led one congressman to observe
that "this issue has generated so much heat
on both sides that it might be more productive to harness the steam generated here in
Congress rather than fool around with plutonium."   Holifield's growing fears during
debate that the Hanford proposal would be
defeated were soon borne out.   On a motion
by Van Zandt, the steam plant was eliminated
from the authorization bill by a "teller"
vote of 176 to 140.   Although no roll-call
vote was requested or taken, it was clear
from the debate that most Republicans and
coal-region Democrats opposed the bill because of two familiar issues: the public
versus private power question and the potential effect on the coal industry.[12]

By all appearances, the battle was
over.   The Hanford issue was renewed, however, as Holifield probably expected it
would be, when the Senate considered the
authorization bill on July 18.   The Senate
retained the Hanford proposal in its version
of the bill and added a five million-dollar
authorization for research on nuclear processes to improve coal and coal products in
order to entice and placate the coal interests.   Unlike the Gore-Holifield confrontation, the opponents of Hanford faced the

issue a second time in the conference version of the bill.[13]

When Holifield called for a conference
on the bill on July 25, he did so with full
knowledge that the conference tradition was
on his side.   It was the conference committee that would decide which house would
consider the final version of the bill
first, and the other body would be given the
opportunity to vote on the bill only as a
whole, rather than on its components. With
Holifield's JCAE majority sure to control
the conference committee, it was clear that
the Senate would be asked merely to pass
upon the ingredients of the bill it approved
on July 18, and the House would then be
faced with a take-it-or-leave-it "money
bill" for the AEC, which would include the
Hanford proposal.[14]

The Republicans were over a barrel.
They were not, however, unaware of the implications of Holifield's seemingly innocu-
ous request for a conference. Minority
Leader Charles Halleck (R-Indiana) objected
personally to Holifield's request, a parliamentary maneuver necessitating a decision
from the Rules Committee on how to deal with
the impasse.[15]

In testimony before the Rules Committee, Holifield shocked and dismayed his
opponents by declaring that his loyalty and
responsibility were divided between the
House and the JCAE. Although he asserted
that he would consider both the House's
wishes and the wishes of the JCAE majority,
he also implied that he would support the
Senate's upholding of the Hanford project.
His cleverly worded position left the Republicans little choice but to use a rare pref-
erential motion to instruct House conferees
not to agree to the Hanford proposal.[16]

On August 8, 1961, another debate on
Hanford ensued in the House as Van Zandt
made the motion that House conferees "be

instructed not to agree to project 62-a-6
[to the authorization bill]." Representatives Van Zandt, Halleck, Craig Hosmer (R-
California), and William H. Bates (R-Massachusetts) stressed the importance of ensuring the elimination of the Hanford project
through Van Zandt's motion, while Majority
Leader John McCormack charged partisanship
on the part of the Republicans, and Appropriations Committee Chairman Clarence Cannon
(D-Missouri) pointed to the importance of
the dual-purpose reactor in the nation's
contest with Russia. Holifield emphasized
the dangerousness of the precedent being set
by Van Zandt's motion and warned his colleagues that "you may be setting an example
which may rise to haunt you." Despite the
display of harmony among the Democratic
leaders, Van Zandt's motion was approved by
a decisive vote of 235 to 164.[17]

Still, the battle was not over, especially for the resourceful Holifield. If
Van Zandt could argue that production of
800,000 kilowatts of power using waste steam
was not "incidental" to other AEC operations,[18] then Holifield could construe nar-
rowly Van Zandt's motion to mean that House
conferees could not agree to the steam plant
"*as contained in* [italics added] the Senate
amendment." What about some other compromise? Holifield's last effort in 1961 with
regard to the Hanford proposal was to attempt to erect a workable compromise proposal that could pass both houses. This
task was difficult and, ultimately, impossible. On August 31, Holifield asked for
and was granted some additional time to file
the conference report.[19]

The compromise worked out by Holifield
and the conference committee called for an
authorization of fifty-eight million dollars
to construct a steam plant half the size of
the one originally proposed, that is, a
plant with a 400,000-kilowatt capacity con-

sisting of one giant turbine instead of two. Rather than being sold, the electricity produced by the steam plant would be used to fill power requirements at the Hanford site, where eight single-purpose, plutonium-production reactors were already in operation. The cost of the steam plant would be paid back to the government in nine years at 4 percent interest, based upon dual-purpose operation of the reactor for that period of time and the estimated cost savings of using this new source of electricity instead of purchasing electricity elsewhere. As with the original proposal, the government would own and operate the new steam plant.[20]

Holifield and the conference committee believed that the steam plant compromise, together with the five million-dollar provision for coal research, would prove palatable to the House. The steam plant would still be the largest of its kind in the world. The public versus private power controversy would be studiously avoided, since the electricity produced by the plant would be used only for AEC operations. Conferees Van Zandt and Senator Hickenlooper thought otherwise, however, and refused to sign the conference report. Van Zandt sent a letter to his House colleagues on September 1 asking them to reject the new Hanford compromise.[21]

While the Senate readily accepted the conference report, House members were not placated by the compromise. Nonetheless, Holifield invoked the biblical invitation of "Come and let us reason together." He observed that the Senate had been about 60 percent in favor of the Hanford proposal and the House, about 60 percent opposed. Thus, he viewed the conference proposal "as a necessary and reasonable solution to the strongly expressed attitudes of two coequal legislative bodies." Holifield declared that "this is not a private versus public power fight" and that "this is not a coal fight." In view of the fact that the Hanford power would be cheaper than the Bonneville power presently used, he emphasized that "if you support the conference report and approve it, you cast a vote for economy."[22]

Van Zandt rebutted Holifield's remarks with six reasons for opposing the Hanford compromise. He argued that the 400,000-kilowatt plant would still put the AEC in the power business, even though the power would be used at Hanford. He also calculated that the reduction from ninety-five million dollars to fifty-eight million dollars for half the electrical capacity would mean a 22 percent increase in cost per kilowatt for the Hanford electricity. In addition, Bonneville Power Administration power would still be needed when the reactor was temporarily shut down for tests or for other reasons. Van Zandt charged that Congress would be in effect authorizing Hanford on the "installment plan" in terms of payback and that the 400,000 kilowatts released back to Bonneville as a result of the new power source "would add to the present surplus and could be used to justify further the proposed Bonneville-California intertie as the first leg of an all-federal giant power grid." Finally, Van Zandt declared that if the proposal passed, "it would be almost impossible to prevent the Government from taking the next step in 1962 by authorizing the addition of another 400,000-kilowatt facility."[23]

The House continued to side with Van Zandt. Not even the implied threat of no AEC authorization bill, if the conference report was rejected so late in the session, impressed opponents of the Hanford plant. With respect to other pressures, Van Zandt declared that "a war of nerves has been conducted," and "in all my legislative expe-

rience . . . never have I encountered the
pressure that was applied in connection with
this issue." When the vote was taken, the
House rejected the conference report by a
decisive vote of 251 to 156, effectively
killing the Hanford project in 1961.[24]

By 1962, it appeared that the Hanford
idea was all but dead. A political realist,
Holifield initially had "no intention of
bringing it up again" because, as he later
explained, "I do not believe in empty ges-
tures."[25] Like the phoenix, however, the
Hanford proposal was reborn from its own
ashes. The late 1961 defeat of the project
inspired a consortium of sixteen public
utilities in the state of Washington to
formulate a plan for financing the Hanford
plant privately. Holifield, who was always
open to workable alternative solutions, was
undoubtedly pleased when the utilities took
their proposal to the AEC and were warmly
received. The AEC kept the House Appropriations Committee and the JCAE informed of its
dealings with the group. In a matter of
months, the AEC reported that it was involved in intense negotiations aimed toward
developing contracts to sell the New Production Reactor's waste steam to the consortium. On July 7, 1962, however, the comptroller general issued an opinion that the
AEC could not negotiate the contracts being
prepared without further congressional authorization. Upon learning of this problem,
Holifield immediately announced hearings to
investigate the proposed arrangements and
decide upon the appropriate legislative
course for authorizing the project.[26]

At the hearings on July 10 and 11,
1962, the JCAE examined the proposed agreements in detail. These called for the sixteen public utilities to organize themselves
into the Washington Public Power Supply
System (WPPSS), which would sell approximately $130 million in tax-free revenue

bonds to finance construction of the generating facilities. WPPSS would then buy the waste steam from the AEC at fixed prices, operate the steam plant, and provide the "infirm" (irregular) power to the Bonneville Power Administration. In return, Bonneville would provide "firm" power to the utilities under power exchange agreements. Thus, the proposed arrangements involved both a contract between the AEC and WPPSS for purchasing the waste steam and for leasing the land on which to build the steam plant and also a contract between WPPSS and Bonneville for exchange of the Hanford power for firm power.[27]

As a result of the hearings, Holifield realized that he had a workable compromise for the Hanford project. Under the proposed agreements, the AEC would not become a power producer, there would be no financial contribution or liability by the federal government, and the United States would still be able to boast of the largest dual-purpose reactor facilities in the world, with the 800,000-kilowatt capacity that Holifield had originally proposed. In addition to the new features of the project, there was greater political support for the new proposal. Representatives Hosmer and Bates, who had vigorously opposed the 1961 provisions in floor debates, were favorable to the 1962 proposal. In fact, all JCAE members except Van Zandt indicated their support for the WPPSS alternative. Still, Van Zandt was a force to be reckoned with. When the Pennsylvania Republican announced that he would seek House approval to stop the Hanford idea once and for all, Holifield set to work feverishly to ensure that the 1962 proposal would not meet the same fate as the one in 1961.[28]

During the week before consideration of the Fiscal Year 1963 AEC authorization bill, Holifield developed a legislative strategy

and amassed support to ensure passage of the
new Hanford project. As a beginning, he
ordered immediate publication of a Joint
Committee print containing all documents
pertinent to the new proposal, so he could
provide comprehensive, printed information
to all of his colleagues. On July 13, two
days after the Hanford hearings ended, he
announced on the House floor the JCAE's
intention to offer two amendments to the
authorization bill to authorize the WPPSS
project, since work on the authorization
bill had been completed and it had been
reported before the Hanford issue had come
up. Holifield also placed in the *Congressional Record* the most important documents
relating to the proposed WPPSS project, so
congressmen could begin studying them.[29] In
addition, with his relatively easy access to
the Democratic White House, Holifield had in
hand by July 14 a letter to him from President Kennedy endorsing the new Hanford alternative. Holifield published the letter
as part of a press release on the same date.
He also solicited a letter from Charles
Luce, head administrator for the Bonneville
Power Administration, to substantiate further the fact that the new proposal would
not result, even indirectly, in any future
liability for the federal government. Finally, on July 16, Holifield sent a letter
to his House colleagues stating the JCAE
majority's reasons for favoring the WPPSS
solution and pointing out the differences
between it and the 1961 proposal. Holifield
attached the newly published Joint Committee
print for further study by his fellow congressmen.[30]
　　Holifield's reasons for his special
efforts on the WPPSS proposal were clear.
In his July 16 letter, he pointed out that
the new arrangement would still assist in
meeting the Pacific Northwest's power requirements and serve the interests of na-

tional defense, both of which were goals of the 1961 proposal. In addition, however, the new Hanford proposal would provide additional guarantees and benefits. Unlike 1961, the government would not be obligated in any way and would realize, moreover, up to $125 million in revenue from sale of the Hanford steam over a twenty-four-year period. Holifield emphasized that the steam would "be made as [a] *byproduct* whether it is *sold* or *wasted*," and for him and the JCAE majority, sale was infinitely preferable to waste. Further, federal acquisition (through Bonneville) of the generating facilities would be prohibited without specific congressional authorization, and private utilities could purchase on a nondiscriminatory basis up to 50 percent of the electricity produced through the project. Holifield and most JCAE members believed that they had avoided the public versus private power controversy altogether and that they had provided an excellent opportunity for congressmen "to cast a *vote for economy*," as embodied in the WPPSS proposal.[31]

Despite his considerable efforts, Holifield failed to gain House acceptance of the new Hanford concept. Holifield's declaration during House debate that "We can either shoot that steam into the air and waste it, or it can be utilized" fell on deaf ears. The majority of House members were more attentive to Van Zandt's charges that the issues were the same as in 1961, that there were "serious defects" in the AEC/WPPSS contract, and that the Hanford project would set a "dangerous precedent." When Van Zandt offered the substitute amendment he had promised, directly forbidding construction or operation of electricity-generating and transmission facilities at the Hanford N-reactor, he prevailed by a vote of 232 to 163.[32]

It appeared to many who remembered 1961 that the WPPSS proposal had been killed by Van Zandt's motion.[33] Holifield probably was not as glum, however, as some of his allies, since the Senate still had to consider the measure, and it did so on August 1, 1962. By a voice vote, it passed the AEC authorization bill, together with the JCAE's Hanford amendments. This action was similar to Senate action in 1961, when the Senate approved the Hanford project after the House had rejected it. At this point, however, the similarity ended. Holifield, not forgetting strategy, made sure that the Senate, rather than the House, asked for a conference on the bill, in order to avoid Van Zandt's and Halleck's 1961 charges that the House had been disadvantaged by Holifield's call for the 1961 conference. Although Holifield and the JCAE majority had been almost as confused as disappointed by the House's earlier rejection of the new proposal, the consensus was that the WPPSS concept had not been made clear or had not been explained in enough detail to House members and that the problem could be resolved during House deliberations on the conference version of the bill. When Van Zandt once again announced his intention to seek instructions for conferees, even Craig Hosmer, Holifield's implacable foe in 1961, sent a brochure to his House colleagues outlining the massive differences between the 1961 and 1962 proposals. Hosmer asked his associates to vote against his fellow Republican's (Van Zandt's) upcoming motion to instruct conferees.[34]

On August 29, Holifield opposed Van Zandt in the floor debate on Van Zandt's proposal. Van Zandt, for his part, observed that the Hanford project had been rejected by the House four times in 1961 and once already in 1962. He also reviewed his reasons for opposing the WPPSS project, referred to its proponents as public power advocates, and appealed to his colleagues from the coal-producing states to stand firm in their opposition. Holifield, still combative and determined, charged that Van Zandt's motion "does violence to the democratic, bicameral legislative process" and that such an action was "an affront to a Member of the House who is asked to serve on a conference committee." He assured his colleagues that the conference would be fair and asserted, "I guarantee you that we will bring back to a vote the issue which is involved in this matter." When former opponents of the bill, including even Rules Committee Chairman Howard W. Smith of the coal-producing state of Virginia, indicated that they would support Holifield, the confident California congressman allowed the debate to end early with an appeal to his colleagues to "let the House proceed in a normal way, send its conferees to conference with open hands, and let them bring back the results to the House for final disposition." This time the House agreed with Holifield, defeating Van Zandt's motion decisively by a vote of 246 to 148.[35]

This first Holifield victory marked the beginning of approval for the proposed Hanford steam plant. Still, Holifield remained cautious and even respectful of his opponent Van Zandt. When the conference committee met, Holifield ensured that the conference version of the Hanford proposal provided (exactly as Van Zandt had proposed) that the AEC was not authorized to enter into any agreement for construction or operation of the electricity-generating facilities for the New Production Reactor *until* (as Van Zandt had *not* proposed) the AEC had formally determined that the reactor's waste steam was usable, that the United States would profit substantially by selling it, and that the national defense posture would be improved by attaching the generating facilities to the reactor. In addition, the conference committee insisted that 50 percent of the power produced would have to be offered on a nondiscriminatory basis to private utilities and that specific congressional approval would be necessary if Bonneville wanted to acquire the facilities later, with any consequent losses in such a transaction to be borne by Bonneville through rate adjustments to its customers. In sum, the conference version of Hanford was the JCAE's proposal carefully rewritten, with some additional safeguards against federal liability and some deference to Van Zandt. Van Zandt was not fooled, of course, by what he believed to be the legislative legerdemain concocted by the JCAE majority, and for a second time because of the Hanford question, he refused to sign a conference report containing the project.[36]

Holifield lost no time in attempting to sell the conference report to his House colleagues. Soon after the House-Senate conference, on September 11, he inserted into the *Congressional Record* the formal statement by House conferees explaining the compromise proposal. The next day, he sent a letter to all House members with a typed copy of the statement attached "for easy reading." In his letter, Holifield asserted that the conferees had reached a "reasonable compromise" and declared that "We believe we have safeguarded the Federal Government against any possible liability and have made it possible for the Federal Treasury to receive . . . up to $125,000,000 for the sale of what would otherwise be wasted steam."[37]

Holifield explained the conference proposal in a September 12 speech on the House floor. He reviewed the mechanics of dual-purpose reactors and their production of steam as an incidental by-product, similar

to other reactors.   He cited four   examples
of   other   reactors to show that   the   AEC's
practice of selling waste steam would not be
new.   Holifield   reiterated the elements   of
the   compromise   proposal and declared   that
they   provided "an iron-clad guarantee   that
the   Federal Government will   neither   spend
any   Federal money nor take any loss in connection with this project."[38]
     With rubber-stamp approval by the   Sen-
ate   expected later,   the final showdown   on
the Hanford proposal took place in the House
on September 14,   1962.   Holifield stressed
that the conference version of Hanford was a
reasonable compromise between the two houses
of Congress.   Van Zandt and his allies made
feverish attempts to discredit the proposal.
Van Zandt called the conference report "misleading"   and   claimed that it "attempts   to
fool Members of the House."   Other opponents
of   the measure referred to the proposal   as
"a subterfuge" and "a sham and a   delusion."
As a last-ditch effort, Van Zandt moved that
the bill be recommitted to the JCAE.   Unlike
his recommittal motion on the Gore-Holifield
bill,   however,   Van Zandt's motion failed by
a   vote of 186 to 151.   Upon failure of the
recommittal attempt,   the House   immediately
passed the conference version of the authorization bill by a voice vote.   As expected,
the   Senate   approved   the House   action   on
September 18, thus ensuring that the Hanford
proposal would go forward.[39]
     A   bitter Van Zandt addressed his   col-
leagues   immediately after Holifield's   victory in the House.   The Pennsylvania Republican   asserted that the Hanford vote   would
prove to be "a completely empty and meaningless   victory   for   the   Pacific   Northwest"
because   of the conference proviso that   the
federal   government could not assist   financially   in the construction or operation   of
the steam plant.   He claimed the venture was
uneconomical   and predicted that   the   steam

plant would never be built.[40]

Van Zandt's prediction proved wrong within approximately five years. The AEC signed the steam plant purchase contract with WPPSS on April 11, 1963. WPPSS sold $122 million in bonds and completed construction of the generating facilities by December 1966, a few months behind schedule. The generating facilities were brought up to full capacity (800,000 kilowatts) briefly on December 9, 1966, and then on a more sustained basis beginning in May 1967. The New Production Reactor remained the world's largest dual-purpose reactor and held the record for electrical production until the mid-1970s. The reactor and generating facilities continued to supply a portion of the electrical needs of the Pacific Northwest into the 1980s, although the AEC halted plutonium production on January 28, 1971.[41]

Still, the outcome of the Hanford steam plant proposal was vastly different from the federal project that Holifield championed in 1961. The Hanford victory was not an unequivocal public power victory, even though more public utilities than private utilities opted to participate in WPPSS.[42] Holifield's willingness to abandon the idea of a federally constructed facility and instead vigorously support a nonfederal, privately financed venture was testimony to his preference for practical solutions over ideological purity. If Holifield tended to support public power interests philosophically, he was also practical and concerned about the public interest. The record clearly shows that he was consistent and telling the truth from the beginning when he asserted in 1961 that he was interested in saving and using the Hanford N-reactor's waste steam in a way that would economically benefit both the Pacific Northwest and the federal government. Ultimately, he accomplished this practical goal.

8

Atomic Energy and Public Safety: Holifield's Role in Civil Defense and Atmospheric Nuclear Testing

Throughout his congressional career, Holifield maintained a remarkable consistency in his thinking and political views on atomic energy issues. From the late 1940s into the 1970s, his advocacy of American leadership in atomic energy development, friendliness toward public power interests, opposition to business monopoly of the atom, and promotion of nuclear power development remained unchanged. On the issue of atomic safety, Holifield was equally consistent. He accepted as a given that atomic energy was here to stay and would necessitate trade-offs and compromises in its use, but he believed that a reasonable degree of safety could be achieved. He maintained that the public should be protected as fully as possible within practical limitations and that the public had a right to be fully informed of the risks associated with the military and peaceful uses of the atom.

From the late 1940s until the end of the Kennedy administration, the focal point of Holifield's safety interests concerned the government's and the public's survival in the event of a nuclear attack. Holifield explored the subject of civil defense extensively in congressional hearings and became an early and persistent advocate of a strengthened civil defense program geared to the atomic age. He also argued eloquently for the public's right to know more about the nation's nuclear capabilities and the potential effects of a nuclear war. Toward that end, Holifield chaired the first congressional hearings to consider the short-term and long-term effects of radioactive fallout from nuclear testing and other sources, in what he hailed as an attempt to educate the public on man-made radiation. By the early 1960s, Holifield had established himself as a well-known congressional authority on civil defense, and he clashed with the Kennedy administration on the choice of space development over civil defense as an administration priority. At the same time, the eminently practical Holifield urged Kennedy in 1961 to resume atmospheric nuclear testing until the Soviets were willing to accept what Holifield believed to be a reasonable nuclear test ban treaty.

From his earliest years on the JCAE, Holifield argued for the public's right to be fully informed on the risks associated with radiation and nuclear war. Notably, in February 1949, Holifield joined other liberal JCAE Democrats in demanding that the AEC provide more information to the American public. While he did not go as far as Senator Brien McMahon's (D-Connecticut) suggestion that the exact number of bombs in the American stockpile be revealed,[1] he did insist that as much data as possible be made public. In a February 1949 House speech expressing chagrin that the American public had not been fully informed on the 1946 Bikini Atoll bomb tests he attended, Holifield declared that he was "alarmed at the [AEC's] policy of ignoring the job of educating the Congress and the American people to the real meaning of the atomic discoveries." He alleged that the American govern-

ment was engaged in "pre-atomic thinking,"
and he expressed concern that "the minds of
many of our leaders are not yet keyed to the
New Mexico explosion which blasted us over
the borderline of a new era." Holifield
further charged that the government's "unjustified margin of secrecy" was "dangerous
to the security of our Nation, not to mention our own personal welfare." He demanded
that the public be told the facts about
atomic warfare because "the truth about
atomic warfare is perhaps the only real
defense we have today against the possibility of [a nuclear war]."[2]

Practical as always, Holifield attempted to define the kind of information
that should be made available to the public:

> What do we have a right to know?
> Let us face that question
> squarely. Let us answer it now.
> We do not, of course, want any
> military secrets disclosed to a
> potential enemy. . . . What we
> are entitled to know is this:
> What will the atom bomb do to you
> and to our children? To our Na-
> tion? To our civilization? These
> are fair questions--questions to
> which people living in a democracy
> have a right to demand the an-
> swers.[3]

Holifield concluded with more specifics. "I
believe the American public is entitled to
know," he declared, "the amount of radiation
released by the Bikini Bombs." He recommended that Congress demand the full facts
on the destructive effects of the Bikini
explosions and that these "be laid bare
before the American public." He also recommended that a congressional investigation be
launched if the information was not provided
in a reasonable time. Holifield showed his

determination on the matter by making a
radio broadcast the next day on the same
subject.[4]

Holifield's interest in civil defense
began to develop a few months later. In a
February 1950 House resolution, he called
for the creation of a commission to investigate measures that could be taken to ensure
continuous operation of the federal government in the event of a nuclear attack.
Holifield was concerned both with establishing an alternate capital in the event Washington, D.C. was destroyed and with replacing the president, the vice president, and
members of Congress if these individuals
were killed in such an attack. A similar
resolution by Holifield the following year
designated the proposed commission as the
Commission on Government Security. In introducing his 1951 resolution, Holifield
expressed his concern that civil defense
efforts "have been dangerously laggard and
too lacking in imagination in the light of
the awful possibilities of the atomic bomb."
In the early 1950s, a third world war with
nuclear weapons seemed a distinct possibility.[5]

Holifield's activities regarding the
purely civilian side of civil defense,
namely, protection of the population in the
event of an atomic attack, also increased
gradually. He participated in 1950 JCAE
hearings on civil defense and generally
supported the Federal Civil Defense Act of
1950, with its establishment of a federal-
state emphasis on action at the local level.
Holifield believed the federal government,
however, should have "an important responsibility for effective planning, guidance and
assistance."[6]

If any event caused Holifield to
sharpen his focus on civil defense, it was
the March 1954 hydrogen bomb test series in
the Marshall Islands. The blast in the

AEC's CASTLE test was larger than anticipated, forcing the evacuation of Marshall
Islanders from islands miles from the point
of the explosion. In addition, the detonation exposed Japanese tuna fishermen outside
the restricted ocean zone to fallout and
radiation poisoning. This news horrified
the Japanese and produced a "tuna scare" in
Japan. In the United States, President
Dwight Eisenhower hardly soothed American
nerves on March 24 by his admission that AEC
scientists had been surprised by the
strength of the blast. AEC Chairman Lewis
Strauss, asked by Eisenhower to reassure the
American people, only increased public fears
by his statement that a single hydrogen bomb
could be developed to destroy an entire
city, including metropolitan New York.[7]
    Holifield stepped into the furor with
civil defense uppermost in his mind. In a
House speech, he commended Strauss, usually
his foe, for "the most important, authoritative statement regarding the development of
hydrogen weapons that has been made to
date." Holifield declared that the Strauss
revelation "should be the basis of a revolutionary change in our concepts of military
offense and defense, and our methods of
civil defense." Holifield wrote Eisenhower,
Strauss, and JCAE Chairman Sterling Cole and
asked that they review security regulations
and "tell the people of the world in plain,
understandable words, exactly what these new
weapons will do." Holifield also used the
occasion to charge that the Eisenhower administration's civil defense plans, which
relied on mass evacuation, were "a confes-
sion of failure and desperation." He noted
that Congress had failed to appropriate
substantial funds for civil defense "because
they know the futility of plans proposed to
date."[8]
    Holifield was not one to criticize
without suggesting alternative solutions.

By early April, scarcely a month later, he was ready to propose a substantial change in civil defense.   House Joint Resolution No. 491, which Holifield introduced on April 12, 1954, proposed that the federal Civil Defense Administration be reconstituted as a cabinet-level department.   Holifield attempted to obtain as much coverage as possible for his resolution by sending a letter to each of his colleagues informing them of his plans to introduce the proposal and inviting them to introduce identical measures.   He also introduced legislation to authorize state governors to fill vacancies in Congress if a majority of senators and representatives were eliminated in a nuclear attack.[9]

Holifield continued his criticism of the Eisenhower administration and called for changes in civilian defense into 1955.   During a speech before a Democratic group in Virginia in January, he lamented that he had to "guard my every sentence, lest I violate security."   He asserted that "a source no less authoritative than the President should tell the American people the truth about our capacity to apprehend surprise enemy attack, and our chances for defense against such an attack." Holifield also believed the president should admit to the "tragic inadequacy" of the administration's civil defense efforts.   He declared that without such an admission and constructive change, "we will continue to live in a fool's paradise until it's too late to develop a plan for survival."[10]

By the end of January 1955, Holifield had begun to formulate the outlines of what he believed would be an adequate civil defense program to replace that of the Eisenhower administration.   In a January 29, 1955, speech before the American Legion, Holifield charged that civil defense was not a priority with the American people and

Congress, as it needed to be, because "they do not understand the present danger because they have not been given the facts which would enable them to understand it." He regretted that there was no information forthcoming from the AEC, the Department of Defense, or the president "concerning the implications of radioactive fall-out for civil defense," and he again challenged Eisenhower to "tell the American people the facts concerning radioactive fall-out." "Without such facts," Holifield declared, "there can be no realistic civil defense program." Holifield advocated new guiding principles to replace Eisenhower's efforts. In place of local resources and volunteer workers, he proposed increased federal funding and a significantly increased, full-time civil defense corps. He asserted that the new program "must also be based on regional planning and unified co-ordination with vital military functions." For Holifield, federal responsibility for civil defense involved "far-reaching programs for utilizing national resources to provide emergency shelters, vital supplies of food, water and medicines, protection of industrial facilities, and trained manpower." He explained that he did not intend a new top-heavy federal bureaucracy, but he did visualize greatly increased federal spending and "a universal system of training for civilian defense," with "a full-time corps drawn largely from young men who had been judged medically unfit for military service."[11]

By mid-1955, Holifield had dropped, at least publicly, the idea of a full-time civil defense corps, but he continued to criticize the Eisenhower program and to emphasize the need for increased federal activity in civil defense. In June, he used the occasion of an evacuation exercise to lambast the administration's approach as "too little" and "too late." He complained that Eisenhower was placing the principle of balancing the budget ahead of protecting American citizens living in areas targeted for destruction by the Soviets in the event of a nuclear war. Holifield concluded that the administration "has woefully failed the American people in the field of Civilian Defense." He now declared that it was "imperative" that the president propose new civil defense legislation based on the two "vital principles" of first, federal responsibility for target-area planning and coordination and second, federal acceptance of major financial responsibility for civil defense on a basis similar to that of national defense.[12]

Holifield's call for a new civil defense program coincided with his preparation for congressional hearings to investigate the need for additional civil defense measures. As chairman of the Subcommittee on Military Operations of the House Committee on Government Operations, he had persuaded subcommittee members early in 1955 of the need for such an investigation. He also had directed the subcommittee staff to research the subject of civil defense so that the subcommittee could be briefed fully before the beginning of the hearings.[13]

In January 1956, Holifield launched his probe into the problems of civil defense. In his opening statement at the hearings on January 31, he conceived his subcommittee's task as a comprehensive assessment of the civil defense program. Hence, the subcommittee would consider the 1950 Civil Defense Act and the institutions erected to administer the act, as well as all new proposals, including his own, that had been introduced in Congress. Holifield observed that "public apathy, congressional indifference and bureaucratic indifference are the three great obstacles to effective civil defense" and that the subcommittee intended to "take a fresh look at the problems to determine how these obstacles can be overcome." Finally, Holifield requested that the subcommittee make the hearings as impartial and nonpartisan as possible. As he viewed them, "the problems are too grave, their solution too important to become the subject of political argument."[14]

As Holifield promised, the hearings were extensive. Besides their hearings in Washington, D.C., the subcommittee visited and solicited testimony in many of the other possible target areas for a nuclear attack, including Los Angeles, Detroit, New York City, Syracuse, and San Francisco. Over two hundred witnesses appeared before the subcommittee, including mayors, governors, scientists, professors, local civil defense officials, and representatives from the AEC, the Department of Defense, the federal Civil Defense Administration, the Office of Defense Mobilization, and the Joint Chiefs of Staff. The hearing record itself ultimately filled seven volumes. As Holifield later observed without exaggeration, "This was the most searching and comprehensive inquiry into civil defense ever made by a congressional committee."[15]

When the subcommittee finished the hearings and completed a report of findings and recommendations in mid-July, it was clear that Holifield's desire for a bipartisan report on civil defense had been achieved. The House Committee on Government Operations approved the subcommittee report with only one dissenting vote. Even President Eisenhower indicated that the subcommittee's study would be seriously considered in future civil defense legislation proposed by his administration.[16]

The Holifield subcommittee report, entitled "Civil Defense for National Survival," criticized the existing civil defense program with regard to both its organ-

izational setting and its principal methods
for protection of the public. The subcommittee found federal authority for civil
defense weak, diffuse, and unclear. The
federal Civil Defense Administration and the
Office of Defense Mobilization duplicated
functions in civil defense planning. Also,
the Civil Defense Administration had not
fully grasped, in the subcommittee's view,
the technical, economic, and administrative
requirements of civil defense. In addition,
the subcommittee described the mobilization
concepts of the Office of Defense Mobilization as "largely outmoded." The subcommittee also found that the basic civil defense
policy of reliance on mass evacuation as the
principal method of protecting the public
was "weak, ineffective, and dangerously
short-sighted."[17]

The recommendations of the report
closely paralleled Holifield's recommended
approach to civil defense. The report
stated that civil defense should be viewed
as a strategic component of national defense
and called for a comprehensive overhaul of
the 1950 act to bring civil defense into the
nuclear age. The subcommittee believed that
the basic responsibility for civil defense
should be vested in the federal government,
with states and local governments having "an
important supporting role." To end administrative confusion and give sufficient importance to the overall program, the subcommittee proposed that a cabinet-level Department
of Civil Defense be created and that the
Civil Defense Administration and the Office
of Defense Mobilization be merged into this
new body. The new department would be responsible for coordinating its efforts with
the Department of Defense and for developing
a master plan for the protection of civilian
populations in target areas. In place of
federal sponsorship of evacuation and encouragement of private, backyard family

shelters, which the subcommittee described as "inexpensive budgetary substitutes" for effective efforts, Holifield and his associates called for a massive, group-shelter construction program as "the core of the civil defense system." As Holifield observed, "A shelter program is the acid test of a national will to build an effective civil defense."[18]

In late 1956, Holifield indicated that the subcommittee would introduce legislation in the next session of Congress to begin implementation of the recommendations. Accordingly, he introduced a bill in 1957 to create a Department of Civil Defense and authorize the shelter program. Holifield also lent his vigorous support to a bill by Representative Ed Edmondson (D-Oklahoma) to authorize a program of school-shelter construction.[19]

With the reelection of the budget-conscious Eisenhower in November 1956, Holifield could not hope to obtain passage of his civil defense proposals. No Republican president would allow a Democrat to preempt such a vital field of public policy. In view of this political reality, Holifield continued to hold hearings on civil defense, keep the existing program's shortcomings in public view, and wait for a more opportune time for action on his proposals. Through his hearings, Holifield continued to call especially for shelter construction as the cornerstone of a strengthened civil defense program. He criticized the Eisenhower administration's new plan to mark existing spaces in big city buildings as creating "an illusion of security," since Holifield believed such shielding from atomic blasts would be inadequate for the heat intensities expected in a nuclear war.[20]

Although Holifield was stymied for a time in his efforts to strengthen civil defense, he was not inactive. Operating on his long-held belief that the public had a right to know about the effects of radiation, Holifield held extensive hearings in 1957 and 1959 on the effects of man-made radiation. His were the first congressional hearings ever on the effects of radiation, and the 1957 hearings were particularly popular with both the public and the press. Ever since the AEC's BRAVO tests of 1954, the American public, press, and scientists had engaged in an on-again, off-again pattern of intense interest in the radiation problem, especially in the nature and danger of fallout resulting from nuclear testing. An AEC report on fallout in February 1955, the creation of a United Nations Scientific Committee on Radiation in December 1955 (proposed by the United States to study radioactive fallout), a report by the National Academy of Sciences in June 1956 on radiation hazards, and the emphasis by Democratic presidential candidate Adlai Stevenson on radiation hazards as his justification for calling for a test ban during the 1956 presidential campaign all testified to the growing importance of the radiation issue.[21]

A number of reasons explain why Holifield was the JCAE member chosen to chair the hearings on radiation. Long an active Democrat, Holifield participated as a consultant to the 1956 Democratic platform committee and saw to it that the party platform contained a provision calling for "a comprehensive survey of radiation hazards from bomb tests." The plank reflected Holifield's call since 1949 for as full a disclosure as possible to the public regarding the dangers associated with radiation and nuclear war and was designed as a companion effort to the congressman's proposal for a strengthened civil defense program. Holifield also called publicly for congressional hearings on radiation in January 1957. He believed that the object of the hearings would be to "sort out the thorny facts in the briar patch of controversy and confusion which had snarled up the radiation issue."[22] JCAE Chairman Carl Durham (D-North Carolina), who in mid-1956 had ordered a JCAE staff study on radiation to "effectually document this matter of fallout and radiation and send it to every Member [of the House]," was convinced by late February 1957 that radiation hearings would be valuable. He appointed Holifield as chairman of a Special Subcommittee on Radiation to conduct the hearings.[23]

Holifield prepared for the radiation hearings with the same degree of thoroughness as he had prepared for his hearings on civil defense. Together with the JCAE staff, he consulted with various scientists and scientific organizations to develop an agenda to consider all facets of the radiation issue. What Holifield intended was a scientific seminar that would "give us all, both Congress and the public at large, a better understanding of the fall-out question and . . . help clear up existing confusion over the character and dimensions of the problem." He was interested in factual information rather than "moral, philosophic and religious convictions," insisting that "an impartial fact-finding and fact-sifting job had to be done first."[24] Holifield also hoped that the printed hearings, which would include scholarly papers, as well as testimony by expert witnesses, would serve as a "textbook" on the radiation issue as "one of the most extensive compendia of expert information on radioactive fallout yet to appear in one document."[25]

The subcommittee hearings were all that Holifield had hoped and planned for. Held in the ornate Senate Caucus Room, site of the famous army-McCarthy hearings three years earlier, the hearings were well attended by the public and the American and foreign press. In opening the hearings, Holifield stressed that the subcommittee's goal was to get the facts rather than justify any predetermined conclusions. Approximately fifty witnesses of all points of view testified on the seven major areas of subject matter laid out in the subcommittee agenda. These areas included the origin and distribution of fallout, the biological effects of radiation, the safety or tolerance levels of exposure for the general population, the effects of past and future atmospheric nuclear tests, and the probable effects of a nuclear war.[26]

The hearings, although often technical, brought out some startling facts. The subcommittee learned from an AEC testing employee that a "clean" bomb (free from fallout) was technically impossible, although this information hardly surprised Holifield, who had ridiculed AEC Chairman Strauss a year earlier for implying that such a bomb might be developed. Much more disturbing was the AEC's admission that it knew of the potential hazards of strontium 90, a byproduct of atomic fission, even before the 1954 BRAVO tests. The subcommittee also learned that fallout was heavier in the northern temperate zone, where the United States was located.[27]

Although the Holifield hearings indicated a general absence of agreement on the dangers of fallout, they were instrumental in educating the public on the potential dangers of atmospheric nuclear testing. From the testimony at the hearings, which was translated by the press into layman's terms, the public learned that strontium 90 and cesium 137, radioactive contaminants from nuclear fission, could spread into the stratosphere and sooner or later fall to earth, entering into the food chain and eventually into human bones and tissues, with potentially lethal or disease-causing results. While there was general agreement that radiation in any amount caused genetic damage in humans, the extent of damage was debatable, as was the effect of radiation in causing nongenetic conditions such as leukemia, bone cancer, or a decrease in life expectancy. Scientists also disagreed over the issue of whether there was a safety limit of exposure below which radiation was harmless, so this issue, too, was left unresolved. Expert testimony indicated that the effects of past testing had caused minimal radiation exposure to humans, but the subcommittee believed similar testing over several generations could be harmful to the world's population.[28]

The Holifield hearings also damaged the credibility of the Eisenhower administration and the Strauss AEC. The disclosures that a clean bomb was impossible, that the AEC had been aware of fallout hazards before the BRAVO tests, and that fallout was heavier in the northern temperate zone all contradicted the administration's pronouncements that testing was safe and the AEC's statements that radiation hazards were minimal. Holifield emphasized these contradictions in a House speech after the hearings. He repeated his assertion that the Strauss AEC had failed to inform the American people of the dangers of fallout. In contrast to the Eisenhower administration's claims that radiation hazards could be largely discounted, Holifield concluded that "we are now dealing with a global health problem." In an article in the *Saturday Review* in September, Holifield charged that the AEC's policy in relation to radiation danger was to "play it down."[29]

Another spin-off of the hearings was Holifield's call for a four-point United States policy on atmospheric testing. In an article he prepared in September for the

Bulletin of the Atomic Scientists, Holifield castigated the AEC for "a lack of frankness" and the Eisenhower State Department for "a lack of vision." He charged that both agencies had "placed the United States on the defensive against the effective campaign of Soviet Russia to identify the Communist cause with peace and the United States with war." In place of the Soviet's "shrewd" and "insincere" call for a halt to nuclear testing, Holifield proposed a policy based on four principles. These included a vigorous radiation education policy, a limitation on annual fission release from total testing of all nations, a serious consideration of the problems of test detection, and a moratorium on testing based on an adequate formula of detection.[30]

Holifield's perceptions about the outlines for a new policy were largely correct. By 1958, American and world opinion had forced the Eisenhower administration to accept, at least in part, three of Holifield's four principles. Eisenhower and Strauss both found themselves insisting that the AEC was providing abundant information about radiation to the American public and declaring it their policy to continue doing so. Strauss also promised a government-wide review of the fallout problem. In addition, Eisenhower sent a letter to Soviet leader Nikita Khrushchev on April 28, 1958, calling for a technical conference on detection. By its wording, the letter also shifted administration policy by allowing negotiations for a test ban to be separated from other disarmament goals. By October 31, 1958, the United States and the Soviet Union had also agreed to a one-year moratorium on atmospheric nuclear testing.[31]

Ironically, the impending moratorium only spurred a hectic round of testing by the United States, Great Britain, and the Soviet Union. The testing produced large

amounts of radioactive fallout, which began
to make its way around the globe. Scientists in the United States detected increased amounts of strontium 90 in various
parts of the country early in 1959. Pronouncements of heightened levels of
strontium 90 in Minnesota wheat and in mid-
western milk caused the greatest concern and
led to a veritable fallout scare in the
nation during the first half of 1959.[32]

Against this radiation background,
Holifield launched his 1959 hearings on
radiation. The California congressman's
intention in holding the new hearings was to
update the scientific information presented
at the 1957 hearings. Holifield also wished
to reconsider certain unresolved matters
from the earlier hearings, examine alternative weapons-testing policies, and learn
what was being done by various federal agencies in the fields of research and monitoring of fallout.[33]

Although Holifield wanted to review all
of the subject areas of his 1957 hearings
except the effects of a nuclear war, plus
examine new areas, he faced more severe time
constraints than in 1957. JCAE Chairman
Durham limited the hearings to four days
because several other hearings were also
scheduled and the JCAE staff was committed
for these hearings and other duties. Thus,
Holifield necessarily had to structure the
hearings very carefully and predetermine all
witnesses to be called to testify.[34] As in
1957, he also consulted with two scientific
groups prior to the hearings in order to
reconcile differences in interpreting data.
Holifield's major objective was to provide
factual scientific data on fallout to the
public. Not taken in by the fallout scare,
he developed his hearing agenda and witness
list with the intent of avoiding sensational
witnesses or those with extreme views or
political motives. Holifield bypassed Linus

Pauling, a prominent scientist and test ban advocate, as well as many others, for this reason. According to Holifield, "The one thing we need is facts and less emotional reaction to propaganda."[35]

Held in a much more emotionally charged atmosphere, Holifield's 1959 hearings were less appreciated than those in 1957. Holifield's determination to get "the facts, just the facts" and his declaration that "the committee does not intend to be swayed by emotional arguments" when cutting off testimony on unknown hazards fell on much more sensitive ears in 1959 and won for Holifield a torrent of negative commentary. The National Committee for a Sane Nuclear Policy (SANE), created after the 1957 hearings, charged that the hearings had ignored the high level of radioactivity in the American food supply and called for a new congressional inquiry. *The New Republic* termed the hearings "a complete farce," while *The Reporter* accused Holifield of conducting a whitewash.[36]

These harsh criticisms stung Holifield. In a letter to a friend, he expressed dismay that some liberal magazines such as *The New Republic* and *I. F. Stone's Newsletter* "were very critical of the hearings." "I honestly believe," he wrote, "that they misrepresented the hearings and cast an unwarranted reflection on my integrity, because the apparent result of the hearings did not support their preconceived conclusions." More charitably, Holifield surmised, "It may have been because there was so much material, documents, etc. submitted for the printed hearings, that they were unable to judge the complete context of the hearings." Holifield was confident that the upcoming printed summary-analysis of the hearings "will be completely objective and very valuable in bringing out the facts that have developed since my hearings on radiation in

1957."[37]

The printed summary of the hearings did attempt to be objective in assessing new scientific information on fallout. Styled as a "systematic compilation of material on fallout for the information of the public," the report indicated that fallout had received a great amount of scientific attention since 1957. In addition to strontium 90 and cesium 137, whose levels were found to have increased significantly since the earlier hearings, scientists had identified strontium 89, iodine 131, barium 140, and carbon 14 (Linus Pauling's "discovery") as other potentially serious radioactive contaminants of atmospheric nuclear testing. The subcommittee paid special attention to carbon 14, concluding that "radioactive carbon 14 from past weapons tests could constitute a genetic hazard to the world's population."[38] The report noted that scientists had also confirmed that distribution of fallout was not uniform and that, indeed, about two-thirds of radioactive debris from nuclear testing had fallen in the northern latitudes. Since no threshold or safety limit of exposure had yet been identified, the subcommittee found it provident to assume "that any dose, however small, produces some biological effect and that this effect is harmful." With regard to past nuclear tests, the findings were reassuring to the public. Scientists forecast that the maximum contamination in human bone from strontium 90 would occur in the period 1962-1965 and would average about six strontium units, or about 10 percent of the "maximum body burden" of sixty-seven strontium units established by the International Commission on Radiation Protection. If tests were to continue at the same intensity as the previous five years for the next two generations, the subcommittee estimated that the level of radioactive contamination could present "a hazard to the world's population."[39]

In the new subject areas covered by the hearings, which included alternative weapons-testing policies and radiation safety research and monitoring activities, the subcommittee's findings were also noteworthy. Testing underground, begun with the RANIER tests, was viewed as radiation-free but appropriate only for small tests. Testing in space had also been considered, but little was known about its effects at the time. Significantly, Holifield's subcommittee viewed atmospheric nuclear testing as "necessary to establish effects of nuclear weapons on military targets, equipment, radiation levels, etc." In the area of radiation safety research and monitoring, the subcommittee concluded that "better coordination by the AEC of fallout information is essential." The Public Health Service, which had begun testing for radiation in milk in July 1958, received honorable mention for its efforts with the comment that its "expenditures and numbers of personnel remain small."[40]

The major result of Holifield's 1959 hearings was to relieve at least some public anxiety over fallout. Holifield's refusal to give in to the fallout hysteria, his quest for hard facts rather than sensational speculations, and his attempt to present the information objectively helped to calm public fears, his liberal detractors notwithstanding. Decreased strontium 90 readings announced by the government also supported the testimony at the Holifield hearings that the increase in strontium 90 was only temporary. The subcommittee's finding that future atmospheric tests might imperil the world's population also provided justification for increased efforts to consummate a test ban treaty.[41]

Another result of the 1959 hearings was

Holifield's call in June 1959 for transfer of the AEC's radiation safety programs to the Public Health Service. In recommending the transfer, Holifield joined Senate critics of the administration and the surgeon general, who had sought the action in March 1959. Senate advocates of the proposed reorganization included JCAE Chairman Clinton Anderson (D-New Mexico), Disarmament Subcommittee Chairman Hubert Humphrey (D-Minnesota), and Lister Hill (D-Alabama). Holifield's interest in the Public Health Service at the hearings probably had been kindled by the earlier calls for the transfer, calls that involved the allegation that the AEC as both promoter and regulator of atomic energy represented a conflict of interest. As a result of the hearings, Holifield decided that the senators were right and joined in recommending the reorganization, but over a period of five to ten years, with responsibilities to be given eventually to states (state health departments) as far as practicable.[42]

The Public Health Service ultimately did not receive the AEC's radiation safety programs. President Eisenhower, realizing that his opponents were gaining the initiative, authorized a study of the possible transfer in April; after the Holifield hearings, he stripped the AEC of its radiation safety responsibilities, placing them in a new Federal Radiation Council. The new council's mission was to determine safety standards and oversee the actual protective measures, which would be carried out by states and federal agencies such as the Food and Drug Administration and the Public Health Service. This arrangement, with the emphasis on allowing states to carry out radiation safety responsibilities, was not wholly unlike Holifield's proposal. Holifield had been wary, however, of getting too many agencies involved "in view of the fact that each type of radiation contributes to the total radiation dose accumulation of the individual."[43]

During the rest of 1959 and 1960, Holifield held additional hearings, which updated available information on radiation hazards associated specifically with nuclear war and civil defense. Unlike his 1957 radiation hearings, the 1959 radiation hearings did not include the subject of the radiation effects of nuclear war, because Holifield had decided to devote a set of hearings to this topic in June 1959. Holifield hoped to "establish for the first time specific data on nuclear war effects, as contradistinct [sic] from general descriptive phrases such as nuclear war is 'unthinkable,' 'will destroy civilization,' 'poison the genetic pool of life,' etc." Holifield wanted to show "the destruction which would occur from blast, heat and most important, from radiation in a war where 1500 to 3000 megatons of bombs would be exploded." Holifield believed that "our only salvation lies in educating as quickly as possible all people in understanding the inevitable horrors of a full scale nuclear war."[44] When the hearings concluded, Holifield wrote to a California assemblyman that he had "been successful in establishing, on authoritative testimony, a computation of probable human casualties and area damage, such as has never been established before." Holifield was "hopeful these facts will awaken enough people so our diplomats will do their best to obtain a genuine peace." He assured the assemblyman that "I will continue my fight to inform the people of the true facts regarding radioactive fallout and nuclear war."[45]

Armed with new knowledge about the effects on the United States of a nuclear war, Holifield held hearings on civil defense again in July 1960 to review the ex-

isting civil defense program. The Holifield
Military Operations Subcommittee reaffirmed
its earlier conclusion that the Eisenhower
evacuation plans and the new plan marking
existing space in big city buildings for
shelters would be ineffective in a nuclear
war. In Holifield's view, the space-marking
plan provided only an "illusion of security"
since the protection these shelters would
afford would be ineffective for the fallout
intensities expected. As for the encouragement of private shelter construction, the
other major component in Eisenhower's civil
defense program, Holifield's subcommittee
concluded that "there is no sense living in
a world of make-believe. If the Federal
government doesn't supply the funds and
direct a construction program for communal
shelters, there will be no national shelter
program."[46]

With the inauguration of President John
F. Kennedy, Holifield had good reasons to be
optimistic about the future of the civil
defense program. His years of research and
hearings on civil defense and radiation
hazards had made him the foremost congressional authority on these subjects. His
accession to the chairmanship of the JCAE in
January 1961 also made him an important
congressional influence and placed him in an
advantageous position to lobby for a
strengthened program. In addition, Holifield could expect that Kennedy, as a Democrat, would be somewhat more receptive than
Eisenhower to the suggestions of Democratic
congressional leaders. The only possible
drawback was that Holifield had not endorsed
Kennedy initially for the nomination. Instead, he had thrown his support behind his
longtime friend and former JCAE associate,
Senate Majority Leader Lyndon B. Johnson (D-
Texas), who was the new vice-president.[47]

Holifield's first attempt to urge Kennedy's support for civil defense got no-

where.   A letter on civil defense he wrote
to Kennedy in the first days of the Kennedy
administration was referred to the Office of
Civil and Defense Mobilization.   Holifield
complained to Special Assistant Lawrence
O'Brien that he "regretted" that O'Brien
"did not think it [the letter] was worthy of
the President's personal attention."   This
complaint brought an immediate conciliatory
message from the White House. Holifield and
Kennedy were more in tune when the issue was
atmospheric nuclear testing.   By summer,
Holifield urged Kennedy to resume testing,
since the Soviets had resumed testing.
Holifield believed this was dangerous for
world health, but necessary. He advocated a
"talk and test" strategy--continue to negotiate for a permanent test ban, but test in
the meantime as a prod to the Soviets. When
Kennedy in effect adopted this strategy in
September 1961, he had the full support of
Holifield.[48]
     If Holifield's first attempt to educate
the president on the need for a strengthened
civil defense program had gone awry, by May
Kennedy had adopted the major tenets of
Holifield's civil defense philosophy.   In a
special message to Congress on May 25, Kennedy called for increased federal involvement in civil defense as a new form of
"survival insurance" against the hazards of
radioactive fallout. Kennedy also announced
that he was transferring civil defense functions of the Office of Civil and Defense
Mobilization to the Department of Defense,
thus accomplishing Holifield's intent of
integrating civil defense with national
defense.   In addition, Kennedy announced
that his administration would introduce
legislation to authorize federal funding for
identifying fallout shelter space in existing buildings, for requiring shelters in
existing and new federal buildings, and for
providing matching grants and other incen-

tives to construct shelters in state and local government buildings. Kennedy predicted that Fiscal Year 1962 civil defense appropriations "will in all likelihood be more than triple the pending [Eisenhower] budget requests; and they will increase sharply in subsequent years."[49]

Holifield was hopeful, but cautious, in response to Kennedy's call for a strengthened civil defense program. In a lengthy letter to Theodore Sorenson, the president's speech writer on the subject, Holifield noted that the president had given civil defense efforts "a needed emphasis" and that the proposed program "could mark a new departure in the civil defense effort." Nonetheless, Holifield expressed his "disappointment and dismay at the tenor or import of certain of the President's remarks." Holifield believed that the concept of civil defense as "survival insurance" appeared to offer "a very narrow base of justification for civil defense." He was also concerned about the president's comment that "many of the civil defense plans proposed have been so far-reaching or unrealistic that they have not gained essential support." Holifield felt the comment subtly criticized all far-reaching programs as unrealistic, and he reminded Sorenson that his own subcommittee's proposals were "not unrealistic in proportion to total annual outlays for national defense." In addition, Holifield asserted that Kennedy's statement about the inability of civil defense to deter a nuclear attack was simply "knocking down another strawman [sic]" since "no one had ever contended that civil defense by itself could deter attack." Holifield repeated his belief that "civil defense is an integral part of the national defense and is an essential part of the deterrent strength and posture of the nation." By his letter, Holifield was hoping to influence further presidential statements on civil defense.[50]

After the president's speech, Holifield continued to exert as much influence as possible to ensure that Kennedy would opt for a comprehensive civil defense program. In early July, he echoed the call of Frank B. Ellis, director of the Office of Civil and Defense Mobilization, for a $20 billion community shelter construction program. Holifield declared that "the important thing is to move as quickly as possible to obtain the protection the American people need." Later in the month, he gave a speech in the House, advocating increased federal involvement in civil defense and urging that "the hour of danger may be nearer than we think." In August, Holifield held lengthy hearings on Kennedy's May 25 reorganization proposal and civil defense needs. The outcome of the hearings, which Holifield offered as a "textbook" on civil defense for the administration, included two program alternatives for Kennedy to consider. The first was a $1 billion to $5 billion program that would save about half of the people otherwise doomed in a nuclear attack, through provision of an evacuation plan, home shelters, shelter space in existing buildings, and a spartan economic recovery program. The second alternative cost $10 billion to $30 billion, and would save all but ten million people. It consisted of large, underground group shelters, a detailed evacuation plan, extensive prewar stockpiles of recovery materials, and a broad reconstruction plan. Holifield himself continued to use the $20 billion (or $19 billion) as the cost of shelters to save most of the population from annihilation.[51]

By late 1961, the crisis over the Berlin Wall had brought a new urgency to civil defense efforts. Kennedy made a personal plea for increased civil defense activities on television during the crisis and caused

near-panic buying of private shelters when
he represented nuclear war as a clear and
present danger. Holifield used the occasion
for another letter to Kennedy, declaring,
"There is a demand for federal leadership
and for a clearly defined civil defense
program." Holifield bemoaned the fact that
"the theme of confusion and irresoluteness
in the Federal government is being played up
in the newspapers," and he asserted that the
situation "requires not only a substantial
and clearly stated program for fiscal 1963,
but *a statement of our national goal for
civil defense in longer range terms.*" For
Fiscal Year 1963, Holifield urged Kennedy to
increase the civil defense budget substantially and concentrate on the construction
of school shelters, since "Congress would
support such a program." He warned Kennedy
that "failure to act promptly and positively
will create heavy political liabilities for
the Administration and the Democratic
party."[52]

Although it is difficult to judge the
influence that Holifield exerted on the
president, the Kennedy administration did
request substantially more funds for Fiscal
Year 1963. In comparison to the $254 mil-
lion it requested for Fiscal Year 1962, the
administration proposed expenditures of $695
million for Fiscal Year 1963. Of this
amount, $460 million was requested for a new
long-range federal incentive program for the
construction of shelters in schools, hospi-
tals, libraries, and similar public centers.
The new program, which certainly mirrored
Holifield's recommendations, required authorizing legislation that the administration could not, however, convince House
Armed Services Committee Chairman Carl Vinson (D-Georgia) to support or act upon. In
addition, the chairman of the House Appropriations Committee, Albert Thomas (D-Texas)
presided over slashing of the remaining

request of $235 million to $75 million.
This action drew a vigorous protest from
Holifield, who called it "a body blow to the
President's civil defense program." Holifield complained that the passing of the
Berlin crisis had made Congress complacent
once again, and he compared the small amount
spent for civil defense to the $600 billion
spent on national defense since 1951. Holifield averred that "if I did not believe in
my heart that this was a necessary program,
I would not be on the floor this afternoon."
For Holifield, it was clear that "the very
life of the Nation is at stake."[53]

The actions of Vinson and Thomas, as
well as the Cuban Missile Crisis in late
1962, led Holifield to attempt once more to
capture the president's ear on civil defense. In a private letter to Kennedy in
February 1963, Holifield asserted that "the
Cuban [Missile] Crisis brought vividly to
mind the fact that the United States has no
effective civil defense." Although he expressed his approval of the "minimal program" in place, Holifield emphasized that it
was his "considered judgment" that even the
president's modest proposals "will not be
supported with adequate funds or legislative
authority unless the President communicates
to key Congressmen such as Mr. Carl Vinson
and Mr. Albert Thomas the significance which
he personally attributes to this program."
Holifield also implied Kennedy would have to
be vocal "from time to time" about the absolute necessity of the program "both privately to key Congressmen and publicly to
the country," if the civil defense effort
was to survive.[54]

By 1963, Holifield was pessimistic
about the future of the civil defense program. In a January 1963 letter to an Arizona civil defense official, Holifield confided that "privately speaking, I am discouraged and doubt we are going to have an

adequate civil defense program to meet the
challenge of nuclear warfare." In a letter
two months later to the same official, Holifield asserted that the problem was "the
lack of attention given to civil defense by
the president and the Pentagon." Holifield
believed that Kennedy and the Joint Chiefs
of Staff were reluctant to look at civil
defense realistically and that "the reluctance to place non-military [civil] defense
in a high priority level is the real root of
the problem."[55]

Holifield's hopes for a higher priority
for civil defense never materialized. Despite his support for civil defense in his
May 25, 1961, speech, Kennedy subsequently
decided that civil defense would not be a
top priority of his administration. In
1963, the shelter bill was dropped as the
subject of a major presidential message and
relegated to the level of a departmental
request.[56]

Although the significance of this blow
to civil defense was somewhat muted by Armed
Services Committee Chairman Vinson's agreement to hold hearings on the shelter bill,
Holifield understood clearly the implications of the president's action. While he
did not directly attack Kennedy, Holifield
demonstrated his unhappiness forcefully in a
speech at Stanford University. In plain
terms, Holifield asserted that the government should be spending more on civil defense and less on the space effort. Pointing out that "we're spending 20 to 30 billion dollars to put a man on the moon,"
Holifield declared that "a national shelter
program, which could save 50 to 100 million
lives, would be better justified than this
project to put a man on the moon."[57]

As a loyal Democrat, Holifield did not
allow his criticism of the administration to
become strident, despite his own views. He
was "encouraged" when the Armed Services

Committee reported a pared-down shelter bill and, probably more so, when the House passed the measure in September. Holifield faced disappointment again, however, when the Senate version failed passage in committee.[58]

The year 1963 essentially brought an end to civil defense as an active national issue. Indicative of the change, the shelter bill did not resurface in the next Congress. Holifield had correctly suspected that "the recent test ban treaty will have a psychological effect on some of the Members and will militate against them being willing to vote appropriations for civil defense."[59] In fact, the test ban treaty was probably the single most important factor in the demise of the civil defense issue. Even so, Holifield supported the limited nuclear test ban treaty, declaring in a press release that the measure would assure "the right of survival." Again, however, Holifield saw the issue as trade-offs, declaring that "we can accept the minimal risks involved, when compared to the increasing danger of an unrestricted nuclear arms race."[60]

After 1963, Holifield had very little to say about civil defense. This silence was partly because of a shift in his beliefs but mostly because of changing political realities and changes in his own personal circumstances. Holifield had always realized that even the best civil defense measures would only minimize the number of immediate deaths in a nuclear attack; ultimately, he came to believe that civil defense would be impossible because of the ever-growing power, sophistication and number of nuclear weapons. In any event, it would have been futile and politically unwise to call for fallout shelters that no longer interested the public and had been rejected by Congress. Also, as a result of Kennedy's 1961 organizational changes in civil defense, Holifield would have had to share jurisdiction over any proposed bills with the Armed Services Committee, thus requiring the agreement of that committee's chairman for any action taken. Kennedy's assassination in November 1963 also produced a different administration with new issues and priorities. Finally, the increasing financial drain of the Vietnam conflict during the later 1960s tended to foreclose any possibility of an ambitious civil defense program.[61]

Holifield's personal circumstances had also changed. Beginning in 1961, he served as chairman (and in alternate congresses, as vice-chairman) of the JCAE and often as acting chairman of the Government Operations Committee because of the frequent illnesses of Chairman William Dawson (D-Illinois).[62] With more of a managing role, Holifield had less time to conduct lengthy investigations. In addition, he was preoccupied, especially in Government Operations, with moving President Lyndon Johnson's Great Society reorganization legislation, and he became the first congressman to be intimately involved in creating two cabinet-level departments, the Department of Housing and Urban Development and the Department of Transportation.[63]

After 1963, the predominant atomic safety issues also changed. From the mid-1960s until the end of his career, Holifield and the nation would be preoccupied with safety problems of a different nature. More and more, the public would become concerned with the safety of nuclear power plants, as more of these plants came on-line and presented new, challenging safety issues in their use. The nuclear power controversy would, in fact, replace civil defense and atmospheric nuclear testing as the paramount safety concern of the 1960s and the 1970s, essentially for the rest of Holifield's congressional career and beyond.

Chet Holifield (fourth from left) with General Dwight Eisenhower in wartime Europe, Fall 1944. Although his 1931 hunting injury prevented him from serving in World War II, Holifield nonetheless served his country well as a member of the House Military Affairs Committee.

President John F. Kennedy and his Chief Congressional Atomic Energy Advisor, Chet Holifield

Holifield's power reached its peak during the administration of his longtime friend from Texas, Lyndon Baines Johnson.

Chet and Cam Holifield with Admiral Hyman G. Rickover (center), chief naval architect of the "Nuclear Navy" and a strong Holifield ally.

9

Defender of the Faiths:
Holifield and the Nuclear Power Controversy

In the 1960s, the predominant public interest in atomic safety shifted toward the
issue of the safety of nuclear power
plants.[1] A newly visible group, the environmentalists, attacked the nuclear power industry as a peril to the environment and
labeled Holifield, now a leader of the JCAE,
as an ideologue of the "Atomic Establishment."[2] While Holifield came to be perceived as an unremitting foe of the antinuclear movement, it was actually the times,
rather than Holifield, that had changed.
Holifield continued to maintain essentially
the same philosophy of atomic safety that he
had held as early as 1949 and through his
civil defense efforts. He believed that
trade-offs and compromises were necessary in
the development of nuclear power, but that a
reasonable degree of safety could be
achieved in its use. The public, he believed, should be protected as fully as
possible within practical limitations, with
the right to be fully informed of the risks
associated with the development of nuclear
power. Environmentalists perceived Holifield as their foe largely because he accepted the existence and necessity of nuclear power as part of the answer to Amer-

ica's growing power needs. The impending
crisis in energy concerned Holifield deeply,
long before the energy crisis of the mid-
1970s emerged on the national scene.

The extremism of some environmentalists
and the media's penchant for presenting
simple dichotomies on public issues helped
to obscure the fact that Holifield was both
a nuclear power supporter and an environmental advocate who supported nuclear safety
and other environmental issues. As early as
1956, at the time Holifield advocated passage of the Gore-Holifield Civilian Power
Acceleration Program, he joined forces with
JCAE colleagues, labor unions, and politicians in Michigan in an attempt to stop
construction of the Fermi reactor at a site
he considered dangerously close to Detroit.
Holifield was also the lone JCAE opponent of
the 1957 Price-Anderson governmental indemnification measure for power reactors, basing his opposition largely on atomic safety
issues. In 1959, he convened his Special
Subcommittee on Radiation for the last time
to investigate an AEC proposal to dump
atomic wastes in offshore areas. Holifield
also supported measures to broaden public
participation in the AEC hearing process on
proposed nuclear plants. During his first
chairmanship of the JCAE, Holifield sponsored successfully a proposal to create
Atomic Safety and Licensing Boards to formalize the hearing process and provide expanded review of nuclear plant construction
permits and operating licenses. As late as
1966, Holifield applauded even the redundancy of reviews of nuclear plant applications on the grounds of safety.

In the late 1960s, however, American
society underwent significant changes. The
Civil Rights Movement, the Vietnam War dem-
onstrations, the feminist movement, and the
youthful counterculture were all both symp-
toms and causes of these changes. Overall,

there seemed to be less respect for authority and for the government in particular,
and added to this change was a growing rejection of scientists and the scientific-
technocratic method for solving society's
problems. For atomic energy, the most significant change was the arrival of the environmentalists as a potent, vocal, and fast-
growing political force. Nuclear energy and
nuclear power plants became a prominent
target of the environmentalists. As this
group grew in numbers and sophistication in
dealing with atomic power safety issues, it
represented a serious threat to the nation's
nuclear power industry.[3]

Holifield changed little, if any, even
in the social and political ferment of the
late 1960s and early 1970s. He considered
nuclear power reasonably safe, although he
never stopped questioning new or untried
designs. Holifield trusted science and the
consensus of scientific thought rather than
individual theories, and he did not hesitate
to counter those scientific opinions he
believed to be unrealistic or extremist. He
remained eminently practical, favoring the
commonsense and consensus approaches to
problem solving. Believing as he did in the
necessity of nuclear power to meet America's
growing energy needs, Holifield sought to
balance the scale between environmental
needs and the nation's energy needs in several ways. He argued for the use of AEC
laboratories for antipollution research but
also fought for the AEC's right to be the
sole regulator of nuclear power safety.
Holifield favored providing the public with
a chance to contest nuclear plant applications in formal hearings, but he also sought
ways to expedite the increasingly long review periods and to devise new ways to
shorten the lead time for constructing nuclear power plants. Holifield's hearings in
1969-1970 on "The Environmental Effects of

Producing Electrical Power," which brought comparative analysis to bear on the environmental effects of nuclear power plants and plants fueled by gas, oil, and coal, represented his major attempt to reconcile environmental needs with power needs.

Atomic safety as a political issue was almost nonexistent before 1956. The McMahon Act of 1946, the nation's first atomic energy legislation, made only two scant references to the safety aspect of atomic energy, although the potential dangers of developing the atom, chiefly for military purposes in the early years, were clearly recognized. In the early AEC, safety research and development research went hand in hand and were essentially indistinguishable. The AEC promulgated only two minor safety regulations prior to the 1954 act. The Atomic Energy Act of 1954, which opened up nuclear power development to private industry, contained no fewer than twenty-five references to "the health and safety of the public." The definition of what was considered "safe" remained with the AEC, however, and the AEC moved only slowly toward enforcing safety as hazardous incidents developed. Even the debate over the Gore-Holifield bill featured little discussion of safety issues associated with nuclear power development. Nuclear power safety as a political issue had simply not come of age.[4]

In 1956, Holifield actively participated in the nation's first nuclear safety incident, involving construction of a research reactor near Detroit, the Enrico Fermi plant. In January 1956, the Power Reactor Development Company (PRDC), a consortium of equipment manufacturers and utility companies, submitted an application for a construction permit for a 100,000-kilowatt fast-breeder plant at Lagoona Beach, Michigan, only twenty miles outside Detroit. The Strauss AEC, operating with its customary secrecy, decided to grant the construction permit despite the opposition of its Advisory Committee on Reactor Safety (ACRS). The ACRS opposed the plant on the grounds that questions were still not resolved about how the commission's own experimental breeder reactor had suffered a recent accident. Holifield and the rest of the JCAE would never have learned about the ACRS's negative evaluation had not AEC Commissioner Thomas Murray leaked word of the report to the JCAE. Up to that time, ACRS reports were not public documents.[5]

Upon learning of the ACRS report, Holifield joined forces with JCAE Chairman Clinton Anderson (D-New Mexico) to oppose construction of the Enrico Fermi Atomic Power Plant, as the Michigan plant eventually came to be known. Anderson called the AEC's method of approval a "star chamber proceeding" and threatened to hold hearings on legislation to require full public disclosure of the safety hazards of each plant and division of the AEC into separate development and regulation agencies. Holifield, for his part, urged organized labor and the governor of Michigan to intervene and demand a hearing on the grounds that the Fermi plant had not been clearly demonstrated to be safe and that the site was too near to Detroit.[6]

Holifield succeeded in mobilizing labor in the initial skirmish with the AEC over the Fermi plant. When the AEC issued a construction permit in August 1956 despite JCAE opposition, the unions asked for a hearing, a proceeding that consumed most of 1957. In 1958, however, the AEC ruled in favor of the PRDC and continued the construction permit in force. The unions appealed all the way to the Supreme Court. The Court refused to rescind the AEC's decision, and the Fermi plant was finally completed in 1966.[7]

Although Holifield and his associates on the JCAE failed to halt the Fermi plant, they took actions that had a profound effect on the AEC regulatory process as a result of the incident. As he had threatened to do, JCAE Chairman Anderson in August 1956 scheduled hearings for the following year on legislation to make AEC safety reviews public information and to reorganize the AEC into separate development and regulatory agencies. The hearings resulted in a JCAE proposal to make the ACRS a statutory body with public reporting responsibilities for each application and another proposal to require public hearings on all applications. These provisions were incorporated into the successful Price-Anderson bill on governmental indemnification insurance, which was actively supported by the AEC. Although Holifield and other JCAE members did not recommend separate development and regulatory agencies in place of the AEC, they exerted enough pressure on the AEC to force the compromise of isolating its safety staff (the Hazards Evaluation Branch) from the rest of the agency.[8]

Ironically, Holifield did not support the Price-Anderson Act, although he supported the added provisions allowing greater public access and involvement in the AEC's safety review process. The veteran congressman was the sole JCAE opponent of the Price-Anderson bill, basing his opposition on safety grounds. He considered the construction of reactors near large population centers dangerous and observed that even "the hard-headed insurance companies declined to place full coverage, public liability policies" on such atomic reactors because their safety and the degree of risk were undetermined because of insufficient knowledge and operating experience. For Holifield, an "aye" vote to provide governmental indemnification as a backup to pri-

vate insurance, as proposed in the Price-
Anderson bill, meant that "you are helping
to place these potential hazards near your
people" and that "you are willing to take
the gamble, not just with dollars liability
but with hundreds of thousands of human
lives in every urban center, where these
atomic reactors will be placed." Holifield
urged instead that "the quickest and safest
way to progress is to build reactors at
present, Government-owned isolated sites,"
which "would obviate the necessity for this
type of legislation." Despite Holifield's
solitary opposition, the Price-Anderson bill
became law in August 1957.[9]

The next nuclear power safety controversy, involving the disposal of radioactive
wastes, did not occur until 1959. In the
meanwhile, Holifield busied himself as
chairman of the JCAE's Subcommittee on Legislation with the Fiscal Year 1959 AEC authorization bill, through which he and the
other JCAE Democrats obtained many of the
government-constructed reactor projects that
they had sought in the Gore-Holifield bill.
Holifield also occupied himself as chairman
of the JCAE Special Subcommittee on Radiation with preparation for his three upcoming
sets of hearings in 1959 on the radiation
hazards of nuclear testing, on the potential
effects of a nuclear war, and on industrial
radioactive waste disposal.[10]

Holifield's hearings on industrial radioactive waste disposal were intended to
"bring out in a thoughtful and objective
manner the various facets of the waste disposal problem."[11] The hearings shifted,
however, to an inquiry on ocean disposal of
low-level wastes when the AEC proposed dumping low-level wastes in offshore areas and
the Gulf of Mexico. Senator Ralph Yarbor-
ough (D-Texas) was the first to attack the
AEC's disposal plans. The AEC's waste proposal soon brought an enormous outcry from

coastal and Gulf states, especially when the
AEC admitted that it was unaware of even the
probable consequences of disposal of such
wastes in some areas where the water was
only 100 feet deep and in other areas close
to major coastal cities. Holifield launched
his investigation as part of the congressional opposition to the AEC's plans. Congressional opposition and Holifield's pressure tactics were instrumental in getting
the AEC to drop the East and West Coast
sites, but the AEC stubbornly refused to
budge on the Gulf sites. The plan was finally shelved when Senator Lyndon Johnson
(D-Texas) persuaded Mexico's ambassador to
the United States to file a formal protest
against the plan on the basis that it also
endangered Mexico's Gulf Coast.[12]
The Fermi reactor and waste disposal
incidents caused Holifield and other members
of the JCAE increasing concern over the role
and performance of the AEC in atomic safety.
From 1959 to 1961, the JCAE pressured the
AEC to reorganize itself to develop credible
radiation standards to avoid similar waste
disposal incidents and create an autonomous
regulatory arm to avoid conflicts of interest with its development functions. The AEC
did, in fact, reorganize twice in 1959 and
1961, although not totally to the satisfaction of the JCAE. In addition to reorganization, Holifield advocated the creation of
independent Atomic Safety and Licensing
Boards to further reduce possible conflicts
of interest within the AEC and to expand and
formalize public review of nuclear power
application decisions. In 1961 and 1962,
Holifield took the lead as the new chairman
of the JCAE in introducing legislation to
create the independent review boards. The
law creating the boards was passed in 1962,
toward the end of Holifield's first chairmanship of the JCAE. Together with the 1961
AEC reorganization, the boards completed a

regulatory system with public access that lasted until the AEC was divided into separate regulatory and development agencies in 1975.[13]

In 1964, Holifield again focused on atomic safety, this time to expand public access to radiation protection information by obtaining passage of a bill to incorporate the National Committee on Radiation Protection and Measurements (NCRP). The NCRP had been a private committee since 1929, when it was first established as an adjunct to the Bureau of Standards. The Advisory Committee on X-Ray and Radiation Protection, as it was then called, represented the United States on the International Commission on Radiological Protection and adopted the radiation exposure standards of the commission although it had no specific statutory authority. Holifield's bill, signed by President Johnson on July 14, 1964, made the NCRP a quasi-governmental corporation with the specified responsibility to "collect, analyze, develop, and disseminate in the public interest" information and recommendations on radiation protection and exposure standards. This NCRP goal reflected Holifield's continuing effort to keep the public informed of radiation hazards and protection in the expanding uses of atomic energy.[14]

In the mid-1960s, Holifield staunchly defended the JCAE's expansion of public access to nuclear power decisions and information. Even the nuclear power industry's complaints of increased costs because of the extended application review process left Holifield unmoved. He disagreed publicly with the Mitchell panel, an outside review body appointed by the AEC in 1965 to study ways to expedite construction permit and operating license reviews. The panel had recommended that the broad review authority of the ACRS and the Atomic Safety and Licensing Boards be curtailed in order to expedite the overall review process. Holifield disagreed, telling a gathering of utility executives, "I think a certain amount of redundancy is desirable in a new field such as this." Holifield favored the "redundancy" because "it is possible that an independent review body may find gaps in the safety analysis performed by the applicant or by other regulatory groups." The trend toward larger nuclear power plants also worried Holifield. He warned the executives that simply extrapolating design data from smaller plants would not be sufficient to guarantee the safety of larger plants. In short, Holifield urged a cautious, deliberative approach to reactor licensing and design, with the question of safety uppermost in his mind.[15]

Holifield's concern with protecting the public and the environment from radiation and other hazards extended back several years. Since the early 1950s, he had participated in a number of studies of environmental pollution and its effects on the public as a member of both the JCAE and the Committee on Government Operations. As a resident of the Los Angeles basin, Holifield was particularly aware of air pollution, which had become a fact of life in Los Angeles long before it became a problem to the rest of the country. In a 1959 speech before a subcommittee of the House Committee on Interstate and Foreign Commerce, Holifield declared: "Smog may seem like something to joke about today when it invades Los Angeles or some other distant city; it won't be funny tomorrow when it comes to your hometown." In keeping with his liberal Democratic philosophy, Holifield urged that "the resources and knowledge of the entire country be mobilized through a Federal program [of pollution control]." For Holifield, environmental pollution was a growing enemy. He warned that "we are in a race with time and we simply cannot afford to fall behind."[16]

In furtherance of his ideas about federal participation in pollution control, Holifield succeeded in the mid-1960s in involving the AEC in pollution control efforts. In 1966, he proposed that the AEC national laboratories conduct research on nuclear pollution problems for other public and private groups as long as the work did not interfere with the AEC's primary mission. Holifield believed that the expertise, methods, and "extensive experience" of the AEC laboratories "especially [qualify] these organizations for coping with the Herculean tasks which must be accomplished in order to safeguard our environment against pollution."[17] Holifield solicited support from Charles Schultze, director of the Bureau of the Budget, and Glenn Seaborg, chairman of the AEC. In 1967, Congress passed an amendment to the Atomic Energy Act of 1954 embodying Holifield's proposal. Holifield also helped to obtain authorization in 1971 legislation for nonnuclear pollution control research by the AEC laboratories.[18]

The mid-1960s were a period of triumph for atomic power in Holifield's eyes. By 1965, his 1956 and 1957 complaints about commercial development of reactors, especially near urban areas, had been mollified by the major government-financed projects he had obtained in his backdoor Gore-Holifield efforts, by the approaching maturity of the light water reactor technology, and by almost another decade of reactor research. In a speech given before members of the Water and Power Committee of the Los Angeles Chamber of Commerce in December 1965, Holifield declared that 1965 was "the year of the breakthrough" for nuclear power. He noted with pleasure that nuclear plant projects with a greater capacity than all existing plants had been announced that year and was gratified that nuclear power was "at a point where decisions are being made in the market-place on the basis of commercial factors."[19]

Holifield's assessment was correct. The commercial success of nuclear power began in 1963 with the first commercial nuclear power plant purchase from General Electric by the Jersey Central Power and Light Company for its Oyster Creek plant. The market for nuclear power reactors blossomed quickly. In 1963 and 1964, nine reactors were sold on a "guaranteed price" or "turnkey" basis by General Electric and Westinghouse, the nation's only reactor manufacturers. Beginning in 1965, the firm price guarantees were abandoned, but reactor orders still grew by leaps and bounds. A "Great Bandwagon Market" ensued in 1966-1967, with utility companies ordering forty-nine plants with a capacity of 39,732 megawatts of generating capacity. From 1963 to 1967, a total of seventy-five plants were ordered with a capacity of over 45,000 megawatts.[20]

If the mid-1960s were boom years for atomic power, they also represented the calm before the storm. Concomitant with commercial development of nuclear power were two significant changes that brought the new industry under increasing scrutiny by the public. Beginning in the early 1960s, the AEC began to approve sites for nuclear reactors closer to urban areas, thus increasing public awareness of the new electrical source. In addition, the average size of reactors increased during 1962-1966 from 325 megawatts of electrical capacity to 780 megawatts. The larger reactors were introduced at the same time that the AEC decreased its emphasis on light water reactor research and development, considering the

technology sufficiently mature to allow
commercial development even though all of
the effects of increased reactor size had
not been fully tested.[21]

Opposition to nuclear power grew gradually. Local, isolated opposition groups in
the early 1960s slowly coalesced into a
sophisticated national movement by the end
of the decade. Up to 1966, only three of
twenty-six proposed reactors were contested,
and two of these were contested on the
grounds of seismic safety by isolated opposition groups in California. During the
period 1967-1971, however, environmental
groups fought twenty-four of seventy-two
proposed nuclear plants. Local opposition
increasingly leaned on outside expertise
from new environmental groups such as Businessmen for the Public Interest, the Lloyd
Harbor Study Group, the New England Coalition, the Union of Concerned Scientists, and
the Scientists' Institute for Public Information. Between 1970 and 1974, over 70
percent of all proposed nuclear power installations drew some form of environmental
opposition.[22]

Holifield was never allied with the
growing opposition to nuclear power for
several reasons. First, he was perceived as
a figure of the "Atomic Establishment" who
had assisted in developing the industry that
the environmentalists opposed. This perception was enhanced by the fact that Holifield
led the JCAE during 1965-1966 and 1969-1970
and was vice-chairman during 1967-1968, when
the environmental movement was growing to
maturity. Holifield's image was perhaps
further "damaged" by the fact that he supported such "establishment causes" as the
Vietnam War.[23]

In contrast to most environmentalists,
Holifield viewed nuclear power as one of the
solutions to environmental pollution. In
the same 1965 speech in which he heralded

nuclear power's breakthrough, Holifield also proclaimed that nuclear power would make for a more pollution-free environment. Citing the problem of excessive carbon dioxide and other pollutants in the air caused by oil-and-coal-burning electric plants, Holifield declared that "this situation could be alleviated in part if a majority of our public utilities were to make the swing to nuclear power."[24] Nuclear power opponents apparently viewed Holifield's environmentally oriented advocacy of nuclear power as political window dressing.

Holifield's position on reactor safety also differed from that of the nuclear power opposition. In his 1965 speech Holifield called nuclear safety "one of the most important responsibilities of the Atomic Energy Commission." The veteran congressman was proud of the AEC's safety record, in that no human lives had been lost during the development or operation of nuclear power plants. Holifield believed that some risk was entailed in all endeavors, but that nuclear power entailed acceptable risk and was reasonably safe.[25]

Holifield's view of safety was mirrored in that of his AEC ally, Milton Shaw. Shaw, who assumed the post of director of the Division of Reactor Development in 1965, considered safety important enough to bring the safety research programs under his personal scrutiny. During his first year, safety research projects were screened so vigorously that Shaw failed to allocate all of his safety budget. Like Admiral Hyman Rickover, another strong Holifield ally, Shaw believed that light water reactor design was basically safe and that the AEC's primary safety mission lay in quality assurance, that is, assuring that components were reliable and that personnel operating the reactors were adequately trained and competent. This belief ran counter to the belief of the nuclear power opposition that nuclear plants were not proven sufficiently safe. Like Holifield, Shaw also favored development and commercialization of the Liquid Metal Fast Breeder Reactor design and technology, hardly a goal of the nuclear power opposition.[26]

Another point of departure between Holifield and the nuclear power opposition was Holifield's concern for energy needs, as well as for environmental protection. For Holifield, here was a necessary trade-off. A balance had to be struck between national power needs and the environmental risks associated with nuclear power. Holifield was deeply concerned with what he believed to be an impending energy shortage. From his perspective in 1970, Holifield predicted that "in the year 2000 we will need eight times the amount of energy that we are producing today."[27] Holifield was "constantly amazed at the lack of attention to the approaching crisis in energy." He confided to a Westinghouse official that the approaching crisis "is so clear to me, and it is so urgent that, for the first time in my life, I am aware of the meaning of my age and the shortness of probable time which I have to work on the problem."[28]

Holifield's attempt to balance energy needs and environmental concerns was apparent in much of his response to the nuclear power opposition. He opposed "impractical" environmentalists and advocated political participation by "solid, practical, responsible people who believe in keeping pollution to the lowest degree possible from the technical and economic standpoint" as an effective means to "offset the loud opposition." Holifield availed himself of every opportunity to speak out against "scare tactics" and "emotionalism" by the opposition. For Holifield, many of the emotional arguments of the environmentalists were reminiscent of the emotionalism he had attempted to assuage in his earlier hearings on radiation hazards and civil defense.[29]

A final, obvious difference between Holifield and the nuclear opposition was in tactics. As a seasoned politician who was obliged to maintain a broader consensus than the nuclear opposition on many issues, Holifield understood and operated within the parameters of political realities on Capitol Hill. In contrast to Holifield and in keeping with the mood of the late 1960s, many environmentalists were confrontationists, a fact that hardly endeared them to the California congressman. Holifield derisively described demonstrators at the Vermont Yankee Nuclear Power Plant in 1969 as "some 2000 kooks and impractical scientists gathered . . . for a confrontation."[30]

Holifield's relationship with the environmentalist movement began to deteriorate from the beginning of the nuclear power controversy. Although there was isolated local opposition to nuclear power in the early 1960s, the nuclear power controversy at the national level essentially began in about 1968 with a scientific dispute over the effects of low-level radiation discharges from nuclear power reactors. The AEC had long subscribed to the threshold hypothesis, which held that there was a threshold below which radiological discharges had no discernible effect on human health. Beginning in 1968, however, Dr. Ernest Sternglass, a professor of radiation physics at the University of Pittsburgh, publicized a correlation he had discovered between radioactive fallout and infant mortality rates. His work, suggesting that fallout increased mortality rates in infants, won wide and sensational press coverage. Sternglass later expanded his theory to include a correlation between nuclear reactor discharges and infant mortality rates, suggesting that even this form of low-level radiation had a harmful effect on human health and indirectly implying that the AEC and nuclear power were instruments of infanticide.[31] Sternglass's theories brought opposition from the AEC, which marshalled its own research forces to counter the professor's implied charges. The AEC scientists selected to rebut Sternglass's hypotheses, Drs. John F. Gofman and Arthur R. Tamplin of the Lawrence Livermore Laboratory, only broadened the crisis by mildly refuting Sternglass and replacing his more drastic infant mortality figure with lesser numbers of their own. In speeches before three congressional committees, including the JCAE, Gofman and Tamplin also called publicly for a tenfold reduction in AEC radiation emission standards. The two scientists soon experienced transfers of their research staff and other administrative actions that they interpreted as AEC reprisals for their views.[32]

The "battle of hypotheses" between the AEC on one side and Sternglass, Gofman, and Tamplin on the other side did not involve Holifield directly. He did show his concern with the issue, however, by attending a 1969 seminar featuring Sternglass. He also heard the testimony of Gofman and Tamplin before the JCAE on January 28, 1970. When Holifield learned some months later of the alleged reprisals against the two scientists, he called for a full AEC investigation of the charges and invited the two scientists to comment on the final report, which found no basis for the scientists' complaints.[33] The two scientists sent scathing denunciations of the report to Holifield, and Gofman vigorously attacked it as an "AEC Staff Whitewash Document." Holifield provided copies of the letters to Senator Edmund Muskie (D-Maine), who was a chief architect of the National Environmental Policy Act

(NEPA) and a leading Senate proponent of environmental protection. Holifield also invited Muskie to comment on the report.[34]

Holifield did not accept Gofman and Tamplin's theory as scientific fact. As he pointed out in his letter to Muskie, the JCAE had "frequently sought and heard testimony from persons critical of the AEC," but "any appraisal at a given point in time must recognize what is theory and what is fact." Holifield did not consider the Gofman-Tamplin theory to be proven sufficiently nor accepted by the scientific community. He later termed their predecessor Sternglass's correlation of nuclear plant discharges with increases in infant mortality as "completely disproven" and noted that Gofman and Tamplin's theory had been "discredited by every reputable scientist in the nuclear energy field." Holifield believed that much of the criticism of the JCAE by environmental sympathizers was unjust and had arisen "because we have not allowed our Committee to be stampeded by the media or the occasional criticism based on theories of individual scientists."[35]

Implicit in his letter to Muskie was Holifield's concern that environmentalists and their cohorts were damaging the nuclear power industry through "sensational media publicity." Holifield felt that nuclear power plants were being singled out for criticism. As he put it, "The unbalanced way in which nuclear energy sources are being considered have [sic] . . . caused me concern." Much of the opposition to nuclear power, Holifield believed, was "based on an emotionalism without basic factual information of the relative environmental impact of conventional fossil fuel plants."[36] Holifield and others on the JCAE suspected that professional agitators might be involved in the environmental movement, and Holifield did not dismiss at least some covert support

by the oil and coal interests, which stood
to gain by the nuclear industry's demise.
In a letter to Senator Lee Metcalf (D-Montana), Holifield declared that "a fight
against nuclear plants by the coal and oil
interests cannot succeed" because nuclear
power was a necessary additional source of
electricity and because "nuclear power plant
proponents will reveal the degree of environmental pollution on a comparative
basis."[37]

Holifield proposed to do just that. In
fact, he had already laid plans to hold
extensive hearings in 1969 and 1970 on "The
Environmental Effects of Producing Electrical Power." Holifield wanted to produce a
"textbook" from the hearings that would
consider comprehensively "the environmental
effects of all types of electrical generating plants."[38] The upcoming hearings, as he
wrote to AEC Chairman Glenn Seaborg, would
"explore . . . what must be done to meet the
country's present and future needs for electrical power, and to what extent alternatives are available or can be provided to
meet the need while . . . minimizing the
potential impact on our environment." Holifield hoped that the public could then decide "not between nuclear and fossil fuel
plants, but how much additional cost they
wish to pay for their electricity in the
interest of obtaining zero or near zero
environmental pollution." For Holifield, it
was "the old, old story," namely that "you
can have pure water and pure air if the
people will pay for it."[39]

As a secondary thrust in his effort to
provide a dispassionate view of nuclear
power, Holifield and his JCAE colleague
Craig Hosmer (R-California) organized a
series of four seminars on "Nuclear Power
and the Environment" for members of the
House of Representatives. Holifield and
Hosmer's purpose was "to provide factual

answers to the questions you are being asked
at home on such current issues as radiation
releases, thermal effects, reactor safety
and regulation." The four nontechnical
subjects of the seminars were "Electrical
Power in America," "The How and Why of Nuclear Power," "Radiation in Perspective,"
and "Nuclear Power and Environmental Effects
Studies." Holifield and Hosmer recruited
AEC Chairman Glenn Seaborg for introductory
remarks at the first session and AEC management staff for the presentations.[40]
     Holifield's attempts to educate Con-
gress and the public probably fell short of
the goal he had intended. The hearings did
not enjoy broad mass or press appeal, and
the first House seminar drew representation
from only about 8 percent of House members.
The hearings did, however, bring together a
wide-ranging discussion of the comparative
environmental effects of fossil-fueled, hydroelectric, and nuclear power plants. As
Holifield related in his closing remarks at
the hearings, "A proper evaluation of the
adequacy of our work on nuclear power can
only be obtained by comparison with the
environmental impact of alternative energy
sources" and "cannot be done in a vacuum."
The JCAE chairman declared that "as fossil
fuel resources become depleted, an increasingly greater reliance will have to be
placed on nuclear fission, and one hopes
even fusion, concepts." He concluded that
he hoped he would live to see solutions to
"this country's spiraling need for available
useful energy and the important goal of a
safe and healthy environment." Holifield
averred, "I believe they are compatible and
I believe we can attain these two goals."[41]
     If the hearings accomplished anything,
they broadened Holifield's perspective on
the nation's energy and environmental protection needs. The comparative statistics
on energy sources convinced him further that

"the atomic generating power is the cleanest
method now available to generate (electrical) energy." Holifield was also convinced
that "we have the technological ability to
prevent damage to our environment." He
argued, however, that a clean environment
would entail public education about and
willingness to accept the costs and incon-
venience involved; a strong economy and
higher taxes to absorb the "massive" costs;
and some form of population control so that
antipollution efforts would not be "overrun
by the sheer weight of numbers."[42] These
prerequisites made the solution difficult.

After the hearings, Holifield also
pushed for the creation of a new congressional organization to meet the changing
public needs for energy. A bill establishing a Joint Committee on the Environment and
Technology, which he cosponsored, would have
provided a vehicle for responding to the
conflicts between environmental protection
and technological growth. The joint committee proposal passed the House on May 25,
1970, by a vote of 287 to 7, but the House
and Senate were never able to agree upon a
mutual version of the bill. Nonetheless,
the bill showed Holifield's support for
measures to ensure that the problems of
environmental protection and technological
growth would be considered as twin, rather
than opposing goals.[43]

Holifield seldom became involved in
environmental and safety disputes regarding
specific nuclear power plants. He did,
however, voice his views and take action
when controversies spilled over into the
national arena or touched on matters of
national significance. Holifield's actions
at these junctures reflected his liberal
Democratic outlook on the role of the federal government in atomic affairs and his
practicality in approaching nuclear safety
issues.

The first national controversy to arise
with regard to nuclear power plants was the
issue of thermal pollution. By the late
1960s, it had become a widely known fact
that nuclear power plants produced compara-
tively more waste heat in the production of
electricity than did fossil-fueled plants.
Rather than add expensive heat-dissipation
or heat-conversion equipment to their nuclear power stations, utilities almost in-
variably chose to build plants on waterways,
where waste heat could be discharged in
running water and carried away. This discharge tended to increase water temperatures
slightly on these waterways. Environmental
groups charged that the increased water
temperature killed some aquatic and plant
life, caused substantial increases in other
aquatic and plant life, and caused other
environmental damage. Between 1966 and
1971, environmental groups contested the
construction or operation of fourteen nuclear power plants on the issue of thermal
pollution.[44]

The thermal pollution issue remained
unresolved for a time because of the AEC's
refusal to consider the problem. In all of
the fourteen cases brought against nuclear
power plants, the AEC refused to consider
thermal pollution as an issue because it
contended it had no purview over the matter.
Because the AEC restricted itself and its
Atomic Safety and Licensing Boards to radiological issues, the environmentalists found
themselves frustrated in their efforts to
expose the issue of thermal pollution in
permit and licensing hearings.[45]

If Holifield was somewhat skeptical of
some environmentalists' tactics, he was
sympathetic to them on the issue of thermal
pollution and opposed the AEC's attempt to
dodge the issue. In 1968 he introduced
legislation to give the AEC regulatory authority for controlling thermal pollution

from nuclear power plants. His proposal
encountered opposition from the AEC and
"bureaucratic infighting . . . over which
Federal agency should have the final word
insofar as the issue of thermal effects is
concerned."[46] The issue of thermal pollution was resolved through passage in 1969 of
the National Environmental Policy Act, which
required all federal agencies having licensing authority to consider the environmental
impacts of their licensing actions. The
Calvert Cliffs court decision of 1971, to be
discussed later in this chapter, finally
forced the AEC to consider thermal pollution
in all of its construction permit and operating license hearings.[47]

At about the time the issue of thermal
pollution was being resolved, another controversy with national implications erupted.
The focal point of the controversy was the
Monticello nuclear plant in Minnesota. In
1966, the Northern States Power Company had
proposed a nuclear power plant on the Mississippi River in open rural country about
thirty-five miles northwest of Minneapolis-
St. Paul. The proposed Monticello plant had
drawn almost immediate opposition on the
issue of thermal pollution and other environmental and safety grounds. Nonetheless,
the AEC granted a construction permit in
June 1967. The environmental opposition
appeared to have been defeated until the new
Minnesota Pollution Control Agency (MPCA),
responsible for issuing a water discharge
permit for the plant, announced that it
would require Northern States Power Company
to adhere to radiological discharge limits
thirty to fifty times more stringent than
those established by the AEC. The AEC disputed the validity of the permit, alleging
that it had the exclusive authority to regulate radiological discharges. The MPCA
refused to budge and issued its more stringent standards for the plant in May 1969.

Northern States filed suit, charging that
the MPCA did not have the authority to regulate radiological discharges.[48]

In the Minnesota affair, Holifield
supported the AEC's position. Reflecting
his liberal Democratic outlook, he believed
a fundamental issue was at stake--the right
of the federal government to control atomic
energy matters. In an attempt to head off
the controversy, Holifield sent letters to
Minnesota Governor Harold Levander, all of
the state's representatives and senators,
and Robert C. Tuveson, head of the MPCA. In
his letters, Holifield argued that there was
"questionable technical justification" for
the MPCA's proposed action, since the AEC
possessed more expertise and developed its
standards with assistance from the Federal
Radiation Council, the National Committee on
Radiation Protection and Measurements, and
the International Commission on Radiological
Protection. Holifield also emphasized that
the MPCA had no legal justification for its
proposed action, since "virtually every
court, legal scholar and state attorney
general who has ever considered this question has concluded that the regulatory control of the radiological effects of the
various atomic energy materials is vested
exclusively in the Atomic Energy Commission." Holifield invited the state's senators and congressmen to meet with him on the
matter and attend "a briefing on the technical points involved." He also invited Tuveson to come to Washington to confer with him
and added that "if there is actual reason to
believe the Commission's standards, and the
internationally-recognized standards on
which they are based, are deficient in certain respects, I would certainly like to
have any such information brought to my
attention and that of my colleagues on the
Joint Committee."[49]

Holifield's offer to confer in the

Monticello dispute apparently did not evoke a response. The Minnesota controversy ultimately was decided in the courts. The Monticello plant received provisional and full operation licenses in 1970 and 1971 as the case brought by Northern States won an initial decision invalidating the MPCA's radiological discharge standards. The state of Minnesota appealed to the Supreme Court. In April 1972, the Court upheld the lower court ruling that the federal government had preemptive control in regulating radiological discharges from nuclear power plants.[50]

Probably the most far-reaching controversy in terms of consequences was the Calvert Cliffs case of 1970-1971. Like other nuclear power controversies that made their way into the national arena, the Calvert Cliffs dispute began with local opposition to a nuclear power facility. A local group, the Calvert Cliffs Coordinating Committee, opposed Baltimore Gas and Electric Company's proposal to construct two 845-megawatt reactors at Calvert Cliffs, Maryland. A major reason for its opposition was the potential thermal pollution from the two reactors. The AEC's Atomic Safety and Licensing Board for the project refused to hear thermal pollution arguments because the AEC had previously ruled that in complying with the National Environmental Policy Act of 1969 (NEPA), it would not further review environmental issues in instances where plants met existing federal or state standards. The AEC held that compliance with the Water Quality Improvement Act of 1970 was sufficient consideration of water quality.[51] The Calvert Cliffs Coordinating Committee took the issue to court, and on July 23, 1971, a three-judge panel of the U.S. Court of Appeals, District of Columbia Circuit, ruled that the AEC had to consider all environmental issues seriously in its review process. In the judges' view, "The Commission's

crabbed interpretation of NEPA makes a mock-
ery of the Act," and "We demand . . . that
the environmental review be as full and
fruitful as possible." In demanding a vigorous interpretation of NEPA by the AEC, the
Calvert Cliffs court decision forced the AEC
to consider thermal pollution in its construction and licensing permit hearings.
More importantly, the decision required the
AEC to conduct a comprehensive review of all
environmental factors of plants issued construction permits and operating licenses
after NEPA took effect in January 1970.[52]

An environmentalist himself, Holifield
sympathized with the national environmental
policies set forth in NEPA. As he asserted
in a 1970 letter to a constituent, "I have
supported every environmental bill during my
past fourteen terms in office." From a
practical standpoint and his own fervent
belief in an impending energy shortage,
however, he was troubled by the implications
of the Calvert Cliffs decision, particularly
the time that it would take for the AEC to
comply with the provisions for full environmental reviews of nuclear plants. In Holifield's eyes, "The impending crisis in the
supply of electrical energy was made even
more acute by the [Calvert Cliffs] decision." Changes in AEC regulations and actions entailed by the decision, he believed,
would mean delays in the development and
licensing of nuclear power plants. His
anxiety was not unfounded. The AEC promulgated new regulations that were made retro-
active to January 1970 and subjected sixty-
one applicants and licensees of eighty-eight
reactors to full environmental reviews,
promising considerable delays in licensing.
Some politicians in energy-scarce regions
were alarmed. Governor Nelson Rockefeller
of New York, fearing electrical shortages
for his state in the summer of 1972, asked
the new chairman of the AEC, James Schle-

singer, to "invoke with all possible speed
whatever extraordinary procedures may be
available" in processing the operating license application for New York's Indian
Point No. 2 reactor."[53]

Two additional court cases in December
1971 added additional problems for reactor
licensing. In a case involving the Quad
Cities nuclear power station in Illinois,
the courts ruled that even a partial-power
license (proposed in the new AEC regulations
as an emergency measure) could not be
granted without completion of the full environmental review required by NEPA. In another case, a court ruling required that an
impact statement be filed prior to the issuance of discharge permits for any plant.[54]

In view of the growing impediments it
saw to granting any operating licenses prior
to completion of lengthy environmental impact reports, the AEC requested legislation
in March 1972 granting it authority to issue
temporary licenses to plants substantially
completed before Calvert Cliffs. JCAE Vice-
Chairman Melvin Price introduced the original AEC bill with the support of Holifield
and others on the JCAE. It called for interim operating licenses of 20 percent of
full power, unless the AEC authorized higher
power, only where "there exists an emergency
situation or other situation requiring the
conduct of the activities in the public
interest." The bill also called for elimination of operating-license hearings except
in cases with evidence that significant
technological advances had been made subsequent to the construction permit that "would
provide substantial additional protection
required for the public health and safety or
the protection of the environment." JCAE
member Craig Hosmer (R-California) introduced a similar bill dealing with temporary
licenses only, with somewhat complex and
legally intricate procedures for the AEC's

exercise of temporary licensing authority, involving a two-step review process.[55]

Although Holifield was no longer chairman or vice-chairman of the JCAE,[56] he quickly took the lead in developing the JCAE's legislation on temporary licensing authority. The California congressman produced a bill less drastic than the AEC bill and simpler than Hosmer's bill. Holifield's bill became the basis for discussion within the JCAE. It called for a single review by the AEC of petitions requesting temporary licenses for plants substantially completed before Calvert Cliffs. Various safety and environmental findings would have to be made by the AEC prior to the granting of temporary licenses, and temporary licenses could be for full-power operation. Holifield originally intended his legislation to be a procedure for issuing temporary licenses in all instances where an operating-license hearing was prolonged, but he accepted amendments extending the legislation only to October 30, 1973, to deal with the immediate problem created by Calvert Cliffs. Rather than eliminating the operating-license hearing as a forum for public discussion of safety and environmental issues, as the AEC wanted, Holifield sought only to prevent the hearings from being used by environmental groups as strategic blocks to operation of completed nuclear power plants.[57]

Holifield's bill as reported with amendments by the JCAE encountered stiff opposition from environmentalists, who considered the bill an "end run" around NEPA.[58] Holifield termed it only as an interim measure designed to deal with "the difficult transitional problems associated with the licensing and operation of plants which were substantially constructed before the new requirements were imposed." He emphasized "the threatened power shortages commencing this summer in certain parts of the country"

as his prime motivation for seeking passage
of the legislation. Despite environmental
opposition, Holifield's bill passed both the
House and the Senate and was signed into law
by President Richard M. Nixon.[59]

By the early 1970s, environmentalism
had made significant inroads into Congress.
Environmentalists and nuclear opponents
found sympathizers in the Senate, including
prominent senators such as Edward M. Kennedy
(D-Massachusetts), Edmund S. Muskie (D-
Maine), Phillip A. Hart (D-Michigan) and
Mike Gravel (D-Alaska). In the House, Representative Richard Bolling (D-Missouri), an
aspirant for the office of Speaker, sought
to abolish the JCAE and divide its functions
among several congressional committees. As
long as Holifield remained in office, he was
able to frustrate Bolling's attempt to dis-
assemble the Joint Committee.[60]

One manifestation of the congressional
attempts to limit the JCAE concerned Holifield's attempt to prevent loss of JCAE
oversight on radiation standards in 1970.
In July 1970, President Nixon used his reorganization prerogatives to create the
Environmental Protection Agency (EPA). The
EPA absorbed the water pollution control
activities of the Department of the Interior; the air pollution control functions of
the Department of Health, Education and
Welfare; pesticide and fungicide regulation
of the Department of Agriculture; and the
setting and regulation of radiation protection standards by the AEC's Division of
Radiation Standards and the Federal Radiation Council. (The Federal Radiation Council was formally abolished.) In response to
the president's action, Holifield and Craig
Hosmer proposed a requirement that the EPA
consult with the National Council on Radiation Protection and Measurement and the
National Academy of Sciences in the setting
of radiation standards and that reports be

filed with the JCAE. Holifield and Hosmer's proposal passed the House on September 30, 1970, by a vote of 345 to 0.[61]

Although Holifield was successful in the House, he encountered resistance first in the press and then in the Senate. Articles appearing in the *Washington Post* and the *New York Times* charged respectively that the proposal would "lessen the independence" and "restrict the authority" of the EPA in setting radiation standards. Holifield found it necessary to refute the argument in a press release. He explained that the roles of the scientific organizations and the JCAE would be advisory only and the principal effect of his proposal would be to assure that protection standards would be "studied comprehensively by the foremost scientific talent in the country" and that their recommendations would be "made known to the Congress and the public at large." Holifield also sent personal letters to Kennedy and Muskie regarding the "misleading" information in the articles. This effort was to no avail. Senators Muskie, Phillip Hart, and Gaylord Nelson (D-Wisconsin) joined the White House in opposition to the measure, and JCAE Chairman John Pastore (D-Rhode Island) felt constrained to withdraw the proposal in the Senate.[62]

The EPA incident and others caused Holifield increasing concern about the role of the media in promoting the nuclear power controversy. He opposed what he called "scare tactics" in the popular literature and on television. Reviewing *Perils of the Peaceful Atom*, a 1968 diatribe against nuclear power, Holifield commented that it was "steeped in ignorance" and that "some of the so-called experts so effusively commemorated on the acknowledgements page wouldn't know the difference between a fuel rod and a pogo stick."[63] At a June 22, 1971, JCAE hearing Holifield was equally critical of televi-

sion. He complained that two television
programs on nuclear power on which he had
been interviewed had been distorted into
"diabolical misrepresentations" designed to
"scare" viewers. "This is why you have
abroad in the land fear and apprehension,"
he told his audience at the hearing. "I
will never again go on a T.V. program. I've
been burned twice."[64]

Holifield had equal disregard for those
who sought to advance their careers by taking up the cudgel against nuclear power.
When a scientist speaking before the JCAE
expanded the Sternglass thesis by suggesting
that tritium releases from nuclear power
plants could cause an additional twelve
thousand birth defects yearly under certain
circumstances, Holifield interposed sarcas-
tically, "There is your headline." Holifield was deeply concerned about many so-
called environmentalists "who, while lining
their own pockets, are going about the country engaging in scare tactics of almost
every type." Of Gofman and Tamplin, Holifield wrote to a constituent that they were
"in great demand on the paid-lecture circuit" although they had been discredited "by
every reputable scientist in the nuclear
energy field." He further complained that
the two scientists had "refused to submit
their theories for review by their peers
and, instead, . . . preferred to report
[sic] to scare tactics."[65]

Holifield's concern about distortion of
facts also brought him into confrontation
with Senator Muskie, one of the Senate's
strongest supporters of environmental protection. The EPA incident was probably the
spark that ignited a long, angry letter by
Holifield to Muskie in October 1970. Not
seeking to alienate Muskie totally, Holifield did not make the letter public. In
his letter, Holifield declared that he had
"tried to be patient in regards to the

criticism, antagonistic news releases and unwarranted attacks on the Joint Committee on Atomic Energy by some of the members of your staff or in the name of your subcommittee," but "I resent deeply any implication that we are either incompetent or irresponsible." Holifield pointed out that he and other members of the JCAE had "served diligently," and "at no time have we lost sight of the absolute need for safety to workers and to the general population." Holifield emphasized that he and the other members had families and that "many have children and grandchildren. . . . Does anyone seriously think that I would countenance or condone hazards to them or to anyone else in this country or that our members are uninformed?" Holifield pointed to "more than 200 thick volumes of hearings and scores of reports" that he emphasized were "evidence of the thousands of hours we have spent listening to literally hundreds of top scientists in every field and discipline of science." Holifield recounted several incidents where Muskie's staff had "unfairly embarrassed" members of the JCAE in their election campaigns or provided sensationalized statements on some subjects to reporters "who use such expressions as a basis for dope stories which stimulate needless fear and concern and tear down the good name and the efforts of our Committee and its members." Holifield urged Muskie to give his personal attention to the incidents that were "polluting the reservoir of good will between our two committees."[66] Because of his reelection campaign schedule, Muskie did not reply to Holifield until about three months later. When he did, Muskie was conciliatory and assured Holifield of his desire to "work out our problems with a minimum of friction and a maximum of cooperation," allowing for the fact that there would be "instances where the two committees will disagree on what is sound policy with respect to protection of the environment."[67]

By the time Muskie replied to him, Holifield no longer chaired the JCAE. House reform rules enacted in 1971 specified that no representative could hold more than one committee chairmanship, and Holifield had opted for the chairmanship of the Government Operations Committee. Although Holifield was no longer able to assume formal leadership of the JCAE, his influence on the committee diminished little, if any. His long-time friend and associate Melvin Price (D-Illinois) assumed the leadership post that Holifield relinquished, enabling Holifield to work closely with the new House leader to design policies he deemed necessary for nuclear power.[68]

From 1971 until his retirement in 1974, Holifield's primary efforts as a JCAE member were geared toward what he believed to be the most pressing need for nuclear power-- revision of licensing procedures for nuclear power plants. Holifield signaled his interest in revising the hearing and licensing process with a letter to AEC Chairman Glenn Seaborg from himself and Craig Hosmer in September 1970, almost at the end of his last chairmanship of the JCAE. Holifield and Hosmer pointed to the "serious deficiencies in AEC's procedural and administrative mechanism for the licensing of nuclear-power plants," complaining that application processing time had tripled and that the licensing process "appears to be degenerating." The two congressmen were particularly concerned about "contested cases," where "all semblance of order seems to be disappearing."[69]

Holifield's concern about the need for public intervention in the nuclear power licensing process had not really changed, nor did he have any intention of eliminating all public opportunities to question the safety of nuclear power.   Public attitudes toward nuclear power had, however, changed. Nuclear power had become or was fast becoming "a moral issue," as one opponent wrote to Holifield.[70] The alleged safety or danger of nuclear power had become an argumentative proposition between nuclear power supporters and its opponents, with the two sides using different scientific assumptions, theories, and findings.   In Holifield's view, the extensive public intervention and review process he had been instrumental in creating had worked well as long as it was not used cynically as a forum for the nuclear opposition or as part of a political strategy to damage nuclear power. Holifield sought to rectify this perceived imbalance.[71]

In 1971, the AEC proposed to streamline the licensing process through two bills it proposed to JCAE members.   One of the bills sought to speed up the licensing process by eliminating the mandatory safety review of applications by the Advisory Committee on Reactor Safety (ACRS). Under the bill, ACRS review would not be made unless specifically requested by the AEC or the ACRS itself. The second bill sought to eliminate operating-license hearings but provided a new mandatory hearing on the suitability of each reactor's proposed site.   Intervention was allowed also at the construction permit stage if intervenors could raise "an unresolved question significantly affecting the health and safety of the public." In addition, the bill gave the AEC authority to issue the construction permit after the site hearing.[72]

Although Holifield cosponsored the two AEC bills at the request of the AEC, he later decided not to report them to the JCAE for consideration.   Hearings on the bills revealed that the AEC bills were controversial in nature and open to charges by envi-

ronmentalists that the bills were merely
instruments to frustrate their intervention
in the licensing process. Also, the Calvert
Cliffs decision of July 1971 presented a
more immediate problem for resolution, since
the court decision required comprehensive
environmental impact reports before any
additional nuclear power plants could be
licensed.[73]

Holifield directed his efforts in 1972
toward the temporary-license authorization
bill discussed earlier in the chapter. After passage of that bill, Holifield once
again concentrated on developing a compromise licensing process which would take into
account the legitimate concerns of both
national power needs and environmental protection. Although some authors have suggested that his and Craig Hosmer's efforts
amounted merely to an attempt to limit public intervention in the licensing process,[74]
this generalization does not withstand close
scrutiny. In fact, Holifield intended to
eliminate redundancies in the review process
at the state and federal levels that, in
Holifield's view, unnecessarily delayed construction and operation of nuclear power
plants. Holifield also favored elimination
of safety hearings at the operating-license
stage because of the practical consideration
that this stage was hardly the time to re-
examine the safety aspects of a completed
plant's design.[75] Holifield's efforts at
reformulating the licensing process appeared
to evolve more from his concern for ensuring
sufficient national energy resources than
from an attempt to frustrate environmentalism. The increasingly long application
approval process, he believed, would eventually create a prolonged electrical power
shortage. He told a group of California
legislators in 1969 that "one fundamental
factor often overlooked is that once a
shortage of electrical energy is permitted

to exist, corrective action to eliminate the
shortage and accommodate the normal growth
in demand of power would in all likelihood
consume the major portion of a decade."[76]

By 1974, Holifield had developed a
comprehensive siting and licensing bill with
assistance and support from JCAE Chairman
Melvin Price, House minority ranking JCAE
member Craig Hosmer and House Majority
Leader Mike McCormack (D-Massachusetts).
The bill, eventually cosponsored by all
House JCAE members, called for a totally
revised licensing process.   Under the proposed bill,   state hearings and approvals on
proposed nuclear reactor sites would have
largely replaced the construction-permit and
operating-license hearings at the federal
level.   States and interstate compacts would
have been authorized to approve nuclear
plant sites in their areas and conduct environmental reviews of the sites in a one-stop
review process under an agreement with the
AEC.   The AEC would have been authorized at
the federal level to grant construction
permits without a hearing where sites were
approved by the state(s) and standardized
units were proposed.   The AEC would still
have conducted shortened construction permit
hearings on radiological safety matters
where requested, using the legislative,
rather than the judicial, hearing model,
which excludes such procedures as right of
discovery and cross-examination.   Also, operating licenses would have been granted
without a hearing except where there were
substantial, unresolved health and safety
problems or where major changes in technology occurred during construction.[77]   In
addition to revising the licensing process,
the bill called for two additional reports
to the public, in keeping with Holifield's
philosophy.   The first report was to be an
AEC survey and designation of sites for
nuclear power parks.   The parks, a favorite

idea of Holifield's,[78] would contain several nuclear plant stations and bring together major elements of the nuclear fuel cycle onto one site, thereby lessening problems such as transportation of hazardous radioactive material to scattered nuclear plant sites (a growing concern of environmentalists). The second report was to be an annual public report by each regional electric reliability council listing the designated nuclear power plant sites and candidate areas in its region, so the public could be fully apprised of actual and proposed nuclear developments in each region.[79]

The siting and licensing bill, which Holifield and others introduced in February 1974, never passed. Holifield, rapidly approaching retirement, placed highest priority on passage of legislation to divide the AEC's functions between two new agencies, the Energy Research and Development Administration and the Nuclear Regulatory Commission. (Holifield's reorganization efforts are discussed in the next chapter.) Still, the siting and licensing bill represented a final attempt by Holifield to erect a workable compromise between environmental protection concerns and the need for sufficient electrical power for the nation.

When Holifield retired at the end of 1974, he must have surprised those environmentalists who viewed him as a tool of the Atomic Establishment because, unlike many before him, he declined offers of employment as a lobbyist or consultant for the nuclear industry at several times his congressional salary. Holifield refused such offers partly because he did not want to be tied to particular industry views that might not represent his own views on nuclear power.[80] Environmental cynics who considered Holifield a puppet of special interests were thus unable to ascribe complicity and personal advantage to Holifield's congressional support for nuclear power. They failed to see that although Holifield supported the AEC and nuclear power in many ways and on many occasions, the congressman was an environmentalist as well.[81]

10

A Power in the House:
Holifield in the Kennedy, Johnson, and Nixon Administrations

In January 1961, as John F. Kennedy ascended
to the presidency, Holifield also became a
power in the House of Representatives. Although he had been influential in atomic
energy affairs almost from the beginning of
his previous eighteen years in office, Holifield now formally took the helm as chairman
of the JCAE. For the remaining fourteen
years of his congressional career, Holifield
became perhaps the most important House
voice and a key national figure in atomic
energy affairs in his capacities as JCAE
chairman (and in alternate congresses, vice-
chairman) during the entire decade of the
1960s and as chairman of the Government
Operations Committee from 1970 until his
retirement at the end of 1974.

As chairman of these two powerful House
committees, Holifield exerted a major influence in domestic atomic energy affairs during the Kennedy, Johnson, and Nixon administrations. To his chairmanships, Holifield
brought a long record of liberal Democratic
activism and friendliness to public power,
which he sustained in his new leadership
roles. During the Kennedy administration,
Holifield worked to strengthen the JCAE's
control over atomic energy affairs and frus-

trated the president's attempts to wrest
control of atomic energy from the legislative branch. As a result, the JCAE increased its influence and reached the pin-
nacle of its power during the administration
of Lyndon Johnson, Holifield's longtime
friend and political ally. With a chief
executive friendly to JCAE initiatives,
Holifield further expanded government research and involvement in the development of
atomic energy for peaceful uses, and he was
instrumental in establishing many new development programs. Although Holifield favored, as a practical matter, increased
business involvement in developing nuclear
power and other peacetime uses of the atom,
he also sought to ensure that the public
power philosophy would remain as a viable
counterweight to private business interests.
During the Nixon administration, Holifield
fought administration attempts to reduce
atomic energy budgets and to turn over certain atomic energy enterprises to private
business. At the same time, Holifield remained personally friendly with the president and eventually persuaded Nixon to adopt
the Liquid Metal Fast Breeder Reactor project as an administration energy development
priority. When the House Reform Rules of
1971 prompted Holifield to choose between
the chairmanships of the JCAE and the Government Operations Committee, Holifield
chose the latter in part to frustrate further administration attempts to reorganize
the atomic establishment along lines more
favorable to takeover by private business.
As chairman of the Government Operations
Committee, Holifield capped his career by
developing and obtaining passage of legislation both to divide the AEC into the Energy
Research and Development Administration and
the Nuclear Regulatory Commission and to
create the Federal Energy Administration.
Through his legislation, Holifield helped to

lay the groundwork for the future cabinet-
level Department of Energy, created after
his retirement.

In the area of foreign affairs involving atomic energy, Holifield remained clear
and consistent in his viewpoint throughout
all three administrations. He favored elimination of nuclear testing in the atmosphere, nuclear disarmament, and nonproliferation of nuclear weapons, but he tempered
his advocacy with the requirement that all
actions must be multilateral, rather than
unilateral. Although he advocated lofty
principles, Holifield was not unaware of the
dangers the United States faced in the
world. Maintaining the caution and vigi-
lance toward the Soviet Union that he had
displayed throughout his career, Holifield
supported measures that strengthened the
United States' position in the atomic age.
During the Kennedy and Johnson administrations, he pushed hard for an expanded civil
defense program and was a major supporter of
a modern, nuclear-powered navy. During the
Nixon administration, he became a major
advocate of the anti-ballistic missile (ABM)
program.

By 1961, when Holifield assumed the
chairmanship of the JCAE, the United States'
atomic energy program had become a very
complex and multifaceted enterprise. As the
new JCAE chairman, Holifield became the
leading congressional overseer of a burgeon-
ing government bureaucracy with expenditures
in the billions of dollars on numerous research and development efforts. These efforts ranged from electrical power generation and medical and business applications
to weapons development and nuclear-powered
submarine and airplane propulsion. Atomic
energy affairs no longer involved single,
overriding issues, like nuclear weapons
development during 1950-1952 and the contest
between public and private power during the

Eisenhower years.[1] To his new managerial role, Holifield brought the enthusiasm that characterized his previous fifteen years on the JCAE.   By his own admission, Holifield declared he "worked the hell out of my staff," and the senior congressman himself often spent six days a week studying the increasingly complex issues he faced as chairman.[2]

As the new congressional manager of atomic energy affairs, Holifield was personally on very good terms with the Democratic president, also newly installed in the White House.   Holifield later described his association with Kennedy as "a pleasant experience."[3] The California congressman's working relationship with Kennedy began soon after the Democratic senator from Massachusetts was elected president. With Kennedy's knowledge, Holifield conducted an inspection tour of North Atlantic Treaty Organization (NATO) installations in Europe to evaluate the strengths and weaknesses of NATO defenses and organization. In addition, Holifield met with representatives of outgoing Secretary of State Christian Herter on proposed changes in NATO weapons arrangements and reported his findings and opinions to Kennedy.[4]

During the first year of the Kennedy administration, Holifield was probably the closest and most important advisor to Kennedy on atomic energy affairs.   Kennedy conferred personally with Holifield on both foreign and domestic issues relating to atomic energy. On the domestic front, Holifield was able to garner Kennedy's support for the Hanford N-reactor, which was hotly contested in 1961. In foreign affairs, Holifield's opinions were important in persuading Kennedy to resume testing in the atmosphere in 1961 and to call for an expanded civil defense program.[5]

There were, of course, limits to the

Holifield-Kennedy relationship. Although
Holifield exerted considerable influence
with the president, he could not save his
friend and JCAE associate Melvin Price's pet
project, the nuclear-powered airplane, from
sudden elimination by the Kennedy administration in March 1961. Kennedy believed
that the project was too expensive and that
"the possibility of achieving a militarily
useful aircraft in the foreseeable future is
still very remote." Then, too, although
Holifield and Kennedy worked together on
friendly terms, Holifield was not a personal
friend of the Kennedy clan. Despite his
years as a representative and senator, Kennedy "was not a man enamored of the legislative way of life," and he numbered very few
congressmen and senators among his personal
friends. The other differences between
Holifield and Kennedy were of degree: Holifield was a liberal Democrat and friend of
public power interests, while Kennedy leaned
more toward the center and had sided often
with private power interests in the public
versus private power controversies of the
Eisenhower era.[6]

In the second year of his administration, Kennedy moved in directions that
brought him into direct conflict with Holifield. The clash erupted in a struggle over
power rather than philosophy. Desiring to be
a strong president, Kennedy wanted to put
his own administration's stamp on the nation's atomic energy program. During 1962,
he skirmished with Holifield's JCAE in three
instances in a futile attempt to seize the
initiative in atomic energy affairs. These
instances involved the Fiscal Year 1963
authorization bill, a study of atomic energy
programs by the Kennedy administration, and
a proposal to reconstitute the AEC.

Kennedy's assault on the JCAE's pre-
dominance in atomic energy affairs began in
January 1962 with the transmittal of the

administration's proposed authorization bill
for Fiscal Year 1963.   The proposal came as
an unpleasant   surprise   to   Holifield and
other   JCAE members because it contained   no
new authorizations of prototype   nuclear
power plants and no additional funds for the
AEC's nuclear power development program, the
Power   Demonstration Reactor Program.[7]   The
president's position was directly counter to
the   JCAE's efforts since 1957 to accelerate
nuclear power development through government
research and development programs.   Kennedy
left   no   doubt of his new direction   in   an
exchange of letters with AEC Chairman   Glenn
Seaborg in March, just before the opening of
JCAE   hearings on the status of the   nuclear
power program.   In his letter,   Kennedy directed the AEC,   in cooperation with private
industry and affected government   agencies,
to   "take a new and hard look at the role of
nuclear   power in our economy."   The   president   intended for the study to   define   the
objectives,   scope,   and   content of the nuclear power program against the backdrop   of
the   nation's   overall energy needs   and   to
provide   recommendations on proper steps   to
assure   correct timing of the various phases
of the program.   In his reply,   Seaborg expressed   enthusiasm for the president's   directive   and indicated he   would   coordinate
the   study   with   one   contemplated   by   the
JCAE.[8]

The   import of the president's   actions
was not lost upon Holifield,   who had fought
hard   after the demise of the Gore-Holifield
bill   in 1956 to strengthen   and   accelerate
government development of nuclear power, and
he   was not to be put off lightly.   Careful
not   to let his criticism of the Democratic
administration   become   strident,   Holifield
nonetheless   assailed the   president's   proposed   study   as unnecessary and   an   action
that   would   needlessly delay nuclear   power
development.   Appealing to the administra-

tion's support of regional power interties, Holifield suggested consideration of new development projects in which larger nuclear power plants could be used as components of regional interties utilizing higher-voltage lines. He also urged the AEC and JCAE staffs to work together to develop a more aggressive development program on promising prototypes. Leaving no doubt as to his own intentions, Holifield served notice on the president and the AEC that the proposed administration authorization bill would not be introduced or considered by the JCAE until it was made more palatable to the JCAE.[9]

In view of Holifield's opposition, which was supported by the majority of JCAE members, the Kennedy administration had no choice but to accede to the demand for a revised authorization proposal. In May, the AEC produced a revised program that provided for one prototype reactor, funds for several development and design studies on other reactor concepts to be authorized later, and authorization and funding for additional activities under the Third Round of the Power Demonstration Reactor Program. The revised administration proposal was acted upon favorably by the JCAE and was passed substantially intact by Congress.[10]

Frustrated in his attempt to change the atomic energy program, Kennedy made one last attempt to seize the initiative in May, just four days after the AEC submitted the revised authorization proposal. Kennedy now proposed that one administrator head the AEC in place of the five-member commission. This proposal, like the earlier maverick authorization bill and the nuclear power study, was another quite transparent attempt to exert greater executive control over atomic energy, since a single administrator would be appointed by and answerable to the president and most likely would be more

responsive to executive pressure than the
five commissioners, who were relatively
equal in terms of power. In a show of
courtesy but not support, Holifield agreed
to hold hearings on the proposal and other
AEC reorganization plans in 1963. Kennedy's
concept was essentially stillborn, however,
because of its implicit threat to JCAE
power. It was never acted upon by the
JCAE.[11]

Like the administration's original authorization bill and the reorganization
proposal, the AEC's study of nuclear power
requested by Kennedy also failed to provide
an opening wedge for administration initiative. In fact, by the time the report was
submitted to the president in November 1962,
Kennedy and the AEC had already acceded to
direction by the JCAE in formulating the
Fiscal Year 1963 program. Thus, in many
ways the report merely blessed the road
taken by Holifield's JCAE and gave credence
to his claim that the AEC study was unnecessary. The AEC report found that nuclear
power would become an increasingly important
source of electrical energy to meet the
nation's electrical needs and predicted that
by the turn of the century it "would be
assuming the total increase in electrical-
energy production." As for nuclear power's
future share of the electricity market, the
report noted that "we have crudely estimated
that by the century's end, nuclear installations might actually be generating half of
the total electric energy in the country."
The AEC believed the development of economically competitive nuclear power to be its
most important goal. Like Holifield, the
AEC report concluded that "the government
can best assure widespread use of nuclear
energy by fostering developments that make
such use economically attractive." It
called for research and development into new
and advanced reactor concepts, including the

breeder reactor.[12] Holifield could not have
asked a more prominent authority to state in
clearer terms what amounted to his own recommendations and program.

Ironically, Kennedy's attempts to increase executive influence in atomic energy
had the opposite effect of increasing the
JCAE's power over the program. In 1963, the
JCAE decided that it should have authorization power over the AEC's operating budget.
It already had gained authorization power
over all AEC construction projects in 1954
and over the civilian reactor program in
1957. Holifield, JCAE vice-chairman in
1963, was definitely a driving force in
overtaking this last major bastion of AEC
autonomy, as he had been in the prior instances. He introduced the legislation in
the House to effect the change, while JCAE
Chairman (Senator) John O. Pastore (D-Rhode
Island) sponsored the legislation in the
Senate. In view of bipartisan JCAE support
for the measure, the Kennedy administration,
already frustrated in its previous efforts
to thwart the JCAE's influence, did not
contest the JCAE initiative, and Kennedy
signed the measure into law.[13]

Although Holifield and Kennedy fought
for control of the atomic energy program in
1962 and Holifield was clearly the victor,
the two men were still able to work together. In part, this cooperation was due
to Holifield's diplomacy, his care in not
criticizing the president personally, and
his caution not to overstate his personal
importance or seek publicity. As a result,
Holifield remained personally friendly and
influential with Kennedy despite their dis-
agreements and garnered the president's
personal support for a key commission appointment and at least two atomic energy
projects in which Holifield had a personal
interest.[14]

The key commission appointment involved

Kennedy's nomination of JCAE Executive Staff
Director James F. Ramey as an AEC commissioner. In 1962, Holifield and the JCAE
recommended Ramey for a vacancy on the five-
member commission. Kennedy was not enthusiastic about Ramey, who was a close associate
and friend of Holifield's. He may have
believed, however, that he could not afford
the luxury of disappointing Holifield and
the Joint Committee in this regard. Ramey
served for over ten years as a commissioner,
until Republican President Richard M. Nixon
declined to renominate him for the post in
1973. With such an ally as Ramey on the
commission, the JCAE was rendered an additional amount of clout over the atomic energy program.[15]

Another notable instance where Holifield obtained Kennedy's personal support
concerned the AEC's problems in 1961 in
obtaining permission to launch a satellite
in space containing a "Special Nuclear Auxiliary Power" (SNAP) device. The State
Department had held up the project for two
years because the device would have to be
launched over Cuba to gain its proper orbit.
The State Department argued that the SNAP
device might fall onto Cuban soil and break
apart, allowing the Cubans to claim that the
United States had dropped an atomic bomb,
with the ensuing radioactive contamination
as evidence. Holifield, a strong supporter
of the SNAP project, thought the State Department's reasoning was ludicrous and personally saw to it that the president was
told. Kennedy agreed with Holifield and
overruled the State Department, thus clear-
ing the way for the launch. The launch was
successful, and SNAP became the first satellite to transmit signals regularly back to
earth. The satellite lasted for fourteen
years, much longer than anticipated, and
became a prototype for development of over
twenty-five similarly powered satellites.[16]

In 1963, Holifield again asked Kennedy's help, this time to obtain land for the first San Onofre nuclear power plant near San Clemente, California. Southern California Edison and San Diego Gas and Electric had jointly submitted a proposal for a major nuclear generating station under the Third Round of the AEC's Power Demonstration Reactor Program in late 1962. The major contingency in their proposal was securing a suitable site for the plant. A ninety-acre site on the coast within the Camp Pendleton marine corps base was considered suitable because of the abundance of available ocean water and the isolated nature of the area. The Department of the Navy balked, however, at the suggestion of granting an easement for a nuclear power station on the site. This problem appeared to halt the project until Holifield lobbied Kennedy on behalf of the project.[17]

Holifield had several reasons for going to Kennedy on the matter. The San Onofre Plant, designed to produce 395,000 kilowatts of electricity per hour and thus one of the largest nuclear plants to be built, would assist in meeting California's growing power needs. It would also be the first major nuclear power plant to be constructed in California. More importantly, the plant was planned to be one of the first nuclear plants on-line that would be competitive, or nearly competitive, with fossil-fueled plants. This fact made the San Onofre plant a symbol of Holifield's and the JCAE's goal for economically competitive nuclear power.[18]

Holifield's intercession with Kennedy was successful. The Navy Department dropped its objections to the plant, and Holifield immediately introduced legislation to provide a legal basis for the easement. Holifield's bill, with technical amendments added by the JCAE, easily passed in the

268 Mr. Atomic Energy

House and was the version of the bill finally passed by the Senate. By the end of
July, Kennedy signed the bill into law. The
AEC went to work immediately to clear the
way for construction of the plant. By early
1964, a provisional construction permit was
issued. Construction and testing of San
Onofre Unit Number One were completed in
1967, and in January, 1968, the nuclear
power station began providing electricity to
thousands of homes in San Diego and Orange
counties. At the dedication of the plant
during the first week of January 1968, Holifield triumphantly pointed to Unit Number
One as the first in a long line of nuclear
plants that could save billions of dollars
in electricity costs and eventually replace
electricity produced by fossil fuels.[19]

The Holifield-Kennedy relationship was
more consistently in tune on the two major
foreign policy issues involving atomic energy during the Kennedy administration. The
two issues were elimination of atmospheric
testing of nuclear weapons and a proposal
for a multilateral nuclear force for the
North Atlantic Treaty Organization (NATO).
Holifield and Kennedy were solidly agreed on
these matters, and Kennedy's approaches to
these problems were certainly reflective of
Holifield's position.

The issue of atmospheric testing of
nuclear weapons had been carried over from
the Eisenhower administration. Eisenhower
had succeeded in getting the Soviet Union to
agree to a test moratorium in 1958 but had
been unable to resolve the atmospheric testing problem on a permanent basis. The
stalemate on test-ban negotiations continued
into the first months of the Kennedy administration. Holifield, who attended the
Geneva Conference on the Discontinuance of
Nuclear Weapons Tests in May 1961, came away
with the feeling that "the Soviets were not
bargaining in good faith." He passed this

information along to Kennedy and became increasingly skeptical that the test-ban negotiations would be fruitful. By August, Holifield was advocating a "T and T" strategy--talk and test--to prod the Soviets into action and to maintain U.S. superiority in weapons development. In a televised debate on test-ban strategies, Holifield publicly doubted that the United States could "risk our national security by delaying [the resumption of some testing] much longer." In September, when the Soviets resumed atmospheric testing without notifying the United States, Kennedy quickly countered with immediate U.S. resumption of underground and laboratory testing. Holifield endorsed the move and recalled his earlier advocacy of test resumption. He noted that "the sober consideration given by the President and his advisors to the resumption question--both before and after the recent Soviet decision--has done much to improve the U. S. posture in world opinion." Henceforth, Kennedy essentially followed the "talk and test" strategy, which culminated in the Test Ban Treaty of July 1963. Although Holifield was critical of some of the aspects of negotiations leading up to the treaty, he supported the treaty wholeheartedly, stating, "We can well afford to take this step."[20]

Like the nuclear test-ban negotiations, the proposal for a multilateral nuclear force originated in the Eisenhower administration. Secretary of State Christian Herter proposed the "multilateral force" (MLF) in 1960 with the approval of President Eisenhower. The MLF was envisioned as a submarine or surface vessel fleet possessing nuclear warheads that would be controlled and manned by crews of mixed nationalities from NATO countries. The goals of the MLF were to provide NATO allies more control over European nuclear deployments, lessen

European demands for separate, national nuclear forces, and serve as a deterrent to the Soviet Union.[21]

As a leader of the JCAE, Holifield became actively involved in the MLF proposal as an early opponent of the concept. Holifield warned Kennedy in November 1960 that the Eisenhower administration's MLF proposal would "perhaps saddle you with an embarrassing situation," and he urged the president-elect to be cautious and to consider the proposal at length before deciding. Kennedy apparently adhered to the advice.[22]

Holifield did not dispute the desirability of the MLF based on its goal of nonproliferation of nuclear weapons. In fact, he was a strong proponent of nonproliferation. He was instead deeply concerned that American atomic secrets not be disseminated even to America's allies because of his commonsense view that proliferation of knowledge on atomic weapons would almost inevitably lead to their development by other countries. In 1958, in an argument reminiscent of his views on passage of the 1954 Atomic Energy Act, Holifield had publicly opposed a "give-away" of American atomic secrets, a giveaway that he believed was envisioned in successful, Eisenhower-sponsored legislation on "agreements for cooperation" with friendly nations. He was also one of the staunchest opponents of providing French President Charles de Gaulle with information on the nuclear-powered *Nautilus* submarine because of his concern with Communist influence in the French government and the fact that a French Communist, Pierre Joliet-Curie, was head of the French atomic energy authority. As Holifield put it, "I began to think that if we turned over the secrets of the *Nautilus* to DeGualle [sic] on a Saturday night, Joliet-Curie would see to it that the plans got into Russian hands by Monday morning."[23]

As the MLF evolved into a more struc-
tured proposal, Holifield increased his
opposition and pointed to specific weaknesses in the proposal. In a speech at
Stanford University in April 1963, Holifield
expressed a preference in a "multinational,"
rather than a multilateral, solution. He
lent his support to an American-British
proposal that a single NATO command would
encompass British nuclear V-bombers, American Polaris-firing submarines, and a European force to launch American nuclear bombs
in the event of war. The United States
would still maintain a clear veto on use of
its nuclear weapons under the proposal.
Even with a clear U.S. veto in place regarding the MLF, Holifield reasoned that such a
concept raised "difficult questions of control, deterrent credibility, and operational
complexity." He believed the United States
should be "extremely cautious" in considering the MLF.[24]

With the assassination of President
Kennedy in Dallas on November 22, 1963, the
MLF issue was left to the Johnson administration for final resolution. Holifield
continued his opposition and added to his
arguments against the concept. In a letter
to President Johnson on October 3, 1964,
Holifield declared his continued opposition
to the MLF and stated his belief that the
MLF "has been vigorously pushed by a small
coterie of enthusiasts at subordinate levels
in the State Department" and that the group
had inexplicably captured the attention of
senior personnel, including Under Secretary
George Ball. Holifield suggested that the
MLF effort might not be totally sincere on
the part of the United States and also noted
that the State Department and the Navy Department had been "unable to answer to my
satisfaction basic operational questions
concerning this force." Holifield let Johnson know that Holifield's own discussions

with European leaders led him to believe
that "there is no real enthusiasm for the
MLF" in Great Britain or Italy, and he reminded the president that France had remained opposed. Holifield added that NATO
allies were concerned about West Germany's
dominant contributions to the MLF in view of
her Nazi past, and he concluded that the MLF
might be divisive within NATO. In a follow-
up letter that Holifield did not send, he
stated his position succinctly: "My position
is that the MLF may, in fact, be a divisive
force in NATO, and I further question the
military and political usefulness of this
scheme."[25]

Holifield wrote his letter to Johnson
shortly before Johnson met with British
Prime Minister Harold Wilson about the MLF.
Holifield's singular concern was soon voiced
by a group of forty-two congressmen, who
sent a joint letter to Secretary of State
Dean Rusk requesting that the administration
not make any critical decisions on the MLF
at least until the Eighty-ninth Congress
convened and congressmen were fully briefed
on the concept.[26]

In November 1965, Holifield once again
prefaced a high-level meeting on the MLF
with his criticisms and suggestions. Just
prior to a meeting of President Johnson and
West German Chancellor Ludwig Erhard, Holifield denounced the MLF as too concerned
with meeting West Germany's particular desire for nuclear participation at the ex-
pense of the overall needs of NATO. As an
alternative to the MLF, Holifield proposed
"greater responsibility" for all NATO countries in deciding when nuclear weapons supplied by the United States would be used.
In view of Holifield's and others' continuing concerns about the MLF, the Johnson
administration eventually withdrew its support for the concept.[27]

Ironically, the MLF served its purpose

in furthering the nonproliferation of nuclear weapons through its own demise. Its
death removed one of the obstacles to Soviet
signing of the Treaty on the Nonproliferation of Nuclear Weapons in July 1968. The
treaty was a major atomic foreign policy
goal of the Johnson administration and a
personal goal of Holifield's. Holifield
served as congressional observer in 1967 at
the eighteen-nation Geneva Conference on
Limiting the Spread of Nuclear Weapons,
which developed the draft language for the
treaty. The Nuclear NonProliferation Treaty
committed the nuclear power signatories not
to transfer nuclear weapons to any country
nor assist any country in developing nuclear
weapons. It also committed the nonnuclear
signers not to seek in any way to possess
nuclear weapons. The treaty also called for
its participants to facilitate peaceful uses
of the atom through sharing of technologies
and to seek eventual world disarmament.[28]

The Nuclear NonProliferation Treaty
was not the only instance in which Holifield
pressed for limiting the spread of nuclear
weapons. He also supported in 1967 the
Treaty of the Peaceful Uses of Outer Space,
which prohibited the use of outer space for
positioning of nuclear weapons. Holifield
also endorsed the United States' signing of
a protocol to a Latin American treaty in
which the United States agreed not to station nuclear weapons in Latin America. In
addition, Holifield conducted a one-man
campaign against the AEC in 1965 to get it
to tighten safeguards in assisting Italy and
Japan in the building of nuclear reprocessing plants in the two countries. Holifield
successfully convinced the AEC that it was
contributing to the weapons-making capability of the two countries by providing extensive information on reprocessing technology.[29]

With Lyndon Johnson in the White House,

Holifield   at last enjoyed the confidence of
a chief executive who possessed views   similar to his own.   Both men were liberal Democrats who had served together on the   JCAE.
They were personal friends and close political allies.   Holifield had supported Lyndon
Johnson for president in 1960 and was present with him when Kennedy's call   came   requesting Johnson to accept the vice   presidential nomination.   The two men also shared
common philosophies on the government's role
in nuclear developments and were friendly to
public power interests.   Above   all,   they
both   accepted   politics as the art   of   the
possible and   were practical and   pragmatic
rather than ideological in their   approaches
to issues.   Holifield believed Johnson to be
the most masterful politician ever to occupy
the executive mansion during his career, and
he did not fail to use his access   to   the
president to overcome obstacles he faced as
a House leader.   With Johnson as an ally and
Holifield's status as JCAE leader and   ranking member of the House Committee on Government Operations,   Holifield reached the pin-
nacle of his personal power and   influence
during the Johnson administration.[30]

     The Holifield-Johnson relationship   was
a two-way street.   In fact, during the first
months of the Johnson administration,   Holifield   was   largely   preoccupied with   nonnuclear   matters   in helping   the   president
implement the "Great Society"   initiatives,
which   became the hallmark and legacy of the
Johnson era.   Shortly after Kennedy's assassination,   Johnson called House leaders   together and asked their help in implementing
Kennedy's legislative program.   Holifield's
particular "assignment" as ranking member of
the Committee on Government Operations   was
expediting hearings on and   ensuring House
passage   of   legislation to   create   the
cabinet-level Department of Housing   and
Urban Development.   This legislation   was

enacted in 1965. Holifield followed this success in 1966 with developing and assuring House passage of legislation to establish the Department of Transportation, another Johnson-sponsored effort, which made Holifield the first congressman in American history to sponsor successfully the creation of two cabinet-level departments. Holifield also vigorously supported the civil rights, education, and other social programs of the Great Society, clearly marking him as a liberal Democrat who followed, like Johnson, in the tradition of Franklin D. Roosevelt and Harry S Truman.[31]

Holifield's special relationship with President Johnson carried over into nuclear-related matters as well. In July 1964, Johnson called upon Holifield to serve as an arbitrator between public and private power interests who were at an impasse in Congress over creation of an interstate electric power project. Johnson wanted Holifield to try to salvage the project, the Pacific Northwest-Southwest Intertie, which had been proposed by the Kennedy administration in 1961 and had been tied up in a congressional struggle between public and private power interests ever since.[32] The Pacific Intertie was a public power initiative of the Bonneville Power Administration (BPA), a federal power agency that had been caught up earlier in the 1961-1962 feud over whether to convert the plutonium-producing Hanford N-reactor to electricity production. The BPA, with the support of the Department of the Interior, envisioned the Pacific Intertie as a vast power interconnection among western states that would be designed to take full advantage of hydroelectric development of the Columbia River under a treaty concluded in 1961 with Canada and that would thus assure widespread U.S. use of this cheap source of electric power. The intertie was designed to save this power, which

would   otherwise be lost,   by opening up new
markets in the Southwest and also by serving
as   an   electrical   source   in   emergency   or
shortage   situations.   Physically,   the Pacific   Intertie   was to consist   of   several
high-voltage   power   lines   running   from   the
state   of   Washington south through   Oregon,
California,   Nevada,   and Arizona.   Private
power   interests opposed the intertie   as   a
giant   federal power grid that would eventually swallow them up.[33]

Holifield stepped into the fray under a
severe deadline.   President Johnson   wanted
the   Eighty-ninth   Congress   to act   on   the
intertie before its close,   a deadline   that
gave   Holifield about one month to effect   a
compromise.   Even   the   president   believed
"the   prospect   of   agreement did   not   look
promising."   Nonetheless,   Holifield went to
work with his characteristic vigor.   He met
with Interior officials,   senators, and congressmen   from the affected states and   with
the   various   public and   private   utilities
participating in or affected by the proposed
intertie.   Within the allotted month, Holifield had obtained agreement for an intertie
that would consist of federal and nonfederal
transmission   lines.   In a July   29,   1964,
letter to the president, Holifield announced
the   agreement and noted that   "the   private
power   companies,   who had stoutly   resisted
our efforts,   have now reluctantly agreed to
support   our position."   At a press   conference   the   same day,   Johnson   endorsed   the
Holifield compromise and termed the proposal
"the   launching of a new era of   cooperation
between   private   power and public power   in
the   United States."   Johnson later   sent   a
personal   letter to Holifield expressing his
appreciation   for Holifield's leadership   on
the   intertie proposal.   Secretary   of   the
Interior   Stewart   Udall   publicly   praised
Holifield   in his press   conference,   noting
that Holifield deserved "an extra measure of

credit for helping reconcile many different points of view."[34]

The Pacific Intertie, in fulfilling public power needs cooperatively with private power interests, was one of Holifield's greatest long-term accomplishments during the Johnson administration. Although it was not strictly a nuclear project, the intertie did include some utilities that possessed nuclear power plants. The final proposal in effect interconnected the BPA with the largest municipally owned electric system (Los Angeles Department of Water and Power); one of the largest privately owned utility groups, comprised of Pacific Gas and Electric Company, Southern California Edison, and San Diego Gas and Electric Company; and two Department of Interior (Bureau of Reclamation) projects, the Colorado River project and the Central Valley project. Congress appropriated funds for the Holifield compromise proposal in August 1964, and construction was begun in 1967 under a series of thirty separate contracts negotiated in the interim. The Pacific Intertie was completed and began operations in 1969.[35]

Two other public power issues affecting nuclear developments during the Johnson administration showed that Holifield remained wedded to the public power philosophy but was eminently practical in his approach to individual issues. These two issues involved opposition to the AEC's installation of power lines to operate the Stanford University Linear Electron Accelerator and a proposed amendment to the Atomic Energy Act to ensure a greater share of nuclear power plant ownership and development for publicly owned utilities. On the first issue, Holifield made his stand both on legal principles and on consideration of practical consequences. On the second issue, Holifield based his position solely on practical considerations, despite his sympathy with the public power position.

The Stanford Linear Accelerator controversy of 1963-1965 arose not from construction of the high-energy physics research
facility itself, but from the AEC's attempt
to supply it with the electrical power necessary for operation. To obtain the most
cost-effective electrical power available,
the AEC proposed routing of a high-voltage
line through the town of Woodside, a bedroom
community of 3,600 people in San Mateo
County. This proposal was opposed by the
county and Woodside on the grounds of aes-
thetics. They argued for an underground
line. The JCAE encouraged the AEC to negotiate, but the AEC was unable to reach
agreement in the dispute because of a lack
of consensus on who would pay the estimated
additional $4.3 million for the underground
line. When it became apparent the two sides
could not reach agreement, Woodside passed a
local ordinance banning the power line and
sued the AEC to prevent construction of the
line under the AEC's asserted right of eminent domain. The courts initially ruled
against Woodside, but the U.S. Court of
Appeals reversed the decision, allowing the
AEC's right of eminent domain but interpreting Section 271 of the Atomic Energy Act to
preclude the AEC from interfering with local
ordinances concerning "the generation, sale,
or transmission of electric power."[36] The
appeal court's decision alarmed Holifield
and convinced him that federal power was at
stake. He believed the court had misinter-
preted congressional "intent" in Section 271
by citing Senator Bourke Hickenlooper's
individual remarks during debate on the
Atomic Energy Act of 1954; he pointed out
that even Hickenlooper had disavowed the
interpretation given to his remarks and
believed the court had reached an erroneous
decision. Holifield was even more concerned
that the court decision would establish a

precedent that would limit the AEC's use of eminent domain guaranteed in the Constitution. As a remedy, he immediately set out to amend the Atomic Energy Act to clarify the intent of Congress.[37]

Holifield's action brought vigorous protests from northern California, where opponents now charged that the Atomic Energy Establishment was seeking to thwart the intent of President Johnson's beautification efforts. The *San Francisco Chronicle* complained that the JCAE was "immorally seeking to rewrite the decision of the courts" and chastised Holifield for behaving "like a common scold." Even Senator Thomas H. Kuchel (R-California) got into the act and asked the JCAE to drop the issue. Holifield remained steadfast in his position, which was bolstered when the JCAE unanimously endorsed his bill. During a lively House debate on the measure, Holifield charged that if the interpretation of the court of appeals was allowed to become a precedent, "an intolerable burden would be placed upon the effective performance of the AEC's responsibilities under the Atomic Energy Act of 1954." Holifield clearly believed that the public power tenet of supremacy of the federal government was at stake and succeeded in convincing a large majority of House members to vote for his bill. The Senate followed suit despite the vigorous opposition of Senator Kuchel, and Holifield's bill became law.[38]

If Holifield could stand on high principle on some public power issues despite intense opposition, he was also a political realist who refused to do battle in the face of insuperable obstacles. This realism was evident with the second public power issue mentioned previously, regarding an Atomic Energy Act amendment to guarantee a greater share of nuclear power plant ownership and development to public power interests. In this instance, Senators Conrad Aiken (R-Vermont) and Robert F. Kennedy (D-New York) had introduced a bill on October 23, 1967, to make a finding of "practical value" by the AEC mandatory before the AEC could issue a reactor construction license to a utility. The Atomic Energy Act had provided that the AEC formally had to find that a reactor had "practical value" before it could issue a "commercial" license for the reactor, which then subjected the project to antitrust review. Because the AEC maintained that the economics of nuclear power was uncertain, no finding of "practical value" had ever been issued for a nuclear power plant. Thus, all projects had been granted "research" licenses instead, which did not make them subject to antitrust review. Aiken and Kennedy were responding to complaints of public power interests that private utilities essentially had taken over the field of constructing large-scale nuclear power installations because they were the only ones with sufficient funds to do so. Because of their "research" licenses, moreover, private utilities did not have to allow participation by publicly owned utilities in the development and ownership of large-scale nuclear plants because there was no fear of an antitrust review. The purpose of the Aiken-Kennedy bill was to ensure that "all utilities, regardless of size, should be able to share in the benefits of nuclear reactors, which were a gift to the utility industry from the taxpayers."[39]

Holifield clearly sympathized with public power interests on the bill. Even during debate on the 1954 Atomic Energy Act, Holifield had argued for government development of nuclear power because of the potential for private monopoly in the field. In later years he also enumerated the many advantages enjoyed by privately owned utilities and declared, "I warn them to restrain

their greed." He sharply criticized private
utilities in the 1960s for seeking an additional tax subsidy under the guise that it
would shorten the time when atomic power
plants would become competitive. Holifield
termed the argument "an insult to the intelligence of the Congress" and averred that
another tax incentive "is about as logical
as giving a dog a luscious bone and then
putting gravy on it to make him eat it." He
declared, "The utilities already have their
bone; let's not be a party to giving them
more gravy, which they neither need nor
merit."[40]

Yet Holifield refused to press for
passage of the Aiken-Kennedy bill. He based
his position on two practical considerations. For one, he told reporters it would
not be reported out of the JCAE in the
Ninetieth Congress because "we haven't got
the votes to get it out." Holifield clearly
was unwilling to make a fight on the bill
without greater JCAE concurrence. Holifield
also believed that the bill unfairly dis-
criminated against nuclear power plants
since it did not seek to ensure the same
requirements for conventional, fossil-fueled
plants. This discrimination, he predicted,
would start a shift by private utilities
back to conventional plants to escape the
antitrust provisions and "would stop the
development of nuclear power."[41]

Eventually, Holifield did support a
modified version of the Aiken-Kennedy bill.
Under Holifield's leadership in 1970, the
JCAE reported a compromise proposal eliminating the "practical value" concept alto-
gether and requiring an antitrust review
process somewhat more limited than the review originally called for in the 1954 act.
While it did not satisfy private or public
power interests entirely, the compromise was
passed by Congress and signed into law by
President Richard M. Nixon.[42]

Although Holifield was friendly to public power interests during his leadership of the JCAE, he was ultimately practical in his approach to private as well as public development of nuclear power. During the Johnson administration, he assisted business development of nuclear power in two important ways. In 1964, as JCAE vice-chairman and chairman of the JCAE Subcommittee on Legislation, Holifield successfully sponsored legislation to provide for private ownership of nuclear fuels for power reactors under stringent safety and security safeguards. Previous to enactment of the legislation, nuclear fuels were owned by and could be leased from only the government, an "additional process" that made nuclear power developments cumbersome. Holifield's legislation was designed as an assist to business development of nuclear power and as a stimulant to the sale of American reactors, components, and services abroad.[43] In 1965, as JCAE chairman, Holifield also sponsored legislation to extend for ten years the Price-Anderson Act, an act he had originally opposed during its passage in 1957. Essentially, the Price-Anderson Act provided a program of government liability for nuclear accidents when damages exceeded the amount of private insurance that owners of reactors were able to purchase commercially. By the 1960s, Holifield was convinced that the technical and safety aspects of the reactor industry had improved to a point where the government was not at substantial risk, and he had come to believe that the government indemnification program was necessary to ensure continued development of nuclear power. He did insist, however, that private insurance pools increase their coverages and that the government indemnification amount (originally $500 million) be reduced by a similar amount. The provision, included in Holifield's bill, easily passed.[44]

Apart from the public versus private nuclear development issues of the Johnson administration, Holifield took a personal interest in many of the AEC's projects, particularly those involving the peaceful uses of atomic energy. The projects Holifield had a hand in promoting included Project ROVER, a project in space rocketry using nuclear energy for propulsion; Plowshare, which involved using nuclear explosives for large land excavations and for gas and oil explorations; the food irradiation program, a nuclear process for killing bacteria in food without changing content or taste of the food; the Southwest Fast Oxide Reactor (SEFOR), a facility to test the feasibility of the breeder reactor concept; the Bolsa Chica Desalting Plant, a project using nuclear power to desalinate seawater for use on land; the Stanford Linear Accelerator and the 200 Billion Electron Volt Accelerator, both high-energy physics research facilities; and at least two power reactor concepts, the seed-blanket reactor and the sodium-graphite reactor. While not all of the projects were successful, they did show Holifield's wide-ranging interest in using nuclear energy for peaceful purposes.[45]

Holifield's avid interest in promoting various AEC projects did not amount to a blind addiction to spending huge sums for impractical research. In fact, Holifield later noted that "even though people thought Holifield was always promoting project[s], I also would lop them off." Holifield was willing to cancel even research projects in California that did not measure up to expectations. It was thus when he cancelled an experimental sodium-graphite reactor project near Santa Susanna. In his opinion, "It didn't warrant authorization." At times, Holifield even embarrassed the AEC when he was displeased with project results. He appalled the AEC and delighted the press with his opinion of the first nuclear-powered merchant ship, the *Savannah*. He termed the ship "the biggest white elephant afloat" and "the biggest flop that ever hit the water."[46]

As during the Kennedy administration, Holifield did not hesitate to go to the president when he believed worthwhile projects were in jeopardy. In 1964 Holifield complained personally to President Johnson that the flight test of a "Special Auxiliary Nuclear Power" (SNAP) device was being cancelled just as it had been completed for testing. This time the device was SNAP 10-A, which contained a five hundred-watt power reactor. Holifield's intercession, with the help of JCAE Chairman John Pastore, was successful, and the flight test for SNAP 10-A was funded and rescheduled. Holifield subsequently learned that the Russians were working on a similar project, hoping to be the first to put an actual nuclear reactor in space. Shortly after the launch of SNAP 10-A in April 1965, Holifield had a field day in Congress explaining how the JCAE had once again ensured America's leadership in nuclear developments, as it had with development of the hydrogen bomb and other projects.[47]

Although Holifield's relations with the Johnson administration were generally cordial, there were notable exceptions. Holifield captured press attention in March 1967 when he dubbed the space program a "Roman circus" and declared that Americans needed "bread, not circuses." In September 1968, Holifield also shocked the Johnson administration as President Johnson and the Kennedy family were in Newport News, Virginia, to dedicate the nation's newest aircraft carrier in honor of the assassinated president. In a House speech the day before the dedication, Holifield declared that it was "unfortunate" that the ship, the last conventionally powered carrier to be built, was "obsolete before ever going to sea." In light of Kennedy's legacy, Holifield bemoaned the fact that the *John F. Kennedy* represented "the end of an era rather than being a symbol of progress."[48]

Holifield's comments on the *John F. Kennedy* actually represented the tip of the iceberg in what was Holifield's biggest confrontation with the Johnson administration. The issue in question was whether the navy's ships should be nuclear-powered. Holifield had been an early and consistent supporter of Hyman G. Rickover, the navy's engineer who had overseen development of nuclear-powered submarines. By the late 1950s, Rickover's and the JCAE's interests had expanded to advocacy of a nuclear-powered surface fleet. By the end of the Eisenhower administration, Congress had authorized a nuclear-powered aircraft carrier, a guided-missile cruiser, and a guided-missile frigate. Robert S. McNamara, defense secretary during the Kennedy administration and much of the Johnson administration, brought an end to expansion of the nuclear surface fleet, based on his contention that nuclear-powered ships were too costly and that it was more cost-effective to build conventionally powered ships. From 1964 to 1968, Holifield used every available occasion, including the commissioning of the *John F. Kennedy*, to speak out in support of a nuclear surface fleet and lambast McNamara's position. The congressman countered McNamara's argument by emphasizing what he believed to be the overriding military advantage of nuclear-powered warships--they did not require logistic (refueling) support and could operate for several years without "refueling." Holifield also took issue with McNamara's bases for comparing costs of nuclear-powered and conventionally powered warships.[49]

In 1966, when Holifield was JCAE chairman, the JCAE and the House Armed Services Committee launched an offensive against McNamara's position by substituting two nuclear-powered destroyers for two conventionally powered ones in the Fiscal Year 1967 Defense Department authorization bill. Holifield followed the lead of Armed Services Chairman L. Mendel Rivers (D-South Carolina) by sending letters in support of the change both to President Johnson and to Secretary McNamara. Congress, again in the Fiscal Year 1968 authorization bill, substituted another nuclear-powered destroyer for two conventionally powered ones. McNamara remained undaunted in his opposition. He delayed construction of the nuclear-powered ships, cancelled plans for the high-speed submarine (an advanced design of nuclear submarine), and in May 1968, halted construction of another class of nuclear submarine, the electric-drive submarine.[50]

McNamara's purported efforts to garner Johnson's personal support for delaying construction of the nuclear ships brought a concerted effort from Holifield to bring the issue to a head. When Holifield's request to Johnson in early 1968 for a face-to-face meeting with McNamara did not bear immediate results, Holifield fired off a five-page letter to the president. In the letter, he detailed McNamara's continuing dispute with Congress, criticized the defense secretary's justifications and cost analyses for favoring conventionally powered ships, and warned Johnson that supporting McNamara's position "could provide ammunition for your opponents to attack you and the Administration in an election year."[51]

President Johnson apparently heeded Holifield's letter. Both Secretary McNamara and his soon-to-be successor, Clark M. Clifford, personally contacted Holifield within a few days of his letter to Johnson. Al-

though McNamara did not back away from his
position, he soon resigned to become head of
the International Bank for Reconstruction
and Development. The new secretary, Clifford, was conciliatory in his approach to
Congress and was particularly attentive to
Holifield and the JCAE. Holifield, with the
support of the JCAE, continued to urge that
the three nuclear programs cancelled or
delayed by McNamara be reinstated. By September 1968, Clifford had reinstated all
three programs.[52]

As "Holifield's Nuclear Navy"[53] steamed
toward success, the administration that
supported it faltered amid American disunity
over the Vietnam War. In March 1968, less
than a month after President Johnson directed his defense officials to confer with
Holifield on the nuclear ships controversy,
Johnson announced that he would not seek
reelection to the presidency. Holifield,
who had supported Johnson's objective of
saving South Vietnam from a Communist takeover, threw his full support to another
longtime friend, Vice-President Hubert H.
Humphrey, in the election of 1968. Humphrey
lost the election by a narrow margin to
another former vice-president, Richard M.
Nixon.[54]

For Holifield, the advent of a Republican administration during his final years as
a congressman moderated his chances for
continued success as a major influence in
atomic energy affairs. He could no longer
count on a friend in the White House to give
an added push to his policy positions. Congress was however, still overwhelmingly
Democratic, and Holifield was able, as a
congressional leader and JCAE chairman during the first two years of the Nixon administration, to parry, if not defeat, the
contrary policy thrusts brought by the new
administration. Through skillful diplomacy
and limited support for some Nixon initia-

tives, Holifield garnered some Nixon endorsements for his own views and thus lessened some areas of friction with the Republican administration.

Holifield's willingness to support some administration initiatives was most apparent in foreign affairs. With regard to the Vietnam War, Holifield was a firm believer in the domino theory in Asia, and he asserted that "the fundamental issue behind the Vietnam War . . . is freedom." He freely admitted in 1970 that "my stand on Vietnam has been one of general support for the President, of whatever party, in his efforts to bring about a peaceful solution to the present confrontation and conflict through negotiation." Holifield opposed a "precipitous withdrawal" by the United States and strongly supported Nixon's efforts to achieve "peace with honor." Holifield's views on Vietnam earned him two personal letters of appreciation from Nixon and undoubtedly enhanced his personal relationship and access to the president on other matters.[55]

Holifield was also in agreement with Nixon administration views during the 1969 congressional debate on the proposed antiballistic missile (ABM) system. In 1967, in response to Soviet deployment of an ABM system around Moscow, Defense Secretary McNamara had announced the Johnson administration's support for the Sentinel area defense system. This decision was one of the few decisions on which both McNamara and Holifield were in full agreement. When the Nixon administration reviewed the Sentinel system proposal in early 1969, Holifield was consulted. On March 14, 1969, he was called to the White House along with other congressional leaders for a briefing by President Nixon on modification of the Sentinel system primarily to a point defense system around Minuteman missile sites. In spite of rela-

tively intense opposition from members of
the liberal Democratic Study Group, of which
he was a prominent member, Holifield developed a position paper for circulation to his
colleagues substantially in favor of Nixon's
"Safeguard" proposal. The paper refuted the
arguments of his liberal Democratic colleagues against the ABM system. Contrary to
his opponents, Holifield believed the ABM
Safeguard system would not be a provocation
to the Soviets because of the existence of
the Soviets' Moscow ABM system. Holifield
also believed that the Safeguard system
would assist in the "mix" of overall weapon
systems in contributing to overall deter-
rence to nuclear war. He correctly predicted that "the forthcoming vote in the
House will be strongly in favor of this
defensive system."[56]

    Similarity of viewpoints between Holi-
field and the Nixon administration did not
translate to domestic affairs. Almost from
the beginning, the JCAE was besieged by
Republican efforts to cut AEC budgets and
reorganize some AEC functions along lines
more favorable to takeover by the private
sector. Holifield found himself having to
defend established AEC programs, such as
Plowshare and the food irradiation program,
from budgetary annihilation. The California
congressman succeeded in avoiding elimination of the programs but had to acquiesce to
lower funding levels.[57]

    Of more intense interest to Holifield
were the Nixon administration's attempts to
reorganize some AEC functions. In April
1969, Holifield received rumors of the administration's plans to operate the government's uranium enrichment plants as a private business, with the intention of eventually selling the plants to private industry.
The government's gaseous diffusion plants,
as they were also called, included installations at Oak Ridge, Tennessee; Paducah,

Kentucky; and Portsmouth, Ohio. They represented a taxpayer investment of $2.3 bil-
lion and, as the sole suppliers of enriched
uranium for the nation's nuclear reactors,
represented the last governmental monopoly
in the atomic power domain.[58]

Nixon's plan for the enrichment plants,
unveiled in November 1969, called for establishment within the AEC of a separate directorate to be managed as a business entity
"with separate accounts fully reflecting
commercial criteria for financial accounting." The president noted that "these facilities should be transferred to the private sector, by sale, at such time as various national interests will best be served."
The AEC also announced simultaneously that
it would be considering whether to increase
its charges for enriching uranium for atomic
power plants.[59]

In a press release on the same day as
the announcement, Holifield publicly doubted
that the proposed AEC directorate could
operate on a businesslike basis when many
decisions "would be subject to approval of
authorities higher than the AEC." Holifield
also questioned the likelihood for normal
business competition "in what is now, and in
all probability for some years to come will
be, a highly concentrated industry." As for
selling the plants, Holifield noted that
such a major policy decision would require
congressional approval, and "there isn't the
slightest doubt in my mind that it [Con-
gress] would want to put any such proposal
under a microscope in order to assure the
protection of the public interest." Privately, Holifield feared another "give-away"
and declared in a private letter to former
JCAE Chairman (Senator) Clinton Anderson,
"It is my opinion that some of the same
forces who tried to carry out the Dixon-
Yates proposal are at work trying to carry
out the sale of the diffusion plants."[60]

Holifield's fears of another "Dixon-Yates" were aired by the press, and the Nixon administration quietly abandoned the idea of selling the plants. The administration also backed away from the separate AEC directorate for the plants but continued the fight by switching the focus to increasing the charges for enriching uranium and changing from "government cost" to commercial criteria for future price increases. Holifield countered by successfully sponsoring legislation to return to the previous pricing criteria, but he was unable to persuade Nixon to roll back the increased uranium enrichment charges, which were raised again only a few months later. Holifield charged the administration with deliberately promoting inflation through what was nearly a 25 percent increase in uranium enrichment charges in one year.[61]

In the episode about increased charges for uranium enrichment, Holifield saw what he considered to be the sinister but unseen hand of the big oil companies, which supported Nixon and which were interested also in damaging the competitive edge enjoyed by nuclear power. As Holifield viewed the matter, "The control of nuclear fuel prices for enrichment fuel units is the key to independent prices," and the loss of that independence "would result inevitably in the melding of this tax-developed industry into the last link in the chain of managed prices for fuel, as now obtains in the oil, coal and gas industries."[62] Other instances similar to the enrichment charge increase added substance to Holifield's perception. In the same bill in which he successfully proposed a return to the previous pricing criteria, Holifield also requested that the Environmental Protection Agency (EPA) be required to consult with the National Academy of Sciences and the National Council on Radiation Protection before revising radiation safety standards. Holifield was defeated in this endeavor (see chapter 9) and was cast as anti-environmentalist for his efforts. Actually, Holifield believed that the "anti-environmental" label was a ruse and that the environmental opposition had been cynically used to defeat him. He was actually attempting to keep the administratively created EPA from being cynically manipulated by the administration through its setting of stricter radiation standards that would be designed only to increase safety-related costs of nuclear power plants and thereby damage the economic competitiveness of nuclear power. In another successful administration foray, the AEC also began programs over Holifield's objections to allow private industry access to gaseous diffusion and gas centrifuge technology. To Holifield, this "unseemly haste to give away advanced technology" pointed to a continued administration drive to give industry eventual access to actual uranium enrichment production. As further evidence of this drive, Holifield found himself having to prod the administration continually to increase the capacity of the government's existing plants.[63]

Although the domestic issues concerning atomic energy were generally a source of confrontation between Holifield and the Nixon administration, there was one notable exception: the Liquid Metal Fast Breeder Reactor (LMFBR) project, strongly supported by Holifield, became an administration energy development priority in June 1971 at least partly because of Holifield's urgings. By remaining personally on friendly terms with President Nixon and supporting administration initiatives in cases where Holifield believed his support was warranted, such as the Vietnam peace initiatives, Holifield retained limited access and influence with the president, which he used to promote programs he considered vital to the nation's interests.

Holifield advocated the LMFBR project as the long-term solution to adequate electrical power generation. In his view, it held the promise of greatly extending available and naturally occurring uranium reserves because it would breed more nuclear fuel than it consumed and would not require extensive dependence on the uranium enrichment process. As AEC Commissioner Clarence E. Larson pointed out in a letter to the congressman, breeders would require about 2 tons of uranium a year, as opposed to about 170 tons for a light water reactor. Holifield emphasized in calling for the LMFBR priority that the plutonium produced by the breeder reactor could be used to fuel both light water reactors and additional breeders, and hence, "the two types of reactors will complement each other."[64]

Development of the breeder reactor was not a new research endeavor. Various phases of breeder reactor development had been conducted by the AEC as early as 1946. Breeder reactor studies were also conducted through construction of demonstration "Experimental Breeder Reactor" projects at the AEC's Idaho testing site in the late 1940s and in 1963. The Enrico Fermi I demonstration plant built in 1963 near Lagoona Beach, Michigan, and the Southwest Fast Oxide Reactor (SEFOR) completed in Arkansas in 1967 also added to knowledge about breeder reactor technology. Although Holifield had, in 1956, opposed construction of the Fermi plant near a populated area (see chapter 9), he was enthusiastic about breeder reactor development and was a strong supporter of the breeder concept from the early 1950s, when the JCAE was first informed of this research area. Both the Kennedy and Johnson administrations supported the breeder reactor concept as an answer to cheap energy in

the future, and Holifield saw to it that the
1968 Democratic national platform called for
development of breeder reactors. During the
1960s, the LMFBR design became the principal
breeder concept being studied by the AEC.
In 1969, Holifield characterized breeder
reactor development as "the most important
challenge . . . of prime importance to the
[utility] industry and to the future development of our nation."[65]

As the Nixon administration prepared an
energy message on proposals to meet the
nation's increasingly perceived shortage of
energy, Holifield received a unique opportunity to speak with the president about the
LMFBR project. In May 1971, he was invited
to accompany the president on *Air Force One*
to California to discuss the president's
reorganization proposals pending before
Holifield's Committee on Government Operations. Holifield turned the discussion
toward the LMFBR, using Nixon's known appreciation for fireplaces to make an analogy
about the LMFBR. Holifield explained that
if the burning logs in a fireplace represented the fission reaction in an LMFBR, the
by-product ashes represented a greater
source of energy than the burning of the
logs. Holifield concluded by requesting
that the president give the LMFBR serious
consideration as an energy alternative to
expand the United States' energy capacity.[66]

President Nixon was apparently impressed by Holifield's presentation. His
June 4, 1971, energy message included the
LMFBR project as the administration's first-
named alternative energy development priority. Holifield was elated, hailing the
president's message as "a momentous and
important event in the history of our country." Holifield lauded the president's
juxtaposition of antipollution efforts and
the need for additional "clean" electrical
energy as inseparable problems. (In a let-

ter to his onetime foe, former AEC Chairman
Strauss, Holifield indicated he had successfully pressed for consideration of the two
issues in tandem.)   The LMFBR, Holifield
declared, was "the solution to our long-term
electrical needs." For a long time after,
this view appeared to be the case.[67]

Holifield basked amid praise and con-
gratulations from friends and associates as
a result of his LMFBR victory. His success
provided only a "breather," however, in what
he considered a continuing effort by the
Nixon administration to gain a "strangle-
hold" on nuclear power and the energy industry in general. In March 1971, Nixon proposed a massive reorganization of the executive branch under four "super agencies."
One of these agencies, a new Department of
Natural Resources (DNR), was to be created
out of the Department of the Interior, the
AEC, and a host of other functions and agencies in other departments concerned with the
use and preservation of natural resources.
Holifield believed the DNR proposal would
"end up as a major drive on the part of the
Nixon administration to destroy the Joint
Committee on Atomic Energy and sell the
Government's uranium enrichment plants to
private industry and put energy and its
research and development into private
hands." He also later declared that "I knew
that if the jurisdiction over the uranium
enrichment plants was transferred to a Department of Natural Resources, the Atomic
Energy Commission would be dead."[68]

Just months prior to Nixon's reorganization proposals, Holifield had become
chairman of the House Committee on Government Operations as a result of the death of
Chairman William Dawson in September 1970.
The Government Operations Committee possessed jurisdiction over all reorganization
proposals.   When the House Reform Rules of
1971 effectively discouraged him from con-

tinuing to hold both the JCAE and Government
Operations chairmanships, Holifield relinquished his JCAE post and retained the
chairmanship of Government Operations in
order to wield greater influence in dealing
with the president's reorganization proposals. For Holifield, the choice of Government Operations meant "the Administration
would then have to bargain with me."[69]

As chairman of the House Government
Operations Committee in the Ninety-second
Congress, Holifield turned a cold shoulder
to DNR as envisioned by Nixon. Holifield
"didn't want nuclear energy put under the
Interior Department people with all the
politics they always had exercised over
oil." He muted his opposition, however, by
holding hearings on another reorganization
that Nixon sought--the proposed Department
of Community Development. Holifield reported a completed bill out of his committee, but the Ninety-second Congress took no
action on it.[70]

In the meanwhile, however, Holifield
sought a middle ground that would appease
Nixon's quest for energy reorganization and
satisfy some of the demands of the growing
environmental opposition to nuclear power
and also leave the AEC-JCAE combination
substantially intact. When he learned in
1972 that a major objective of the Nixon
administration was an energy research and
development administration, Holifield began
to work toward a limited reorganization,
involving separation of the AEC's research
and regulatory functions. The AEC's research function would be combined with other
energy research and development programs,
while its regulatory portion would be made a
separate entity to meet environmentalist
demands to have development and regulatory
functions in separate agencies. Holifield
wrote to the president on November 28, 1972,
urging that the AEC's capability be used as

a base for creation of an energy research
and development organization outside of, but
compatible with DNR.[71] President Nixon saw
the wisdom in this structuring of energy
functions, and on June 29, 1973, he called
for a Department of Energy and Natural Resources (DENR), along with an independent
Energy Research and Development Administration (ERDA) and a nuclear regulatory body,
the Nuclear Energy Commission (NEC). Holifield responded favorably and agreed to hold
hearings on the new proposal. It only remained for Holifield to "split off" ERDA and
NEC from the DENR proposal. As Holifield
noted before the House Rules Committee on
December 11, 1973, "Our committee had just
about decided on this move when the President, in his energy message of November 8
[1973], called for prompt action along the
same line."[72]

Holifield faced powerful opposition on
many fronts in his effort to guide his
ERDA/NEC bill to passage. As evidenced by
Nixon's several energy messages since 1971
in which the president advocated various
reorganization strategies, the administration had not made up its mind about energy
policy. Even after the president's November
8, 1973, energy message, Nixon's energy
chief William E. Simon and Office of Management and Budget Director Roy L. Ash won
press coverage for their continued urgings
that ERDA be included as part of the administration's proposal for a Federal Energy
Administration (FEA). The environmental
opposition was also working toward the
breakup and destruction of the AEC. Even in
Congress, there was a widening antinuclear
attitude that threatened Holifield's efforts. In the House, Richard Bolling (D-
Missouri), head of a select committee studying committee reorganization, targeted the
JCAE for annihilation. In addition, Holifield faced a significant jurisdictional

squabble as Morris K. Udall (D-Arizona), chairman of the Environment Subcommittee of the Committee on Interior and Insular Affairs, attempted to offer a substitute for Holifield's proposal. In the Senate, the antinuclear climate was even more severe, as a significant number of prominent senators, including Edward Kennedy (D-Massachusetts), Edmund S. Muskie (D-Maine), Philip A. Hart (D-Michigan), Mike Gravel (D-Alaska), and others increasingly turned a friendly ear to environmentalists' concerns.[73]

Holifield's most significant political problem in passage of his bill was Senator Henry M. Jackson (D-Washington), chairman of the Senate Interior Committee and JCAE member. Jackson, with the assistance of Representative Morris Udall in the House, launched an alternative to Holifield's bill. Jackson essentially proposed that an additional general manager for nonnuclear research be added to the AEC and that joint government-industry corporations be formed to conduct research on nonnuclear energy sources. Holifield remained friendly with Jackson and his staff and pointed to the obvious weaknesses in the proposal. In a memorandum to Jackson, Holifield emphasized, among other points, that a second general manager would create an administrative and legal anomaly within the AEC and promote program confusion. More importantly, Holifield asserted that Jackson's proposal would not separate the development and regulatory functions of the AEC, a separation that Holifield believed to be a necessary goal to respond to the legitimate concerns of the environmental opposition. Only after Holifield outmaneuvered Udall in the House did Jackson acquiesce in some degree to Holifield's proposal.[74]

Ultimately, Holifield successfully shepherded his ERDA/NEC bill to passage in the House on December 19, 1973. In the

Senate, however, his bill was besieged by amendments. Jackson boldly appended his entire proposal to the Holifield bill. Senator Kennedy proposed financial assistance for intervenors (opponents in hearings for permits), while an amendment by Senator Lee Metcalf (D-Montana) would have required the AEC to provide technical assistance to groups opposing nuclear developments in hearings. Still other amendments provided that no energy technology be given an "unwarranted priority" and provided minimum percentages of research funds for various energy technologies. The Senate version of the bill also called for abolition of the AEC, rather than redesignation of its remainder (after the research portion was removed as ERDA) as the NEC, and named the "new" entity the Nuclear Safety and Licensing Commission. The Senate version also prohibited the administrator and deputy administrator of ERDA from having nuclear research backgrounds.[75]

At the first meeting of the House-Senate conference on his bill, Holifield emphasized that "the Senate version goes too far afield" and that House conferees "will press to free H. R. 11510 from all this extra cargo." Holifield was also clear in his opinion that the Senate version had "a distinct anti-nuclear bias," and he indicated House conferees would work to eliminate it. Holifield felt there was "no need for . . . concern" that nuclear energy would dominate ERDA. The real issue, as he saw it, was "how we can obtain all the clean energy the nation needs for sustained economic growth without undue dependence on foreign sources." Holifield recalled the 1971 JCAE-sponsored law that provided for nonnuclear research in AEC laboratories and restated his frequently declared belief that "we must have all these energy programs [fossil fuel, nuclear, and nonnuclear]" and

that "other energy potentials also must be
investigated with vigor, and promising developments fully supported for our longer-
range needs."[76]

The Energy Reorganization Act of 1974,
as signed by the president, was remarkably
close to Holifield's original proposal.
During the conference on the bill, Holifield
managed to eliminate most of the Senate's
"antinuclear bias" and achieve a relatively
large amount of operational flexibility for
ERDA. The NEC was renamed the Nuclear Regulatory Commission (NRC) but was the linear
successor to the regulatory portion of the
AEC, as Holifield had wanted, rather than an
entirely new entity. Holifield proudly
considered his role in developing and enacting the bill as "a crowning achievement in
my legislative career" because, he explained, "I deeply feel that a sustained and
systematic attack on the energy problem is
absolutely critical to the nation's security
and economic vitality."[77]

Concurrently, Holifield pressed on a
second front for passage of the other major
energy reorganization proposal of the
Ninety-third Congress. This was the proposal for a Federal Energy Administration
(FEA), a temporary agency requested by Nixon
to handle fuel allocation, rationing, and
other emergency programs associated with the
national energy shortage brought on by the
Arab Oil Embargo of 1973. Nixon intended
the FEA to be a temporary stopover agency in
the quest for a cabinet-level department to
deal with the energy problem and to be a
replacement for the Federal Energy Office he
had established earlier by executive order.
Holifield's bill provided the organizational
framework of the FEA to implement emergency
powers considered in various House and Senate measures. The bill also stood alone as
the blueprint for a temporary energy agency
to deal with pressing needs of the energy

crisis, and for that reason, Holifield expe-
dited its development and passage. Under
the bill, several energy functions of the
Department of the Interior and the entire
Cost of Living Council were transferred to
the new entity. As with the ERDA proposal,
Holifield sought to give the FEA maximum
organizational flexibility, rather than attempting to dictate closely its internal
structure. Holifield's and his committee's
position was that "the [FEA] Administrator
must have flexibility to accommodate programs authorized by substantive legislation
and to adjust to rapidly-changing circumstances."[78]

During consideration of the FEA bill,
Holifield stressed the need to act quickly.
He also inveighed against what threatened to
become another round of amendments, as increasingly energy-conscious congressmen
sought to make their political influence
felt in the energy field. Holifield sternly
warned his House colleagues: "You load this
bill down . . . and you'll get this bill
vetoed." Holifield's warning apparently
succeeded, since action was relatively
swift. The president signed the FEA bill in
early May 1974.[79]

By the time Holifield retired at the
end of 1974, both the ERDA and the FEA bills
had been signed into law. The veteran California congressman could look back at the
Ninety-third Congress as a very significant
period in his career. Through his extensive
committee work and his status as a major
House legislator, he left behind a legacy of
energy organizations that would be the major
building blocks for future administrations'
responses to the energy question. One of
the organizations legislated into being by
Holifield, the NRC, was still functioning in
1989, a decade and a half after he retired.
The other two organizations, ERDA and FEA,
provided the basic organizational ingredi-

ents of the Department of Energy established during the Carter administration. Holifield thus influenced not only most aspects of atomic energy affairs during his tenure in office, but also the future course in atomic energy affairs long after his retirement.

Epilogue:
Mr. Atomic Energy

About midway through his sixteenth term in
Congress, Holifield decided that the time
had come to retire. In a letter to a relative in February 1974, Holifield wrote that
he and his wife had recently passed their
seventieth birthdays. "The time comes," he
continued, ". . . when a chapter in the book
of life must end and I have decided to
retire from Congress."[1] When he retired at
the end of 1974, Holifield had completed
thirty-two years of congressional service,
one of the longest tenures of any California
congressman.

Although Holifield had worked on many
subject areas while in Congress, his most
prominent legacy was in atomic energy affairs. His work of over twenty years on the
Government Operations Committee was certainly substantial, since it included his
involvement in legislation to create the
General Services Administration, the Department of Housing and Urban Development, the
Department of Transportation, the Office of
Procurement Policy, the Federal Catalog
System, the U.S. Disarmament Agency, the
Consumer Protection Agency, and other government organizations as well,[2] including
the reorganization of the AEC into the En-

ergy Research and Development Administration
and the Nuclear Regulatory Commission described in chapter 10. If Holifield's reorganization work was distinguishing, however,
his efforts in the novel field of atomic
energy and his long-term leadership of the
JCAE extended his influence far beyond the
House of Representatives and made him a
truly national figure. As a relative newcomer to the national arena in 1945, he had
grasped the significance of the bombings of
Hiroshima and Nagasaki as a startling new
force in national and international affairs
and had read all the material he could obtain on the possibilities of atomic energy.
He was in the fortuitous position of being a
member of the House committee that drafted
the nation's first atomic energy legislation, and he used his opportunity well. His
enthusiasm in pursuing passage of what became the Atomic Energy Act of 1946 brought
him to the attention of the House leadership, who gave him a place on the JCAE,
which was created by the legislation. The
JCAE quickly became the driving force in
developing, directing, and promoting atomic
energy policies and programs in the United
States, even more so than the president or
the AEC, in no small part because of the
tenacity, persistence, and determination of
this onetime haberdasher from Montebello,
who had not even completed high school.

As early as 1946, Holifield heralded
atomic energy as a force with myriad possibilities for peaceful applications. The
peaceful uses of atomic energy remained
foremost in Holifield's thinking and received the most attention during his twenty-
eight-year career as a JCAE member, although
he recognized America's need for continuing
superiority in nuclear weapons. By the time
he retired, Holifield had witnessed an incredible growth in the peaceful applications
of atomic energy to over two thousand prac-

tical applications in business, medicine, space technology, electricity production, and other areas.

While Holifield's predominant interest in atomic energy was not nuclear weaponry, he nonetheless made himself felt in this area as well. His role in the decision to build the hydrogen bomb, his years of support for Admiral Hyman Rickover's nuclear submarine and surface ship propulsion program, and his advocacy of the antiballistic missile programs showed him to be sensitive to the realities of international politics and the need for America to maintain superiority in nuclear weapons. His interest and leading role in advocacy of an expanded civil defense program and his attempts to inform the public about the hazards of nuclear testing were also indicative of his concern in this area. If nuclear weaponry was not his particular area of concentration, it was nonetheless an area in which Holifield put considerable time and study.

One area that greatly concerned Holifield, and the area in which he became most controversial, was the use of atomic energy for electricity production. From the Eisenhower period until his retirement, Holifield stood at the forefront of advocacy of atomic power development to meet the nation's growing energy needs. He preferred and fought for an expanded government development program, instead of a development program by private business, because he believed the considerable taxpayer investment in atomic power development should be preserved and because he was wary of a possible monopoly of atomic power by a few large corporations. Although not an ideologue, he was friendly to public power interests and also sought to ensure that municipal and other publicly owned utilities would share in atomic power development. What he could not obtain immediately, Holifield was willing to gain gradually through persistence.

For much of Holifield's career, atomic power development rode a wave of general public acceptance. Holifield was an unabashed promoter of nuclear power as the future answer to the nation's power needs. The public's approval of nuclear power eroded during the 1960s, however, and Holifield found himself having to defend further development of this energy source. A review of Holifield's record shows his concern about pollution of the environment, but he parted ways with most environmentalists in arguing that nuclear power, on balance, was as clean an energy source as any of the other sources available for broad public consumption and was part of the answer to the pollution problem. He attempted to educate the public on the comparative environmental merits of atomic energy and fossil fuels as producers of electrical power, but without the success he had enjoyed in educating the public in the 1950s about the radiation hazards of atmospheric nuclear testing. Holifield's emphasis on the necessity of some trade-offs between environmental quality and adequate electricity production was an unpopular and not very glamorous view in a controversy that increasingly became polarized between the "environmental position" and the "nuclear power position." His own concern for environmental quality received far less attention than his promotion of nuclear power, as he was increasingly associated by many environmentalists with the "Atomic Establishment."

The question of one's legacy is largely a matter of viewpoint. It is also a matter of perspective, as time and subsequent events change the landscape and color the understanding of the past. Part of Chet Holifield's legacy has hopefully been made clear, however, by this study. In his twenty-eight years on the JCAE, Holifield

was a significant force to be reckoned with.
Through hard work and intensive study, he
became one of the most knowledgeable members
of the JCAE, and he made his views felt.
Whether one likes Holifield or appreciates
his views on atomic energy issues, he
clearly deserves his reputation as one of
the principal "movers and shakers" in Congress who shaped atomic energy policy during
the formative years of the nation's atomic
energy program. And with the demise of the
JCAE in 1977 after his retirement, certainly
there was no congressman following him who
enjoyed such a confluence of power in atomic
energy affairs that Holifield enjoyed while
a member and chairman of the JCAE. Given
his longevity in Congress, his influence
from the early years of the JCAE in atomic
energy affairs, his many years as a JCAE
leader, and his hard work and amassed knowledge and influence over most facets of the
nation's atomic energy program, Holifield
fully deserves the title "Mr. Atomic Energy"
bestowed upon him by his colleagues.

Notes

Note to the Reader: Throughout these notes,
the author's interviews with Chet Holifield
are cited as "Holifield interview" and are
followed by the date of the interview.
Holifield's collection of his personal papers is referred to as "HP";   the phrase in
parentheses following the box number indicates the file name from which the material
was taken. See the introduction to the
Bibliography for a full description of the
Holifield papers.

PREFACE

      1.   Nicknames associated with one's
reputation   are often difficult to pin down,
since   they   are more often a product of
thought and the spoken word than of the
written word. That Holifield was closely
associated in many minds with atomic energy
can not be doubted. Holifield himself notes
that "in Congress, some called me 'Mr.
Atomic Energy.'" (Warren Unna, "Atomic Energy," unpublished typescript [1974],   1.)
In writing a biographical sketch on Holifield, Enid Douglass notes that "beginning
in 1946 he [Holifield] served on the JCAE,

much of the time as chairman, earning the nickname 'Mr. Atom' because of his tireless efforts." (*Chet Holifield, United States Congressman*, typed transcripts of five tape-recorded interviews by Enid H. Douglass, Oral History Program, Claremont Graduate School, Claremont, California, 1975, vol. 1, v.) Certainly Holifield is unique and most remembered for his work and influence in atomic energy affairs. Carl Albert (D-Oklahoma) noted in 1972 that Holifield had been "outstandingly active in the field of atomic energy legislation," and predicted that "his [Holifield's] contribution in the field of nuclear energy will come to be recognized, in my opinion, as 'statesman-like' in the classic sense of the word." (7 Mar. 1972, *Congressional Record*, 93d Cong., 2d sess., vol. 118, reprinted as part of Holifield constituent publication, "Your Congressman Chet Holifield Reports From Washington," n.d., courtesy of Mr. Holifield.)

2. Actually, Holifield served formally as a JCAE member for twenty-eight years and five months. The JCAE held its first organizational meeting on 2 Aug. 1946, just before the Seventy-ninth Congress adjourned. See Harold P. Green and Alan Rosenthal, *Government of the Atom: The Integration of Powers* (New York: Atherton Press, 1963), 5, for the first organizational meeting of the Joint Committee. Both the House and the Senate leadership appointed their respective members to the committee on 2 Aug., the day after President Truman signed the Atomic Energy Act of 1946 into law.

3. Representative Melvin Price (D-Illinois) is the representative mentioned. Price was a close friend and associate of Holifield who began service on the JCAE at the same time Holifield did. He succeeded Holifield as JCAE chairman and served until

the JCAE was dissolved in 1977.

    4. Holifield to Senator Henry M. Jackson (D-Washington), 1 Oct. 1973, Box 60 (H. R. 11510 - Energy Reorganization Act of 1973--Correspondence, 1973 [File #2]), HP. Actually, Holifield never sent the completed letter to Jackson. He wrote on it: "Never used, substituted a memorandum." The memorandum, Holifield to Jackson, 16 Oct. 1973, is in the same file. It does not contain Holifield's comment, which the author quoted.

CHAPTER 1:   BEFORE ATOMIC ENERGY

    1. Warren Unna, "Boyhood, My Own Family, and My Own Business" (1974), unpublished typescript, 6-7. Mr. Holifield graciously provided the author with this manuscript and others, which appear to be drafts of chapters of a biography or autobiography. The documents are written in the first person. They apparently were prepared for Holifield by Warren Unna, a reporter for the *Washington Post*. The titles of the nine "chapters" and their apparent order of appearance (given in the first "chapter") are as follows: (1) "Holifield Biography Outline," (2) "Boyhood, My Own Family, and My Own Business," (3) "Politics," (4) "Civil Liberties," (5) "Atomic Energy," (6) "Government Operations Committee," (7) "Legislating," (8) "Nixon," and (9) "Vietnam."

    2. Holifield to Roy L. Holifield, 12 Sept. 1969, and Holifield to Robb Hicks, 13 Aug. 1971, Box 1 (Relatives), HP.

    3. Unna, "Boyhood," 3.

    4. Ibid., 3-5.

    5. Ibid., 4.

    6. Ibid., 6.

    7. Ibid., 7. Another helpful source of information on Holifield's early life and his congressional career is *Chet Holifield,*

United States Congressman, 3 vols., typed transcripts of five tape-recorded interviews by Enid H. Douglass, Oral History Program, Claremont Graduate School, Claremont, California, 1975. (Hereafter cited as Holifield interviews by Enid H. Douglass.) The three volumes are 170, 160, and 99 pages long, respectively, and each includes an index. Volume 1 consists of Douglass's interviews with Holifield on 25 Apr. 1975 and 7 May 1975 and concentrates on Holifield's early life up to his first election to Congress. Volume 2 includes interviews on 15 May 1975 and 25 July 1975 and centers on Holifield's congressional committee work and some of his early atomic energy efforts. Volume 3 is a closing interview held on 12 Nov. 1975 and is about Holifield's participation in various atomic energy events and issues. All of the interviews were conducted at 2001 Lincoln Avenue, Montebello, California, Holifield's residence for most of his congressional career. For Holifield's description of his early life in Paragould and Springdale, see vol. 1, 10-17.

    8. Holifield interview, 19 Feb. 1980.

    9. Holifield to John Reich, 18 Dec. 1970, Box 47 (JCAE Outgoing Letters, 1970 [Blue Copies]), HP. In 1975, Holifield explained that he had read the New Testament twice and the Old Testament once under his father's direction. Holifield also credited his sixth-grade teacher, Harriet B. King, with assisting in development of his reading skills. (Holifield interviews by Enid H. Douglass, vol. 1, 16-17.)

    10. Warren Unna, "Holifield of California," *Atlantic Monthly* 205 (April 1960):79.

    11. Unna, "Boyhood," 8.

    12. Holifield interview, 19 Feb. 1980.

    13. Unna, "Boyhood," 7; Holifield to Robb Hicks, 13 Aug 1971, Box 1 (Relatives), HP.

14. Unna, "Boyhood," 8.

15. Ibid.

16. Paul Houston, "Holifield: A 32-Year Flashback on His Congress Career," *Los Angeles Times*, 21 Feb. 1974, Part II.   A copy of this newspaper article may be found loose (no file) in Box 1, HP.

17. Unna, "Boyhood," 10;   Holifield interviews by Enid H. Douglass, vol. 1, 20.

18. Unna, "Holifield of California," 79; "Boyhood," 10-11.

19. Holifield interview, 19 Feb. 1980; Unna, "Boyhood," 10, 12.

20. Unna, "Boyhood," 11.   In 1975, Holifield remembered that his father left the business in 1927 in order to concentrate on his real estate interests.   (Holifield interviews by Enid H. Douglass, vol. 1, 39.)

21. Holifield interview, 19 Feb. 1980; Holifield, completed fact sheet requested by *Congressional Quarterly*, 30 Jan. 1968, Box 1, HP; Unna, "Boyhood," 11.

22. Unna, "Boyhood," 12.

23. Unna, "Holifield of California," 79; "Boyhood," 12-13; Holifield interviews by Enid H. Douglass, vol. 1, 41, 50-51.

24. Holifield, "Candidates Biographical Fact Sheet," 1 Aug. 1968, requested by *East Whittier Review*, et al., Box 1 (Biographical Material), HP.

25. Holifield interview, 19 Feb. 1980.

26. Ibid.

27. Ibid.   An account of the hunting accident is also in Unna, "Boyhood," 13.   In his 1960 article on Holifield, Unna also mentions some details of the mishap and notes that "that stray shot from nowhere kept him bedridden or in a wheel chair for four [*sic*] years." (Unna, "Holifield of California," 79.) In 1975, Holifield explained that the hunting accident left him disabled for three and one-half years. (Holifield interviews by Enid H. Douglass, vol. 1, 42.)

28. Holifield interview, 19 Feb. 1980; Unna, "Boyhood," 14.

29. Unna, "Boyhood," 13-15; Holifield interview, 19 Feb. 1980; Unna, "Holifield of California," 79; Holifield interviews by Enid H. Douglass, vol. 1, 44-46.

30. Holifield interview, 19 Feb. 1980.

31. Unna, "Holifield of California," 79.

32. Unna, "Boyhood," 15. During the interview on 19 Feb. 1980, Holifield remembered the books he had read during his convalescence.

33. Unna, "Boyhood," 15. Holifield became a member of the Young Democrats Club of East Los Angeles, undoubtedly a major influence in his budding political philosophy. (Holifield interviews by Enid H. Douglass, vol. 1, 58.)

34. Holifield interview, 19 Feb. 1980; Unna, "Politics," 1-2.

35. Unna, "Politics," 2; Unna, "Holifield Biography Outline," 4. During the interview 19 Feb. 1980, Holifield remembered that Voorhis was dressed incongruously in a blue shirt and suit and plowshoes. Holifield was very impressed with Voorhis's speaking ability and his idealism, sincerity, and enthusiasm.

36. Unna, "Boyhood," 16; Holifield interview, 19 Feb. 1980; Holifield, "Candidates Biographical Fact Sheet."

37. Unna, "Politics," 2.

38. Holifield interview, 19 Feb. 1980.

39. Unna, "Politics," 2-3; Holifield interviews by Enid H. Douglass, vol. 1, 48.

40. Voorhis decided not to run for the Senate in 1940 because he could not raise enough money. (Unna, "Politics," 3.) Beginning in 1940, Holifield attended every Democratic convention as a delegate until the 1972 convention. See, for example, the typewritten and published copies of his entry for the *Congressional Directory* in

Box 1 (Biographical Material), HP. In discussing his lifelong Democratic party affiliation, Holifield noted that "I had voted the Democratic ticket at 21 and cast my presidential vote for FDR in 1932." (Unna, "Politics," 1; Holifield interview, 19 Feb. 1980.)

41. Unna, "Holifield Biography Outline," 4; Unna, "Politics," 3. See also Unna, "Holifield of California," 80.

42. Ibid. Holifield interviews by Enid H. Douglass, vol. 1, 57.

43. Houston, "Holifield: A 32-Year Flashback on His Congress Career." Holifield himself acknowledged that his was the longest career of any California congressman. (Holifield to Ralph Jacques, 11 Feb. 1974, Box 1 [Relatives--Personal], HP.)

44. Holifield noted that the most he ever spent for reelection was fourteen thousand dollars and that he usually won with well over 60 percent of the vote. (Holifield interview, 19 Feb. 1980.) In three of his sixteen campaigns, Holifield was endorsed by both the Democrats and the Republicans. (Unna, "Holifield of California," 80.) In discussing his strength in his district, Holifield noted that he had never solicited donations from the oil companies in oil-rich Montebello. He also commented: "I've never had a dinner to raise money. That's another unusual thing. And I've never published a list of sponsors." (Holifield interviews by Enid H. Douglass, vol. 1, 79-80.)

CHAPTER 2: PRESENT AT THE DAWNING

1. *New York Sunday News*, 10 Jan. 1943, Box 1, HP.

2. Holifield interview, 7 Mar. 1981.

3. "Notes for Mr. Holifield's Address to Postal Employees," n.d., Box 1, HP.

Early in his career, Holifield was also appointed to the Committee on Executive Expenditures, which would later become the powerful Committee on Government Operations. (*Chet Holifield, United States Congressman*, typed transcripts of five tape-recorded interviews by Enid H. Douglass, Oral History Program, Claremont Graduate School, Claremont, California, 1975, vol. 1, 100.)

4. Holifield interview, 7 Mar. 1981.

5. Richard G. Hewlett and Oscar E. Anderson, *The New World, 1939/1946*, vol. 1 of *A History of the United States Atomic Energy Commission* (University Park, Pennsylvania: The Pennsylvania State University Press, 1962), 10-11.

6. Frank G. Dawson, *Nuclear Power: Development and Management of a Technology* (Seattle: University of Washington Press, 1976), 12-14.

7. Ibid., 13-14; Hewlett and Anderson, *The New World*, 7.

8. Harold P. Green and Alan Rosenthal, *Government of the Atom: The Integration of Powers* (New York: Atherton Press, 1963), 3; Hewlett and Anderson, *The New World*, 402, 415.

9. Warren Unna, "Atomic Energy," (1974), unpublished typescript, 2.

10. Ibid; Holifield interviews with Enid H. Douglass, vol. 2, 93.

11. Hewlett and Anderson, *The New World*, 436.

12. Ibid., 422-23, 429; Green and Rosenthal, *Government of the Atom*, 2.

13. For a thorough discussion of the origins of the May-Johnson bill, see Hewlett and Anderson, *The New World*, 408-427.

14. Ibid., 414.

15. Ibid., 429, 431, 435; Green and Rosenthal, *Government of the Atom*, 2; Dawson, *Nuclear Power*, 16-18.

16. Hewlett and Anderson, *The New World*, 421-23, 431-35, 445-48.

17. Holifield interview, 7 Mar. 1981; Warren Unna, "Holifield of California," *Atlantic Monthly* 205 (April 1960), 80; Paul Houston, "Holifield: A 32-Year Flashback on His Congress Career," *Los Angeles Times*, 21 Feb. 1974, Part II.

18. Hewlett and Anderson, *The New World*, 433, 436, 482.

19. House of Representatives, Committee on Military Affairs, *Atomic Energy Act of 1945*, 79th Cong., 1st sess., 5 Nov. 1945, H. Rept. 1186, 3–4.

20. Ibid., 16–18; Holifield interview, 7 Mar. 1981; Unna, "Atomic Energy," 2; Holifield interviews with Enid H. Douglass, vol. 2, 84–89. Holifield reads part of his minority report into the record in his interview with Douglass. See vol. 2, 86–87.

21. Quotations are from House of Representatives, Committee on Military Affairs, *Atomic Energy Act of 1945*, 16–18.

22. Hewlett and Anderson, *The New World*, 482–91.

23. Unna, "Atomic Energy," 4–5.

24. Hewlett and Anderson, *The New World*, 436, 445.

25. James R. Newman and Byron S. Miller, *The Control of Atomic Energy: A Study of Its Social, Economic, and Political Implications* (New York: McGraw-Hill Book Company, Inc., 1948), 8. Newman and Miller, in fact, dedicated this book to Senator McMahon and Congresswoman Helen Gahagan Douglas as "two of the people's representatives who saw far and who saw clearly."

26. H. R. 5365, 79th Cong., 2d sess., 4 Feb. 1946, Box 51 (H. R. 5365), HP.

27. Hewlett and Anderson, *The New World*, 443–44, 449–54.

28. Ibid., 452, 485–86, 491–92, 505.

29. Ibid., 483–84, 492, 507.

30. Byron S. Miller, "A Law is Passed--The Atomic Energy Act of 1946,"

University of Chicago Law Review 15   (Summer 1948):811.

31.   Alice Kimball Smith, *A Peril and a Hope: The Scientists' Movement in America: 1945-47* (Chicago: The University of Chicago Press, 1965), 397-98.

32.   Holifield interview,   7 Mar. 1981; Smith,   *A Peril and a Hope*,   400.   See also Holifield interviews with Enid H. Douglass, vol. 2, 91-94 for Holifield's comments on his 1945-1946 activities toward promotion of civilian control of atomic energy and his role   in   the   Emergency   Conference   for Civilian Control of Atomic Energy.

33.   Smith,   *A Peril and a Hope*,   400-402;   Holifield   interviews   with   Enid   H. Douglass, vol. 2, 91-94.

34.   Hewlett   and   Anderson,   *The New World*, 512-13, 516.

35.   Ibid., 519-21;   Smith, *A Peril and a Hope*, 417.

36.   Hewlett   and   Anderson,   *The   New World*, 529-30.

37.   "Atomic   Bomb Tests: Bikini, July 1st and 25th, 1946;   also 'Conditions in the Far   East'   as observed by   Chet   Holifield, Congressman,   19th   District,   California," pamphlet   "prepared from notes by Chet Holifield,   M.   C.,"   n.d.,   9, 29, Box 41 (Bikini Atom Test), HP.

38.   Ibid., 8.

39.   Ibid., 28.

40.   Ibid., 7.

41.   Holifield interview,   7 Mar. 1981. Holifield   believes that   Rayburn   conferred with   Senator McMahon in selection of   House members   for   the Joint Committee   and   that this conference aided the selection of Holifield   and   Price.   Holifield is quoted   as saying,   "Speaker Rayburn must have said   to himself: 'Mel   and   Chet were right.'   He appointed us to the first Joint Committee on Atomic   Energy   even   though   we   were   down fourth and fifth from the bottom [in senior-

ity] of the House Military Affairs Committee." (Unna, "Atomic Energy," 6.)

42. Green and Rosenthal, *Government of the Atom*, 3, 25-30.

CHAPTER 3:   IN DEFENSE OF THE NATION

1. Richard G. Hewlett and Oscar E. Anderson, *The New World, 1939/1946*, vol. 1 of *A History of the Atomic Energy Commission* (University Park, Pennsylvania: The Pennsylvania State University Press, 1962), 483, 507, 512-13.

2. Corbin Allardice and Edward R. Trapnell, *The Atomic Energy Commission*, Praeger Library of U. S. Government Departments and Agencies (New York: Praeger Publishers, Inc., 1974), 219-22.   These pages, which comprise Appendix C, provide helpful listings of members of the Senate Special Committee on Atomic Energy, the House Committee on Military Affairs (Seventy-ninth Congress), and the Joint Committee on Atomic Energy.   See Harold P. Green and Alan Rosenthal, *Government of the Atom: The Integration of Powers* (New York: Atherton Press, 1963), 5, for the first organizational meeting of the Joint Committee.

3. For reconstitution of the Joint Committee, see Green and Rosenthal, *Government of the Atom*, 5.   For information on Thomason and his resignation, see Hewlett and Anderson, *The New World*, 520.   For details on Forand, see *Facts on File 1947* (New York: Facts on File, Inc., 1947).

4. Richard G. Hewlett and Francis Duncan, *Atomic Shield, 1947/1952*, vol. 2 of *A History of the Atomic Energy Commission* (University Park, Pennsylvania: The Pennsylvania State University Press, 1969), 1-7.

5. Ibid., 48-53, 90-91.

6. Green and Rosenthal, *Government of the Atom*, 38-44.

7. W. W. Waymack, "Four Years Under Law," *Bulletin of the Atomic Scientists* 7 (February 1951):54.

8. Hewlett and Duncan, *Atomic Shield*, 89-95.

9. Holifield, "Smearing the Scientists: Attempt to Discredit Civilian Atomic-Energy Control," reprint of Holifield House speech, 22 July 1947, 3, 12, Box 50 (Dr. E. U. Condon/Civil Liberties), HP. Hewlett and Duncan provide a summary of the speech. (*Atomic Shield*, 95.)

10. Holifield, "Sabotage of American Science: The Full Meaning of Attacks on Dr. Condon," reprint of Holifield House speech, 9 Mar. 1948, 4-5, Box 50 (Dr. E. U. Condon/Civil Liberties), HP.

11. Holifield, copy of typewritten House floor speech, 17 Jan. 1949, Box 79 (January 17, 1949, Speech--Floor, Re Frank Havenner), HP; Holifield, "The Present Crisis in Civil Liberties," copy of floor speech, 11 Mar. 1948, Box 79 (March 11, 1948, Speech, "The Present Crisis in Civil Liberties"), HP. Holifield criticized the House Committee on Un-American Activities specifically in a letter to the publisher of the *Los Angeles Sentinel*. (Holifield to Leon H. Washington, Jr., 8 Dec. 1947, Box 51 [Chet's Bill, H. R. 4641], HP.)

12. See, for example, Holifield's bill, H. R. 4641, 80th Cong., 1st sess., Box 50 (Dr. E. U. Condon/Civil Liberties), HP. The purpose of the bill was "to prescribe the procedures of investigating committees of the Congress and to protect the rights of parties under investigation by such committees."

13. Green and Rosenthal, *Government of the Atom*, 63.

14. Hewlett and Duncan, *Atomic Shield*, 328-31; Green and Rosenthal, *Government of the Atom*, 63.

15. Green and Rosenthal, *Government of*

the Atom, 8. See Hewlett and Duncan, *Atomic Shield*, Appendix 1, "Table of Organization," 665, for Joint Committee composition in the Eighty-first Congress.

16. McMahon to Johnson, 14 July 1949, quoted in Hewlett and Duncan, *Atomic Shield*, 183. The Joint Committee's draft report, *The Influence of the Joint Committee on Atomic Energy on the Decision to Build the Hydrogen Bomb*, [1969], Part 2, 10, Box 44 (Decision to Build the Hydrogen Bomb 1966), HP, contains larger portions of McMahon's letter, from which one of the quotations was taken. For McMahon's statement to the press, see Hewlett and Duncan, *Atomic Shield*, 179.

17. Hewlett and Duncan, *Atomic Shield*, 352.

18. Ibid., 355-58.

19. Ibid., 357. For the Holifield quotations, see "The Present Crisis in Civil Liberties," last page (pages are unnumbered), 11 Mar. 1948, Box 79 (March 11, 1948, Speech, "The Present Crisis in Civil Liberties"), HP.

20. Holifield to G. P. Wachtell, Sec., Princeton Association of Scientists, 22 June 1949, Box 50 (1950 David Lilienthal), HP.

21. Transcript of 1 Oct. 1949 broadcast on Bert Andrews Program at the Trans Lux Building, Washington, D. C., Box 79 (October 1, 1949, Broadcast, Re: First Russian Atomic Explosion), HP.

22. Holifield, "81st is Hard-Working Congress," copy of Holifield speech, [1950], 10-11, Box 79 (1950 [undated], "81st is Hard-Working Congress"), HP.

23. Harry S Truman, *Years of Trial and Hope*, vol. 2 of *Memoirs by Harry S Truman* (Garden City, New York: Doubleday & Company, Inc., 1956), 306-07; Hewlett and Duncan, *Atomic Shield*, 362-67.

24. Hewlett and Duncan, *Atomic Shield*, 368.

25. Ibid., 369; U.S. Congress, Joint Committee on Atomic Energy, "The Influence of the Joint Committee on Atomic Energy on the Decision to Build the Hydrogen Bomb," typewritten draft report, [1969], Part 2, 14, Box 44 (Decision to Build the Hydrogen Bomb 1966), HP (hereafter cited as *JCAE Hydrogen Bomb History*).

26. Warren Unna, "Atomic Energy" (1974), unpublished typescript, 8; Holifield interview, 7 Mar. 1981.

27. Transcript of 1 Oct. 1949 broadcast on Bert Andrews Program.

28. Edward Teller and Allen Brown, *The Legacy of Hiroshima* (Garden City, New York: Doubleday & Company, Inc., 1962), 36.

29. U.S. Congress, Joint Committee on Atomic Energy, *The Hydrogen Bomb and International Control: Technical and Background Information*, 81st Cong., 2d sess., July 1950, Committee Print, 1. *JCAE Hydrogen Bomb History*, Part 1, 3-4, also provides a helpful layman's description of the fusion, or thermonuclear, reaction.

30. *JCAE Hydrogen Bomb History*, Part 1, 4-5, 49-53.

31. Lewis L. Strauss, *Men and Decisions* (Garden City, New York: Doubleday & Company, Inc., 1962), 216-17.

32. Hewlett and Duncan, *Atomic Shield*, 374, 478.

33. Ibid., 369. According to Holifield, Strauss and Teller were well acquainted and were, in fact, friends. (Holifield interview, 7 Mar. 1981.) Writing later of his unsuccessful nomination to be secretary of commerce, Strauss mentions that "Dr. Edward Teller left a hospital bed in California to come to Washington to testify [in support of Strauss's nomination]." (Strauss, *Men and Decisions*, 392.)

34. Holifield interview, 7 Mar. 1981. Holifield also describes the meeting in *Chet Holifield, United States Congressman*, typed

transcripts of five tape-recorded interviews by Enid H. Douglass, Oral History Program, Claremont Graduate School, Claremont, California, 1975, vol. 3, 4-7. Warren Unna mentions this meeting, although the meeting place was allegedly "the security-guarded back room of the Joint Committee suite." ("Atomic Energy," 8.)

35. Holifield interview, 7 Mar. 1981; Holifield interviews by Enid H. Douglass, vol. 3, 7. Holifield names the subcommittee members in a 1954 letter to former AEC Chairman Gordon Dean. (Holifield to Dean, 6 Oct. 1954, Box 41 [JAEC Originating Leg., Early Misc.], HP.) Note: The acronym "JAEC" in the last file named above is not a misprint or error; it stands for "Joint Atomic Energy Committee," which is an alternate, less-formal title for the Joint Committee on Atomic Energy (JCAE). Holifield's usage of the acronym "JAEC" is part of the common congressional vernacular in referring to committees.

36. Hewlett and Duncan, *Atomic Shield*, 377. This meeting is also discussed in Strauss, *Men and Decisions*, 218, and *JCAE Hydrogen Bomb History*, Part 2, 19-20.

37. *JCAE Hydrogen Bomb History*, Part 2, 23-25, 27-29.

38. Ibid., 39-41. JCAE staff member Walter Hamilton assumed the laborious task of taking notes on all subcommittee meetings and later wrote a fifteen-page memorandum summarizing the subcommittee's trip. In Holifield to Dr. Norris E. Bradbury, 19 July 1969, Box 46 (JCAE Correspondence--1969, Outgoing June-December), HP, Holifield himself describes all of those present at Los Alamos and reiterates the fact that Hamilton wrote the report on the trip. Holifield briefly mentions his subcommittee's tour to Enid Douglass, but appears incorrect on some of the details. (Holifield interviews with Enid H. Douglass, vol. 3, 7-8.)

39.   *JCAE Hydrogen Bomb History*, Part 2, 40-41.

40.   Ibid., 41-42.

41.   Ibid., 42.

42.   Ibid., 42-43.

43.   Ibid., 43-44.

44.   Ibid., 44-45.

45.   Ibid., 45. According to Part 1, 53, both the military and the AEC "were depending greatly on Oppenheimer" for their information on the super weapon, rather than on field visits or other firsthand methods.

46.   Holifield interview, 7 Mar. 1981. Sterling Cole wrote to Holifield in 1969 stating that he had not been "overly impressed with the need or desirability" of building the hydrogen bomb. His view was "based on the preponderance of scientific judgment that it could not be done, upon the estimated cost of $2 billion and, more importantly, upon the horrendous prospect of the destruction which such a weapon would work." Cole wanted Truman to pursue an agreement with Russia whereby both nations would renounce development of the weapon. (Cole to Holifield, 25 Sept. 1969, Box 45 [Hydrogen Bomb], HP.)

47.   David E. Lilienthal, *The Atomic Energy Years, 1945-1950*, vol. 2 of *The Journals of David E. Lilienthal* (New York: Harper and Row, 1966), 582.

48.   Those present for the GAC meeting are listed in a JCAE memorandum, [JCAE Executive Director] Edward J. Bauser to Holifield, 1 Apr. 1969, Box 46 (JCAE Correspondence--1969, Outgoing, January-May), HP. Dr. Glenn T. Seaborg, the principal discoverer of the transuranic elements and professor of chemistry at Berkeley, was in Sweden and unable to attend the meeting. (Hewlett and Duncan, *Atomic Shield*, 378.) Other sources on the GAC meeting include *JCAE Hydrogen Bomb History*, Part 2, 48-52; Robert Gilpin, *American Scientists and Nuclear Weapons*

Policy (Princeton, New Jersey: Princeton University Press, 1962), 87-94.

49. *JCAE Hydrogen Bomb History*, Part 2, 52; Teller and Brown, *Legacy of Hiroshima*, 44-45; Hewlett and Duncan, *Atomic Shield*, 388.

50. Hewlett and Duncan, *Atomic Shield*, 391; *JCAE Hydrogen Bomb History*, Part 2, 55; Margaret Truman, *Harry S Truman* (New York: William Morrow & Company, 1973), 417; Hewlett and Duncan, *Atomic Shield*, 389.

51. *JCAE Hydrogen Bomb History*, Part 2, 66-67. Hewlett and Duncan mention McMahon's 15 Nov. 1949 trip to Los Alamos but do not mention his 8 Nov. trip. (*Atomic Shield*, 392-93.)

52. *JCAE Hydrogen Bomb History*, Part 2, 70-76, contains large portions of McMahon's five-thousand-word letter to Truman, from which the quotes in the paragraph are taken. In his 12 Nov. 1975 interview with Enid Douglass, Holifield claimed to have a copy of the letter in his possession and viewed it as the major result of his subcommittee's work. (Holifield interviews with Enid H. Douglass, vol. 3, 10.)

53. Ibid.

54. Ibid.

55. The exact date of the meeting with the president is unclear. In a 1967 letter to Holifield, Dr. Richard G. Hewlett thanked Holifield for an interview Holifield granted to Hewlett and Dr. Francis Duncan during their research for *Atomic Shield*. Hewlett also asserted that the researchers "were especially happy to have your recollections on the meeting of the Joint Committee members with President Truman in November, 1949." (Hewlett to Holifield, 16 Oct. 1967, Box 44 [1967 Atomic Energy Commission], HP.) In a letter to former AEC Chairman Gordon Dean, Holifield wrote that after returning from the subcommittee trip, "several of us went to the White House (I cannot remember

exactly who, but believe it was McMahon, Jackson, Price and I), and urged Truman to give the order, which a few days later was done." (Holifield to Dean, 6 Oct. 1954, Box 41 [JAEC Originating Leg., Early Misc.], HP.) Holifield recalled later that Vice-Chairman Carl Durham also accompanied the group to the White House. (Holifield interview, 7 Mar. 1981.) Also regarding the meeting with President Truman, Green and Rosenthal assert that McMahon "wrote Truman repeating his views, and JCAE members 'marched down to the White House' where they consulted the President personally prior to his decision to proceed with the hydrogen bomb." (*Government of the Atom*, 235.) David Alan Rosenberg relates that according to the president's appointment schedule, McMahon saw Truman for forty minutes on January 5, 1950. ("American Atomic Strategy and the Hydrogen Bomb Decision," *Journal of American History* 66 (June 1979): 86, n. 92.) This date could have been when Holifield, McMahon, and the others met with Truman on the hydrogen bomb. Another Holifield account of the meeting is in Unna, "Atomic Energy," 10. In 1975, Holifield included Carl Hinshaw among the JCAE members who went to the White House, and he estimated the date of the meeting to be between 28 Nov. 1949 and 30 Nov. 1949. (Holifield interviews with Enid H. Douglass, vol. 3, 15.)

    56. Hewlett and Duncan, *Atomic Shield*, 394; Margaret Truman, *Harry S Truman*, 417.

    57. Hewlett and Anderson, *The New World*, 621; Hewlett and Duncan, *Atomic Shield*, 394.

    58. Dean Acheson, *Present at the Creation: My Years in the State Department* (New York: W. W. Norton & Company, Inc., 1969), 348. With regard to the Pentagon's development of a position on the hydrogen bomb project, David Alan Rosenberg ("American Atomic Strategy and the Hydrogen Bomb Deci-

sion," *Journal of American History* 66 [June 1979]:86) points out that most of the proponents and opponents of the hydrogen project had made their views known to Truman by November 1949 and that the Joint Chiefs of Staff (JCS) "in contrast, presented its views to the president three times during the final three weeks of January when Truman was under enormous pressure from Congress and the press to make a public statement regarding the hydrogen bomb." Since the JCS each time provided "an orderly and dispassionate presentation backed up with evidence and analysis," Rosenberg concludes that "in the final analysis it can be said that the JCS played a significant role in the policy-making process by offering Truman a historical context and a strategic justification for what was essentially a political decision." This conclusion is a clever overstatement, especially in view of the fact that Rosenberg observes in note 92 on the same page (86) that McMahon visited the president for forty minutes on January 5, 1950, and followed up with a letter of January 18, indicating that McMahon did not waver in his effort to convince Truman that the hydrogen bomb project should go forward. The January 5 meeting may have been the one in which Holifield and other JCAE members met with Truman on the weapon. In any event, there is no tangible indication that Truman used any particular report or was influenced by any one person in his decision. In addition, Holifield's assertion that McMahon and he knew of the president's decision by "late December or early January" would tend to negate any appreciable effect that the military viewpoint might have exercised during the last three weeks of January. (Holifield interview, 7 Mar. 1981; Unna, "Atomic Energy," 10.) Finally, at least one AEC commissioner, Sumner Pike, was not impressed with the military's perform-

ance in the months before and after the
hydrogen bomb decision.   One of Pike's two
major reasons for rejecting hydrogen bomb
development (and thus voting with Lilienthal
and Smyth against development) was that "we
had not at that time had any word from the
military establishment that they wanted such
a weapon," and "it seemed to me that until
they gave us a requirement for one that we
shouldn't go ahead." Pike also noted that
"we had had many instances of delay while
the Joint Chiefs of Staff were considering
proposals." After Truman's January 31 decision, Pike attended a meeting of the National Security Council as acting chairman
of the AEC (because of Lilienthal's resignation) regarding the implementation of the
president's decision, and he remembered that
he "stressed the point that the military, on
several occasions had been very slow in
coming to decisions and that in this case,
since time was of the essence, we could not
wait until the military had finally made up
their minds but would have to go along,
using our own judgement [*sic*] if we felt
the Pentagon was unduly delaying a decision." (Sumner T. Pike to Holifield, 20
Oct. 1969, Box 45 [Hydrogen Bomb], HP.)
Only by extending the concept of the hydrogen bomb decision to Truman's March 10 directive is Rosenberg able to show significant movement by the military in regard to
the hydrogen bomb.   Even with this extension, Rosenberg apparently fails to appreci-
ate the extent to which military planners,
like most bureaucrats, adjust their ideas to
mirror what is currently in fashion politically.   After January 31, it was clear that
the United States would have a hydrogen bomb
and attempt to get it as soon as possible,
so there was little for the military planners to do except adjust to this reality.

    59. Acheson, *Present at the Creation*,
348; Truman, *Years of Trial and Hope*, 309.

60. Warner R. Schilling, "The H-Bomb Decision: How   to Decide Without   Actually Choosing,"   *Political Science   Quarterly*   76 (March 1961):37.

61. Ibid.,   36-37;   Rosenberg, "Ameri-can Atomic Strategy and the Hydrogen Bomb Decision," 62.

62. Schilling, "The   H-Bomb Decision," 24-25, 37.

63. Unna, "Atomic Energy,"   10;   Holi-field interview, 7 Mar. 1981.

64. Hewlett and Duncan, *Atomic Shield*, 401.

65. *Washington Post*,   1 Feb. 1950, Box 46 (JCAE Fact Sheets--1969), HP.

66. Schilling, "The   H-Bomb Decision," 37, 45-46.

67. Holifield,   "Item   for   Reader's Digest Article,   Submitted by   Congressman Chet Holifield of California,"   [1957],   5, Box 41 (Atomic Energy 1956-60 Misc.), HP.   A revised version of this article was   later published in Donald Robinson, ed., *The Day I Was Proudest to be an American* (Garden City, New York: Doubleday & Company, Inc., 1958), 86-89.

68. The   report is   the *JCAE   Hydrogen Bomb History*.   Hewlett and Duncan state they were not granted access to the Joint Commit-tee's classified files.   (*Atomic Shield*, 599.)   The *JCAE Hydrogen Bomb History* con-tains some (censored) information from the Joint Committee's classified files   (for example, Hamilton's memorandum on the Holi-field subcommittee trip) which heretofore have apparently not been used by scholars.

69. Holifield,   "Item   for   Reader's Digest Article," 5.

CHAPTER 4: PUBLIC POWER ON THE DEFENSIVE

1. Actually, Durham was "acting chair-man."   The House's claim to equal   partner-

ship with the Senate with regard to who could be chairman of the JCAE was not settled until the "Alternate Chairmanships Controversy" of January–April 1953, which is discussed later in this chapter. For discussions of Durham's status as acting chairman, see Harold P. Green and Alan Rosenthal, *Government of the Atom: The Integration of Powers* (New York: Atherton Press, 1963), 55, and Morgan Thomas, in collaboration with Robert M. Northrop, *Atomic Energy and Congress* (Ann Arbor, Michigan: The University of Michigan Press, 1956), 136.

2. Thomas and Northrop, *Atomic Energy and Congress*, 136.

3. Holifield interview, 8 Feb. 1982. The fact that House Republican JCAE members agreed to join with House Democratic JCAE members in the Alternate Chairmanships Controversy is corroborated in Green and Rosenthal, *Government of the Atom*, 55–56, who utilize Madeline W. Losee (comp.), *Legislative History of the Atomic Energy Act of 1954/Public Law 703, 83rd Congress* (Washington, D.C.: U.S. Atomic Energy Commission, 1955), vol. 3, 3964, for Holifield's comments in 1954 on the House–Senate JCAE controversy. See also *Chet Holifield, United States Congressman*, typed transcripts of five tape-recorded interviews by Enid H. Douglass, Oral History Program, Claremont Graduate School, Claremont, California, 1975, vol. 3, 103–106.

4. Holifield to Carl T. Durham, 24 Mar. 1954, Box 41 (JAEC Originating Leg., Early Misc.), HP.

5. Green and Rosenthal, *Government of the Atom*, 56.

6. Frank G. Dawson, *Nuclear Power: Development and Management of a Technology* (Seattle: University of Washington Press, 1976), 40, 53; Green and Rosenthal, *Government of the Atom*, 122–23. Thomas and Northrop point out (*Atomic Energy and Con-*

gress, 161-62) that weapons testing resulting from the H-bomb and the nuclear weapons
expansion program of the early 1950s under
the McMahon chairmanship tended to lead the
United States away from weapons issues and
toward the peaceful uses of atomic energy in
the international arena. In discussing a
1 Mar. 1954 test, they note that the United
States realized that nuclear weapons of
almost unlimited size could be easily and
cheaply constructed, and "this knowledge
gave renewed impetus to the need to develop
the peaceful uses of the atom, and to make
this a basis for increased international
understanding and good will."

7. Quoted in Dawson, *Nuclear Power*,
36-37.

8. Richard G. Hewlett and Francis
Duncan, *Atomic Shield, 1947/1952*, vol. 2 of
A History of the Atomic Energy Commission
(University Park, Pennsylvania: The Pennsylvania State University Press, 1969), 15-
23, 129-32; Dawson, *Nuclear Power*, 39-40,
49-53.

9. Dawson, *Nuclear Power*, 53.

10. Cole and Hickenlooper's announcement of the hearings is quoted in Green and
Rosenthal, *Government of the Atom*, 123.
Dawson lists a series of questions put forward by JCAE Chairman Cole at the beginning
of the hearings, which identify the concerns
and purposes of the hearings. (*Nuclear
Power*, 54.)

11. 1 June 1953, *Congressional Record*,
83rd Cong., 1st sess., vol. 99, 5858-63.
See also Holifield press release, 1 June
1953, Box 79 (June 1, 1953, Speech--Floor,
"Atomic Energy and Private Enterprise") and
Box 79 (June 1, 1953, Press Release, Re:
Moves to Change the Atomic Energy Act), HP.
(There is a copy of the press release in
both files.) In his speech, Holifield also
characterized the movement to change the
Atomic Energy Act as "a bold-faced bid to

withdraw from the United States government
the exclusive ownership of bomb-making materials and to make possible the issuance of
restrictive patents to private firms."

12.   Dawson summarizes the major points
of the 1953 hearings.   (*Nuclear Power*, 53-
58.)   The AEC's "Statement of Policy on
Nuclear Power Development," which served as
one of the background documents for the
hearings, was criticized by Holifield on the
House floor on 22 June 1953. This speech is
in Box 79 (June 22, 1953, Speech--Floor,
"Atomic Energy Commission Proposals on
Atomic Power"), HP.   Holifield also gave
another speech on 10 June 1953 in the House,
which is contained in Box 79 (June 10, 1953,
Speech--Floor, "Are We Ready to Give the
Atom to Private Enterprise?"), HP.

13.   29 July 1953, *Congressional Record*, 83rd Cong., 1st sess., vol. 99, 10426-
28.   This speech is also in Box 79 (July 29,
1953, Speech--Floor, "Atomic Power Development"), HP.

14.   House Joint Resolution No. 317 is
printed in 29 July 1953, *Congressional Record*, 83rd Cong., 1st sess., vol. 99, 10427-
28.   It is also summarized in Thomas and
Northrop, *Atomic Energy and Congress*, 148.
In addition, a copy of the resolution is in
Box 52 (H. J. Res. 317), HP.

15.   Aaron B. Wildavsky, *Dixon-Yates:
A Study in Power Politics* (Westport, Con-
necticut: Greenwood Press, 1976), 21.   In
July 1953, there were 221 Republicans in the
House, compared to 210 Democrats.   In the
Senate, there were 48 Republicans, 47 Demo-
crats, and 1 Independent (Wayne Morse of
Oregon).

16.   Lewis L. Strauss, *Men and Decisions* (Garden City, New York: Doubleday and
Company, Inc., 1962), 319; Green and Rosenthal, *Government of the Atom*, 12-13.

17.   Strauss is quoted in Green and
Rosenthal, *Government of the Atom*, 124.

18. Holifield press release, 29 Oct. 1953, Box 79 (October 29, 1953, Speech at the Nat. Indus. Conf. Board Meeting, Re; [*sic*] Atomic Energy Act Changes), HP.

19. Holifield, "Atomic Power Legislation: Remarks Prepared by Honorable Chet Holifield for the Meeting of the Federation of American Scientists, Washington, D.C., November 17, 1953," Box 79 (November 17, 1953, Speech before Federation of American Scientists, Re: Atomic Energy "Give-Away"), HP.

20. Corbin Allardice and Edward R. Trapnell, *The Atomic Energy Commission*, Praeger Library of U. S. Government Departments and Agencies (New York: Praeger Publishers, Inc., 1974), 45; Dawson, *Nuclear Power*, 59-60; Green and Rosenthal, *Government of the Atom*, 124-25; Thomas and Northrop, *Atomic Energy and Congress*, 161. A copy of Eisenhower's 17 Feb. 1954 speech is in Box 41 (Correspondence, White House, 1954), HP.

21. Holifield, "The Hope of Electric Power from Atomic Energy: Address by Congressman Chet Holifield, Member of the Joint Committee on Atomic Energy, to the National Rural Electric Cooperative Association, Miami, Florida, Wednesday, January 13, 1954," Box 79 (January 13, 1954, Speech--NRECA, "The Hope of Electric Power from Atomic Energy"), HP. There is also a separate press release file on this speech. (Box 79 [January 13, 1954, Press Release, "The Hope of Electric Power from Atomic Energy"], HP.

22. Ibid.

23. Ibid.

24. Holifield press release, 1 Mar. 1954, Box 79 (March 1, 1954, Press Release, Re: Atomic Energy Patents), HP.

25. Ibid.

26. Ibid.

27. Green and Rosenthal, *Government of the Atom*, 125.

28. Dawson, *Nuclear Power*, 62, 131; Green and Rosenthal, *Government of the Atom*, 125-26.

29. Holifield press release, 20 Apr. 1954, Box 79 (April 20, 1954, Press Release, <u>Re</u>: Atomic Energy Bill), HP.

30. Green and Rosenthal, *Government of the Atom*, 130, n. 30; 131, n. 31 and n. 32; Dawson, *Nuclear Power*, 62.

31. Dawson, *Nuclear Power*, 62-64.

32. Holifield and Price's minority report on the 1954 act is quoted and discussed in detail by Dawson. (*Nuclear Power*, 68-70.)

33. Quoted in Dawson, *Nuclear Power*, 70. Later, Holifield averred that he "wasn't against the act *per se*. I was against certain things they tried to write into the act." (Holifield interviews by Enid H. Douglass, vol. 2, 121 [see n. 3].)

34. Green and Rosenthal, *Government of the Atom*, 156.

35. Green and Rosenthal provide Table IV-1 regarding "House Roll-Call Votes on H. R. 9757." (*Government of the Atom*, 160.) See also Dawson, *Nuclear Power*, 70-71; 26 July 1954, *Congressional Record*, 83rd Cong., 2d sess., vol. 100, 11697-98.

36. Wildavsky notes that "in June 1954, the Republican party controlled the House by a margin of 219 to 215 and the Senate by 48 to 47, with Senator Wayne Morse of Oregon classifying himself as an independent." (*Dixon-Yates*, 99.)

37. Wildavsky, *Dixon-Yates*, 101-105, 110-11, 114-16. See also Table IV-2, "Key Senate Roll-Call Votes on S. 3690," in Green and Rosenthal, *Government of the Atom*, 162; Dawson, *Nuclear Power*, 70-71.

38. Green and Rosenthal, *Government of the Atom*, 165-66; Dawson, *Nuclear Power*, 71-72.

39. Green and Rosenthal, *Government of the Atom*, 165-66; 9 Aug. 1954, *Congres-*

sional Record, 83rd Cong., 2d sess., vol. 100, 13783-84.

40. 9 Aug. 1954, *Congressional Record*, 83rd Cong., 2d sess., vol. 100, 13784-85. A copy of Holifield and Price's opposition statement on the conference report and a Holifield press release on the subject may be found in Box 79 (August 9, 1954, Statement, Melvin Price and Chet Holifield, Re: Atomic Energy Legislation), and Box 79 (August 9, 1954, Press Release, "Holifield and Price Oppose Conference Bill on Atomic Energy"), HP, respectively.

41. Wildavsky, *Dixon-Yates*, 117; Green and Rosenthal, *Government of the Atom*, 167; Dawson, *Nuclear Power*, 71-72.

42. Dawson, *Nuclear Power*, 72-73; Thomas and Northrop, *Atomic Energy and Congress*, 151-52, 155.

43. The new powers of the Joint Committee under the 1954 act are discussed in Thomas and Northrop, *Atomic Energy and Congress*, 153-56.

CHAPTER 5: PUBLIC POWER FIGHTS BACK

1. Aaron B. Wildavsky, *Dixon-Yates: A Study in Power Politics* (Westport, Connecticut: Greenwood Press, 1976), 6.

2. Ibid., 10-15.

3. Ibid., 8, 15-16.

4. Ibid., 7, 47.

5. Ibid., 42, 48-49.

6. Ibid., 53-54, 59-60, 67, 76-77, 167.

7. Henry D. Smyth and Eugene M. Zuckert to Rowland Hughes, 16 Apr. 1954. A copy of this letter is contained in "Analysis of Dixon-Yates Proposal," a speech delivered by Holifield in the House on 8 July 1954. A typescript of this speech is in Box 79 (July 8, 1954, Speech--Floor, "Analysis of Dixon-Yates Proposal"), HP. See also

Wildavsky, *Dixon-Yates*, 81-82, for a discussion of the letter and 84 for a general discussion of TVA and AEC wrangling over the proposal.

8. Wildavsky, *Dixon-Yates*, 85-86.

9. Holifield mentions his investigation and information requests in his 4 June 1954 prepared statement to JCAE Chairman Cole, calling for an investigation of Dixon-Yates. Congressman Price's name was added in ink after the statement was typed, suggesting that Holifield probably asked Price to join in the statement after it was prepared. See the statement in Box 79 (June 4, 1954--Statement, Re: Atomic Energy Bill), HP. Wildavsky mentions Holifield's 28 May 1954 letter to the General Accounting Office. (*Dixon-Yates*, 87, and 87, n. 31.)

10. Holifield statement, 4 June 1954, typescript, Box 79 (June 4, 1954--Statement, Re: Atomic Energy Bill), HP. Congressman Price's name was added in ink after the statement was typed, signifying probably that Holifield asked Price to join in the statement after it was prepared. Holifield enlisted Price's support on a number of occasions, in projects such as the minority reports on the May-Johnson bill and the 1954 Atomic Energy Act.

11. Wildavsky, *Dixon-Yates*, 99.

12. Ibid., 100.

13. In 1951 and 1952, the AEC worked out a plan in which existing private utilities formed two new corporations, Electric Energy, Inc. and Ohio Valley Electric Corporation, to build additional steam plants to assist the TVA in providing electricity to the Paducah, Kentucky, and Portsmouth, Ohio, installations, respectively. This plan was the result of greatly increased power needs of the AEC because of the outbreak of the Korean War. AEC Commissioner Thomas E. Murray, a Truman appointee, was (ironically enough) the greatest influence behind the

contracts. See Wildavsky, *Dixon-Yates*, 13-14. Holifield provides a fuller discussion in his remarks in the *Congressional Record*. (6 July 1954, *Congressional Record*, 83rd Cong., 2d sess., vol. 100, 9865-66.)

14. Holifield to Ralph H. Demmler, 21 June 1954. A copy of this letter is attached to a Holifield press release on the subject, in Box 79 (June 22, 1954--Press Release, "Holifield Requests Securities and Exchange Commission Investigation of Dixon-Yates Proposal"), HP.

15. 6 July 1954, *Congressional Record*, 83rd Cong., 2d sess., vol. 100, 9865-67.

16. Holifield, "Analysis of Dixon-Yates Proposal," 8 July 1954, floor speech typescript, Box 79 (July 8, 1954, Speech--Floor, "Analysis of Dixon-Yates Proposal"), HP. See also 8 July 1954, *Congressional Record*, 83rd Cong., 2d sess., vol. 100, 9970-77.

17. Holifield interview, 8 Feb. 1982.

18. 21 July 1954, *Congressional Record*, 83rd Cong., 2d sess., vol. 100, 10689. Pages 10687-93 of the *Congressional Record* are in Box 79 (July 21, 1954, Speech--Floor, "The Dixon-Yates Contract"), HP.

19. 21 July 1954, *Congressional Record*, 83rd Cong., 2d sess., vol. 100, 10690.

20. Wildavsky, *Dixon-Yates*, 111-13. See Dawson, *Nuclear Power*, 68-70, for the Holifield-Price minority report.

21. Holifield, "Holifield Asks Full Inquiry on Dixon-Yates Contract," press release, 22 Sept. 1954, Box 79 (September 22, 1954--Press Release, "Holifield Asks Full Inquiry on Dixon-Yates Contract"), HP. See also Wildavsky, *Dixon-Yates*, 126-28.

22. Wildavsky, *Dixon-Yates*, 136-37.

23. Ibid., 137-38.

24. Lois Laycook, "GOP Lines Up to Kill Move: Cancellation Probably Will Start Court Action by Bidders," no newspaper name given, 6 Jan. 1955, newspaper clipping sent

to Holifield from Estes K[efauver], Box 41 (Dixon-Yates #4), HP.

25. Wildavsky, *Dixon-Yates*, 226.

26. Ibid., 225-26; Holifield, "Cancel Dixon-Yates and Restore Unity to the A. E. C.," floor speech typescript, 14 Feb. 1955, Box 79 (February 14, 1955, Speech--Floor, "Cancel Dixon-Yates and Restore Unity to the A. E. C."), HP.

27. Wildavsky, *Dixon-Yates*, 229-31. On page 231, Wildavsky notes that a JCAE staff member bluffed the security officer at the AEC into providing photostatic copies of passes issued to Wenzell. The staff member claimed that Senator Lister Hill (D-Alabama) knew that Wenzell had been there, and that the AEC security officer "would be accused of serious violations of security procedures designed to protect the nation's defense secrets," if the AEC security officer had no proof of Wenzell's visits. According to Holifield, the JCAE staff member, unnamed by Wildavsky, was Frank Cotter, who is now a corporate executive. (Holifield interview, 8 Feb. 1982.) Holifield also names Cotter in his discussion with Enid Douglass. (*Chet Holifield, United States Congressman*, typed transcripts of five tape-recorded interviews by Enid H. Douglass, Oral History Program, Claremont Graduate School, Claremont, California, 1975, vol. 2, 128.) Holifield apparently mispronounces Wenzell's name, which gets "translated" by Douglass as "Adolph Winslow." (See the Dixon-Yates discussion, vol. 2, 123-29.)

28. Wildavsky, *Dixon-Yates*, 237-38, 245-47, 261.

29. Holifield, "Public Agencies and Atomic Power: Address by the Honorable Chet Holifield (D-Calif.), Before the American Public Power Association 12th Annual Convention, Jacksonville, Florida, May 5, 1955," speech typescript, Box 79 (May 5, 1955, Speech--American Public Power Association,

"Public   Agencies and   Atomic   Power"),   HP;
Wildavsky, *Dixon-Yates*, 264.
    30.   Wildavsky,   *Dixon-Yates*,   275-79,
283-88.
    31.   Holifield, "Holifield Urges Appeal
of Dixon-Yates Decision," press release,   n.
d.,   Box 41 (Dixon-Yates #4), HP.   A copy of
Holifield's   speech,   "The Dixon-Yates Decision Should be Appealed," is attached to the
press release.

CHAPTER 6:   SILENT VICTORY

    1.   30 July 1955, *Congressional Record*,
84th Cong., 1st sess., vol. 101, 12198.   See
also   U.S.   Congress,   Joint   Committee   on
Atomic Energy (JCAE), *Providing for a Civilian   Atomic Power Program: A Report to Accompany H. R. 10805*, 84th Cong., 2d sess., 5
July 1956, H. Rept. 2622, 4.
    2.   JCAE, *Accelerating Civilian Reactor
Program: Hearings   on S.   2725 and   H.   R.
10805*,   84th Cong., 2d sess., (May) 1956, 1.
JCAE   Chairman Anderson notes that   S.   2725
and   H.   R.   10805 are identical   bills   and
provides   the text of the bills.   A copy of
H. R. 10805 is in Box 53 (H. R. 10805), HP.
    3.   Frank   G.   Dawson, *Nuclear   Power:
Development   and Management of a   Technology*
(Seattle: University   of Washington Press,
1976), 93-96.   A brief overview of the AEC's
reactor development program is in Richard G.
Hewlett and Francis Duncan, *Atomic   Shield,
1947/1952*, vol. 2 of *A History of the Atomic
Energy Commission* (University Park, Pennsylvania: The   Pennsylvania State   University
Press,   1969),   208-209,   219.   See Dawson,
Nuclear Power, 84-100, for a longer summary.
    4.   Warren   Unna, "Legislating" (1974),
unpublished typescript, 1;   Holifield, H. R.
10805,   84th Cong.,   2d sess., Box 53 (H. R.
10805),   HP;   JCAE, *Accelerating   Civilian
Reactor Program*, 1.

5. The lack of signed contracts from Round One and Round Two of the Power Demonstration Reactor Program was stressed by Holifield as a major reason for his cosponsoring the bill with Senator Gore. (Holifield interview, 8 Feb. 1982.) See Dawson, *Nuclear Power*, 98-100, for a discussion of Round Two and its differences from Round One.

6. Holifield had been concerned with the issue of maintaining American leadership in atomic energy from his earliest days on the JCAE. His strong advocacy of expeditious development of the hydrogen bomb was clear testimony to his belief that the United States must stay ahead of Russia in atomic energy developments. Holifield also maintained the idea of American leadership as a distinct, though secondary theme in many of his speeches and statements against passage of the 1954 act. Holifield and Price's call for a billion-dollar program for atomic power development over five years near the end of the national debate on the 1954 act also presaged Holifield's eventual sponsorship and Price's support of the Gore-Holifield bill. (See 1 June 1953, *Congressional Record*, 83rd Cong., 1st sess., vol. 99, 5858; Holifield, H. J. Res. No. 317, 83rd Cong., 1st sess., Box 52 [H. J. Res. No. 317], HP; 29 July 1953, *Congressional Record*, 83rd Cong., 1st sess., vol. 99, 10426; Holifield press release, 29 Oct. 1953, Box 79 [October 29, 1953, Speech at the Nat. Indus. Conf. Board Meeting, Re; [*sic*] Atomic Energy Act Changes], HP; Holifield and Price, copy of statement [typescript], 9 Aug. 1954, Box 79 [August 9, 1954, Statement, Melvin Price and Chet Holifield, Re: Atomic Energy Legislation], HP; 9 Aug. 1954, *Congressional Record*, 83rd Cong., 2d sess., vol. 100, 13784.)

7. For Democratic dissatisfaction with the AEC's progress in atomic power develop-

ment, see Harold P. Green and Alan Rosenthal, *Government of the Atom: The Integration of Powers* (New York: Atherton Press, 1963), 256. This dissatisfaction is corroborated by Holifield. (Holifield interview, 8 Feb. 1982.) For Holifield's and Anderson's introduction of legislation to curb Strauss's alleged "one-man rule" of the AEC, see Richard Dudman, "2 Democrats Think Time is Ripe to Curb Strauss 'Rule' of AEC," *St. Louis Dispatch*, 23 July 1955, Box 41 (Dixon-Yates #4), HP.

   8. The Report of the Panel on the Impact of the Peaceful Uses of Atomic Energy is mentioned and quoted at length by Robert McKinney, chairman of the panel, in his statement on 28 May 1956 at the hearings on the Gore-Holifield bill. (JCAE, *Accelerating Civilian Reactor Program*, 315.) The panel spent "from the late spring of 1955, until January of 1956" on its study and submitted it to the JCAE in January 1956. (JCAE, *Providing for a Civilian Atomic Power Acceleration Program*, 3.)

   9. 26 Apr. 1956, *Congressional Record*, 84th Cong., 2d sess., vol. 102, 7054, 7056; JCAE, *Accelerating Civilian Reactor Program*, 4; Dawson, *Nuclear Power*, 88.

   10. JCAE, *Accelerating Civilian Reactor Program*, 14-15.

   11. Strauss to JCAE, 18 May 1956, quoted in JCAE, *Providing for a Civilian Atomic Power Acceleration Program*, 4. Strauss's defense of his position is in JCAE, *Accelerating Civilian Reactor Program*, 28-30.

   12. For examples of private industry views on the Gore-Holifield bill, see JCAE, *Accelerating Civilian Reactor Program*, 140, 180, 336, 356. See Dawson, *Nuclear Power*, 102-106, for additional details on the hearings.

   13. JCAE, *Accelerating Civilian Reactor Program*, 165. For examples of views of

public power groups, see JCAE, *Accelerating Civilian Reactor Program*, 259, 445, 485. For a view by a labor organization, see page 165. The JCAE employed Dr. Walter H. Zinn as a part-time consultant on 6 June 1956. Zinn completed a paper for the JCAE on "reactor types that could be given added emphasis in an expanding development program for power reactors," which is included in Appendix 1 of JCAE, *Civilian Atomic Power Acceleration Program: Hearing on the June 26, 1956 Draft of the Gore-Holifield Bill*, 84th Cong., 2d sess., 28 June 1956, 13–19. (This hearing is sometimes referred to as Part 2 of the Gore-Holifield Bill hearings.) See also Zinn's colloquy with Alfred Iddles, president of Babcock and Wilcox. (JCAE, *Accelerating Civilian Reactor Program*, 336.)

14. JCAE, *Civilian Atomic Power Acceleration Program*, 18.

15. Ibid., 10. As reintroduced in Congress, the revised bill (S. 4641/H. R. 12061) retained the phrase "authorized and directed" throughout, similar to the language in the original bills introduced by Gore and Holifield (S. 2725/H. R. 10805). A copy of H. R. 12061 is in Box 53 (H. R. 12061), HP.

16. Holifield's bill, H. R. 12061, in Box 53 (H. R. 12061), HP, shows the date of introduction as June 29, 1956. See also 29 June 1956 *Congressional Record*, 84th Cong., 2d sess., vol. 102, 11509.

17. The texts of the original and revised bills may be compared by consulting JCAE, *Accelerating Civilian Reactor Program*, 1, and JCAE, *Civilian Atomic Power Acceleration Program*, 1–2, respectively. Green and Rosenthal also provide an analysis of the differences between the two bill versions. (*Government of the Atom*, 135, n. 41.)

18. JCAE, *Accelerating Civilian Reactor Program*, 1; JCAE, *Civilian Atomic Power Acceleration Program*, 1–2; Green and Rosen-

thal, *Government of the Atom*, 135, n. 1. In addition, a brief comparison of H. R. 10805 and H. R. 12061 in the Holifield Papers was helpful in identifying the additional programs and provisions appended to the original version. See H. R. 10805 and H. R. 12061 files, Box 53, HP.

19. Green and Rosenthal, *Government of the Atom*, 153 and 153, n. 92. The fact that the bill passed without amendments is confirmed in a letter from Carl Durham to "Dear Colleague," 19 July 1956, Box 41 (1956 Gore), HP. Durham writes that "this bill H. R. 12061 passed the Senate recently without amendment as S. 4641."

20. Holifield to Howard W. Smith, 7 July 1956; Smith to Holifield, 10 July 1956; William M. Colmer to Holifield, 10 July 1956, all in Box 53 (H. R. 12061), HP. Colmer (D-Mississippi) was ranking member on the Rules Committee.

21. Green and Rosenthal, *Government of the Atom*, 154, n. 93.

22. Saylor's "Dear Colleague" letter and attachment, dated July 7, 1956, is in Box 53 (H. R. 12061), HP.

23. Ibid. Representative James E. Van Zandt (R-Pennsylvania), a member of the JCAE, actually used the term "atomic TVAs" to describe the Gore-Holifield efforts during House debate on the bill. (24 July 1956, *Congressional Record*, 84th Cong., 2d sess., vol. 102, 14260.)

24. Durham to "Dear Colleague," 19 July 1956, Box 41 (1956 Gore), HP. The attachment to Durham's letter is in Box 41 (1956 Gore-Holifield fight [*sic*] "Ammunition,")), HP.

25. Green and Rosenthal's statement that "sarcasm is an interrogating tool Mr. Holifield employs often and effectively" could be stated more generically. (*Government of the Atom*, 134, n. 40) Holifield also employed sarcasm very effectively in

many of his speeches, such as in "The Development of Atomic Power (H. R. 12061)," floor speech typescript, 17 July 1956, 1-4, Box 79 (July 17, 1956, Press Release, "The United States Must Lead in Atomic Power Development"), HP.

26. Holifield, "The Development of Atomic Power (H. R. 12061)," 1-4. See also 17 July 1956 *Congressional Record*, 84th Cong., 2d sess., vol. 102, 13195-99.

27. Holifield, "The Development of Atomic Power (H. R. 12061)," 4-8.

28. Ibid., 6-8, 13.

29. Ibid., 15-17.

30. Green and Rosenthal, *Government of the Atom*, 155-56. The debate on the Gore-Holifield bill covers over forty pages of the *Congressional Record*. See 24 July 1956, *Congressional Record*, 84th Cong., 2d sess., vol. 102, 14246-88.

31. 24 July 1956, *Congressional Record*, 84th Cong., 2d sess., vol. 102, 14246-52. The four Republicans were Representatives Saylor (R-Pennsylvania), Bray (R-Indiana), Thomson (R-Wyoming), and Phillips (R-California). Although Phillips did not speak directly to the public power and coal issues initially, he offered a complex amendment later to ensure that the bill would not have a public power orientation. (Ibid., 14282-84.)

32. 24 July 1956, *Congressional Record*, 84th Cong., 2d sess., vol.102, 14249-50, 14252.

33. Ibid., 14253.

34. Other issues presented during the debate included America's leadership in atomic power development, the question of sufficient manpower, and the radiation effects of atomic power plants. With regard to American leadership, see Van Zandt's (R-Pennsylvania) and Flood's (D-Pennsylvania) remarks. (Ibid., 14259, 14262, 14266.) On the manpower issue, see Van Zandt's and

Thomas's (D-Texas) views. (Ibid., 14260, 14264.) On radiation effects, see Representative Saylor's (R-Pennsylvania) remarks. (Ibid., 14264.)

35. 24 July 1956, *Congressional Record*, 84th Cong., 2d sess., vol. 102, 14260, 14262, 14264. The speakers representing similar public power and/or coal views included (particularly) members from the coal-producing states of Pennsylvania, Kentucky, and Ohio. (Ibid., 14261-71.)

36. For amendments to the Gore-Holifield Bill, see 24 July 1956, *Congressional Record*, 84th Cong., 2d sess., vol. 102, 14272-79. Cole's amendment reducing the authorization from $400 million to $50 million was defeated by a voice vote. (Ibid., 14280-81.) For Cannon's attempt to kill the bill, see pages 14276-78. See pages 14287-88 for Van Zandt's motion to recommit the bill.

37. Green and Rosenthal, *Government of the Atom*, 155.

38. 26 July 1956, *Congressional Record*, 84th Cong., 2d sess., vol. 102, 14890-91; 27 July 1956, *Congressional Record*, 84th Cong., 2d sess., vol. 102, 15454. A reprint of Holifield's July 27 speech is in Box 79 (July 27, 1956, Speech--Floor, "Holifield Bill for Peacetime Atomic Power"), HP.

39. 27 July 1956, *Congressional Record*, 84th Cong., 2d sess., vol. 102, 15454.

40. George T. Mazuzan and J. Samuel Walker, *Controlling the Atom: The Beginnings of Nuclear Regulation 1946-1962* (Los Angeles: University of California Press, 1984), 119-120; Green and Rosenthal, *Government of the Atom*, 146, n. 72, and 152, n. 89. Mazuzan and Walker note that "the fate of Price-Anderson in the Eighty-Fourth Congress depended on Congress' decision on the Gore-Holifield legislation."

41. Dawson, *Nuclear Power*, 95, 100-101, 135, and 294, n. 53. The cutoff date

for one reactor type, the homogeneous reactor, was extended to 30 June 1962. See also
Green and Rosenthal, *Government of the Atom*,
16, 257-58. On page 258, Green and Rosenthal note that "the AEC's invitation was
coupled with the indication that it was
prepared to initiate construction of these
reactors as federal projects if industry
could not do the job within the specified
time."

42. Green and Rosenthal, *Government of
the Atom*, 187-88.

43. Atomic Energy Act of 1954, Public
Law 83-703 (68 Stat. 919) (1954), Section
261. The 1946 act had authorized "such sums
as may be necessary and appropriate to carry
out the provisions and purposes of this
act," which was a "blanket authorization"
that meant the AEC could bypass the JCAE and
go directly to the appropriations committees
for funds. See Green and Rosenthal, *Government of the Atom*, 169.

44. Green and Rosenthal, *Government of
the Atom*, 172-73, 175-76.

45. Ibid., 16, 176.

46. JCAE Subcommittee on Legislation,
*Authorizing Legislation for AEC's Fiscal
Year 1958 Construction Budget*, 85th Cong.,
1st sess., 1957, 73; Green and Rosenthal,
Government of the Atom, 177.

47. JCAE, *Congressional Review of
Atomic Power Program*, hearings on 23 May and
10 June 1957, 85th Cong., 1st sess., 1957,
10.

48. Ibid.

49. Ibid., 69-70. Page 40 contains
the quotations by Strauss. In assuring the
JCAE that the AEC would not oppose the legislation being considered, Strauss declared,
"If there is any implication or any feeling
in your mind that we are going to take any
steps to oppose this, let me disabuse you of
that at once." (Ibid., 41.) For the unanimous vote on the authorization bill, see

Green and Rosenthal, *Government of the Atom*, 179.

50. Green and Rosenthal, *Government of the Atom*, 179-80; Dawson, *Nuclear Power*, 108.

51. Dawson, *Nuclear Power*, 108.

52. Green and Rosenthal, *Government of the Atom*, 180.

53. Ibid., 180-81; Dawson, *Nuclear Power*, 108. Holifield described the Russian concentration on dual-purpose reactors in a 1982 interview with the author. (Holifield interview, 8 Feb. 1982.) Dr. Walter Zinn discusses the Canadian, British, and Russian reactor development efforts in JCAE, *Accelerating Civilian Reactor Program*, 333.

54. Green and Rosenthal, *Government of the Atom*, 180-81.

55. Ibid., 181; Dawson, *Nuclear Power*, 108.

56. Green and Rosenthal, *Government of the Atom*, 181-82.

57. Ibid., 182.

58. Ibid., 188.

59. For Holifield's floor speech, see 5 Aug. 1957, *Congressional Record*, 86th Cong., 1st sess., vol. 103, 13685. The legislation Anderson threatened to kill included the government indemnification bill, the International Atomic Energy Agency participation bill, and legislation granting a salary increase to AEC executives. (Green and Rosenthal, *Government of the Atom*, 183.)

60. Dawson, *Nuclear Power*, 108; Green and Rosenthal, *Government of the Atom*, 181.

61. Green and Rosenthal, *Government of the Atom*, 182-85; Dawson, *Nuclear Power*, 108-109.

62. JCAE Subcommittee on Legislation, *AEC Authorizing Legislation: Hearings on Fiscal Year 1959 Authorization Legislation (H. R. 13121)*, 86th Cong., 2d sess., 1958, 4. Fields notes, in answer to a question from Representative Van Zandt, that "the

Commission and the Joint Committee last fall
undertook to hold conversations as well as
committee hearings . . . to determine the
objectives and needs of the program and what
should be the program of the Government in
the civilian power field."
    63. Green and Rosenthal, *Government of
the Atom*, 188-89.
    64. Ibid., 189-90.
    65. Ibid., 192-93.

CHAPTER 7: TO WASTE ENERGY OR NOT

    1. Even during one of the House de-
bates on the proposed Hanford steam plant,
Holifield made clear the importance he
placed on compromise: "Mr. Speaker, we, who
practice the art of legislating, know that
reasoned compromise is the single most important ingredient in successful legislative
activity." (8 Aug. 1961, *Congressional
Record*, 87th Cong., 1st sess., vol. 107,
14953.)
    2. Harold P. Green and Alan Rosenthal,
*Government of the Atom: The Integration of
Powers* (New York: Atherton Press, 1963),
189. Dawson incorrectly cites the cost of
the convertibility feature as $20 million,
instead of $25 million. (Frank G. Dawson,
*Nuclear Power: Development and Management
of a Technology* [Seattle: University of
Washington Press, 1976], 110.) The dual-
purpose reactor itself, as opposed to the
controversy surrounding it, was born in the
Fiscal Year 1958 AEC authorization bill,
which authorized $3 million for the AEC to
conduct a development-design and engineering
study for a plutonium-production reactor,
either single-purpose (plutonium production
only) or dual-purpose (plutonium and electricity production). The Fiscal Year 1959
authorization bill authorized $145 million
for actual construction of the reactor and

facilities, including the dual-purpose aspect, and triggered the controversy. Although Green and Rosenthal (*Government of
the Atom*, 239) credit Senator Henry M. Jackson (D-Washington) with first proposing in
1956 a dual-purpose reactor for the Hanford
AEC facility, Holifield also had long been a
supporter of the dual-purpose reactor concept and was chief legislative architect of
the proposal as chairman of the JCAE and,
earlier, as chairman of the JCAE Subcommittee on Legislation. In an interview, Holifield maintained that the dual-purpose reactor was held up for three years because of
opposition from private power interests.
(Holifield interview, 8 Feb. 1982.)

3. Dawson, *Nuclear Power*, 112-13.
4. Green and Rosenthal, *Government of
the Atom*, 189, 192-93.
5. The studies mentioned are included
in a JCAE committee print. (JCAE, *Power
Conversion Studies: Hanford New Production
Reactor*, 87th Cong., 1st sess., [March]
1961.) See page XII of the committee print
for a summary. See also Green and Rosenthal, *Government of the Atom*, 262-63.
6. JCAE, *AEC Authorizing Legislation
Fiscal Year 1962*, 87th Cong., 1st sess., 21
June 1961, H. Rept. 562, 6-11.
7. Holifield emphasized the practical
concern of saving the New Production Reactor's waste steam many times during speeches
and debates on the proposed Hanford steam
plant. (*Congressional Record*, 87th Cong.,
1st and 2d sess.: 13 July 1961, vol. 107,
12441, 12448, 12455; 13 July 1962, vol.
108, 13508; 17 July 1962, vol. 108, 12836;
12 Sept. 1962, daily edition, 12836, and 14
Sept. 1962, daily edition, 18133, 18135,
both in Box 54 (H. R. 7576), HP.
8. Holifield to "Dear Colleague," 7
July 1961, Box 54 (H. R. 7576), HP. Holifield makes reference to "the five Republican Members who signed the minority report."

9. The minority report   is included in the JCAE report on H. R.   7576.   (JCAE, *AEC Authorizing Legislation Fiscal Year 1962.*) See   also Holifield's "Analysis of Minority Objections   to Project for Installing Electric Generating Facilities for the Hanford, Washington, New Production Reactor in AEC Authorization Bill for Fiscal Year 1962," attached to Holifield's letter, Holifield to "Dear Colleague," 7 July 1961, Box 54 (H. R. 7576), HP.   Holifield's analysis of the opposition's ten points was the subject of one of his presentations on the House floor in July 1961.   (10 July 1961, *Congressional Record*,   87th Cong.,   1st sess.,   vol. 107, 12239-42.)

10. 13 July 1961, *Congressional Record*, 87th Cong., 1st sess., vol. 107, 12441.

11. Ibid., 12443-44.

12. Ibid., 12452, 12471. The remark about congressional "steam" was made by Representative Hechler of West Virginia.

13. Van Zandt noted the Senate amendments in a history of the Fiscal Year 1962 authorization bill he presented on 13 Sept. 1961 during House consideration of the conference version of the bill.   (13 Sept. 1961, *Congressional Record*, 87th Cong., 1st sess., vol. 107, 19214.) The Senate vote was fifty-four to thirty-six in favor of the Hanford project.   See Van Zandt's and Holifield's discussions of the Senate bill, respectively, in 8 Aug. 1961 *Congressional Record*, 87th Cong., 1st sess., vol. 107, 14949, and 13 Sept. 1961, 19213-14.

14. The conferencing tradition and its effect on the authorization bill are explained by Minority leader Charles Halleck (R-Indiana) and Representative Brown (R-Ohio) in 25 July 1961, *Congressional Record*, 87th Cong., 1st sess., vol. 107, 13386, and 8 Aug. 1961, 14947-48. Van Zandt also discussed the subject in 8 Aug. 1961, 14949.

15. 25 July 1961, *Congressional Record*, 87th Cong., 1st sess., vol. 107, 13386. That the Rules Committee had to deal with the impasse brought about by Halleck's objection to Holifield's request for a conference is related by Representative Brown (R-Ohio), a member of the Rules Committee. (8 Aug. 1961, *Congressional Record*, 87th Cong., 1st sess., vol. 107, 14947.)

16. 8 Aug. 1961, *Congressional Record*, 87th Cong., 1st sess., vol. 107, 14947.

17. Ibid., 14949-50, 14950, 14954, 14951, 14950, and 14954-55 for remarks of Van Zandt, Halleck, Hosmer, Bates, McCormack, and Cannon, respectively. See page 14953 for Holifield's comment and page 14958 for the vote.

18. 13 July 1961, *Congressional Record*, 87th Cong., 1st sess., vol. 107, 12443. Van Zandt's and Holifield's dispute over the word "incidental" was semantical but central to their positions. As part of its background philosophy, the 1954 act permitted the production of power by the AEC as long as it was *incidental* to the production of plutonium or to AEC operations in other areas. Van Zandt interpreted the word to mean "insignificant" or "minor," while Holifield took it to mean "likely to happen as a result of." Both definitions are equally valid semantically. Hence, Van Zandt argued that the Hanford project was not in keeping with the 1954 act because production of Hanford power would not be a *minor* (800,000 kilowatts was not minor) by-product of the production of plutonium, while Holifield argued that the Hanford project was consistent with the act because the power was a *natural result* of the design of the New Production Reactor and of the production of plutonium by the reactor.

19. 31 Aug. 1961, *Congressional Record*, 87th Cong., 1st sess., vol. 107, 17863.

20. The conference report on H. R. 7576 (H. Rept. 1101, 31 Aug. 1961) is reprinted in 13 Sept. 1961, *Congressional Record*, 87th Cong., 1st sess., vol. 107, 19209-13.

21. Van Zandt notes that he and Senator Hickenlooper refused to sign the conference report in 13 Sept. 1961, *Congressional Record*, 87th Cong., 1st sess., vol. 107, 19215. Holifield mentions Van Zandt's letter in 13 Sept. 1961, *Congressional Record*, 87th Cong., 1st sess., vol. 107, 19214.

22. 13 Sept. 1961, *Congressional Record*, 87th Cong., 1st sess., vol. 107, 12913-14.

23. Ibid., 12915.

24. Ibid., 12917-20. In answer to Van Zandt's assertion that Congress would never adjourn without an AEC authorization bill, Melvin Price (D-Illinois) replied, "I say he [Van Zandt] can give no such guarantee."

25. 17 July 1962, *Congressional Record*, 87th Cong., 2d sess., vol. 108, 12828.

26. For additional background on the new Hanford financing proposal, see Bonnie Baack Pendergrass, *Public Power Politics and Technology in the Eisenhower and Kennedy Years: The Hanford Dual-Purpose Reactor Controversy, 1956-1962* (New York: Arno Press, 1979), 127-37. A JCAE document ("Analysis of Committee Amendments to H. R. 11974 . . ."), reprinted in 13 July 1962 *Congressional Record*, 87th Cong., 2d sess., vol. 108, 13509, lists the date of the comptroller general's opinion as 7 July 1962, but Holifield referred to "Friday, July 6, 1962" as the date when he announced hearings on the new proposal. (17 July 1962, *Congressional Record*, 87th Cong., 2d sess., vol. 108, 12829.)

27. JCAE, *Utility Proposal for Power-plant Addition to Hanford New Production Reactor*, hearings on 1962 proposed Hanford project, 87th Cong., 2d sess., (July) 1962,

8-9, provides a good discussion of the WPPSS proposal. See also the JCAE committee print, *Utility Proposal for Powerplant Addition to Hanford New Production Reactor*, 87th Cong., 2d sess., (July) 1962, for an in-depth consideration of the proposal. Holifield describes the proposal and provides descriptive JCAE documents in 13 July 1962, *Congressional Record*, 87th Cong., 2d sess., vol. 108, 13505-12.

28. Both Hosmer and Bates vigorously opposed the 1961 Hanford proposal but expressed support for the 1962 alternative. (13 July 1961, *Congressional Record*, 87th Cong., 1st sess., vol. 107, 12449-51; 17 July 1962, *Congressional Record*, 87th Cong., 2d sess., vol. 108, 12830, 12843.) Holifield acknowledged that there was only one JCAE opponent of the 1962 Hanford proposal [Van Zandt] in 12 Sept. 1962, *Congressional Record*, daily edition, 87th Cong., 2d sess., vol. 108, 18135, Box 54 (H. R. 11974), HP.

29. The JCAE committee print is JCAE, *Utility Proposal for Powerplant Addition to Hanford New Production Reactor*, Box 54 (H. R. 11733), HP. (H. R. 11733 is an older version of H. R. 11974.) For Holifield's placement of the important documents in the *Congressional Record*, see 13 July 1962, *Congressional Record*, 87th Cong., 2d sess., vol. 108, 13505-12. It was with not-a-little sarcasm that Holifield built his justification of the proposal around ten points, as Van Zandt had done for the opposition the year before. (See page 13508 for Holifield's "10 points.")

30. A copy of the press release entitled "President Kennedy Endorses Utility Proposal for Construction of Hanford Electric Plant," together with a copy of the letter to Holifield from Kennedy, is in Box 54 (H. R. 11974), HP. Holifield placed the letter addressed to him from Charles Luce in the *Congressional Record* during the first

floor debate on the 1962 Hanford proposal. He noted that he had sought the letter from Luce. (17 July 1962, *Congressional Record*, 87th Cong., 2d sess., vol. 108, 12831.) For Holifield's letter to his colleagues, see Holifield to "Dear Colleague," 16 July 1962, Box 54 (H. R. 11974), HP.

31. Holifield to "Dear Colleague," 16 July 1962.

32. See 17 July 1962, *Congressional Record*, 87th Cong., 2d sess., vol. 108, 12831, 12833, 12836 for Holifield's comments. For Van Zandt's arguments, see page 12838. The vote is given on pages 12860-61.

33. Holifield received letters of regret but appreciation for his efforts from such notables as J. R. Wiggins, editor of the *Washington Post*, and Alex Radin, head of the American Public Power Association. (Wiggins to Holifield, 26 July 1962, and Radin to Holifield, 23 July 1962, both in Box 54 [H. R. 11974], HP.)

34. Following Senate passage of the new Hanford proposal, Senator John O. Pastore (D-Rhode Island), vice-chairman of the JCAE, formally made the motion for a conference with the House and appointment of conferees. (1 Aug. 1962, *Congressional Record* 87th Cong., 2d sess., vol. 108, 15236.) In his brochure, Representative Craig Hosmer (R-California) declared that his colleagues could "just blame me and the other Joint Committee members for not making the difference between Hanford *1961* and Hanford *1962* clear during debate!" and that his colleagues "could have been mislead [*sic*] because we couldn't unravel these complications during 5-minute rule debate." A copy of the brochure ("Dear Colleague, Only the Name's the Same"), dated 28 Aug. 1962, is in Box 54 (H. R. 11974), HP.

35. 29 Aug. 1962, *Congressional Record*, 87th Cong., 2d sess., vol. 108, 18029-30.

36. The conference committee's compromise is contained in an attachment to a letter from Holifield to his House colleagues. (Holifield to "Dear Colleague," 12 Sept. 1962, Box 54 [H. R. 11974], HP.) Van Zandt was appointed as one of the conferees. (29 Aug. 1962, *Congressional Record*, 87th Cong., 2d sess., vol. 108, 18036.) His name, however, does not appear on the "Statement by Managers on the Part of the House, from Conference Report on Atomic Energy Authorization Bill (H. R. 11974)," the attachment to Holifield's 12 Sept. 1962 letter to his colleagues, because Van Zandt refused to sign the conference report.

37. Holifield mentions placing the conference report in the *Congressional Record* on 11 Sept. 1962. (12 Sept. 1962, *Congressional Record*, 87th Cong., 2d sess., daily edition, 18135, Box 54 [H. R. 11974], HP.) The Holifield quotations are contained in Holifield to "Dear Colleague," 12 Sept. 1962.

38. 12 Sept. 1962, *Congressional Record*, 87th Cong., 2d sess., daily edition, 18129-35, Box 54 (H. R. 11974), HP.

39. 14 Sept. 1962, *Congressional Record*, 87th Cong., 2d sess., daily edition, 18373-81, Box 54 (H. R. 11974), HP. For Senate approval of the conference report, see 18 Sept. 1962, *Congressional Record*, 87th Cong., 2d sess., vol. 108, 19759.

40. 14 Sept. 1962, *Congressional Record*, 87th Cong., 2d sess., daily edition, Box 54 (H. R. 11974), HP.

41. Dawson, *Nuclear Power*, 112-14; Holifield interview, 8 Feb. 1982. In an attachment to a personal communication to the author (21 Mar. 1989), Holifield notes that "the plant is still operating, (1989) 21 years."

42. According to Dawson, the Washington Public Power Supply System was ultimately comprised of five private utilities

and seventy-one public utilities.   (*Nuclear Power*, 113.)

CHAPTER 8:   ATOMIC ENERGY AND PUBLIC SAFETY

1.   Richard G. Hewlett and Francis Duncan, *Atomic Shield, 1947/1952*, vol. 2 of *A History of the Atomic Energy Commission* (University Park, Pennsylvania: The Pennsylvania State University Press, 1969), 179, 352.

2.   24 Feb. 1949, *Congressional Record*, 81st Cong., 1st sess., daily edition, 1536-37, Box 79 (February 24, 1949, Speech-- Floor, "Atomic Warfare Leaves Mankind Nowhere to Hide"), HP.

3.   Ibid., 1536.

4.   Ibid., 1537;   Holifield, speech typescript, 25 Feb. 1949, Box 79 (February 25, 1949, Speech on WOL, "Mutual Newsreel of the Air, *Re* A-Bombs"), HP.

5.   Holifield, H. J. Res. 419, 81st Cong., 2d sess., 20 Feb. 1950, Box 51 (Alternate Capitol), HP;   H. J. Res. 259, 82d Cong., 1st sess., 15 May 1951, Box 52 (H. J. Res. 259), HP.   For Holifield quotation, see memorandum, Holifield to Committee on the Judiciary, 15 May 1951, Box 52 (H. J. Res. 259), HP.   Of the seemingly imminent possibility of a nuclear war, Holifield declared that "the problem of maintaining the continuity of Federal government operations in the event of a catastrophic attack . . . has given us anxious concern for many months," and that "it has caused me many sleepless nights." (Memorandum, Holifield to Committee on the Judiciary, 15 May 1951;   Holifield, "Statement by Congressman Holifield Before the Bryson Subcommittee Number Three, Judiciary Committee, on H. J. Res. 259 [Holifield]," Box 52 [H. J. Res. 259], HP.)

6.   Holifield mentions the JCAE hearings on civilian defense in a speech en-

titled "Civilian Defense," n.d., 3, Box 52 (H. J. Res. 259), HP.

7. Robert A. Divine, *Blowing on the Wind: The Nuclear Test Ban Debate, 1954-1960* (New York: Oxford University Press, 1978), 4-5, 7-8, 13.

8. Holifield, "Power of 1952 Model Hydrogen Bomb," 12 Apr. 1954, 1, Box 79 (April 12, 1954, Speech--Floor, "Power of Model Hydrogen Bomb"), HP; Holifield, "Tell the People the Facts About the Atomic-Hydrogen Weapons," typescript, 29 Mar. 1954, 5-6, Box 79 (March 29, 1954, Speech--Floor, "Tell the People the Facts About the Atomic-Hydrogen Weapons"), HP; Holifield, press release on civil defense, 30 Mar. 1954, Box 79 (March 30, 1954, Press Release, Re: Civil Defense"), HP.

9. Holifield, H. J. Res. 491, 83d Cong., 2d sess., 12 Apr. 1954, Box 52 (H. J. Res. 491), HP. (Holifield reintroduced the legislation in 1955. See Holifield, H. J. Res. 98, 84th Cong., 1st sess., 6 Jan. 1955, Box 53 [H. J. Res. 98], HP.); Holifield to "Dear Colleague," 9 Apr. 1954, Box 52 (H. J. Res. 491), HP; Holifield, H. J. Res. 525, 83d Cong., 2d sess., 13 May 1954, Box 52 (H. J. Res. 525), HP. Holifield confined a later piece of legislation to replacement of representatives only. (Holifield, H. J. Res. 322, 84th Cong., 1st sess., 26 May 1955, Box 53 [H. J. Res. 322], HP.)

10. Holifield, "The Challenge of Atomic Energy: Address Before the Dinner Meeting of the Democratic Club for the 10th District of Virginia, Hunting Towers, Alexandria, Virginia, Tuesday, January 18, 1955," Box 79 (January 18, 1955, Speech Before Democratic Club, Alexandria, Va., "The Challenge of Atomic Energy"), HP.

11. Holifield, "Civilian Defense--A Federal Obligation in the Atomic-Hydrogen Age: Address Before the National Security Commission of the American Legion, Washing-

ton, D.C., Saturday, January 29, 1955," Box 79 (January 29, 1955, Speech--Before the American Legion, "Civilian Defense--A Federal Obligation in the Atomic-Hydrogen Age"), HP. For a summary of the speech, see Warren Unna, "Full-Time Civil Defense Corps Urged," *Washington Post and Times Herald*, 30 Jan. 1955, sec. A, 9, Box 52 (Civil Defense Legislation), HP.

12. Holifield, "Administration has Woefully Failed the American People in Civilian Defense," press release, 15 June 1955, Box 79 (June 15, 1955, Press Release, "Administration has Woefully Failed the American People in Civilian Defense"), HP.

13. Holifield, typescript of untitled opening statement of Subcommittee Chairman Holifield before members of the House Subcommittee on Military Operations, 31 Jan. 1956, Box 79 (January 31, 1955 [*sic*], Statement--Re: Civil Defense), HP.

14. Ibid.

15. Holifield, "Congress Looks at Civil Defense: Address Before the National Medical Civil Defense Conference Sponsored by the Council on National Defense of the American Medical Association, Chicago, Illinois, June 9, 1956," Box 79 (June 9, 1956, Speech--AMA, "Congress Looks at Civil Defense"), HP; Holifield, "Civil Defense for National Survival--Report of the Holifield Subcommittee," floor speech reprint from *Congressional Record*, 27 July 1956, Box 79 (July 27, 1956, Speech--Floor, "Civil Defense for National Survival"), HP; Holifield, "Holifield Subcommittee Issues Civil Defense Report," press release, 26 July 1956, Box 79 (July 26, 1956, press release, "Holifield Subcommittee Issues Civil Defense Report"), HP.

16. Holifield, "Holifield Subcommittee Issues Civil Defense Report"; Holifield, "Congressional Report on Civil Defense: Address Before the County Medical Societies

Civil Defense Conference Sponsored by the Council on National Defense of the American Medical Association, Chicago, Illinois, November 10, 1956," 7, 19, Box 79 (November 10, 1956, Speech before County Medical Societies CD Conference, "Congressional Report on Civil Defense"), HP.

17. Holifield, "Holifield Subcommittee Issues Civil Defense Report."

18. Holifield, "Congressional Report on Civil Defense," 12–13.

19. Ibid., 20. The Holifield bill mentioned is H. R. 2125, 85th Cong., 1st sess., Jan. 1957. See 20 May 1957, *Congressional Record*, 85th Cong., 1st sess., daily edition, Box 53 (H. R. 7623), HP, for Holifield's support of school-shelter construction.

20. "New Frontier's Backyard Shelters Another Case of 'Warmed Over Eisenhower,'" *I. F. Stone's Weekly*, 23 Oct. 1961, 2, Box 42 (Civil Defense 1961), HP.

21. For good discussions of Holifield's 1957 and 1959 hearings, see George T. Mazuzan and J. Samuel Walker, *Controlling the Atom: The Beginnings of Nuclear Regulation 1946–1962* (Los Angeles: University of California Press, 1984), 48–53, 255–56; Divine, *Blowing on the Wind*, 129–38, 271–77. For the various facets of the growing radiation issue, see Divine, *Blowing on the Wind*, 27, 38, 55–56, 78–79, 86, 110.

22. Divine, *Blowing on the Wind*, 85; Warren Unna, "Atomic Energy" (1974), unpublished typescript, 27; Holifield, "Congressional Hearings on Radioactive Fallout," typescript draft of an article for *Bulletin of the Atomic Scientists*, 3 Sept. 1957, Box 41 (1959 Fallout), HP.

23. For Durham's remarks, see 24 July 1956, *Congressional Record*, 84th Cong., 2d sess., vol. 102, 14271. Durham made the comment during debate on the Gore-Holifield bill. For Holifield's appointment as sub-

committee chairman, see Holifield, "Congressional Hearings on Radioactive Fallout," 2. Holifield discusses the hearings in *Chet Holifield, United States Congressman*, typed transcripts of five tape-recorded interviews by Enid H. Douglass, Oral History Program, Claremont Graduate School, Claremont, California, 1975, vol. 3, 56-57.

24. "Scientists and Reporters," *The Reporter* 16 (May 1957):27-28, Box 44 (1966), HP. See also Divine, *Blowing on the Wind*, 129; Holifield, "Congressional Hearings on Radioactive Fallout," 2-3.

25. Holifield, "Congressional Hearings on Radioactive Fallout," 4.

26. Divine, *Blowing on the Wind*, 129; Holifield, "Congressional Hearings on Radioactive Fallout," 4-6.

27. Holifield, typescript of untitled floor speech, 25 July 1956, Box 79 (July 25, 1956, Press Release, Speech of CH on floor RE Atomic Energy), HP; Divine, *Blowing on the Wind*, 130-32, 137-38.

28. Mazuzan and Walker, *Controlling the Atom*, 48-53; Divine, *Blowing on the Wind*, 131-35; Holifield, "Congressional Hearings on Radioactive Fallout," 4-6.

29. Divine, *Blowing on the Wind*, 131, 137-38; Holifield, "Who Should Judge the Atom," *Saturday Review* (3 Aug. 1957):34-37.

30. Holifield, "Congressional Hearings on Radioactive Fallout," 8-10.

31. Divine, *Blowing on the Wind*, 210-11, 215, 269.

32. Ibid., 229-30, 238, 263-67.

33. JCAE, *Fallout from Nuclear Weapons Tests: Summary-Analysis of Hearings, May 5-8, 1959*, 86th Cong., 1st sess., (August) 1959, Committee Print, 1. See Mazuzan and Walker, *Controlling the Atom*, 255-56, for a good summary of the 1959 hearings.

34. Holifield to Eli Isenberg, 18 May 1959, Box 41 (Atomic Energy 1956-60 Misc.), HP.

35. JCAE, *Fallout from Nuclear Weapons Tests*, 3; Holifield to (California Assemblyman) George E. Brown, 25 June 1959, Box 41 (Atomic Energy 1956-60 Misc.), HP.

36. Divine, *Blowing on the Wind*, 272, 277, and 362, n. 21.

37. Holifield to Eli Isenberg, 18 May 1959.

38. JCAE, *Fallout from Nuclear Weapons Tests*, 1, 5-8 (the quotation is taken from page 7); See also Divine, *Blowing on the Wind*, 186.

39. Ibid., 5-8.

40. Ibid., 8-9.

41. Divine, *Blowing on the Wind*, 271, 277-78.

42. Ibid., 265-66; "Plan to Give States Authority for Radiation Safety Outlined: Rep. Holifield Discloses at Canisius Workshop a Program to Transfer Responsibility from AEC," *Buffalo Evening News*, 9 June 1959, Box 41 (1959), HP.

43. Divine, *Blowing on the Wind*, 270, 278; "Plan to Give States Authority for Radiation Safety Outlined."

44. Holifield to Eli Isenberg, 18 May 1959.

45. Holifield to George E. Brown, 25 June 1959.

46. "New Frontier's Backyard Shelters Another Case of 'Warmed Over Eisenhower,'" 2.

47. Holifield to the author, 19 Feb. 1980 (pers. comm.). President Johnson served on the JCAE as a House member during the Eightieth Congress (1947-1948) and as a Senate member during the Eighty-second Congress (1951-1952). See Corbin Allardice and Edward R. Trapnell, *The Atomic Energy Commission*, Praeger Library of U. S. Government Departments and Agencies (New York: Praeger Publishers, Inc., 1974), 220.

48. Holifield's first letter to Kennedy could not be located. It is mentioned,

however, in Holifield to Lawrence O'Brien, 8 May 1961, Box 42 (Civil Defense: Exec. Branch Communications, 1961-63), HP. For Holifield's "talk and test" strategy, see David Burnham, "Holifield to Scan 'Lag' in A-Test Detection," *Washington Post*, 5 July 1961; "Holifield Favors 'Talk and Test' Atom Policy," *Los Angeles Times*, 28 Aug. 1961; "Congress Chiefs Back Atom Tests," *Los Angeles Examiner*, 6 Sept. 1961, all in Box 42 (1961 Nuclear Testing), HP. Holifield discusses his views on nuclear testing in detail in a three-page letter to Representative Leonard Farbstein regarding a letter to Farbstein from the chairman of the Greenwich Village Committee for a Sane Nuclear Policy and in a three-page letter to Jerry Littman, editor of the *East Los Angeles Gazette*. (Holifield to Farbstein, 5 Feb. 1960, Box 41 [Atomic Energy 1956-60 Misc.], HP; Holifield to Littman, 18 Sept. 1962, Box 42 [1962 Nuclear Test Ban], HP.)

49. Theodore C. Sorenson, *Kennedy* (New York: Bantam Books, 1966), 691-92; Holifield, "Remarks on Civil Defense Excerpted from President Kennedy's Special Message on Urgent National Needs, May 25, 1961," (typescript) attachment to Holifield to Sorenson, 7 June 1961, Box 42 (Civil Defense: Exec. Branch Communications 1961-63), HP.

50. Holifield to Sorenson, 7 June 1961, Box 42 (Civil Defense: Exec. Branch Communications, 1961-63), HP. The letter to Sorenson is over three pages long, typed single-spaced, with a two-page attachment.

51. For Holifield's support of Frank B. Ellis, see "Holifield Urges Vast U. S. Shelter Program," *Los Angeles Times*, 8 July 1961, Part I, 3; "$20 Billion Atom Shelter Fund Asked," *Los Angeles Examiner*, 8 July 1961, both in Box 42 (Holifield Civil Defense Speeches; Statements 1961-63), HP. The quotation from Holifield's floor speech is taken from 17 July 1961, *Congressional*

Record, 87th Cong., 1st sess., daily edition, 11821, Box 42 (Holifield Civil Defense Speeches; Statements 1961-63), HP. On the civil defense hearings, see Richard Fryklund, "How Worthwhile is Civil Defense? Government Studies Experts' Views," *The Evening Star*, 12 Aug. 1961, sec. A, 11, Box 42 (Civil Defense 1961), HP. The citation for the actual hearings is House Committee on Government Operations, Subcommittee on Military Operations, *Civil Defense 1961*, 87th Cong., 1st sess., 1961. In Holifield, "The Political Arena: Solon Outlines Steps for Civil Defense Plan," *Los Angeles Examiner*, 6 Sept. 1961, Box 42 (Civil Defense 1961), HP, Holifield rounds off the shelter figure to nineteen billion dollars.

52. Sorenson, *Kennedy*, 692-93; Holifield to President John F. Kennedy, 14 Nov. 1961, Box 42 (Civil Defense: Exec. Branch Communications 1961-63), HP.

53. 30 July 1962, *Congressional Record*, 87th Cong., 2d sess., daily edition, 13995-96, Box 42 (Civil Defense: Exec. Branch Communications 1961-63), HP; Leon H. Weaver, *The Civil Defense Debate: Differing Perceptions of a Persistent Issue in National Security Policy* (East Lansing, Michigan: Michigan State University Press, 1967), 2.

54. Holifield to President John F. Kennedy, 8 Feb. 1963, Box 42 (Civil Defense: Exec. Branch Communications 1961-63), HP. At the top of his copy of the letter, Holifield wrote: "Letter requests the President to take certain actions with Vinson and Thomas on a personal contact basis. Publication would nullify the chance of him taking such informal action--and therefore defeat the purpose of the letter."

55. Holifield to Colonel Albert E. Stoltz, 17 Jan. 1963 and 26 March 1963, both in Box 42 (Civil Defense 1963), HP.

56. Sorenson, *Kennedy*, 695.

57. "Holifield Urges More Shelters, Cutback of Space Exploration," *San Jose Mercury*, 17 Apr. 1963, Box 42 (Civil Defense 1963), HP.

58. Holifield to Stoltz, 19 Aug. 1963, Box 42 (Civil Defense 1963), HP; "House Passes First Measure to Construct Fallout Shelters," *Washington Municipal News*, 30 Sept. 1963, 3-4, Box 42 (Civil Defense 1963), HP; Weaver, *Civil Defense Debate*, 3-6.

59. Holifield to Stoltz, 19 Aug. 1963.

60. Holifield, "Nuclear Test Ban," press release, 24 July 1963, Box 43 (1963 Nuclear Test Ban #2), HP.

61. Holifield had repeatedly complained, as discussed in this chapter, of the general apathy of the president, the Pentagon, and the public regarding civil defense issues. Even Divine speaks of the on-again, off-again interest of the public on the hazards of nuclear testing. (*Blowing on the Wind*, 27.) Holifield would probably not agree that his view of civil defense had shifted, but in later years, he appears to emphasize the impossibility of civil defense. In 1975, for example, he claimed that "I knew that civil defense could not be effective in a nuclear war." (Holifield interviews by Enid H. Douglass, vol. 3, 61 [see n. 23].) In 1989, Holifield asserted that the reason for his advocacy of civil defense was "to prove [that] 'civil defense of population' was imposible [*sic*]." (Holifield to the author, 21 Mar. 1989 [pers. comm.].) With regard to changes from the Kennedy administration to the Johnson administration, Weaver notes "The Johnson-McNamara approach to civil defense can therefore be summarized as a low-key continuation of Kennedy administration programs." Weaver does allow, however, that Johnson extended the fallout shelter identification program to private homes and other small

structures, and proposed a ten-million-dollar experimental program of subsidizing incremental costs (up to 1 percent of total costs) of fallout shelters in new private buildings and public school buildings in those areas where existing shelters would not house all of the population. (*Civil Defense Debate*, 7.) As such, Johnson's programs appear to be a concession to Holifield for the congressman's efforts in this field. Weaver also notes that "Congress has not, however, seen fit to appropriate money for this experimental program [as of 1966]." Holifield's influence in civil defense had already diminished during the Kennedy administration when the president in effect brought civil defense under the jurisdiction of the House Armed Services Committee by transferring civil defense to the Department of Defense during his reorganization of civil defense functions.

62. Holifield interview, 8 Feb. 1982. Dawson died in September 1970, and Holifield ascended to the chairmanship of the Committee on Government Operations in November 1970 as a result.

63. Box 30, HP, contains files on the Department of Housing and Urban Development and Department of Transportation bills. See also House Committee on Government Operations, *Department of Housing and Urban Development: Report to Accompany H. R. 6927*, 89th Cong., 1st sess., 1965, H. Rept. 884. This is the conference report on the bill.

CHAPTER 9: DEFENDER OF THE FAITHS

1. ˙Elizabeth Rolph, *Nuclear Power and the Public Safety: A Study in Regulation* (Lexington, Massachusetts: D. C. Heath and Company, 1979), 101.

2. Holifield is referred to or included implicitly as a member of the "Atomic

Establishment" by several authors sympathetic to environmentalism. Ralph Nader and John Abbotts write that "Chet Holifield and [AEC Commissioner] James T. Ramey represented the classic characteristics of the old 'Atomic Establishment.'" (*The Menace of Atomic Energy* [New York: W. W. Norton and Company, 1977], 272.) Richard S. Lewis implicitly includes Holifield as a member of the "Atomic Establishment" and writes that "eventually, the Congressional Joint Committee on Atomic Energy became its board of directors." (*The Nuclear-Power Rebellion: Citizens Vs. the Atomic Industrial Establishment* [New York: The Viking Press, 1972], 14, 269.) H. Peter Metzger also includes Holifield as a member of the "Atomic Establishment." (*The Atomic Establishment* [New York: Simon and Schuster, 1972], 1.)

3. Rolph, *Nuclear Power and the Public Safety*, 101-102; Frank G. Dawson, *Nuclear Power: Development and Management of a Technology* (Seattle: University of Washington Press, 1976), 198-99.

4. Rolph, *Nuclear Power and the Public Safety*, 22-23; Dawson, *Nuclear Power*, 176. It is somewhat ironic that there are so many references to "health and safety" in the 1954 act, since Rolph notes that "no questions regarding the possible safety hazards of nuclear technology were ever explored in the hearings and there were no discussions of what might constitute an acceptable 'level of risk.'" Rolph also points out that "since Congress chose not to define 'adequate protection' or 'undue risk,' that job fell to the AEC." (*Nuclear Power and the Public Safety*, 28-29.) Safety issues were mentioned in the Gore-Holifield bill debate in the House, but only by opponents of the bill, who used the safety issue as a one of their minor reasons for opposing the bill. (14 July 1956, *Congressional Record*,

84th Cong., 2d sess., vol. 102, 14262-64, 14266.)

5. George T. Mazuzan and J. Samuel Walker, *Controlling the Atom: The Beginnings of Nuclear Regulation 1946-1962* (Los Angeles: University of California Press, 1984), 122-82, provide the best, in-depth review of the controversy surrounding the Fermi plant. Dawson and Rolph also discuss the Fermi reactor incident in detail. (Dawson, *Nuclear Power*, 192-94; Rolph, *Nuclear Power and the Public Safety*, 38-42.) The Fermi reactor proposal was the first to be made for support under the AEC's Power Demonstration Reactor Program. (Rolph, *Nuclear Power and the Public Safety*, 39.)

6. Dawson, *Nuclear Power*, 193; Rolph, *Nuclear Power and the Public Safety*, 39.

7. Mazuzan and Walker, *Controlling the Atom*, 178-82; Dawson, *Nuclear Power*, 194; Rolph, *Nuclear Power and the Public Safety*, 40.

8. Rolph, *Nuclear Power and the Public Safety*, 40-42. Mazuzan and Walker, *Controlling the Atom*, 213, note that "The PRDC episode was the catalyst for Joint Committee action to allow a larger public role in licensing procedures."

9. Holifield's minority report on the Price-Anderson bill, from which quotes in the text are taken, was reprinted in the *Congressional Record* as part of the Gore-Holifield debate. Representative John Saylor (R-Pennsylvania) included it as a part of his comments. See 14 July 1956, *Congressional Record*, 84th Cong., 2d sess., vol. 102, 14263. Mazuzan and Walker, *Controlling the Atom*, 211, note that Holifield actually tried to amend the Price-Anderson bill during floor debate to increase the power of the Advisory Committee on Reactor Safety by forbidding the AEC to issue licenses when the Advisory Committee issued an adverse report. The two authors devote an entire

chapter (pages 183-213) to the Price-
Anderson bill, characterizing it as "the
most important piece of atomic energy legislation brought to the floor since the 1954
act." (See page 211.)

10. Holifield's three 1959 hearings on
radiation hazards, potential effects of a
nuclear war, and nuclear waste disposal are
discussed in a twelve-page, typewritten
report by JCAE staff. See JCAE staff, "Organization and Functions of the Joint Committee on Atomic Energy," 14 Jan. 1960, 9-
10, Box 41 (Organization and Functions of
JCAE), HP.

11. JCAE staff, "Organization and
Functions of the Joint Committee on Atomic
Energy," 9.

12. Mazuzan and Walker, *Controlling
the Atom*, 353-66, provide an excellent summary of the AEC's handling of the ocean
atomic waste disposal problem, including a
discussion of Holifield's 1959 hearings.
See also JCAE staff, "Organization and Functions of the Joint Committee on Atomic Energy," 9-10; Rolph, *Nuclear Power and the
Public Safety*, 109-110. The JCAE staff
report indicates that five days of hearings
were held in January and February of 1959 on
"industrial radioactive waste disposal."
The report notes that "an additional day of
hearings was held on July 29, 1959, to cover
more specifically the subject of ocean disposal of low level wastes" with the objective of obtaining "better public understanding regarding the criteria and procedures
now being used to protect the [public]
health and safety." Rolph notes that the
AEC refused to drop the Gulf sites.

13. Mazuzan and Walker, *Controlling
the Atom*, 398-99; Rolph, *Nuclear Power and
the Public Safety*, 45, 48-49; Dawson, *Nuclear Power*, 178. Holifield's advocacy of
establishment of an internal but independent
Atomic Safety and Licensing Board stemmed

from a 1962 JCAE review of AEC organization.
A JCAE study recommended establishment of
the boards by the AEC. Two other studies
recommended the status quo, and a University
of Michigan Law School study team recommended separate development and regulatory
agencies. For Holifield's bills on establishment of the boards, see H. R. 8708, 87th
Cong., 1st sess., 15 Aug. 1961, Box 54 (H.
R. 8708), HP; H. R. 12336, 87th Cong., 2d
sess., 27 June 1962, Box 54 (H. R. 12336),
HP.

14. Rolph, *Nuclear Power and the Public Safety*, 108. The quotation is taken
from Public Law 88-376 (78 Stat. 320) (1964)
Section 3. A copy of this law is in Box 55
(H. R. 10437), HP.

15. "Holifield Outlines Views on Major
Policy Questions," *Nuclear Industry* 13 (June
1966):29, 32, Box 44 (1966 Misc. #2), HP.
Another article on Holifield's speech to the
Edison Electric Institute's June 1966 con-
vention in San Francisco is "Holifield Calls
for Caution in Reactor Licensing," *Nucle-
onics* 24 (July 1966):17-18, Box 54 (1966),
HP. See also Rolph, *Nuclear Power and the
Public Safety*, 71.

16. Holifield, "Statement by Congressman Holifield in Behalf of H. R. 3730," 19
May 1959, Box 54 (H. R. 3730), HP. In his
testimony before the Subcommittee on Health
and Safety of the House Committee on Interstate and Foreign Commerce, Holifield declared that "I have been particularly interested in the problem of air pollution for a
number of years." He mentioned his participation in a 1957 study of the air pollution
control program by the House Government
Operations Committee and his involvement as
chairman of the JCAE's Special Subcommittee
on Radiation in studies of pollution from
radioactive sources.

17. Holifield to Charles L. Schultze,
15 Nov. 1966, Box 44 (1966 JAEC General

Correspondence), HP.   (The acronym *JAEC* is
not a misprint or error;   it stands for
Joint Atomic Energy Committee, which is an
alternate, but less often used, title for
the Joint Committee on Atomic Energy
[JCAE].)

18. Holifield to Schultze, 15 Nov.
1966, and Holifield to Elmer B. Staats, 15
Nov. 1966, both in Box 44 (1966 JAEC General
Correspondence), HP. Holifield sent copies
of his letter to Schultze to AEC Chairman
Glenn Seaborg and to Comptroller General
Elmer B. Staats.   The Schultze letter contained a "cc" to Seaborg, while Holifield
included a cover letter to Staats, with the
Schultze letter as an attachment. Holifield
notes passage of the 1967 and 1971 legislation in a letter to Dr. Melvin Calvin, a
chemistry professor and laboratory director
at the University of California at Berkeley.
(Holifield to Calvin, 9 May 1972, Box 49
[JCAE Outgoing Correspondence (Blue Copies)
1972], HP.)

19. Los Angeles Chamber of Commerce,
"Holifield Sees Nuclear Power Breakthrough,"
Southern California Business, 27 Dec. 1965,
1, Box 43 (1965), HP.

20. Irvin C. Bupp and Jean-Claude
Derian, *Light Water: How the Nuclear Dream
Dissolved* (New York: Basic Books, 1978),
42, 49; Rolph, *Nuclear Power and the Public
Safety*, 55-56.   Three other corporations
eventually entered the reactor manufacturing
market.   These were Combustion Engineering,
Babcock and Wilcox, and Gulf-General Atomic
Corporation.

21. Rolph, *Nuclear Power and the Public Safety*, 62-63, 71, 91.

22. Ibid., 102-103, 139. Rolph points
out in footnote 6 on page 102 that besides
the Bodega Bay and Malibu interventions in
California on environmental and seismic
grounds, the Turkey Point No. 3 reactor in
Dade County, Florida, was opposed unsuccess-

fully on the grounds that it could not withstand sabotage or acts of war.

   23. See n. 2 for characterizations of
Holifield as a member of the "Atomic Establishment."   With regard to the Vietnam   War
issue, Holifield was a firm believer   in
saving Vietnam from Communist takeover   and
Chinese designs on the Southeast Asian country.   As he wrote to one   constituent,   "My
stand on Vietnam has been one of general
support for the President,   of whatever
party, in his efforts to bring about a
peaceful solution [to the Vietnam   con-
flict]."   (Holifield to Harry A. Lindsay, 17
Mar. 1970, Box 22 [Vietnam--1970], HP.)
Holifield's Vietnam stand brought him two
personal letters of appreciation from President Nixon.   See Nixon to Holifield, 11 May
1972, Box 62 (White House, 1972), HP; Nixon
to Holifield, 24 Jan. 1973, Box 63 (President Richard Nixon 1971-1974), HP.

   24. Los Angeles Chamber of Commerce,
"Holifield Sees Nuclear Power Breakthrough,"
4.   Holifield's belief that nuclear energy
was a cleaner source of energy was still in
evidence in 1970 when he wrote to a constituent that "electrical power is clean energy
and the atomic generating plant is the
cleanest method now available to generate
that energy."   (Holifield to Miss Laura
Burts, 1 Nov. 1970, Box 22 [Pollution--
1970], HP.)

   25. Los Angeles Chamber of Commerce,
"Holifield Sees Nuclear Power Breakthrough,"
1.   In a letter to the author, Holifield
noted that Americans have accepted thousands
of highway deaths and millions of injuries
because of the automobile.   He went on to
write: "In my opinion the carefully engi-
neered technology of nuclear use is *unavoid-
able* and *relatively far less dangerous* than
all the rest of modern technology. 30 years
of use for national defense weapons and
2,000 peacetime applications--including the

production of 13% of our electricity--*with-out one nuclear death to our citizenry.*" (Holifield to the author, 22 Apr. 1980, [pers. comm.]. Emphases are Holifield's.) See *Chet Holifield, United States Congressman*, typed transcripts of five tape-recorded interviews by Enid H. Douglass, Oral History Program, Claremont Graduate School, Claremont, California, 1975, vol. 3, 65, for Holifield's argument along these same lines.

26. Rolph, *Nuclear Power and the Public Safety*, 90-91. Holifield was an ally of Shaw, and was particularly upset with AEC Chairman Dixy Lee Ray when she pressured Shaw to resign in 1973. Holifield was perhaps even more closely allied with Admiral Hyman G. Rickover than he was with Shaw. In Warren Unna, "Atomic Energy" (1974), unpublished typescript, which consists of Holifield's first-person recollections of his years in Congress, Holifield devotes more time to Rickover than any other subject. Holifield is convinced that Rickover "will go down in history." He notes that Senators Henry Jackson (D-Washington) and Clinton Anderson (D-New Mexico) and Representative Melvin Price (D-Illinois) and himself were "Rick fans" and that "we believed in him, and the more he performed, the more we believed in him." (Unna, "Atomic Energy," 19.) Holifield and other JCAE allies of Rickover saw to it that Rickover was promoted to full Admiral. (Unna, "Atomic Energy," 19-26.)

27. Holifield to R. O. Smith, 17 Dec. 1970, Box 22 (Oil--Oil Drilling--1970), HP.

28. Holifield to Frederick Forscher, 30 Nov. 1970, Box 47 (JCAE Outgoing Correspondence 1970 [Blue Copies]), HP. Forscher was consulting engineer for the Nuclear Fuel Division of Westinghouse Electric Corporation in Pittsburgh, Pennsylvania.

29. The quotation in this paragraph is taken from Holifield to William A. Warne, 12

Sept. 1969, Box 46 (JCAE Outgoing Letters 1969 [Blue Copies]), HP. Holifield often employed the terms "scare tactics" and "emotionalism" to describe the message of environmentalists he thought to be extremists. In letters to constituents he noted that some environmentalists had resorted to "scare tactics." (Holifield to R. O. Smith, 17 Dec. 1970, Box 22 [Oil--Oil Drilling--1970], HP; Holifield to T. V. Arredondo, 13 June 1972, Box 49 [JCAE Outgoing Correspondence (Blue Copies) 1972], HP.) In at least two instances, Holifield asserted his belief that much of the nuclear opposition was "based on an emotionalism without basic factual information of the relative environmental impact of conventional fossil fuel plants" and "based on emotion rather than reason." ("Quotable Quotes on Nuclear Power," *North American Rockwell News* [El Segundo, California], 3 Sept. 1971, 3, Box 1 [Speech Material 1971], HP; Holifield, "Statement of Congressman Chet Holifield of California, (D-19th District), Chairman, Joint Committee on Atomic Energy, before California Legislature, Joint Committee on Atomic Development and Space, Eureka, California, September 26, 1969," 3, Box 46 [9/25/69--Letter to Senator Aiken from Cong. Holifield re Amchitka], HP.)

30. Holifield to William A. Warne, 12 Sept. 1969.

31. Rolph, *Nuclear Power and the Public Safety*, 110-11; Lewis, *Nuclear-Power Rebellion*, 68-69, 73, 93, 95, 98. One sensational article by Sternglass in *Esquire* was entitled "The Death of All Children."

32. Rolph, *Nuclear Power and the Public Safety*, 111-12. See also Lewis, *Nuclear-Power Rebellion*, 48-49, 79-82, 98-101. Tamplin estimated that the radiation dosage from bomb test fallout for the years 1953-1957 and 1959-1965 increased the death rate of fetuses and infants between .3 and 3

percent, instead of the twofold increase
suggested by Sternglass. Gofman and Tamplin
found from their studies that both fetal and
infant deaths and increasing incidents of
cancer resulted from the operation of nuclear power reactors and from bomb test
fallout. They postulated an additional
thirty-two thousand cancer deaths a year
from these sources *if* the population was
exposed uniformly to the maximum radiation
dosage permitted under AEC standards.
(Lewis, *Nuclear-Power Rebellion*, 81, 86.)

33. Lewis, *Nuclear-Power Rebellion*,
68, 98, 101-102. Letters to Holifield from
both Gofman and Tamplin mention Holifield's
invitation to comment on the AEC's report
concerning the scientists. (John W. Gofman
to Holifield, 28 and 29 July 1970 [plus a
cover letter dated 29 July 1970]; Arthur R.
Tamplin to Holifield, 27 July 1970, all in
Box 50 [Drs. Gofman and Tamplin], HP.)

34. The Gofman quotation is taken from
Gofman to Holifield, 29 July 1970 (cover
letter), Box 50 (Drs. Gofman and Tamplin),
HP. For the Holifield-Muskie correspondence, see Holifield to Edmund S. Muskie, 5
Aug. 1970, and Muskie to Holifield, 18 Aug.
1970, both in Box 50 (Drs. Gofman and
Tamplin), HP. These last two letters mention an additional 24 July letter from Holifield to Muskie, which could not be located.
In his August 18 reply, Muskie alleged that
the AEC report contained "possible bias"
because the report contained an Appendix O,
which disputed Gofman and Tamplin's theories.

35. Holifield stated his belief during
an interview on a television program that
Sternglass had been "completely disproven."
(Don Widner [producer], "Powers That Be,"
transcript of a KNBC public affairs documen-
tary, n.d., 9, Box 48 ["The Powers That Be"
KNBC Public Affairs Documentary], HP.)
Holifield's comment that Gofman and

Tamplin's theories had been disproven is
included in a letter to a constituent.
(Holifield to T. V. Arredondo, 13 June 1972
[see n. 29].) The last quotation in the
paragraph is taken from Holifield to Muskie,
5 Aug. 1970.

36. In his 5 Aug. 1970 letter to
Muskie, Holifield stated that he was making
Gofman and Tamplin's letters (their commentary on the AEC report) available to Muskie
because "the charges advanced by Drs. Gofman
and Tamplin contain the substance for sensational media publicity." (Holifield to
Muskie, 5 Aug. 1970.) For Holifield's remarks on the "unbalanced" consideration
being given to nuclear energy, see Holifield
to Oliver Townsend, 26 May 1969, Box 46
(JCAE Correspondence--1969, Outgoing, January-May), HP. Holifield's comment on the
emotionalism of the nuclear opposition is
taken from "Quotable Quotes on Nuclear
Power," (see n. 29), 3.

37. Holifield to Lee Metcalf, 27 May
1969, Box 47 (Thermal Pollution), HP. At
the 30 Oct. 30, 1969 session of Holifield's
hearings on the "Environmental Effects of
Producing Electric Power," AEC Commissioner
James Ramey expressed his belief that there
were "some professional stirrer-uppers" at
some AEC public hearings in Vermont, New
Hampshire, and Minnesota. Holifield expressed his approval of Ramey's characteri-
zation of the nuclear dissidents. (JCAE,
*Environmental Effects of Producing Electric
Power*, 91st Cong., 1st sess., [November]
1969, Part 1, 128-29, quoted in Nader and
Abbotts, *Menace of Atomic Energy*, 271-72.
See also Lewis, *Nuclear-Power Rebellion*,
104-105.)

38. Holifield states his intentions to
hold hearings in Holifield to Metcalf, 27
May 1969, and Holifield to Townsend, 26 May
1969. See also Holifield's press release
announcing the hearings: JCAE, "Joint Com-

mittee on Atomic Energy to Hold Hearings on Environmental Effects of Producing Electric Power," 25 Sept. 1969, typescript draft, Box 46 (9/25/69--Letter to Senator Aiken from Cong. Holifield re Amchitka) HP. Holifield's reference to compiling a "textbook" on the effects of all types of electricity-generating plants is contained in Holifield to Douglas G. Stenson, 11 June 1970, Box 22 (Pollution--Water--1970), HP. Holifield's attempt to compile a "textbook" on environmental effects of electrical plants was similar to his efforts to compile "textbooks" on radiation hazards and civil defense. For other Holifield references to compiling of a "textbook," see Holifield to Miss Cathy Williams, 21 July 1970, Box 22 (Pollution--1970), HP; Holifield to William A. Warne, 12 Sept. 1969, Box 46 (JCAE Outgoing Letters 1969 [Blue Copies]), HP.

39. Holifield to Glenn Seaborg, 10 Oct. 1969, Box 47 (Environmental Problems), HP; Holifield to Metcalf, 27 May 1969.

40. Holifield and Craig Hosmer to "Dear Colleague," n.d., Box 47 (Seminar on Nuclear Power and the Environment), HP. This letter was written before 9 June 1970, since it announces four seminars to be held on June 9, 16, 23, and 30, and a follow-up letter in the same file from Hosmer to Glenn Seaborg thanks Seaborg for his participation on 9 June 1970. (Hosmer to Seaborg, 11 June 1970, Box 47 [Seminar on Nuclear Power and the Environment], HP.) See also "Congressional Seminar on 'Nuclear Power and the Environment,'" n. d., Box 47 (Environmental Problems), HP. This is a one-page schedule and summary of the contents of the four seminars.

41. "Closing Remarks by Chairman Holifield, February 26, 1970, 'Environmental Effects of Producing Electric Power,'" 1190-93, Box 47 (Environmental Problems), HP. (This typescript appears to be a portion of

a draft of the hearing record, prior to its publication.) With regard to attendance at the congressional seminars, Hosmer noted that twenty-one representatives had indicated that they would attend, but only two showed up. However, a total of thirty-four congressmen (about 8 percent) were represented by the two congressmen and congressional staff members who attended. (Hosmer to Seaborg, 11 June 1970.) See also Holifield to T. V. Arredondo, 13 June 1972 (see n. 29); in this three-page letter, Holifield provides a wide-ranging discussion of the comparative effects of various types of electrical plants, a discussion doubtlessly based upon his accumulated knowledge from the hearings.

    42. The quotations in this paragraph are from Holifield to Miss Laura Burts, 1 Nov. 1970; Holifield to Larry S. Cahn, 12 Mar. 1970; "Statement of Congressman Chet Holifield on the Environment," typescript, [1970], all three in Box 22 (Pollution-- 1970), HP.

    43. 25 May 1970, *Congressional Record* 91st Cong., 2d sess., 16981-82, 16995; 9 March 1970, 6419; 18 Nov. 1970, 37917-18; 19 Nov. 1970, 38068. In a letter to a constituent, Holifield incorrectly states the May 25 vote as 285 to 7. (Holifield to Miss Cathy Williams, 21 July 1970 [see n. 38].)

    44. Rolph, *Nuclear Power and the Public Safety*, 104. While there is agreement that nuclear plants produce more waste heat, there is disagreement over how much more. Rolph states that about only 30 percent of the heat in nuclear plants is translated into electricity, whereas the comparative figure for fossil-fueled plants is 40 percent. Dorothy Nelkin rates nuclear plants at 25-33 percent and fossil-fueled plants at 40 percent. (*Nuclear Power and its Critics: The Cayuga Lake Controversy* [Ithaca, New

York: Cornell University Press, 1971], 25-26.)   Nader and Abbotts rate nuclear plants at "about 33 percent" as compared to 40 percent for fossil-fueled plants.   (*Menace of Atomic Energy*, 129-30.) Plants for which thermal pollution was an issue included Vermont Yankee (New York), Palisades (Michigan), Turkey Point No. 3 (New York), Monticello (Minnesota), Shoreham (Long Island), Indian Point No. 2 (New York), Zion (Illinois), and Calvert Cliffs (Maryland).

45. Dawson, *Nuclear Power*, 182; Rolph, *Nuclear Power and the Public Safety*, 104-105;   Lewis, *Nuclear-Power Rebellion*, 259.

46.   The quotation is from Holifield to Muskie, 26 Feb. 1969, Box 46 (JCAE Correspondence--1969, Outgoing, January-May), HP. For Holifield's thermal pollution legislation, see Holifield, H. R. 18867, 90th Cong., 2d sess., 17 July 1968, Box 56 (H. R. 18867), HP. See Rolph, *Nuclear Power and the Public Safety*, 106, for AEC opposition to the thermal effluents bill. Although Holifield fully supported requiring the AEC to regulate thermal effects, he later dropped his bill in favor of a more comprehensive bill drafted by Senator Muskie's Subcommittee on Air and Water Pollution. Muskie's bill required regulation of thermal pollution by all federal agencies granting licenses and permits for electrical plants. Holifield was very concerned, however, that Muskie's bill not present unnecessary obstacles to civilian nuclear power development. See Holifield to Muskie, 20 May 1969; Holifield to Representative Ed Edmondson, 14 Apr. 1969;   Holifield to (Senator) John O. Pastore, 19 May 1969; Memorandum, Holifield to All Senate JCAE Members, 19 May 1969, all in Box 46 (JCAE Correspondence--1969, Outgoing, January-May), HP.

47. Rolph, *Nuclear Power and the Public Safety*, 106;   Dawson, *Nuclear Power*,

182-84,   199-201;   Lewis, *Nuclear-Power Rebellion*, 282-85.

48. Dawson, *Nuclear Power*, 194-95, and Rolph, *Nuclear Power and the Pubic Safety*, 112, provide background details on the Minnesota affair.

49. Holifield to Robert C. Tuveson, 3 May 1969, Box 46 (JCAE Correspondence--1969, Outgoing, January-May), HP. Holifield indicated to Tuveson in a postscript that he was sending a copy of the letter to Governor Levander.   In the same file are Holifield's letters to Senators Eugene McCarthy and Walter F. Mondale and Representatives Archer Nelson, Albert H. Quie, John A. Blatnik, and Donald M. Fraser, all dated 8 May 1969. Dawson notes that Governor Levander later appeared as a witness at Holifield's Environmental Effects hearings in January 1970 and supported Tuveson's position.   Levander also acknowledged support from the states of Michigan,   Illinois, Vermont, Wisconsin, Hawaii, Kentucky, Maine, North Dakota, Pennsylvania, Utah, Virginia, and the territory of Guam.   (Dawson, *Nuclear Power*, 196.) In New York, Governor Nelson A. Rockefeller was presented with bills authorizing state agencies to regulate thermal and radiological discharges from nuclear power plants. Holifield sent a letter to Rockefeller voicing the JCAE's concern with the state legislation proposing to regulate radiological discharges. (Holifield to Rockefeller, 19 May 1969, Box 46 [JCAE Correspondence--1969, Outgoing, January-May], HP.)

50. Dawson, *Nuclear Power*, 196, 198.

51. Roger R. Trask, "The Calvert Cliffs Case: The Atomic Energy Commission and the National Environmental Policy Act, 1969-1972," 4, paper presented at meeting of the Pacific Historical Association, Los Angeles, California, August 1980, courtesy of Mr. Trask and used with his permission. Trask also mentions that the National Wild-

life Foundation and the Sierra Club opposed
the Calvert Cliffs plants. Compare Lewis,
Nuclear-Power Rebellion, 277. Nader and
Abbotts note that the two reactors at Calvert Cliffs have an electrical capacity of
845 megawatts. (*Menace of Atomic Energy*,
130.) For additional background information
on Calvert Cliffs, see Lewis, *Nuclear-Power
Rebellion*, 269-82, and Dawson, *Nuclear
Power*, 199.

52. *Calvert Cliffs Coordinating Committee vs. A. E. C.*, 449 F 2d. 1109 (D. C.
Circuit, 1971), quoted in Trask, "Calvert
Cliffs Case," 7, 9-10. Trask provides an
excellent summary of the Calvert Cliffs
decision. Liroff notes that "Calvert Cliffs
was the most widely cited of all NEPA opinions." (Richard A. Liroff, *A National Policy for the Environment: NEPA and Its Aftermath* [Bloomington: Indiana University
Press, 1976], 164.) See also Dawson, *Nuclear Power*, 199-201; Lewis, *Nuclear-Power
Rebellion*, 282-85; two JCAE memoranda,
Melvin Price to All Committee Members, 30
July 1971, and [JCAE Executive Director]
Edward J. Bauser to All Members, 24 July
1971, both in Box 49 (Calvert Cliffs vs.
AEC), HP.

53. The Holifield quotations are from
Holifield to Mrs. R. Arellanes [1970], Box
22 (Pollution, Air, 1970), HP; 2 Nov. 1971,
Congressional Record, 90th Cong., 2d sess.,
daily edition, E11661, Box 48 (Plant Siting
1971), HP. For the AEC's response to the
Calvert Cliffs decision, see Dawson, *Nuclear
Power*, 200. In a memorandum a few days
after the Calvert Cliffs decision, JCAE
Chairman Melvin Price estimated that the
decision would affect sixty license applicants and eighty-three reactors. (Memorandum, Price to All Committee Members, 30 July
1971, Box 49 [Calvert Cliffs vs. AEC], HP.)
Rockefeller is quoted in Dawson, *Nuclear
Power*, 201-202.

54. Trask, "Calvert Cliffs Case," 15-16. See also Dawson, *Nuclear Power*, 202, and Lewis, *Nuclear-Power Rebellion*, 293-96. The second case was the Kalur case. It is briefly discussed in a JCAE memorandum, Edward J. Bauser to All Committee Members, 8 Mar. 1972, 2, Box 59 (H. R. 13731), HP.

55. Quotations are taken from letter, [AEC Chairman] James R. Schlesinger to Senator John O. Pastore, 8 Mar. 1972. This letter is Attachment B of a memorandum, Edward J. Bauser to All Committee Members, 8 Mar. 1972 (see n. 54). Attachment A to this memorandum summarizes both the AEC bill (H. R. 13731) introduced by Holifield upon request and Congressman Hosmer's bill. In his memorandum, Bauser notes that Hosmer's bill predated the AEC bill, having been "disclosed in its original form at the authorizations hearing on January 26, 1972." Attachment A notes that "the procedures in this [Hosmer's] bill are quite similar to preliminary injunction procedure and concepts in Federal District and State Courts." Hosmer's bill, H. R. 13731, called for a designated AEC commissioner to make the initial decision on a temporary license, with optional review by the full panel of AEC commissioners within ten days after the decision. For a copy of the AEC bill, see Holifield, H. R. 13731, 92d Cong., 2d sess., 9 Mar. 1972, Box 59 (H. R. 13731), HP.

56. Under the House Reform Rules of 1971, Holifield could hold only one chairmanship, and he opted for the continuous chairmanship of the House Committee on Government Operations, rather than the chairmanship of the JCAE in alternate congresses. Holifield also considered the important additional power of subpoena possessed by Government Operations in his decision. (Holifield interview, 20 Dec. 1980.) Holifield noted that he could have fought for keeping the JCAE chair based on the fact

that it was a joint committee, but he decided to relinquish the position to his close friend and associate, Melvin Price (D-Illinois).

57. Holifield, H. R. 14065, 92d Cong., 2d sess., 23 Mar. 1972, Box 59 (H. R. 14065), HP. A concept paper answering potential opposition arguments notes that "each of these bills [AEC's and Hosmer's bills] involved more drastic changes than does H. R. 14065." (Untitled concept paper, n.d., typescript, Box 59 [H. R. 14065], HP.) The concept paper cites 6 opposition arguments and provides answers to each. See also two memorandums, Edward J. Bauser to All Committee Members, 13 Apr. 1972 and 22 Apr. 1972, Box 59 (H. R. 14065), HP. The 22 Apr. memorandum includes the amended version of H. R. 14065 as an attachment and notes that the amended version "takes into account, with one exception, all of the comments made by the members on that bill at the Committee's executive sessions of April 11 and 20." The exception was Senator Howard H. Baker's (R-Tennessee) proposal to establish a Division of Nuclear Power Safety Research within the AEC. A "clean" bill, H. R. 14655, was introduced by Holifield on 26 Apr. 1972 with the support of all House JCAE members. (Holifield, H. R. 14655, 92d Cong., 2d sess., 26 Apr. 1972, Box 59 [H. R. 14655], HP.) At least two authors have incorrectly ascribed authorship to Hosmer. (See Dawson, *Nuclear Power*, 202, and Lewis, *Nuclear-Power Rebellion*, 295.) Hosmer's bill was H. R. 13732, although he was a cosponsor of H. R. 14655, the amended bill introduced by Holifield. As documentation that the bill was Holifield's, see the JCAE's own report, "Activities and Accomplishments of the Joint Committee on Atomic Energy in the 92D Congress, Second Session (1972)," 4-5, Box 49 (Joint Committee on Atomic Energy 1972), HP.

58. Representative Paul N. McCloskey (R-California), a leader of the opposition to the temporary licenses legislation, charged that "this is only an end run around our environmental protection law" during debate on companion legislation necessary to implement Holifield's proposal. (UPI-151, 17 Apr. 1972, Box 59 [H. R. 13731], HP.) To implement Holifield's proposal, separate legislation to amend both NEPA and the Atomic Energy Act of 1954 was necessary. Representative John D. Dingell (D-Michigan), chairman of the House Subcommittee on Fisheries and Wildlife Conservation, worked closely with Holifield in handling the NEPA amendments. There are various documents in Box 59 (H. R. 14065), HP, that deal with the Holifield-Dingell effort.

59. The Holifield quotation in the paragraph is from "Statement by Mr. Holifield, H. R. 13752, April 17, 1972," Box 59 (Floor Statement for Mr. Holifield re H. R. 13752), HP. H. R. 13752 was Representative Dingell's bill to amend NEPA. For passage of Holifield's temporary licensing legislation, see "Activities and Accomplishments of the Joint Committee on Atomic Energy in the 92D Congress, Second Session (1972)," 4-5. It should be noted that the fight over the temporary licensing bill turned out to be a "tempest in a teapot." The new law proved to be neither a significant "end run" around NEPA as claimed by the environmentalists, nor a highly successful method to prevent power shortages. It was applied to only one nuclear power plant before its expiration in 1973. (Trask, "Calvert Cliffs Case," 18.)

60. Holifield averred that he was the major stumbling block to Representative Bolling's designs on the JCAE. (Holifield interview, 20 Dec. 1981.) See Nader and Abbotts, *Menace of Atomic Energy,* 287-91, for a discussion of congressional opposition to the JCAE. The growing list of congres-

sional opponents of nuclear power varied in the degree of their opposition. Edward Kennedy tended to favor the nuclear opposition, even proposing public financing for intervenors. (Duncan Burn, *Nuclear Power and the Energy Crisis* [London: The Macmillan Press, Ltd., 1978], 69, and 80, n. 43.) Corbin Allardice and Edward R. Trapnell refer to Muskie's "efforts to strengthen environmental safeguards" and declare he is "too wise to make a frontal attack" on the JCAE and the AEC in seeking his aims. (*The Atomic Energy Commission*, Praeger Library of U.S. Government Departments and Agencies [New York: Praeger Publishers, Inc., 1974], 171.) Liroff refers to "environmentalist Senator Philip Hart." (*A National Policy for the Environment*, 204.) Nader and Abbotts refer to Senator Gravel and Representative Jonathon Bingham (D-New York) as "nuclear power skeptics." (*Menace of Atomic Energy*, 287.)

61. E. W. Kenworthy, "Radiation Standards Bill Seen as Yielding Federal Authority," *New York Times*, 2 Oct. 1970, Box 47 (H. R. 18679--JCAE Omnibus Bill), HP; Thomas O'Toole, "Agency's A-Pollution Control Diluted," *Washington Post*, 3 Oct. 1970, Box 47 (Environmental Problems), HP. See also JCAE, "Atomic Energy Chairman Rebuts News Story Charges that Environmental Protection Agency Controls are Diluted by Joint Committee Legislation," press release, 3 Oct. 1970, Box 47 (H. R. 18679--JCAE Omnibus Bill), HP. Another copy of the O'Toole article is in Box 47 (H. R. 18679--JCAE Omnibus Bill), HP.

62. Kenworthy, "Radiation Standards Bill Seen as Yielding Federal Authority,"; O'Toole, "Agency's A-Pollution Control Diluted"; JCAE, "Atomic Energy Chairman Rebuts News Story Charges"; Holifield to Edward Kennedy, 3 Oct. 1970, and Holifield to Muskie, 2 Oct. 1970, both in Box 47

(H. R. 18679--JCAE Omnibus Bill), HP; Thomas O'Toole, "Pastore Withdraws Restraint on Radiation Safety Control," *Washington Post*, 7 Dec. 1970, Box 48 (Radiation Standards), HP.

63. "Statement by Mr. Holifield re *Perils of the Peaceful Atom*," typescript, 14 July 1969. This is an attachment to a memorandum, Edward J. Bauser to Honorable Chet Holifield, 14 July 1969, Box 46 (JCAE Correspondence 1969, Outgoing, June-December), HP.

64. Quoted in Lewis, *Nuclear-Power Rebellion*, 265. One of the televison programs Holifield was referring to was probably "The Dangers of Radiation," a segment of the "CBS Morning News," hosted by Joseph Benti during the week of August 10-14, 1970. Holifield was interviewed by Benti and later sent a letter to Frank Stanton, CBS president, criticizing the show and analyzing several page proofs from the show's transcripts. Holifield deeply resented what he believed to be an inference by Benti that Holifield told only the results of some scientific experiments that favored atomic energy and neglected those that were unfavorable. See Holifield to Stanton, 11 Sept. 1970, and Stanton to Holifield, 5 Oct. 1970, both in Box 48 (Benti Program on Radiation), HP.

65. The first Holifield quotation of this paragraph is from Lewis, *Nuclear-Power Rebellion*, 271. The other quotations are from Holifield to R. O. Smith, 17 Dec. 1970 (see n. 27); Holifield to T. V. Arredondo, 13 June 1972 (see n. 29).

66. Holifield to Muskie, 17 Oct. 1970, Box 47 (H. R. 18679--JCAE Omnibus Bill), HP. This letter and other materials are grouped together with a cover sheet on contents in Edward J. Bauser's handwriting. Bauser defines the attachments as "Documents on Sen. Muskie et. al. Objections to JCAE Omni-

bus Bill re Radiation Standards," indicating
that the EPA incident probably was the reason (or final reason) Holifield wrote the
letter to Muskie. Holifield's letter to
Muskie is marked "Personal and Confidential"
in two places on the first page.

67. Muskie to Holifield, 5 Jan. 1971,
Box 48 (JCAE--Correspondence With Members of
Congress), HP. Muskie's letter to Holifield
was marked "Personal and Confidential" and
was signed by someone other than Muskie. At
the bottom of the letter is the following
statement in parentheses: "Dictated but not
read, signed in Senator Muskie's absence."

68. Allardice and Trapnell, *Atomic
Energy Commission*, 174. The authors mention
Holifield's relinquishing of his JCAE chairmanship but do not give the date. They note
that "when Representative Holifield relinquished his JCAE chairmanship to become
chairman of the House Committee on Government Operations, he *designated* [italics
added] Representative Price as vice-chairman." (The chairmanship of the JCAE went to
the Senate side in the Ninety-third Congress.)

69. Holifield and Hosmer to Seaborg,
24 Sept. 1970, quoted in Lewis, *Nuclear-
Power Rebellion*, 260-61.

70. Mrs. Galen C. Radle to Holifield,
18 Oct. 1973, Box 49 (JCAE Incoming Correspondence, 1973), HP. Radle repeated many
of the arguments against nuclear power and
expressed her sentiment that "speeding up on
licensing of nuclear power plants is wrong."
She concluded: "This is a moral issue, just
like the Vietnam War was."

71. In a letter to Oliver Townsend,
director of New York's Office of Atomic and
Space Development Authority, Holifield asserted that "the unbalanced way in which
nuclear sources are being considered have
also caused me concern." Holifield declared
that Townsend's efforts and the efforts of

others "to assure that the various energy sources are considered in a balanced way" were very important, "if we are to meet the energy requirements of our society and limit environmental pollution." (Holifield to Townsend, 26 May 1969 [see n. 36].)

72. Lewis, *Nuclear-Power Rebellion*, 263-64; Rolph, *Nuclear Power and the Public Safety*, 119, n. "a." For copies of the two bills, see H. R. 9285, 92d Cong., 1st sess., Box 58 (H. R. 9285), and H. R. 9286, 92d Cong., 1st sess., Box 58 (H. R. 9286), HP. Holifield introduced the bills at the AEC's request.

73. Lewis, *Nuclear-Power Rebellion*, 267-69.

74. At least two authors have used this generalization. See Rolph, *Nuclear Power and the Public Safety*, 119, n. "a," and Lewis, *Nuclear-Power Rebellion*, 261.

75. JCAE, *Amending the Atomic Energy Act of 1954, as Amended, to Add New Section 192 to Authorize the Atomic Commission to Issue Temporary Operating Licenses for Nuclear Power Reactors: Report to Accompany S. 3543*, 92d Cong., 2d sess., 9 May 1972, S. Rept. 92-787, 5, Box 59 (H. R. 13731), HP. S. 3543 was the counterpart of H. R. 14655, Holifield's temporary licensing bill. A draft copy of the H. R. 14655/S. 3543 report is in Box 59 (H. R. 14065), HP. (See p. 8 of draft report.) Both reports stated that "after a plant is fully constructed at a particular site and is ready to operate is hardly the time for prolonged and meaningful debate on . . . [safety and environmental] questions." This Holifield view was subscribed to by a majority of JCAE members.

76. "Statement of Congressman Chet Holifield, September 26, 1969," (see n. 29), 5.

77. For Holifield's siting and licensing legislation, see H. R. 11957, 93d Cong., 1st sess., 13 Dec. 1973, Box 61 (H. R.

11957), HP; H. R. 12823, 93d Cong., 2d sess., 14 Feb. 1974, Box 61 (H. R. 12823), HP; and H. R. 13204, 93d Cong., 2d sess., 4 Mar. 1974, Box 61 (H. R. 13204), HP. John McCormack introduced the bill with Holifield, Price, and Hosmer as cosponsors. As McCormack noted, however, in a letter to William Simon, head of the Federal Energy Office, H. R. 12823 included parts of an earlier bill on the AEC review and licensing process (H. R. 11957) introduced by Price, Holifield, and Hosmer. (McCormack to Simon, 18 Feb. 1974, Box 61 [H. R. 12823], HP.) H. R. 13204, which was the same bill as H. R. 12823 (with more cosponsors), is explained in detail in two attachments to a letter McCormack sent to Holifield. (McCormack to Holifield, 14 Feb. 1974, Box 61 [H. R. 12823], HP.) This letter appears to be a form letter probably sent to all House members.

78. In a 1969 letter to California Governor Ronald Reagan, Holifield and Craig Hosmer (R-California) suggested centralized "power parks" as an effective approach to California's need for additional power and environmental protection. (Holifield and Hosmer to Reagan, 5 Aug. 1969, Box 47 [Plant Siting, 1969-70], HP.) Holifield reiterated the concept in his speech before the California Legislature's Joint Committee on Atomic Development and Space. ("Statement of Congressman Chet Holifield, September 26, 1969" [see n. 29], 7-8.)

79. H. R. 12823/H. R. 13204 is explained in detail in two attachments to a letter from McCormack to Holifield. (McCormack to Holifield, 14 Feb. 1974.)

80. Holifield interview, 19 Feb. 1980. In a personal letter to a friend, Holifield admitted he had "had some approaches from corporation people to consider leaving Congress to work for them. But I cannot conceive of maintaining an interest in a narrow

field of endeavor after the breadth of in-
teresting subjects I deal with as a congressman." He also noted that "Frankly, the
reason I have worked so long is the interest
I've had in my work and not the income."
(Holifield to Margaret Boyce, 3 July 1973,
Box 1 [Margaret Boyce], HP.)

81. In his 1969 speech before the
California Legislature's Joint Committee on
Atomic Development and Space, Holifield
summarized his overall position: "Let me
make it crystal clear that I am not a champion of those who wish to pollute our environment. But neither am I a champion of
those who are so unrealistic that they would
go back to the use of kerosene lamps and
candles." ("Statement of Congressman Chet
Holifield, September 26, 1969" [see n. 29],
4.) Holifield's reference to lamps and
candles was a reference to a statement by
environmentalist Ralph Nader that Americans
would be better off using lamps and candles
than abiding further development of nuclear
power. (Arthur Murphy [ed.], *The Nuclear
Power Controversy* [Englewood Cliffs, New
Jersey: Prentice-Hall, Inc., 1976], 3.)

CHAPTER 10:   A POWER IN THE HOUSE

1. Harold P. Green and Alan Rosenthal,
*Government of the Atom: The Integration of
Powers* (New York: Atherton Press, 1963),
18.

2. Warren Unna, "Atomic Energy"
(1974), unpublished typescript, 14; Holifield interview, 8 Feb. 1982.

3. Holifield interview, 8 Feb. 1982.

4. Holifield to Kennedy, 26 Nov. 1960,
Box 45 (Nuclear Weapons 1960-1968), HP.
Holifield noted that he met with William
Macomber and Phil Farley "at urgent request
of the Secretary of State," and they ex-
plained "the Administration's proposal with

respect to changes in nuclear weapons arrangements between the United States and NATO." Holifield closed his letter with the statement, "As you know, we leave tomorrow for a thorough tour of NATO installations in the next two weeks," and he offered to make the findings available to Kennedy or Kennedy's representative upon his return.

5. Harold L. Nieburg, *Nuclear Secrecy and Foreign Policy* (Washington, D.C.: Public Affairs Press, 1964), 55. See chapter 7 for Holifield's role in obtaining Kennedy's support for the N-reactor. See chapter 8 for Holifield's roles in securing Kennedy's support for resumption of atmospheric nuclear testing and expansion of the civil defense program.

6. Kennedy is quoted on the nuclear-powered airplane in Green and Rosenthal, *Government of the Atom*, 19, n. 17. See also page 247. For the quotation on Kennedy's lack of enthusiasm for legislating, see Richard Neustadt, "Kennedy in the Presidency: A Premature Appraisal," in Franklin D. Mitchell and Richard O. Davies (eds.), *America's Recent Past* (New York: John Wiley & Sons, Inc., 1969), 384. Holifield and others have viewed Kennedy as a moderate Democrat. (Holifield interview, 8 Feb. 1982. See also Leo Rennert, "Public Power Runs Into Familiar Cold Shoulder – Vintage 1930s," *Sacramento Bee*, 10 Sept. 1967, Box 44 [1967 Atomic Energy Commission], HP.)

7. Green and Rosenthal, *Government of the Atom*, 263; Nieburg, *Nuclear Secrecy*, 55.

8. The Kennedy-Seaborg correspondence is quoted in Green and Rosenthal, *Government of the Atom*, 264.

9. Green and Rosenthal, *Government of the Atom*, 264-65. See also Nieburg, *Nuclear Secrecy*, 55.

10. Green and Rosenthal, *Government of the Atom*, 265.

11. George T. Mazuzan and J. Samuel Walker, *Controlling the Atom: The Beginnings of Nuclear Regulation 1946-1962* (Los Angeles: University of California Press, 1984), 401-403; Green and Rosenthal, *Government of the Atom*, 114, n. 106; Nieburg, *Nuclear Secrecy*, 34.

12. Quoted in Richard S. Lewis, *Nuclear-Power Rebellion: Citizens Vs. the Atomic Industrial Establishment* (New York: The Viking Press, 1972), 6, 27, 244. For the full report, see U.S. Atomic Energy Commission, *Civilian Nuclear Power--A Report to the President--1962* (Washington, D.C.: Government Printing Office, 20 Nov. 1962). Mazuzan and Walker, *Controlling the Atom*, 410, suggest that Kennedy "hoped it [the nuclear power study] would placate Holifield" as Kennedy's motivation for approving the new AEC study.

13. Virginia Kelly, "Holifield, Hosmer Successful in Atomic Spending Control," *P. T.* (?), 26 July 1963, editorial page, Box 42 (1963), HP. This is a newspaper clipping. For Holifield's role in expanding the JCAE's authorization power over the atomic energy program, see Green and Rosenthal, *Government of the Atom*, 169-72, 175-80.

14. Holifield interview, 8 Feb. 1982. Holifield believes his "low-key" approach was instrumental in maintaining his relationship with Kennedy.

15. Ibid. Green and Rosenthal note that "the President's reluctance to name Ramey was matched by the JCAE's insistence that it would block any other nominations to the Commission." (*Government of the Atom*, 107.) Nieburg posits that Kennedy's ultimate nomination of Ramey "seemed to indicate an effort by the chief executive to conciliate the powerful committee and avoid another head-on collision." (*Nuclear Secrecy*, 55.)

16. Unna, "Atomic Energy," 29; Holifield to President Lyndon B. Johnson, 12

Dec. 1967, Box 44 (1967 JAEC General Correspondence), HP. In his letter to Johnson, Holifield notes, "You may remember that I enlisted your support when you headed the Space Council, in obtaining the approval of President Kennedy to launch the satellite."

17. Holifield interview, 19 Feb. 1980; Frank G. Dawson, *Nuclear Power: Development and Management of a Technology* (Seattle: University of Washington Press, 1976), 95, 97, 100-101; Southern California Edison Company, 67th Annual Report (1962), Box 55 (H. R. 2940), HP.

18. Dawson, *Nuclear Power*, 135; "Atomic Power Plant at San Onofre Dedicated," *Fullerton, California, News-Tribune*, 6 Jan. 1968, Box 45 (1968 JAEC General Correspondence #2), HP.

19. The Holifield Papers contain several significant items on Holifield's San Onofre bill. (H. R. 2940, 88th Cong., 1st sess., 28 Jan. 1963; *Congressional Record*, 88th Cong., 1st sess., 15 July 1963, 11818-19; and 16 July 1963 [no page number visible]; Public Law 88-82 [77 Stat. 115] [1963], all in Box 55 [H. R. 2940], HP.) Holifield introduced his bill at the same time that Senator Clair Engle (D-California) introduced S. 546. Although Engle's bill got the nod to become law, it was an exact copy of Holifield's bill as amended by the JCAE. Kennedy signed the bill on 30 July 1963. For progress on the San Onofre plant and Holifield's dedication speech, see United States Atomic Energy Commission, "AEC Schedules Public Hearing in California on Reactor Proposed at Camp Pendleton," press release, No. F-205, 15 Oct. 1963, and United States Atomic Energy Commission, "AEC Issues Permit for Construction of Nuclear Power Plant in California," press release, No. G-52, 4 March 1964, both in Box 55 (H. R. 2940), HP; "Atomic Power Plant at San Onofre Dedicated," *Fullerton, California*

News-Tribune, 6 Jan. 1968, Box 45 (1968 JAEC General Correspondence #2), HP; Southland's First A-Fuel," *Los Angeles Herald-Examiner*, 27 June 1966, Box 44 (1966 Misc. #2), HP.

20. Holifield states in a letter to the editor of the *East Los Angeles Gazette* both his doubts about Soviet good-faith bargaining and the fact that he informed Kennedy of his doubts. (Holifield to Jerry Littman, 18 Sept. 1962, Box 42 [1962 Nuclear Test Ban], HP.) For Holifield's "talk and test" strategy, see "Holifield Favors 'Talk and Test' Atom Policy," *Los Angeles Times*, 28 Aug. 1961, Box 42 (1961 Nuclear Testing), HP. On nuclear test resumption, see "Congress Chiefs Back Atom Tests," *Los Angeles Examiner*, 6 Sept. 1961, Box 42 (1961 Nuclear Testing), HP. Holifield's comments on the Test Ban Treaty are taken from one of his press releases. ("Nuclear Test Ban," press release, 24 July 1963, Box 43 [1963 Nuclear Test Ban #2], HP.)

21. Nieburg, *Nuclear Secrecy*, 9, 13, 206-207, 212-213; "Statement on Multilateral Force," *F. A. S. Newsletter*, 17 (June 1964):1-2.

22. Holifield to John F. Kennedy, 26 Nov. 1960, Box 45 (Nuclear Weapons 1960-68), HP.

23. For Holifield's atomic secret "give-away" opinions, see "Holifield Opposes A-Secret Giveaway: Dangers in Sharing Atom Data Cited by Lawmaker," *Los Angeles Examiner*, n.d. [1958], and "A-Secret 'Giveaway' Opposed: 'Share Atom Plan' Called Kremlin Propaganda Aid," *Los Angeles Examiner*, 15 Mar. 1958, both in Box 41 (1958 Misc. Atom), HP. Both of these articles are actually installments of a speech that Holifield gave opposing the Eisenhower administration's "agreements for cooperation" proposal. The *Nautilus* episode is discussed in Unna, "Atomic Energy," 36. Holifield was men-

tioned prominently as a senatorial candidate in 1958 and averred that the French request for information on the *Nautilus* was "one of the reasons I didn't run for the U. S. Senate." As Holifield further explained it, "I had a deep feeling that if I ran for the Senate, maybe the fight against giving the secrets to DeGaulle [*sic*] and Joliet-Curie might not be fought with the same vigor and determination if I were not around." (Unna, "Atomic Energy," 36-37.)

24. Murrey Marder, "2 A-Moves Questioned by Holifield: Caution on Mixed NATO Crews and Test-Ban Urged," *Washington Post*, 17 Apr. 1963, Box 42 (1962 Nuclear Test Ban), HP. See also "Top Democrat's Worry About Atom Policy," *U. S. News and World Report* (29 Apr. 1963):16, Box 42 (1963 Misc. Articles), HP.

25. Holifield to Lyndon B. Johnson, 3 Oct. 1964, Box 43 (Multi-lateral Nuclear Force), HP. Holifield's follow-up letter, marked "Proposed letter - not sent" was actually a proposed response by Holifield to a letter Holifield received from McGeorge Bundy in reply to Holifield's letter to the president. (McGeorge Bundy to Holifield, 5 Oct. 1964, and proposed letter, Holifield to Bundy, 8 Oct. 1964, both in Box 43 [Multi-lateral Nuclear Force], HP.)

26. Don Edwards, Bob Kastenmeier, et. al., to "Dear Colleague," 24 Nov. 1964, Box 43 (Multi-lateral Nuclear Force), HP, is the letter that solicits participation in the letter to Rusk. The letter to Rusk is Joseph P. Addabbo, Thomas L. Ashley, et. al., to Dean Rusk, 7 Dec. 1964, Box 43 (Multi-lateral Nuclear Force), HP. See also Carroll Kilpatrick, "Rusk Urged to Delay MLF Commitment," *Washington Post*, 8 Dec. 1964, Box 43 (Multi-lateral Nuclear Force), HP.

27. John W. Finney, "Greater Voice on Nuclear Arms Urged for NATO," *New York Times*, 16 Nov. 1965, Box 43 (1965), HP.

28. Holifield, "Geneva Conferences on Limiting the Spread of Nuclear Weapons," n.d. [1967], Box 1 (Biographical Material), HP. This apparently is a short speech by Holifield in which he discusses the draft treaty. See also "Congressman Sees Signing of Treaty," *La Habra Review/East Whittier Review*, 11 July 1968, 2D, Box 43 (1968 Misc. Articles), HP. This is a newspaper clipping from a small newspaper in Holifield's congressional district. Holifield was also a cosponsor of a resolution to support President Johnson's efforts to obtain a nuclear nonproliferation treaty. (Memorandum, Holifield to All House Members of the Joint Committee on Atomic Energy, 18 Jan. 1966, and untitled Holifield press release, No. 495, 19 Jan. 1966, both in Box 56 [H. Res. 673], HP.) For details on the treaty, see U.S. Congress, Senate Committee on Foreign Relations, "Treaty on the Nonproliferation of Nuclear Weapons," 90th Cong., 2d sess., 26 Sept. 1968, S. Exec. Rept. 9.

29. "Congressman Sees Signing of Treaty," *La Habra Review/East Whittier Review*; John W. Finney, "AEC Puts a Curb on Its Foreign Aid: New Policy Seeks to Slow Spread of Weapons," *New York Times*, 3 July 1965, Box 43 (1965), HP.

30. Holifield interview, 8 Feb. 1982. Lyndon Baines Johnson served on the JCAE during the Eightieth Congress when he was a representative and during the Eighty-second Congress when he was a senator. See Corbin Allardice and Edward R. Trapnell, *The Atomic Energy Commission*, Praeger Library of U.S. Government Departments and Agencies (New York: Praeger Publishers, Inc., 1974), 220. In a letter to the author, Holifield mentions he was with Johnson when Johnson received Kennedy's offer of the vice presidential slot on the 1960 Democratic ticket. (Holifield to the author, 19 Feb. 1980 [pers. comm.].)

31. Holifield interview, 8 Feb. 1982. For Holifield's work on legislation to create the Department of Housing and Urban Development (HUD), see Box 30 (Creating the Department of HUD 1962), HP; "Remarks by Mr. Holifield at the Dedication of the New Quarters of the Committee on Government Operations, Room 2154, Rayburn House Office Building, May 5, 1965," Box 44 (1966 JAEC General Correspondence), HP; and various materials in Box 56 (H. R. 6927 [HUD]), HP. For Holifield's work on the Department of Transportation (DOT), see Box 30, HP, which contains various DOT files. Warren Unna, "Government Operations Committee" (1974), unpublished typescript, 1, 4-6, contains Holifield's reminiscences of his roles in creating the two cabinet-level departments (HUD and DOT). In two letters, Holifield acknowledges his support for civil rights and social programs legislation. (Holifield to Andrew J. Biemiller, 15 Dec. 1969, Box 22 [Voting - 1970], HP; Holifield to Ralph Jacques, 11 Feb. 1974, Box 1 [Relatives - Personal], HP.)

32. Holifield mentions in his letter to President Johnson on the subject that Johnson asked him on 1 July 1964 to begin to work toward agreement on the intertie. (Holifield to Johnson, 29 July 1964, Box 4 [Intertie 2# (*sic*)], HP.)

33. Bonnie Baack Pendergrass, *Public Power, Politics, and Technology in the Eisenhower and Kennedy Years: The Hanford Dual-Purpose Reactor Controversy, 1956-1962* (New York: Arno Press, 1979), 106-111, provides background on the intertie.

34. President Johnson's quotation on prospects for agreement is taken from his letter of appreciation to Holifield. (Johnson to Holifield, 11 Aug. 1964, Box 4 [Intertie], HP.) Holifield mentions his meetings with various individuals and organizations in his letter to Johnson. (Holifield

to Johnson, 29 July 1964.) See also "Long Distance Call from Congressmen Bernie Sisk and Congressman Chet Holifield to Mr. Gerdes (P. G. & E.), Piedmont, California . . . OLney 3-6423," transcript of telephone conversation, n.d., Box 4 (Intertie Meeting), HP. Johnson's press conference comments are taken from Pacific Gas and Electric Company (PG & E), "The Pacific Intertie," pamphlet, n.d. (1974?), 15, Box 4 (Pacific Intertie), HP. This pamphlet was sent to Holifield as an attachment to a letter. (Ralph B. Dewey, assistant to the chairman of the board, to Holifield, 27 Mar. 1974, Box 4 [Pacific Intertie], HP.) Secretary Udall's comments are on page 18 of the same pamphlet.

35. Pacific Gas and Electric Company, "The Pacific Intertie," 1.

36. For a brief summary of the controversy, see "Three Poles and a Principle," *Washington Atomic Energy Report and the Atomic Energy Guideletter* 11 (19 July 1965):1-3, Box 56 (H. R. 8856), HP; "Three Poles and a Principle (Replay)," *Washington Atomic Energy Report and the Atomic Energy Guideletter* 11 (2 Aug. 1965):1-2, Box 43 (1965), HP; Holifield to Ralph G. Carley, 8 Sept. 1965, Box 43 (Stanford Linear Accelerator 1964-1965), HP.

37. "Three Poles and a Principle," 2; Holifield to Charles de Young Thieriot, 21 June 1965, Box 43 (1965 Misc. #1), HP. Mr. de Young Thieriot was editor and publisher of the *San Francisco Chronicle*, which was highly critical of Holifield's role in the Woodside controversy. Holifield charged de Young Thieriot with "biased news and editorial coverage."

38. Holifield cites the *Chronicle's* criticisms in his letter to de Young Thieriot, 21 June 1965. Senator Thomas H. Kuchel asked the JCAE to drop the Woodside issue in a letter to JCAE chairman (Senator) John O. Pastore. (Kuchel to Pastore, 26

Mar. 1964, Box 48 [Stanford Linear Accelerator Ctr. 1964-1974], HP.) Holifield's House debate comments are included in "Three Poles and a Principle," 2.   Holifield's bill passed on the second try in the House by a vote of 275 to 125. The Senate passed Holifield's bill (H. R. 8856) without amendment despite Senator Kuchel's attempt to attach an amendment.   See "Three Poles and a Principle (Replay)," 1, and 10 Aug. 1965 *Congressional Record*, 89th Cong., 1st sess., 19087, both in Box 56 (H. R 8856), HP. In his previously mentioned letter to Ralph Carley, Holifield also pointed out that Woodside already had "2488 unsightly poles," and he declared he was trying to save the extra $4.35 million that would have gone for "the benefit of a few wealthy property owners in the exclusive little community of Woodside."   These facts helped Holifield's case. (Holifield to Carley, 8 Sept. 1965.)

39. Lewis, *Nuclear-Power   Rebellion*, 35-36; Leo Rennert, "Public Power Runs into Familiar Cold Shoulder - Vintage 1930s," *Sacramento Bee*, Box 44 (1967 Atomic Energy Commission), HP. The quotation is taken from Lewis, *Nuclear-Power Rebellion*, 35.

40. Holifield, "Another   Unjustified Tax Bonanza for Privately Owned Electric Utilities" (marked "draft"), n.d., 1, Box 45 (1967 Public Power), HP. According to the contents of this speech, it was written in the early 1960's.

41. Quoted in Leo Rennert, "Public Power Loses Fight for Nuclear Power Plants," *Sacramento Bee*, 3 July 1968, Box 45 (1968 Atomic Energy Commission), HP.

42. Lewis, *Nuclear-Power   Rebellion*, 39-40.   Holifield's bill (H. R. 18679) was passed by Congress and signed by President Nixon on 19 Dec. 1970.   Public Law No. 91-560 (84 Stat. 1472) (1970). A copy of this law is in Box 57 (H. R. 18679), HP. Other files with helpful materials on this subject

are Box 43 (1965), and Box 47 (H. R. 18679 - JCAE Omnibus Bill), HP.

43. See "Congressman Holifield Attends White House Ceremony of Signing of Atomic Energy Bill," press release, n.d., Box 42 (1963 Misc. Articles), HP.

44. "JCAE Urges Change: Congress Amends Price-Anderson Act to Set New Ground Rules for Handling Claims," *Nuclearpower Newsletter* (September 1966):1-4, Box 44 (1966 Public Power), HP; Holifield to Representative Clarence D. Long, 22 Dec. 1969, Box 46 (JCAE Correspondence--1969, Outgoing, June-December), HP; "The Industry Goes on Record," *Nuclear Industry*, 12 (July 1965):3, Box 44 (1966 Misc. #2), HP.

45. With regard to Project ROVER, Holifield and other JCAE members wanted to use it as a base to expand AEC research activities to outer space development. (Green and Rosenthal, *Government of the Atom*, 18-19, 218, and 231, n. 95.) For Holifield's enthusiastic support for Plowshare, see Holifield to Lyndon Johnson, 12 Dec. 1967, Box 44 (JAEC General Correspondence), HP, and Holifield to Professor Paul Kruger, 22 Dec. 1969, Box 46 (JCAE Correspondence--1969, Outgoing, June-December), HP. For Holifield's support of the food irradiation program, see 15 Apr. 1965, *Congressional Record*, 89th Cong., 1st sess., 6661, Box 43 (1965), HP. For the Southwest Experimental Fast Oxide Reactor (SEFOR) program, see Leroy Donald, "Ozark Ceremonies Mark Formal Start on Reactor Designed in Quest for Cheaper Power From Atom," *Arkansas Gazette*, 28 Oct. 1965, Box 43 (SEFOR), HP. For the Bolsa Chica Desalting Plant, see "Holifield Hails Desalting Program," *Montebello Messenger*, 27 Apr. 1967, 3, Box 45 (Desalting), HP; H. R. 17558, 89th Cong., 2d sess., Box 56 (H. R. 17558), HP. For the Stanford Linear Accelerator, see 13 July 1961, *Congressional Record*, 87th Cong., 1st

sess., vol. 107, pt. 9, 12441. For the Two Hundred Billion Electron Volt (200 BEV) Accelerator, see Holifield to Carlyle Reed, 11 July 1966, Box 45 (1967 Site Selection: The 200 Bev Accelerator), HP. For the seed-blanket reactor project, see "Holifield Indicates Effort Will be Made to Have Joint Committee Re-Study Seed-Blanket Reactor for Possible Construction in California," *National Coal Policy Conference, Inc. Newsletter* 7 (13 Jan. 1966), 3, Box 44 (1966), HP. For the gas-graphite reactor project, see Dawson, *Nuclear Power*, 90-91.

46. The first two quotations are from Unna, "Atomic Energy" (see n. 1), 15. Holifield is quoted regarding the *Savannah* in "Retire the NS Savannah?" *Houston Post*, 5 Mar. 1967, Box 45 (Savanah [*sic*] JCAE), HP. See also "Unionist Decries Holifield View That Nuclear Vessel Is 'a Flop,'" *New York Times*, 27 Mar. 1966, 88, Box 45 (Savanah [*sic*] JCAE), HP.

47. See Holifield to Johnson, 12 Mar. 1964, Box 43 (Snap [*sic*] 10A 1964), HP. Holifield and Pastore had written a prior letter to Johnson requesting that the SNAP-10A project be retained. (Holifield and Pastore to Johnson, 17 Feb. 1964, Box 43 [Snap [*sic*] 10A 1964], HP.) For Holifield's "field day" in Congress declaring the success of SNAP-10A, see 5 Apr. 1965, *Congressional Record*, 89th Cong., 1st sess., 6661, Box 43 (1965), HP. During his talk, Holifield mentioned the Soviets' "almost identical project" known as "Romashka."

48. Holifield is quoted on the space program in"Holifield Attacks NERVA-II Go-Ahead," *SPACE Daily*, 35, Box 45 (Space Priorities), HP. Holifield's comments on the *John F. Kennedy* are taken from a paste-up of a section from the *Congressional Record* that includes Holifield's statement. The section apparently is Congressman Melvin Price's (D-Illinios) extension of remarks in

the 9 Sept. 1968 *Congressional Record.*
Paste-up is entitled "Congressional Record--
House - Sept. 9, 1968 (H-8423 - H8424," in
Box 45 (1968 JAEC General Correspondence),
HP. Holifield also put most of his speech
in a press release he issued. ("Statement
by Congressman Chet Holifield, Vice Chair-
man, Joint Committee on Atomic Energy on the
Commissioning of the Aircraft Carrier JOHN
F. KENNEDY," press release, 6 Sept. 1968,
Box 45 [1968 Atomic Energy Commission], HP.)
See also Edward W. O'Brien, editorial, "From
the Globe's Bureaus: Washington," *St. Louis
Globe Democrat*, 3-4 June 1967 [*sic*], Box 45
(USS Kennedy), HP.

    49. Richard G. Hewlett and Francis
Duncan, *Nuclear Navy, 1946-1962* (Chicago:
University of Chicago Press, 1974), 311,
374, provides background on the nuclear-
powered fleet. One example showing McNa-
mara's policy position against building
nuclear-powered ships is John W. Finney,
"M'Namara Scored on Nuclear Navy: Holifield
Criticizes Policy at Submarine Ceremony,"
New York Times, 18 Jan. 1966, Box 45 (Nu-
clear Navy 1966-1968), HP. For other Holi-
field comments in favor of the "Nuclear
Navy," see "Holifield's Nuclear Navy,"
*Atomic Energy Report and the Atomic Energy
Guideletter* 10 (28 Dec. 1964):2, Box 45
(Nuclear Navy 1961-1968), HP; "Holifield
Boosts Nuclear Ships," *Nucleonics*, 23 (Feb-
ruary 1965), 22, Box 45 (Nuclear Navy 1966-
1968), HP; "The Case for a Nuclear Surface
Navy," *Atomic Energy Report and the Atomic
Energy Guideletter* 12 (18 July 1966):4, Box
44 (1966), HP; Holifield to Johnson, 19
Oct. 1966, and Holifield to Robert S. McNa-
mara, 20 Oct. 1966, Box 44 (1966 JAEC Gen-
eral Correspondence), HP; "Naval Nuclear
Surface Fleet Strongly Urged by Chairman of
Joint Committee on Atomic Energy," JCAE
press release, No. 518, 11 July 1966, Box 45
(Nuclear Navy 1966-1968), HP; Holifield to

President Johnson, 9 Feb. 1968, Box 45 (Nuclear Navy 1966-1968), HP. The 1968 letter to Johnson is five pages long. Holifield also discusses his support for Admiral Rickover and the nuclear navy in *Chet Holifield, United States Congressman*, typed transcripts of five tape-recorded interviews by Enid H. Douglass, Oral History Program, Claremont Graduate School, Claremont, California, 1975, vol. 3, 46-51.

50. Holifield to Johnson, 19 Oct. 1966, and Holifield to McNamara, 20 Oct. 1966. Holifield mentions Rivers in both letters. He attached his letter to Johnson to the letter he sent to McNamara. McNamara's decision to delay construction of the authorized nuclear warships and his purported attempt to persuade Johnson to back him were the reasons for Holifield's 1968 letter to Johnson. (Holifield to Johnson, 9 Feb. 1968.) Holifield notes in his press release on the USS *Kennedy* that McNamara "had previously deleted" the high speed submarine from the navy's planned shipbuilding program. ("Statement by Congressman Chet Holifield, Vice Chairman, Joint Committee on Atomic Energy on the Commissioning of the Aircraft Carrier JOHN F. KENNEDY," 4.) A JCAE press release acknowledges that construction was halted in May 1968 on the electric-drive submarine. ("Hearings on Advanced Nuclear Submarines Released by the Joint Congressional Committee on Atomic Energy," JCAE press release, No. 589, 20 Sept. 1968, Box 45 [Nuclear Submarines], HP.)

51. Holifield to Johnson, 9 Feb. 1968.

52. There is a typewritten note, dated "2/15/68," regarding calls from Clifford and Secretary McNamara, who both wanted Holifield to call them. According to the note, Clifford wanted to talk to Holifield before Holifield met with McNamara. (Note in Box 45 [Nuclear Navy], HP.) As McNamara's suc-

cessor, Clifford was much more conciliatory in his dealings with the JCAE; in one letter, he assured Holifield that Holifield's concerns about the electric drive submarine had Clifford's "personal attention." (Clifford to Holifield, 9 Aug. 1968, Box 45 [1968 JAEC General Correspondence], HP.) On page 4 of his press release on commissioning of the USS *Kennedy*, Holifield expressed satisfaction that Clifford had decided to go ahead with construction of a nuclear-powered ship and with the high-speed submarine. ("Statement by Congressman Chet Holifield, Vice Chairman, Joint Committee on Atomic Energy on the Commissioning of the Aircraft Carrier JOHN F. KENNEDY.")

53. "Holifield's Nuclear Navy," *Atomic Energy Report and the Atomic Energy Guideletter* 10 (28 Dec. 1964):2.

54. "Final 1968 Presidential Returns Show 499,704-Vote Nixon Lead," *New York Times*, 12 Dec. 1969, Box 63 (Nixon, Richard M.), HP. Holifield was chairman of the California State Committee for Humphrey in 1972. See materials in Box 62 (Humphrey Campaign 1972 Correspondence), HP.

55. The Holifield quotations are from Holifield to John D. Coty, 14 Jan. 1970, and Holifield to Harry A. Lindsay, 17 Mar. 1970, both in Box 22 (Vietnam - 1970), HP. For President Nixon's letters of appreciation, see Nixon to Holifield, 11 May 1972, Box 62 (White House, 1972), HP, and 24 Jan. 1973, Box 63 (President Richard Nixon 1971-1974), HP. In both letters, Nixon addressed Holifield as Chet.

56. "Statement by Congressman Chet Holifield Before the House of Representatives," 19 Sept. 1967, Box 44 (Anti-Ballistic Missile 1967 Legisl. Info.), HP; Holifield's handwritten notes entitled "Conference at White House, Congressional leaders with Pres. Nixon, March 14, 1969, 8:30 a m [*sic*] to 10:15," and Holifield to "Dear

Colleague," 19 Sept. 1969, both in Box 65 (ABM 1969), HP. Attached to Holifield's letter is a twelve-page position paper entitled "The Case for the Safeguard ABM System." See also "Holifield Defends Safeguard Plan," *Long Beach Independent Press-Telegram*, 17 June 1969, Box 65 (ABM 1969), HP. For opposition views within the liberal Democratic Study Group, see Jonathan B. Bingham and Lucien N. Nedzi to Colleague, 19 Sept. 1969, Box 65 (ABM 1969), HP.

57. Holifield to Professor Paul Kruger, 22 Dec. 1969 (see n. 45); Edward S. Josephson to Captain Edward J. Bauser, 24 Mar. 1970 (cc. Mr. Holifield), Box 47 (Food Irradiation), HP.

58. Transcript of 1969 authorization hearing entitled "Auth. Hrg - A M, 17 Apr 69," 74-78, Box 47 (Gaseous Diffusion Plants 1970), HP.

59. White House Press Release, 10 Nov. 1969, and "AEC Proceeds to Implement Presidential Decision on Uranium Enrichment," AEC press release, No. M-255, 10 Nov. 1969, both in Box 47 (Uranium Enrichment Facilities), HP.

60. "Representative Chet Holifield Comments on Administration Plan for Future Ownership and Operation of Uranium Enrichment Facilities," JCAE press release, No. 618, 10 Nov. 1969, Box 47 (Uranium Enrichment Facilities), HP; Holifield to Clinton P. Anderson, 25 Nov. 1969, Box 46 (JCAE Correspondence--1969, Outgoing June-December), HP.

61. For an example of the Dixon-Yates theme aired by the press, see "Ghost Rattles in Atom Plant Sale Proposal, *Long Beach Independent Press-Telegram* 7 Dec. 1969, Box 47 (Uranium Enrichment Facilities), HP. On uranium enrichment cost increases, see Leo Rennert, "Nuclear Fuel Issue is Heating Up," *Sacramento Bee*, 25 Oct. 1970, Box 47 (Speech Material: Monopoly of Electrical Energy

1969-1970), HP. See also Holifield to Nixon, 15 June 1970, and accompanying untitled statement, 15 June 1970 (both apparently in draft form), Box 47 (Uranium Enrichment Facilities), HP. Holifield has written "my copies letter and statement" on them. For Holifield's views on the cost increases, see "Holifield Plans Hearings on Uranium Enrichment Service Price Boost," *Nuclear Power Newsletter* (January 1971):1, Box 48 (Uranium Enrichment 1971), HP.

62. Holifield to Henry M. Jackson, 1 Oct. 1973, Box 60 (H. R. 11510 - Energy Reorganization Act of 1973--Correspondence, 1973 [File #2]), HP. Holifield has written "Never used, substituted a memorandum" on the letter. The memorandum to Jackson, dated 16 Oct. 1973, is in the same file. Holifield has written "Written Before Split of D. E. N. R. by Pres." on it.

63. The quotation is from "Statement by Congressman Chet Holifield on Granting Access by U. S. Industry to AEC Gas Diffusion and Gas Centrifuge Technology," n.d., Box 47 (Gaseous Diffusion Plants 1970), HP. Holifield has written "To be used only if the matter comes up" at the top of this statement. See Dawson, *Nuclear Power*, 171-72, for additional information on industry access to enrichment technology, and Rennert, "Nuclear Fuel Issue is Heating Up" (see n. 61) for Holifield's unsuccessful amendment to the "pricing criteria" bill. For Holifield's prodding to increase government plant capacity, see Holifield to James R. Schlesinger (AEC chairman), 8 Oct. 1971, Box 49 (International Nuclear Power 1972), HP.

64. In a floor speech, Holifield declared, "I believe that the solution to our long-term electrical needs is the atomic fast breeder nuclear reactor." (4 June 1971, *Congressional Record*, 92d Cong., 1st sess., H4722, Box 26 [Presidential Energy

Message June 4, 1971], HP.) For Larson's letter and the Holifield quotation in the paragraph, see Larson to Holifield, 2 Oct. 1973, Box 49 (Fast Breeder Reactor 1973), HP, and "Why LMFBR Now? Presentation by Congressman Chet Holifield of California," *The Time is Now* (publication of Westinghouse), n.d. (1971?), Box 48 (Fast Breeder Reactor 1971), HP.

    65. For background on the breeder reactor, see Lewis, *Nuclear-Power Rebellion*, 243-44; "Data Sheet, SEFOR (Southwest Experimental Fast Oxide Reactor)," n.d., Box 43 (1965 Misc. #2), HP; Leroy Donald, "Ozark Ceremonies Mark Formal Start on Reactor Designed in Quest for Cheaper Power From Atom," *Arkansas Gazette*, 28 Oct. 1967, Box 43 (SEFOR), HP. As examples of Holifield's comments on the breeder reactor in 1951, 1953, and 1965, see transcript of questions and answers, untitled, n.d. (1951), Box 79 (1951 [undated], Questions and Answers on Atomic Energy Program "Can Atom Secrets be Kept"), HP; "Atomic Energy Commission Proposals on Atomic Power: Remarks by Congressman Chet Holifield in the House of Representatives," Holifield press release, 22 June 1953, Box 79 (June 22, 1953, Speech--Floor, "A. E. C. Proposals on Atomic Power"), HP; "Holifield Sees Nuclear Power 'Breakthrough,'" *Southern California Business* (weekly publication of Los Angeles Chamber of Commerce), 27 Dec. 1965, Box 43 (1965), HP. For the Kennedy administration's support for the breeder reactor, see Lewis, *Nuclear-Power Rebellion*, 244. For President Johnson's support of the breeder, see Appendix C, "Letter From President Johnson on AEC Programs," 53, U.S. Congress, Joint Committee on Atomic Energy, *Authorizing Appropriations for the Atomic Energy Commission for Fiscal Year 1966*, 89th Cong., 1st sess., 13 May 1965, H. Rept. 349, Box 56 (H. R. 8122), HP. (In his letter of 17 Apr.

1965 to AEC Chairman Glenn T. Seaborg, Johnson expresses support for other programs
favored by Holifield as well, including the
SNAP and desalting programs.) For the Democratic party's 1968 support of the breeder,
see copy of page 40 of the 1968 Democratic
National Platform (*Toward a More Perfect
Union: The Platform of the Democratic Party
1968*) in Box 62 (National Convention - Presidential Campaign 1968), HP. Support for the
breeder reactor also cut across party lines.
California Republican Governor Ronald Reagan, who would later become President of the
United States, vigorously supported the
breeder. (Governor Reagan to Holifield, 24
Mar. 1971, Box 48 [Fast Breeder Reactor
1971], HP.) Holifield acknowledges that the
LMFBR had become the principal breeder concept in a letter to Representative John B.
Anderson (R-Illinois). (Holifield to Anderson, 18 Mar. 1969, Box 46 [JCAE Correspond-
ence--1969, Outgoing, January-May], HP.)
The 1969 Holifield quotation is from Holifield, "A Quarter Century of Atomic Development," n.d. [1969], Box 46 (Statements -
1969), HP.

66. Holifield interview, 20 Feb. 1984.

67. For a copy of the president's 4
June 1971 energy message, see 4 June 1971,
Congressional Record, 92d Cong., 1st sess.,
H4715-H4719, Box 26 (Presidential Energy
Message June 4, 1971), HP. (Holifield's
quoted remarks are on page H4722.) In a
letter to his onetime foe, former AEC chairman Strauss, Holifield indicated that he had
successfully pressed President Nixon for
consideration of antipollution efforts and
additional "clean" energy in tandem as inseparable issues. (Holifield to Admiral
Lewis L. Strauss, 11 June 1971, Box 48 [JCAE
Outgoing Correspondence (Blue Copies) 1971],
HP.) Holifield discusses the LMFBR in
Holifield interviews by Enid H. Douglass,
vol. 3, 55-56 (see n. 49).

68. In a congratulatory letter to Holifield, AEC Commissioner James Ramey mentions Holifield's "concurrent release" (of the President's energy message) and Holifield's "willingness to let the President take the lead." (James F. Ramey to Holifield, 7 June 1971, Box 48 [Fast Breeder Reactor 1971], HP.) For other congratulatory letters, see William E. Kriegsman to Holifield, 4 June 1971, and John T. Conway to Holifield, 7 June 1971, both in Box 48 (Fast Breeder Reactor 1971), HP. For Holifield's remarks on the Nixon administration's intentions, see Unna, "Government Operations Committee" (see n. 31), 16-17, and Unna, "Atomic Energy" (see n. 2, 46), 30.

69. Unna, "Government Operations Committee," 16.

70. Ibid., 17. Holifield mentions the failure of the Department of Community Development legislation in his opening statement at hearings on Nixon's DENR proposal. (Typewritten opening statement, "Hearings by the Legislation and Military Operations Subcommittee on H. R. 9090, A Bill to Establish a Department of Energy and Natural Resources and an Energy Research and Development Administration: Opening Statement by Chairman Holifield, July 24, 1973," Box 60 [H. R. 9090], HP.)

71. Holifield learned of Nixon's plans for an energy research and development administration late in 1972. (JCAE Executive Director Captain Edward J. Bauser's two-page handwritten notes to Holifield, dated "WED 15 NOV" (1972), Box 49 [JCAE Staff Memoranda 1972], HP. Actually, the second page is a "FRI - 10 NOV" Bauser note to Senator Pastore, which describes "ADMINISTRATION PLANS . . . RE ENERGY." [Bauser writes exclusively in capital letters.] On the first page of the two-page note, Bauser tells Holifield, "PLEASE DESTROY ENCLOSED [I

HAVE COPY - AND I THOT (*sic*) ENCLOSED IS
SENSITIVE]."') Holifield's letter to Nixon
could not be located in the Holifield Papers. It is mentioned by Holifield and a
paragraph from the letter is included, however, in a memorandum, Holifield to Henry M.
Jackson, 16 Oct. 1973, Box 60 (H. R. 11510 -
Energy Reorganization Act of 1973--Corre-
spondence, 1973), HP.
     72. For Nixon's introduction of the
Department of Energy and Natural Resources
proposal, see U.S. Congress, House Committee
on Government Operations, *Draft of Proposed
Legislation to Promote More Effective Management of Certain Related Functions of the
Executive Branch* (Communication From the
President of the United States), 93d Cong.,
1st sess., 16 June 1973, H. Doc. 93-119.
Holifield introduced Nixon's DENR proposal
at the request of the administration. (H.
R. 9090, 93d Cong., 1st sess., 29 June 1973,
Box 60 [H. R. 9090], HP; form letter, Holi-
field to "Dear:," 18 July 1973, Box 60 [H.
R. 9090] HP.) A cover memorandum and press
release also provide details on the hearing
schedule and witness list. (Memorandum,
Holifield to Members of the Legislation and
Military Operations Subcommittee, 18 July
1973, and "Hearings Scheduled on Energy
Reorganization Bill," news release, 18 July
1973, both in Box 60 [H. R. 9090], HP.)
Holifield acknowledged in a memorandum to
Senator Jackson that he had been working
with administration officials on the pro-
posal. (Holifield to Jackson, 16 Oct. 1973,
Box 60 [H. R. 11510 - Energy Reorganization
Act of 1973--Correspondence, 1973], HP.)
For Holifield's quoted remark at the end of
the paragraph, see "Statement of Chet Holi-
field, Chairman, Committee on Government
Operations, before the Committee on Rules on
H. R. 11510, December 11, 1973," 5, Box 60
(H. R. 11510 - Energy Reorganization Act of
1973--Misc. #1), HP. H. R. 11510 was intro-

duced by Holifield on 15 Nov. 1973, and was essentially Nixon's proposal for ERDA and NEC without DENR.

73. For the Simon-Ash advocacy regarding ERDA, see Edward Cowan, "Simon, White House Split on Nuclear Power Control," *New York Times*, 3 Jan. 1974, Box 60 (H. R. 11510 - Energy Reorganization Act of 1973--Miscellaneous #1), HP. Another copy of this article is in Box 60 (H. R. 11510 - Energy Reorganization Act of 1973--correspondence, 1974), HP. Also in this file are a letter to Simon from Congressman (soon-to-be Speaker) Mike McCormack endorsing the concept of consolidating ERDA and FEA and also a later letter from Simon and Ash to Morris Udall backing away from the consolidation proposal. (Mike McCormack to William Simon, 2 Jan. 1974, and Roy L. Ash and William E. Simon to Morris K. Udall, 6 Feb. 1974.) For environmentalists' attacks on the AEC, see Jerome B. Price, *The Antinuclear Movement*, Social Movements Past and Present (Boston: Twayne Publishers, 1982), 11; Duncan Burn, *Nuclear Power and the Energy Crisis: Politics and the Atomic Industry* (London: Macmillan Press, 1978), 15-16. Holifield mentions Bolling's designs on the JCAE in his previously cited memorandum to Senator Jackson. (Holifield to Henry M. Jackson, 16 Oct. 1973 [see n. 71, 72].) Morris K. Udall, chairman of the Subcommittee on the Environment of the House Committee on Interior and Insular Affairs, attempted unsuccessfully to obtain a rule for a substitute bill in place of or as an alternative to Holifield's bill. (Morris K. Udall to Ray J. Madden [chairman, House Rules Committee], 7 Dec. 1973, Box 60 [H. R. 11510 - Energy Reorganization Act of 1973--Misc. #1], HP; "Remarks by Mr. Holifield In Rebuttal to Those of Mr. Udall Before the Rules Committee, December 12, 1973, 2:00," Box 61 [H. R. 11793 - Federal Energy Administration--Gen-

eral], HP.) Holifield discusses the
creation of ERDA with Enid Douglass.
(Holifield interviews by Enid Douglass, vol.
3, 84-91 [see n. 49].)

74. A Senate Interior Committee
"markup copy" of Senator Jackson's bill is
in Box 60 (H. R. 11510 - Energy Reorganization Act of 1973--Misc. #1), HP. (See U.S.
Congress, Senate, "S. 1283, [March 19,
1973]," copy of bill designated "For Discussion by the Committee on Interior and Insular Affairs," 93d Cong., 1st sess., 7 Nov.
1973, Committee Print 3.) Holifield describes the contents of the bill in his
previously mentioned memorandum to Jackson.
(Holifield to Jackson, 16 Oct. 1973.) S.
1283 passed the Senate late in 1973. Holifield outmaneuvered Udall in the House with
the help of his friend and JCAE colleague,
Craig Hosmer (R-California). Hosmer, ranking House minority member on the JCAE, was
also ranking minority member on Udall's
subcommittee. Hosmer harassed Udall by
offering still another substitute proposal
and by slowing the subcommittee's work by
various maneuvers. Hosmer made no secret of
his real intentions. ("Hosmer Proposal to
By-Pass Political Stall on ERDA Bill," Hosmer press release, 6 Mar. 1974, Box 60 [H.
R. 11510 - Energy Reorganization Act of
1973--correspondence, 1974], HP.) Early in
April 1974, Jackson made it clear in a letter to Holifield that he was "prepared to
support prompt establishment of ERDA," and
Holifield replied gratefully. (Jackson to
Holifield, 3 Apr. 1974, and Holifield to
Jackson, 12 Apr. 1974, Box 60 [H. R. 11510 -
Energy Reorganization Act of 1973--corre-
spondence, 1974], HP.) In his letter, Holifield was also conciliatory and declared he
was "prepared to help develop and support
enactment of an H. R. 13565-type bill [Jack-
son's proposal] that follows and carefully
complements the statute establishing ERDA."

75. Holifield mentions that his bill passed in the House on 19 Dec. 1973 by a vote of 355 to 25 in a letter to Senate Government Operations Committee Chairman Sam J. Ervin (D-North Carolina). (Holifield to Ervin, 20 May 1974, Box 60 [H. R. 11510 - Energy Reorganization Act of 1973--correspondence, 1974], HP.) For Senate amendments to Holifield's bill, see "ERDA Outlook: Holifield Stews Over Senate's 'Anti-Nuclear' Bill," *Nucleonics Week* 15 (5 Sept. 1974):6, Box 61, (H. R. 11510 - Energy Reorganization Act of 1973--Miscellaneous #2), HP. In addition, there are two typewritten papers in Box 61 (H. R. 11510 - Energy Reorganization Act of 1973--Miscellaneous #2), HP, which succinctly present Senate changes to the House-passed Holifield bill. See "ERDA/NEC ISSUES," 22 Aug. 1974 (one page), and "Major Senate Changes to ERDA/NEC (NSLC) Bill (H. R. 11510)," 22 Aug. 1974 (three pages). In the same file, see House Government Operations Committee Staff Director Herbert Roback's memorandum to Holifield on the status of conference matters on H. R. 11510. (Memorandum, Roback to Holifield, 4 Oct. 1974.) There are other extensive materials on the House-Senate conference on the Holifield bill in Box 61. There is a black binder (title is missing) that includes well over fifty pages of analysis of differences between the House and Senate versions, with Government Operations Committee staff recommendations for positions to be taken by House conferees. Also included in the binder are what appear to be a draft cover memorandum and the actual cover memorandum sent by Holifield to House conferees along with the staff analyses. In the dated actual cover memorandum, Holifield asserts, "The purpose of ERDA is not to roll back or curtail nuclear energy, but to build up on existing AEC resources to provide a broader organizational base for meeting the nation's

energy needs." (Memorandum, Holifield to House Conferees, 16 Sept. 1974.) Also included in Box 61 is a separate, oversized committee print of the Senate Government Operations Committee that compares Senate and House versions of the reorganization bill. See U.S. Congress, Senate Committee on Government Operations, *Comparison of H. R. 11510 as Passed by Senate and as Passed by House With Comments on Differences*, 93d Cong., 2d sess., 26 Aug. 1974, Committee Print (no number). Holifield has (helpfully) written liberally on many of the conference documents.

76. "House-Senate Conference on H. R. 11510, to Establish an Energy Research and Development Administration, Wednesday, October 2, 1974: Opening Statement by Chairman Holifield," Box 61 (Chairman Holifield Opening Remarks at House-Senate ERDA Conference), HP. The "Chairman Holifield Opening Remarks" file was found by the author in the middle of the oversized Senate Committee on Government Operations committee print previously described.

77. Holifield to Ervin, 20 May 1974, Box 60 (H. R. 11510 - Energy Reorganization Act of 1973--correspondence, 1974), HP. See also a previously cited memorandum, Herbert Roback to Holifield, 4 Oct. 1974, Box 61 (H. R. 11510, Energy Reorganization Act of 1973--Miscellaneous #2), HP, for additional information on the NRC. Although the NRC was the regulatory successor to the AEC, Holifield told Enid Douglass that "I cut my own child's throat when I dissolved the AEC." (Holifield interviews by Enid H. Douglass, vol. 3, 90 [see n. 49].) Holifield had been willing to divide the AEC into regulatory and development units to meet the environmentalists' criticism that the regulatory and development functions should be separate. Holifield felt, however, that this criticism was "phony," since "The

only people that knew anything about atomic energy was [*sic*] the people that were promoting it and therefore they were the only ones that could regulate it." (Holifield interviews by Enid H. Douglass, vol. 3, 87.) Although Holifield was willing to compromise, he nonetheless believed that the AEC had a good safety record and was better qualified than most environmentalist groups to regulate atomic power plants.

78. For a discussion of the FEA legislation, see "Remarks by Mr. Holifield (During floor debate on H. R. 11740, the bill providing emergency energy authorities, reported from the Committee on Interstate and Foreign Commerce), December 12, 1973," Box 61 (H. R. 11793 - Federal Energy Administration--General), HP; U.S. Congress, House Committee on Government Operations, *Federal Energy Administration*, 93d Cong., 1st sess., 28 Dec. 1973, H. Rept. 93-748, 2-4. The Holifield quotation at the end of the paragraph is from "Statement of Honorable Chet Holifield for Inclusion in the Congressional Record of March 4, 1974: Federal Energy Administration (H. R. 11793)," 3, Box 61 (H. R. 11793 - Federal Energy Administration--General), HP.

79. Holifield is quoted in "UPI 189 (Propane)," 5 Mar. 1974, copy of United Press International press bulletin, Box 61 (H. R. 11793 - Federal Energy Administration--General), HP. For passage of the FEA legislation, see "Energy Crisis Still With Us, Nixon Warns," *Los Angeles Times*, 8 May 1974, Box 61 (H. R. 11793 - Federal Energy Administration--General), HP.

Epilogue: Mr. Atomic Energy

1. Holifield to Ralph Jacques, 11 Feb. 1974, Box 1 (Relatives--Personal), HP.

2. Holifield interview, 19 Feb. 1980.
Boxes 27-37 and 89 of the Holifield Papers
provide a good starting point for an in-
depth study of Holifield's influence in the
field of governmental reorganization.

Select Bibliography

THE HOLIFIELD PAPERS

Although the Holifield Papers were first
cited in George T. Mazuzan and J. Samuel
Walker's *Controlling the Atom* (1984), *Mr.
Atomic Energy* is the first book to make
extensive use of these papers. The Chet
Holifield Papers are part of the Regional
Cultural History Collection of Edward L.
Doheny, Jr., Memorial Library at the University of Southern California. The papers
cover the entire period of Holifield's congressional service from 1943, when he first
entered the House of Representatives, to his
retirement at the end of 1974. The subject
matter varies from strictly California and
local congressional district issues to items
of national importance, including atomic
energy. The papers on Holifield's later
years in Congress are more numerous, at
least in part bec... of his growing importance as a leader in the House and in national atomic energy affairs. There are
ninety boxes in the collection, and an ar-
chival calendar of over two hundred pages is
available for use by scholars. The papers
are arranged according to broad subject
categories, as follows:

Subject	Box Number(s)
Biographical and Personal	1
California and District Services and Issues	2-7
California Political	8-10
Commission on Government Procurement	11-12
Congressional Reform	13
Correspondence	14-24
Democratic Caucus	25
Economy	25-26
Energy	26
Federal Departments and Commissions	27-29
Government Operations Committee	30-37
House Committees	38-39
Issues (Air Pollution, Taxation, Electoral Reform)	40
Joint Committee on Atomic Energy	41-50
Legislation (78th through 93rd Congresses)	51-61
National Political (By subjects, individuals)	62-63

Holifield's role as an atomic energy legislator is best presented in Boxes 41 through 50, since these are Holifield's JCAE papers. Also of importance are the boxes on legislation, since many files contain correspondence and other information central to understanding atomic energy and other issues. The correspondence files, national political files, the research files, and especially the files on speeches, statements, and press releases and on insertions into the *Congressional Record* are very useful in surveying Holifield's views on specific problems and issues. Energy and the economy are important enough to Holifield to warrant nearly two boxes of material. Box 13 is noteworthy for its information on Holifield's role in House procedural reforms spearheaded by Holifield and other liberal Democrats in the 1960s.

The Holifield Papers are open to scholars and others wishing to explore them in detail. Interested persons should contact:

Regional Cultural History Collection
Department of Special Collections
Doheny Memorial Library
University of Southern California
Los Angeles, California 90089-0182

OTHER PRIMARY AND SECONDARY SOURCES

This listing consists of works cited in the notes and the text and does not represent a comprehensive listing of all the works relating to atomic energy or of all the materials consulted by the author but not used. In addition, many of the articles, government documents, and other materials found in the Holifield Papers are not cited separately here.

During his thirty-two years in Congress, Holifield conducted or participated in over two hundred sets of hearings. Copies of many hearing documents may be found in the Holifield Papers. Holifield himself has bound copies of all of his hearings, which cover one wall of his study in Balboa, California.

Acheson, Dean. *Present at the Creation: My Years in the State Department.* New York: W. W. Norton & Company, Inc., 1969.

Allardice, Corbin, and Edward R. Trapnell. *The Atomic Energy Commission.* Praeger Library of U.S. Government Departments and Agencies. New York: Praeger Publishers, 1974.

Bupp, Irvin C., and Jean-Claude Derian. *Light Water: How the Nuclear Dream Dissolved.* New York: Basic Books, 1978.

Burn, Duncan. *Nuclear Power and the Energy Crisis.* London: The Macmillan Press, Ltd., 1978.

Congressional Record, 1943-1974. Washington, D. C.

Curtis, Richard, and Elizabeth Hogan. *Perils of the Peaceful Atom.* Garden City, New York: Doubleday & Company, Inc., 1969.

Dawson, Frank. *Nuclear Power: Development and Management of a Technology.*

Seattle: University of Washington Press, 1976.

Del Sesto, Steven L. *Science, Politics, and Controversy: Civilian Nuclear Power in the United States 1946-1974*. Westview Special Studies in Science, Technology and Public Policy. Boulder, Colorado: Westview Press, Inc., 1979.

Divine, Robert A. *Blowing on the Wind: The Nuclear Test Ban Debate, 1954-1960*. New York: Oxford University Press, 1978.

Facts on File. New York: Facts on File, Inc., 1947.

Fenn, Scott. *The Nuclear Power Debate*. Praeger Special Studies/Praeger Scientific. New York: Praeger Publishers, 1981.

Foreman, Harry, ed. *Nuclear Power and the Public*. Minneapolis: University of Minnesota Press, 1971.

Gilpin, Robert. *American Scientists and Nuclear Weapons Policy*. Princeton, New Jersey: Princeton University Press, 1962.

Green, Harold P., and Alan Rosenthal. *Government of the Atom: The Integration of Powers*. The Atherton Press Political Science Series. New York: Atherton Press, 1963.

Halberstam, David. *The Best and the Brightest*. Greenwich, Connecticut: Fawcett Publications, Inc., 1972.

Hewlett, Richard G., and Oscar E. Anderson. *The New World, 1939/1946*. Vol. 1 of *A History of the Atomic Energy Commission*. University Park, Pennsylvania: The Pennsylvania State University Press, 1962.

Hewlett, Richard G., and Francis Duncan. *Atomic Shield, 1947/1952*. Vol. 2 of *A History of the Atomic Energy Commission*. University Park, Pennsylvania:

The Pennsylvania State University Press, 1969.

Hewlett, Richard G., and Francis Duncan. *Nuclear Navy, 1946-1962.* Chicago: The University of Chicago Press, 1974.

Holifield, Chet. United States Congressman. Typed transcripts of five tape-recorded interviews by Enid H. Douglass (interviewer). Oral History Program, Claremont Graduate School, Claremont, California, 1975.

Holifield, Chet. "Who Should Judge the Atom?" *Saturday Review,* 40 (3 Aug. 1957):34-37.

Lewis, Richard S. *The Nuclear-Power Rebellion: Citizens Vs. the Atomic Industrial Establishment.* New York: Viking Press, 1972.

Lilienthal, David E. *The Atomic Energy Years 1945-1950.* Vol. 2 of *The Journals of David E. Lilienthal.* New York: Harper and Row, 1966.

Liroff, Richard A. *A National Policy for the Environment: NEPA and its Aftermath.* Bloomington: Indiana University Press, 1976.

Los Angeles Times, 1958-1984.

Mazuzan, George T. and J. Samuel Walker. *Controlling the Atom: The Beginnings of Nuclear Regulation 1946-1962.* Los Angeles: The University of California Press, 1984.

Metzger, Peter H. *The Atomic Establishment.* New York: Simon and Schuster, 1972.

Miller, Byron S. "A Law is Passed--The Atomic Energy Act of 1946." *University of Chicago Law Review* 15 (Summer 1948):811-22.

Mitchell, Franklin D., and Richard O. Davies, eds. *America's Recent Past.* New York: John Wiley & Sons, 1969.

Moore, Thomas Gale. *Uranium Enrichment and Public Policy.* American Enterprise Institute - Hoover Policy Studies.

Washington, D.C.: American Enterprise Institute for Public Policy Research, 1978.

Murphy, Arthur W., ed. *The Nuclear Power Controversy.* Englewood Cliffs, New Jersey: Prentice-Hall, Inc., 1976.

Nader, Ralph, and John Abbotts. *The Menace of Atomic Energy.* New York: W. W. Norton & Company, 1977.

Nelkin, Dorothy. *Nuclear Power and Its Critics: The Cayuga Lake Controversy.* Science, Technology and Society series. Ithaca, New York: Cornell University Press, 1971.

Newman, James R., and Byron S. Miller. *The Control of Atomic Energy: A Study of Its Social, Economic and Political Implications.* New York: McGraw-Hill Book Company, Inc., 1948.

New York Times, 1961-1974.

Nieburg, Harold L. *Nuclear Secrecy and Foreign Policy.* Washington, D.C.: Public Affairs Press, 1964.

Orlans, Harold. *Contracting for Atoms: A Study of Public Policy Issues Posed by the AEC's Contracting for Research, Development and Managerial Services.* Washington, D.C.: The Brookings Institution, 1967.

Pendergrass, Bonnie Baack. *Public Power, Politics and Technology in the Eisenhower and Kennedy Years: The Hanford Dual-Purpose Reactor Controversy, 1956-1962.* New York: Arno Press, 1979.

Polach, Jaroslav G. *Euratom: Its Background, Issues and Economic Implications.* Dobbs Ferry, New York: Oceana Publications, Inc., 1964.

Price, Jerome. *The Antinuclear Movement.* Social Movements Past and Present. Boston: Twayne Publishers, 1982.

Robinson, Donald, ed. *The Day I Was Proudest to be an American.* Garden City, New York: Doubleday & Company, Inc., 1958.

Rolph, Elizabeth S. *Nuclear Power and the Public Safety: A Study in Regulation.* Lexington, Massachusetts: Lexington Books, 1979.

Rosenberg, David Alan. "American Atomic Strategy and the Hydrogen Bomb Decision." *Journal of American History* 66 (June 1979):62-87.

Schilling, Warner R. "The H-Bomb Decision: How to Decide Without Actually Choosing." *Political Science Quarterly* 76 (March 1961):24-46.

Smith, Alice Kimball. *A Peril and a Hope: The Scientists' Movement in America: 1945-1947.* Chicago: The University of Chicago Press, 1965.

Sorenson, Theodore C. *Kennedy.* New York: Bantam Books, 1966.

Staats, Elmer B. *Questions on the Future of Nuclear Power: Report to the Congress of the United States by the Comptroller General.* Washington, D.C.: Government Printing Office, 21 May 1969.

Stephens, Mark. *Three Mile Island.* New York: Random House, 1980.

Strauss, Lewis L. *Men and Decisions.* Garden City, New York: Doubleday & Company, Inc., 1962.

Teller, Edward, and Allen Brown. *The Legacy of Hiroshima.* Garden City, New York: Doubleday & Company, Inc., 1962.

Thomas, Morgan, in collaboration with Robert M. Northrop. *Atomic Energy and Congress.* Ann Arbor: The University of Michigan Press, 1956.

Trask, Roger R. "The Calvert Cliffs Case: The Atomic Energy Commission and the National Environmental Policy Act, 1969-1972." Paper presented at meeting of the Pacific Historical Association, Los Angeles, California, August 1980. Used by permission of Dr. Trask.

Truman, Harry S. *Years of Trial and Hope.* Vol. 2 of *Memoirs by Harry S Truman.*

Garden City, New York: Doubleday & Company, Inc., 1956.

Truman, Margaret S. *Harry S Truman.* New York: William Morrow & Company, Inc., 1973.

Unna, Warren. "Holifield Biography Outline" and eight subsequent chapters, unpublished typescript, 1974. Prepared for Chet Holifield. Obtained from Mr. Holifield and used with his permission.

Unna, Warren. "Holifield of California." *Atlantic Monthly* 205 (April 1960):79-82.

U.S. Atomic Energy Commission. *Civilian Nuclear Power--A Report to the President--1962.* Washington, D.C.: Government Printing Office, 20 Nov. 1962.

U.S. Congress. House. Committee on Appropriations. *Second Supplemental Appropriations Bill, 1957: Report to Accompany H. R. 12350.* 84th Cong., 2d sess., 1956. H. Rept. 2849.

U.S. Congress. House. Committee on Government Operations. Subcommittee on Military Operations. *Civil Defense--1961.* 87th Cong., 1st sess., 1961.

U.S. Congress. House. Committee on Military Affairs. *The Atomic Energy Act of 1945.* 79th Cong., 1st sess., 5 Nov. 1945. H. Rept. 1186.

U.S. Congress. Joint Committee on Atomic Energy. *Accelerating Civilian Reactor Program: Hearings on S. 2725 and H. R. 10805.* 84th Cong., 2d sess., 1956.

U.S. Congress. Joint Committee on Atomic Energy. *AEC Authorizing Legislation Fiscal Year 1962.* 87th Cong., 1st sess., 1961. H. Rept. 562.

U.S. Congress. Joint Committee on Atomic Energy. *Civilian Atomic Power Acceleration Program: Hearings on the June 26, 1956 Draft of the Gore-Holifield Bill.* 84th Cong., 2d sess., 1956.

U.S. Congress. Joint Committee on Atomic Energy. *Congressional Review of Atomic Power Program: Hearings.* 85th Cong., 1st sess., 1957.

U.S. Congress. Joint Committee on Atomic Energy. *Power Conversion Studies: Hanford New Production Reactor.* 87th Cong., 1st sess.,1961. Committee Print.

U.S. Congress. Joint Committee on Atomic Energy. *Providing for a Civilian Atomic Power Program: Report to Accompany H. R. 12061.* 84th Cong., 2d sess., 1956. H. Rept. 2622.

U.S. Congress. Joint Committee on Atomic Energy. Subcommittee on Legislation. *AEC Authorizing Legislation: Hearings on Fiscal Year 1959 Authorizing Legislation (H. R. 13121).* 85th Cong., 2d sess., 1958.

U.S. Congress. Joint Committee on Atomic Energy. Subcommittee on Legislation. *Authorizing Legislation for AEC's Fiscal Year 1958 Construction Budget.* 85th Cong., 1st sess., 1957.

U.S. Congress. Joint Committee on Atomic Energy. *Utility Proposal for Powerplant Addition to Hanford New Production Reactor: Hearings on 1962 Proposed Hanford Project.* 87th Cong., 2d sess., 1962.

U.S. Congress. Joint Committee on Atomic Energy. *Utility Proposal for Powerplant Addition to Hanford New Production Reactor.* 87th Cong., 2d sess., 1962. Committee Print.

Weaver, Leon H. *The Civil Defense Debate: Differing Perceptions of a Persistent Issue in National Security Policy.* East Lansing, Michigan: Michigan State University Press, 1967.

Wildavsky, Aaron B. *Dixon-Yates: A Study in Power Politics.* Yale Studies in Political Science, no. 3. Westport, Connecticut: Greenwood Press, 1976.

Zink, Thomas Andrew. "The Joint Committee on Atomic Energy and the Formation of the Civilian Atomic Power Program: 1945-1963." Master's thesis, University of Southern California, June 1977.

Index

About the Author

RICHARD WAYNE DYKE graduated in 1972 with a major in history and political science from Pasadena College, now Point Loma Nazarene College in San Diego. He holds a Master's Degree in history (1974) from California State University, Long Beach and a Master's Degree in Public Administration (1977) from the University of Southern California, and earned the Ph.D. in history from the University of Southern California in 1984. He is currently employed as a Community Services Analyst with the County of Los Angeles, Department of Community and Senior Citizens Services.